DEFUSING ARMAGEDDON

Inside **NEST**, America's Secret
Nuclear Bomb Squad

DEFUSING A

 W. W. NORTON & COMPANY | NEW YORK · LONDON

RMAGEDDON

JEFFREY T. RICHELSON

For information about permission to reproduce selections from this book,
write to Permissions, W. W. Norton & Company, Inc.,
500 Fifth Avenue, New York, NY 10110

For information about special discounts for bulk purchases, please contact
W. W. Norton Special Sales at specialsales@wwnorton.com or 800-233-4830

Manufacturing by RR Donnelley, Harrisonburg
Book design by Judith Stagnito Abbate
Production manager: Julia Druskin

Library of Congress Cataloging-in-Publication Data

Richelson, Jeffrey.
Defusing Armageddon : inside NEST, America's secret
nuclear bomb squad / Jeffrey T. Richelson. — 1st ed.
p. cm.
Includes bibliographical references and index.
ISBN 978-0-393-06515-2 (hardcover)
1. Nuclear terrorism—United States. 2. Nuclear terrorism—United
States—Prevention. 3. Nuclear weapons information. 4. Nuclear arms
control—United States. 5. Terrorism—United States. I. Title.
HV6433.86R54 2009
363.325'570973—dc22

2008042966

W. W. Norton & Company, Inc.
500 Fifth Avenue, New York, N.Y. 10110
www.wwnorton.com

W. W. Norton & Company Ltd.
Castle House, 75/76 Wells Street, London W1T 3QT

1 2 3 4 5 6 7 8 9 0

CONTENTS

LIST OF LETTERS, MAPS, FIGURES, AND TABLES

PREFACE

In 1961, and again in 1965, a British Vulcan bomber carrying two nuclear weapons was hijacked during a NATO training exercise. Eventually, the hijacker landed the plane at the bottom of the ocean off the coast of Nassau in the Bahamas. The plot originated with an international criminal organization, which then attempted to extort a huge ransom in diamonds from the American and British governments—threatening to detonate the bombs in one American city (Miami, as it turned out) and one British city (presumably London) if its demand was not met. But a heroic British agent identified the location of the bombs, and after the leader of the criminal effort escaped during a raid on the undersea location where the bombs were hidden, taking one of the bombs with him, the agent prevented that nuclear device from reaching Miami.

Of course, the international criminal organization was the Special Executive for Counterintelligence, Terrorism, Revenge, and Extortion (SPECTRE), and the British agent was James Bond. And those events occurred not in the real world but first in the pages of Ian Fleming's 1961 novel *Thunderball* and then, beginning in late 1965, on movie screens throughout the world. Essentially the same plot would be repeated in *Never Say Never Again*, the 1983 remake of *Thunderball*. But James Bond's 1965 confrontation with SPECTRE was not the first encounter British filmgoers had had with nuclear extortion.

About fifteen years earlier, in August 1950, *Seven Days to Noon* appeared in British cinemas. As in *Thunderball*, a nuclear weapon is stolen, and its new owner threatens to detonate the device if his demands are not met. But the thief is not some elaborate criminal organization but rather a lone individual. Professor Willingdon, a British nuclear scientist, is not looking for a huge payoff, at least not one measured in dollars or diamonds. Instead, he threatens to detonate the stolen weapon in London unless his government halts its production of nuclear weapons. In a final similarity to *Thunderball*, it all ends badly for the extortionist. The British cabinet refuses to negotiate, and Scotland Yard's Special Branch initiates a huge manhunt for Willingdon, ending with his being gunned down with only seconds (but probably not 007 seconds) to spare before the bomb would have been detonated.[1]

Stolen nuclear weapons have figured prominently in other films and one television series, although the objectives of those in possession of the deadly devices have varied considerably. In 1996's *Broken Arrow*, a renegade Air Force major, played by John Travolta, seizes control of his "B-3" bomber, steals its two nuclear weapons, and threatens to destroy a city unless he receives a payoff. The next year, in *The Peacemaker*, starring George Clooney and Nicole Kidman, a Yugoslav seeking revenge for the death of his wife and daughter, and blaming the United Nations for not protecting them, tries and fails to detonate a stolen nuclear device at UN headquarters.[2] Then, in Season 6 (2007) of *24*, Islamic terrorists buy "suitcase" bombs from a rogue Russian general and manage to detonate one on the outskirts of Los Angeles.

While theft is one way to get hold of a nuclear weapon, an alternative for a prospective nuclear terrorist is to build one, or to have someone else build one—even if that requires threatening to kill the scientist or his loved ones should he refuse to cooperate. With the help of American physicist Peter Zimmerman, Nicolas Freeling, the detective novelist best known for his Inspector Van der Valk mysteries, produced *Gadget*, published in 1977. The central character of the book is Jim Hawkins, a physicist who works at a nuclear research facility in Hamburg. After a traffic accident he wakes up to find himself, as well as his wife and two daughters, the prisoner of "Herr Doktor," a terrorist who demands that he use his expertise to build a nuclear device. Before the novel concludes, the reader witnesses Hawkins going through the process, involving both theoretical calculations and industrial work, to produce the "gadget." This time things end badly for the city of Geneva and the group of international leaders who had assembled there for a UN conference.[3]

Probably the best-known novel involving a nuclear device built on behalf of a terrorist, *The Fifth Horseman*, appeared in 1980, coauthored by Larry Collins and Dominique Lapierre, renowned for their collaboration on the nonfiction work *Is Paris Burning?* In the novel the terrorist is Libyan strongman Muammar al-Qaddafi, who threatens to detonate a three-megaton device in New York City unless an autonomous Palestinian state is established. Unlike Herr Doktor, Qaddafi's first preference is not to detonate the device but to attain a political objective. And, unfortunately for the fictional version of the Libyan dictator, like the extortionists in *Thunderball*, neither his first nor his second objectives are accomplished. No Palestinian state is established and New York survives unscathed.[4]

Sometimes, terrorists just get lucky and virtually have a nuclear weapon handed to them. That was a premise of 1991's *The Sum of All Fears*, the work of best-selling author Tom Clancy. In the inevitable "techno-thriller" prologue, which is set during the October 1973 Yom Kippur War, an Israeli A-4 warplane carrying a nuclear bomb is shot down. Years later it is recovered and eventually winds up in the hands of Muslim extremists, who succeed in detonating it in Denver during (and at) the Super Bowl.[5]

In one film there was nothing virtual about the villain being handed a nuclear weapon. In 1964's *Goldfinger*, the third James Bond film, as part of a plot to destroy the value of the U.S. gold supply, the People's Republic of China provides the appropriately named Auric Goldfinger with a nuclear device to be detonated within the chambers of Fort Knox. Of course, as unlikely as it was that such a plot would be hatched or succeed in the real world, it was even less likely to be successful in a James Bond film.

On television, terrorists have attempted to do radioactive harm on a lesser scale than the terrorists in Clancy's book or *24*. In 2005, BBC and HBO viewers had the opportunity to watch *Dirty War*, which featured Islamic terrorists detonating a "dirty bomb"—in which radioactive material, such as cesium-137 or cobalt-60, is combined with conventional explosives. There are two effects of such a bomb. One is the damage done by conventional explosives. The second is the dispersal of the radioactivity. Such a bomb need not, and unless cleverly designed will not, produce mass casualties, since individuals can quickly escape the scene. But it does have the ability to contaminate the immobile buildings and structures for a significant area around ground zero and make them uninhabitable for years to come. In the 2006 Showtime series *Sleeper Cell*, Islamic terrorists attempt but, thanks to an undercover FBI agent, fail to do the same to Los Angeles.

Decades earlier, in the 1961 novel *The Removers*, secret agent Matt Helm halts a Soviet operation that involved smuggling "very ingenious" sabotage devices into the United States. The devices consisted of radioactive wastes packed into a shielded container with a small explosive charge that "would distribute the radioactive material over a fairly wide area."[6]

A step below detonating anything is stealing radioactive material that can be employed in a dirty bomb or nuclear device. Novelists and scriptwriters have not neglected this possibility. Michael Connelly's *The Overlook*, featuring his now-legendary detective Harry Bosch, involved the theft of medical radioactive sources that were feared at first to be earmarked for use in a dirty bomb. In the 2007 HBO film *PU-239*, a technician suffering from radiation poisoning pilfers the weapons-grade substance that gives the film its title in order to sell it and provide economic security for his family after his demise.[7]

Not surprisingly, such films and novels take liberties with scientific and other facts—which can produce laughter from the initiated.* Thus, a team rather than an individual is likely to be necessary to build a bomb. But the depiction of how nuclear devices or dirty bombs might be obtained or used does mirror concerns by officials in the U.S. and other governments and international organizations such as the International Atomic Energy Agency.

Within the U.S. government a nuclear device constructed by a terrorist or extortionist is known as an "Improvised Nuclear Device" or IND. Theft, seizure, or loss of a nuclear weapon would be reported under the designation "Empty Quiver." A dirty bomb has the more formal, less literary, designation "Radiological Dispersal Device" or RDD.[8]

Many of the organizations that appear in films, novels, and government exercises dealing with nuclear terrorism or extortion—from SPECTRE to GLODO—are fictional. Others are very real. One of those that is a frequent participant in exercises, and makes an occasional appearance in film and fiction, is the Nuclear Emergency Support Team, known until 2002 as the Nuclear Emergency Search Team (NEST). If a similar organization did not exist in the real world, Hollywood probably would have created one. NEST has appeared in *24, The Fifth Horseman,* and *The Peacemaker.* In such works it has not been the central focus of the story. But in this book it is.

---

*When Alan Mode of Lawrence Livermore National Laboratory took some of his staff, who were experts in weapons design, to see the film version of *The Sum of All Fears,* he cautioned them not to laugh at errors, telling them that their laughter, by revealing errors, might be classified. Interview with Alan Mode, Pleasanton, Calif., April 12, 2007.

DEFUSING ARMAGEDDON

Chapter 1

"BYE-BYE BOSTON"

By 1946, J. Robert Oppenheimer was no stranger to nuclear secrecy. During World War II, as scientific director of the Manhattan Project, he had supervised America's quest to build an atomic bomb from Los Alamos, where everything was secret. He was also present at the Trinity test site in July 1945, when the design for a plutonium bomb was secretly and successfully tested. So his appearance at a closed Senate hearing in 1946 to discuss nuclear matters was rather unexceptional.[1]

But his response to one senator's question was a surprise, at least to the senator. When Oppenheimer was asked "whether three or four men couldn't smuggle units of an [atomic] bomb into New York and blow up the whole city," he responded politely, "Of course it could be done, and people could destroy New York." Following up, the shocked senator asked, "What instrument would you use to detect an atomic bomb hidden somewhere in a city?" Oppenheimer's response was probably even more shocking, and certainly disheartening: "A screwdriver"—to open every crate or suitcase big enough to hold a bomb.[2]

A few years later, in the early 1950s, Oppenheimer sought help in giving the United States a better, more high-tech means of detecting a smuggled nuclear weapon than a screwdriver. He asked physicist Wolfgang Panofsky, another Manhattan Project veteran, to produce a top-secret study, which became known as the "Screwdriver Report," on how to neutralize any enemy efforts to smuggle nuclear weapons or radioactive materials into the United States. The result was the discrete placement of radiation detectors at airports and ship terminals during the 1950s. Their primary accomplishment was detecting a woman smuggler who was carrying a hundred radium-dial watches in her corset.[3]

Another branch of the U.S. government would also worry about smuggled nuclear weapons in the early 1950s and beyond. On Thursday, August 30, 1951, the United States was fighting two wars—one hot and one cold. The hot war was being fought on the Korean Peninsula, the result of North

Korea's June 1950 invasion of South Korea. Truce talks had broken down and there was little prospect of a cease-fire.[4] The Cold War, with the Soviet Union as America's main antagonist, was being fought on every continent and in a multitude of ways—through diplomacy and propaganda, espionage and covert action, and the buildup of conventional and nuclear forces.

The Soviet Union's detonation of an atomic device in August 1949 had created the prospect that not only could the Cold War between the two superpowers turn into a hot one but also it could lead to atomic bombs exploding on American territory. Soviet Tu-4 bombers bearing the red Soviet star, on one-way missions, might drop their deadly payloads on the residents of New York, Boston, Washington, and other major American cities, leaving those cities and millions of lives in ruins.[5] It was possible, however, that the Soviets might also employ more clandestine means of attack. Undoubtedly, the senator who asked Oppenheimer about smuggled nuclear weapons had Soviet agents in mind as the most likely smugglers.

And on that Thursday in late August 1951, in downtown Washington, D.C., Director of Central Intelligence (DCI) Walter Bedell Smith, or his representative, was chairing a meeting of the Intelligence Advisory Committee (IAC), whose functions included approving national intelligence estimates. Also attending were representatives of the intelligence organizations of the State Department, Army, Navy, Air Force, Federal Bureau of Investigation (FBI), and Atomic Energy Commission (AEC). Under consideration was a newly completed national intelligence estimate with a rather ponderous title—*Soviet Capabilities for Clandestine Attack against the US with Weapons of Mass Destruction and the Vulnerability of the US to Such Attack (mid-1951 to mid-1952)*—which examined how the Soviets might attack with stealth.[6]

Among the methods American intelligence analysts identified as options for the Soviet Union, should it wish to conduct a clandestine nuclear attack, were atomic bomb–carrying merchant ships and smuggling. "The delivery of atomic weapons into key harbors by merchant ships is feasible and therefore constitutes a serious threat," they wrote. They also identified a number of factors that would "seriously hamper" the Coast Guard in detecting a hidden weapon—most importantly that "there is no device for detecting an atomic weapon within the hold of a merchant ship." Further complicating the Coast Guard's task was the Soviet operation of fishing trawlers similar to U.S. ships as well as the 140 Western ships under charter to countries in the Soviet orbit.[7]

An atomic bomb might be smuggled in whole, or broken down into relatively small components that could be brought into the United States over a period of time—with the components packaged so that "radiation detection would be most improbable." Smuggling, whether of components or a complete bomb, could be accomplished in a number of ways. Shipments to Soviet diplomats in the United States, which were not subject to inspection by the Bureau of Customs, and not limited in size, could be labeled household effects but actually contain far more deadly items. Alternatively, bombs or their components might be smuggled in as commercial shipments.[8]

While customs inspectors had been alerted to watch for shipments with the weight and size characteristics of a bomb, the bureau "would have considerable difficulty detecting bomb shipments," the U.S. intelligence analysts concluded. A third possibility, which was characterized as "well within Soviet capabilities," was the smuggling of a bomb, particularly a disassembled one, into an isolated section of the United States. According to the estimate a smuggling operation could involve the transfer of a bomb from a Soviet-controlled merchant vessel or submarine to a small boat, which would bring it ashore. From there it could be loaded into a truck for assembly and delivery to the target area, where the truck might be parked and the bomb detonated. Yet another possible means of sneak attack was placing a nuclear bomb on a civilian aircraft used by U.S. or foreign airlines.[9]

The estimate also informed its readers that no coordinated overall plan had been completed for the detection and prevention of the smuggling of atomic weapons into the country at secluded points. It warned that "until such a plan is complete and put into effective operation, the US will remain vulnerable to this threat."[10]

One attempt to reduce that vulnerability was the creation of "Committee B," also known as the Committee on Countermeasures, in 1953. The group was a joint enterprise of the Interdepartmental Intelligence Conference and the Interdepartmental Committee on Internal Security—both of which reported to the National Security Council (NSC) until June 1962, when President John F. Kennedy transferred responsibility for oversight to his brother Attorney General Robert Kennedy. Committee B's mission was to "consider ways and means of safeguarding against the clandestine introduction of nuclear weapons."[11]

The Intelligence Community also periodically produced new estimates concerning the threat of clandestine nuclear attack, estimates that reflected both continuity and change. In 1963, the community presented one in response to President Kennedy's concern, in the wake of the Cuban missile crisis, that Weapons of Mass Destruction (WMD) might be smuggled into the United States just as they had been smuggled into Cuba. The estimate was not reassuring. Nuclear weapons with yields up to three hundred kilotons "could be brought into the United States by a variety of means such as by ground or air transport across land borders or at points along U.S. seacoasts."[12]

But the majority view in that estimate—that a Soviet clandestine attack of any sort was unlikely and if attempted would be only as a supplement to an overt attack—held through the 1960s and beyond. Problems the Soviets faced in carrying out a clandestine attack included getting any significant number of bombs to their targets without detection, the possibility of a leak or defection, and the amount of time the devices would have to be concealed before they were detonated. Yet there were always some skeptics among the nation's intelligence agencies. In 1963 the FBI, the National Security Agency (NSA, the nation's foreign eavesdropping agency), the Air Force's assistant chief of staff for intelligence, and the Joint Staff's J-2 (the intelligence unit of the Joint Chiefs of Staff) argued that "as long as the Soviets have the capability for clandestine nuclear attack against selective important targets in the US, with minimal risk, there is not enough evidence to make the judgment that such an attack is unlikely."[13]

One change in the estimates was in the evaluation of port security. The 1960 estimate stated that existing port security measures would probably prevent the employment of merchant ships for carrying nuclear weapons into U.S. ports (although use of fishing boats or similar small vessels was still viable). In 1968, a new estimate, prepared at the request of the Joint Chiefs of Staff, reflected China's having entered the nuclear club in October 1964. It noted that since China had no other means of attacking the United States with nuclear weapons, its leaders might consider clandestinely placing nuclear weapons on U.S. territory for deterrence purposes. The ultimate targets would be U.S. population centers. Then, in 1970, analysts for the first time suggested that a nation might consider a clandestine nuclear attack on the United States "as an act of deception designed to embroil the US with a third power." One particular scenario, mentioned despite being considered highly unlikely, had China detonating a nuclear device on U.S. territory during a period of great tension between the United States and Soviet Union in the hope that the United States would strike back at the Soviets.* Another scenario had China constructing a bomb

---

*During this era the concept of China's seeking to provoke a war between the United States and Soviet Union and pick up the pieces was not uncommon in film and fiction.

to appear to be of Soviet origin and then have it discovered by the United States so as to provoke a crisis between the two superpowers.[14]

During the Cold War the scenarios created by U.S. intelligence analysts— of Soviet or Chinese nuclear weapons hidden in the United States—never became more than unlikely possibilities. The United States never experienced the devastation of a clandestine nuclear attack or had to send out search teams in a desperate attempt to locate foreign atomic weapons hidden on its territory. But in the 1950s and 1960s the U.S. government would spend considerable time and expense trying to locate U.S. nuclear weapons after nuclear-armed aircraft had crashed.

On February 4, 1958, Maj. Howard Richardson, age thirty-six, and his two-man crew took off from Homestead Air Force Base in Florida in a Strategic Air Command (SAC) B-47 Stratojet, the country's first swept-wing, multiengine bomber, and headed west toward New Orleans. Their plane was carrying a 7,600-pound, eleven-foot-seven-inch-long thermonuclear weapon—although it was not armed with the removable nuclear capsule required to actually produce a nuclear detonation. Richardson and his crew were participating, along with a second B-47, in a practice mission designed to simulate wartime attacks on targets in the Soviet Union.[15]

Usually the flight, an almost 5,000-mile round trip at speeds up to 600 miles per hour, included aerial refueling and the dropping of an electronic "bomb" before returning to its home base. On this run, Richardson turned north near New Orleans, flew to a point near the Canadian border, headed south for a bombing run on the radar scoring facility at Radford, Virginia, and then turned toward home. At this point the crew had been in the air for eight hours and had covered 4,000 miles. Headquarters then told Richardson he had entered friendly territory and would not be encountering any "enemy" fighters during the last several hundred miles of the flight.[16]

Unfortunately, three pilots at Charleston Air Force Base in South Carolina had been told that as part of the exercise, they could "attack"

Peter George's 1965 novel *Commander-1* featured such a plot, as did the 1967 James Bond film *You Only Live Twice*. A recent nonfiction book claimed that in 1968 rogue elements in the Soviet navy were going to use a missile attack from a submarine to instigate a war between the United States and China. See Kenneth Sewell with Clint Richmond, *Red Star Rogue: The Untold Story of a Soviet Submarine's Nuclear Strike Attempt on the U.S.* (New York: Pocket Books, 2006).

Richardson's plane anytime before it landed in Florida. At the time, each of the pilots, including Lt. Clarence Stewart, were flying F-86L Sabre Dog aircraft. First introduced in 1956, the forty-foot-long planes could fly just fast enough (715 miles per hour) to break the sound barrier. At 12:09 a.m. on February 5, the alert shack's horn began blaring. Three minutes later the planes were in the air, heading to intercept Richardson's plane. But while the Air Defense Command's radar had detected the second plane, it had missed Richardson's B-47. Ground control therefore gave the pilots a target several thousand feet above and fifteen miles behind Richardson's plane. As a result, Stewart descended while watching the other B-47 on the radar screen. When he looked up, he found the sky "filled with airplanes." He rolled his plane to the right.[17]

Stewart's maneuver couldn't prevent a collision. Richardson and his copilot felt a tremendous jolt and witnessed a bright flash. Richardson could see that the far right engine had been bent to a thirty-degree angle while the right external fuel tank was missing. Meanwhile, Stewart's fighter was without its left wing and then, after the fuel accumulation tank exploded, its right wing—although Stewart would manage to land his wingless plane safely, "in a little clearing in the biggest damn swamp in South Carolina." Richardson took his plane down to 20,000 feet, reduced the speed, extended the flaps, and lowered the wheels to determine if a safe landing was possible. He headed for Hunter Air Force Base, outside of Savannah, Georgia. But repair work at the base had left an eighteen-inch drop at each end of the runway, and if his plane landed short, the landing gear and dangling engine could snag. As a result, Richardson was told, the bomb could be propelled through the cockpit and down the runway at over 200 miles per hour. He then decided to jettison the bomb in the Atlantic and, not long after telling SAC of his plans, let it loose into the water near Tybee Island, Georgia, before landing safely at Hunter. On April 16, 1958, after a nine-week search, which covered an area of three square miles, the Air Force declared the bomb to be "irretrievably lost."[18]

A little less than eight years later, another U.S. nuclear weapon landed in the water after an accident—only this accident was far more devastating. Its immediate aftermath included seven U.S. airmen dead, four nuclear weapons on foreign territory, and a public relations nightmare not only for SAC but also for the U.S. government.[19]

At 10:22 a.m., on Monday, January 17, 1966, a B-52G bomber and

KC-135 tanker aircraft collided over Palomares, a small remote village about a mile inland from the Spanish Mediterranean Coast. About fifteen hundred people, whose principal activity involved raising tomatoes, lived in the vicinity. The B-52G was piloted by Capt. Charles F. Wendorf, age twenty-nine, a 1958 graduate of Duke University. The captain's crew included another five officers, and Tech. Sgt. Ronald P. Snyder, the B-52's gunner. Also on board, as the B-52 was on airborne alert, were four nuclear weapons, each of which could explode with a force equivalent to 1.5 million tons of TNT (1.5 megatons), but they were not armed. Arming the weapon required the crew to activate two switches (a readiness switch and an inflight control switch) after receiving orders from higher authority.[20]

After twenty-three hours in the air, having departed Seymour Johnson Air Force Base in North Carolina at about 5:00 a.m. on Sunday, January 16, the B-52G was scheduled to be refueled by a KC-135 stationed at the joint U.S.-Spanish air base at Torrejón, nineteen miles from Madrid. At the helm of that plane was Maj. Emil J. Chapla, a forty-two-year-old Ohio native who flew B-24 bombers in the Pacific during World War II. Also along for the ride were Chapla's copilot, his navigator, and the boom operator, who ranged in ages from twenty-seven to forty-one.[21]

The B-52G had entered Spanish territory near the port of Cartagena and was flying, at an altitude of 30,500 feet, along the coastline toward what was known as the Saddle Rock Refueling Area, and Palomares. In preparation for refueling, Captain Wendorf began to reduce his plane's speed, from its cruising speed of 600 miles per hour. Chapla had also cut his plane's speed and lowered his KC-135 to enter a "racetrack" orbit twenty-one miles ahead of the approaching bomber, which was to edge up behind and slightly below the tanker. If nothing went wrong, the tanker's forty-two-foot fuel boom would be lowered and connected to the B-52's nose, refueling would be completed, and the two planes would go their separate ways.[22]

But something did go wrong. The B-52 came in too fast, at 275 miles per hour, and the top of its fuselage rammed the KC-135. A few seconds later the tanker was consumed by flames as its enormous load of fuel exploded. Both planes began falling to earth, breaking into hundreds of fragments as they did. The Associated Press reported that "school children walking to their classes heard the rending of metal, then watched as smoke clouds erupted from the big planes as they spiraled down, scattering burning wreckage over a wide area." The four bombs, along with their parachutes, slid out through the bomb bay door. Miraculously, no one on the ground was killed by the debris, but the tanker had no ejection mechanisms and all four of its crew died as a result of the explosion. Three of the B-52 crew also perished, while the four in the aircraft's forward section survived. Wendorf, Capt. Ivens Buchanan, the radar-navigator, 1st Lt. Michael Rooney, the copilot, and Maj. Larry G. Messinger, who had been serving as the relief pilot on the long flight, were able to parachute to safety.[23]

Word that there had been a nuclear accident, a "Broken Arrow" in Pentagon terminology, reached Washington—specifically, Col. Charles Burtyk, the duty officer at the National Military Command Center—at 5:35 a.m. A flurry of notifications, from the center and other sources, followed, as did orders. SAC's chief of staff, Maj. Gen. Charles M. Eisenhart, informed Maj. Gen. A. J. Beck, the head of SAC's Disaster Control Team, of the event. By 4:13 a.m. Omaha time, every member of Beck's team had been awakened and instructed to get to the SAC airfield by five o'clock ready to board a plane for Spain.[24]

Also receiving notice of the accident, courtesy of the Air Force Nuclear Safety directorate, was the Joint Nuclear Accident Coordinating Center (JNACC), an organization that reported to both the AEC and the Department of Defense. It was described by one author in 1967 as "America's nuclear fire station": "if a reactor blew its stack, if a radiation laboratory had an accident, if an atomic-weapon storage depot caught on fire, if a train carrying uranium logs to a nuclear munitions plant was derailed, if a B-52 loaded for air-alert duty crashed with its cargo, [JNACC] would be the place to turn for emergency assistance."[25]

JNACC headquarters, in Albuquerque, New Mexico, consisted of two rooms a few blocks apart. Inside those rooms were metal maps of the United States and the rest of the world. Magnetic markers showed the locations of nuclear emergency teams. A card index provided extensive details on the capabilities, current strength, and deployment of individuals and machines that might be called on to deal with nuclear accidents or disasters. Manning one of the two rooms were representatives from the AEC, while personnel from the Defense Atomic Support Agency manned the other.[26]

Experts from JNACC and two AEC laboratories, the Los Alamos Scientific Laboratory and the Albuquerque-based Sandia Corporation, were sent to Spain, along with Air Force personnel, to observe the effort to locate the bombs and detect any signs of radiation. Among those arriving from Los Alamos were Douglass Evans, from the high-explosives division, and William H. Chambers, of the lab's weapons division.[27]

Chambers, a native of White Plains, had graduated from Cornell University in 1943 and immediately entered the Army. Once the war ended, he returned to physics and received his doctorate from Ohio State. While there he coauthored two papers that appeared in *Physical Review*—"The

Nuclear Magnetic Moment of Praseodymium[141]" and "Nuclear Gyromagnetic Ratios II." In the course of his graduate studies Chambers met several physicists who had worked at Los Alamos during World War II. When he interviewed there in 1950, Chambers looked the facility over and thought it would be a good place to spend five years (he was still there fifty-seven years later). At the lab he became involved in weapons design work and, as a sideline, preparing explosive ordnance disposal manuals for America's nuclear weapons. He recalls that the order to head for Palomares came from lab director Harold Agnew "in the midst of a midnight phone call."[28]

Detection, location, damage limitation, and bomb disassembly were the primary responsibilities of the Air Force, including the Disaster Control Team attached to the 16th Air Force (headquartered at Torrejón) and the 7410th Explosive Ordnance Disposal (EOD) Squadron from United States Air Forces Europe. Sgt. Raymond Howe of the 16th Air Force arrived with a PAC-1S, the military's standard monitor for alpha rays, an AN/PDR-39, similar to a Geiger counter, and a device (the "27-C") that could detect beta and gamma rays.[29]

One objective was to keep even a single bomb out of the hands of the Russians, whose experts would examine the device to determine its electronic arming, firing, and fusing mechanisms. But the United States also did not want any of its hydrogen bombs to fall into the hands of friendly nations, particularly France. French President Charles de Gaulle was pressing his nuclear scientists to present him with a hydrogen device before the end of 1968.[30]

By the time the plane bringing Air Force and AEC experts to Spain landed, Air Force reconnaissance planes, including five RF-4Cs, one RF-101, and an RB-66, had obtained pictures of the wreckage. It does not appear those photos played a role in the detection of any of the bombs. The first was discovered on the same day as the accident by a member of the Guardia Civil, who saw something that appeared to be "a kind of weapon" lying in the soft sand near the river bed. The EOD men, who were trained to "render safe" such devices by disconnecting bomb components so a nuclear reaction could not occur, examined the policeman's find for signs of damage. But it was too dark for them to proceed, so disabling the bomb had to wait until the following morning.[31]

The next day also brought the discovery of two more bombs. Within an hour after first light, the crew of a search helicopter had spotted a parachute with a metal tube protruding from the ground on a hill well behind the Palomares cemetery. The location of the third bomb also came from the Guardia Civil in the form of a story about a torpedo in a tomato patch. It was clear to Sergeant Howe that there had been a partial detonation of the bomb's conventional explosives and that the detonation had shattered the connections in the bomb, eliminating the need for EOD personnel to disassemble it.[32]

In about twenty-four hours from the time of the accident, U.S. and Spanish authorities had been able to locate three of the four bombs. But locating bomb number four would be a far more difficult task. U.S. aerial reconnaissance missions produced plenty of photographs but none that showed the resting place of weapon number four. Hundreds of American servicemen searched the vicinity of Palomares, some armed with Geiger counters, but also came up empty. North American Aviation (NAA) offered to provide a device capable of detecting gamma rays from the decay of uranium and plutonium. On January 26, Dr. W. R. Laidlaw, the company's vice president for research and engineering, arrived with the three thousand pounds of equipment, and the technicians to install it on a C-54 aircraft landed the following day.[33]

During four flights made between January 29 and January 31, five radioactive areas were discovered, with three of the detections considered to be the result of natural sources. Another hit was believed to be the result of the detonation of the conventional explosives on weapon number two. The fifth was judged to be the result of weapon number three's explosives detonating or due to natural sources. While use of the detector was halted, other search methods—on land and in the air—continued. Those methods included almost every available PAC-1S detector, fifty-one of fifty-five, in Spain.[34]

According to an official history of the recovery operation, "sand, rocks, hills, ravines, every inch of this area of Spain was covered." That history was referring to the search on land. But every inch in that area of Spain was also covered from space by the Corona spy satellite that had been launched on February 2. Dino Brugioni, a senior executive of the CIA's National Photographic Interpretation Center at the time, recalls that "we didn't see anything" in the images produced by the satellite. On March 3, Maj. Gen. Delmar Wilson informed SAC that "all land areas presenting even a remote possibility of success have been searched at least four times, and other areas have been covered seven or more times. Appraisal of all search efforts to date places increasing emphasis on the probability that the intact weapon went into the sea," as had been suggested in a February 7 report by experts from the AEC's Albuquerque office, Sandia, and the Air Force.[35]

Shifting the search to sea did not produce an immediate success, but it did yield success. Almost two months after Broken Arrow, the twenty-two-foot-long, 23,000-pound *Alvin*, a Navy deep-sea submersible vessel, located weapon number four, much of it covered by its parachute, resting in an underwater canyon 2,500 feet below the surface. One attempt to raise it, using an electronic recovery apparatus known as CURV (Cable-Controlled Underwater Recovery Vehicle), which had been developed in the early 1960s to recover test ordnance lost off California's San Clemente Island, failed when the cable lifting the bomb snapped, and the bomb fell to 2,850 feet. But on April 7, the Navy succeeded in getting the weapon out of the Mediterranean so it could be shipped back to the United States—although not until EOD personnel had completed their render-safe work.[36]

On January 21, 1968, only a few days after the second anniversary of the Palomares incident, SAC was confronted with another Broken Arrow. This time a B-52 went down about seven hundred miles above the Arctic Circle, near Thule Air Base in ice-covered Greenland—the site of one of three Ballistic Missile Early Warning System (BMEWS) radars designed to provide advance warning of a Soviet missile attack. SAC had instituted what it labeled the Thule Monitor Mission in August 1961, altering one northern route flown as part of its airborne alert program. One purpose of the "Hard Head" route was to allow SAC to determine the cause of any interruption in communications between the site and U.S. warning centers. There had been two outages in 1961 when the cable carrying the BMEWS data, which ran under North Atlantic fishing grounds, had been cut—either by accident or as the result of enemy action.[37]

Confronted with a fire in the navigator's compartment that was raging out of control, the thirty-six-year-old pilot of the B-52, Capt. John M. Haug of Phoenix, Arizona, abandoned his attempt to make an emergency landing at the air base and ordered his crew to bail out. Haug and five other crew members were successful in escaping the plane and serious injury, except for the unfortunate crew member whose feet froze before he was rescued. Even less fortunate was the copilot, Capt. Leonard Svitenko, who was killed while bailing out. At a brief news conference about a week after the crash, Captain Haug explained that "we used up all our fire-fighting equipment and we even tried to smother the fire, but the smoke got so bad I had no choice but to bail out my crew." When the plane crashed, 225,000 pounds of jet fuel exploded and the conventional high explosives in each bomb detonated.[38]

Like the B-52 that fell apart over Palomares, Haug's plane carried four unarmed nuclear bombs, each capable of detonating with the force of over a megaton. With the crew quickly rescued, the next steps were to collect the wreckage, locate the bombs, and determine if any of Greenland had been contaminated by radioactivity—an effort designated Project Crested Ice. The SAC Disaster Control Team arrived at Thule approximately ten hours after the crash, as did an initial element from the Defense Atomic Support Agency's Nuclear Emergency Team, which was there to provide radiation- and contamination-control support for the operation. To provide additional assistance, the AEC dispatched a three-man team, selected from Los Alamos, Sandia, and the AEC operations office in Albuquerque. By the evening of January 22, sixty-eight people had arrived at Thule for the disaster control operation, a number which grew to 565 within a few days. They faced conditions that included morning temperatures of twenty degrees below zero and winter darkness.[39]

There was no mystery as to where the plane crashed (about seven miles southwest of the Thule Air Base's runway on the ice of Wolstenholme Fjord) or its velocity when it did (518 miles per hour). The recovered aircraft debris filled 163 drums, fourteen engine containers, and eleven large tanks with a total capacity of 14,720 cubic feet. Parts of the bombs, which had been blown apart when their conventional explosives had detonated, were found scattered within a one-mile-wide swath that extended about three miles south of where the B-52 had crashed.[40]

To determine whether the debris, ice, and snow in the vicinity of the crash site had been contaminated with plutonium from the fractured bombs, all of it needed to be removed, packed, and shipped back to the United States. On January 23, an eleven-man team of radiation monitors and EOD personnel, accompanied by their AEC advisors, traveled by dog sled to the crash site to do so. The snow, ice, and debris that was removed weighed in at 10,000 tons, and the entire effort would extend into the summer of 1968.[41]

A variety of devices would be employed to detect radiation. Over seventy of the PAC-1S alpha-ray monitors, also used at Palomares, would be enlisted in the effort. Other devices bore designations such as AN/PDR-27 and PAC-3G. A key element in identifying the contaminated territory was the emergency team's use of six FIDLERs, FIDLER being an acronym for

Field Instrument for Detection of Low Energy Radiations. At the time of the crash the device was being tested by Lawrence Livermore Laboratory, which reported to the AEC. It could effectively plot plutonium contamination by measuring gamma radiation from americium-241, a by-product of plutonium production and plutonium decay.[42]

On July 11, 1970, an Air Force Athena missile was launched from Green River, Utah, toward a target in New Mexico's White Sands Missile Range. The missile, fifty feet tall and weighing 16,000 pounds, was part of an effort to study the reentry characteristics of warheads and other space vehicles. While the first part of the flight went smoothly, the second part did not. Pat Quinlan was in the Range Control building monitoring telemetry and radar data. He recalled that rather than the Athena coming into view in its usual spot to the north and about forty-five degrees above the horizon, "the glow appeared almost straight overhead and the reentry streak trailed to the south."[43]

That southerly course took the missile to a crash landing in Mexico— just as the flight of a Pershing missile fired from Blanding, Utah, in September 1967 had ended up just across the border from Van Horn, Texas. The missile's nose cone contained cobalt-57, an extremely dangerous radioactive substance used to measure the ablative material on the outside of the nose cone that burned off and protected the vehicle during its reentry phase. The presence of radioactive material exacerbated the difficult diplomatic situation created by the off-course missile.[44]

While it was clear that the missile had landed in Mexico, it was not clear exactly where in Mexico it was to be found. Initial estimates focused on an area 450 miles into Mexico, in the vicinity of the boundary between Durango and Chihuahua. On July 16, an Air Force team assigned to find the missile left to begin the hunt. Subsequently, the first estimate was refined and the missile's nose cone was said to be in an area one and a half miles long and a half-mile wide, but the absence of reference points made it difficult to specify exact boundaries. Air Force personnel, along with Mexican government representatives, then began aerial surveys of the area where they hoped to locate the nose cone and its cobalt-57.[45]

Two weeks later, on July 30, the nose cone was still proving to be elusive. On that day, the AEC instructed one of its contractors, Edgerton, Germeshausen and Grier (EG&G), to discontinue a survey of background radiation in Illinois that required use of an Aerial Radiological Monitoring

System (ARMS) aircraft. The crew and plane were ordered to proceed to Holloman Air Force Base in New Mexico and then on to Torreón, Mexico, to assist in the effort to recover the nose cone. The aircraft was equipped with an assortment of detection equipment, including one calibrated for cobalt-57.[46]

The first mission was flown on July 31 to familiarize the crew with the search area and pinpoint the sector marked by ground personnel about 2.2 miles north of the impact point computed at White Sands. A second mission, flying over the mountains at three hundred feet and 200 miles per hour, followed on August 1 and detected radiation that was twice as great as the background level. On August 2, the ARMS aircraft, along with a ground party, found the missing nose cone.[47]

In the 1970s a new fear emerged. In addition to Soviet or Chinese agents with hidden atomic bombs, or bombs lost through accidents, there was the fear of terrorists. Terrorism had taken on a much higher international profile in the late 1960s, thanks to the activities of the Palestine Liberation Organization (PLO) and other Arab terrorist groups.

In 1971, at a symposium concerning the prevention of a nuclear theft, an official from the AEC asked his audience to imagine what would happen if the mayor of New York received a note that read, "I've got two bird cages of plutonium and if you don't release all your prisoners and leave Vietnam, I'll blow up New York City." The mayor, according to the AEC official, would seek help in understanding the meaning of "two bird cages" and learn that it was a reference to the shipping containers for bomb-grade plutonium, containers with welded tubular frames that separate and confine pieces of the silvery, heavier-than-lead substance to prevent them from becoming close enough to start a chain reaction. The writer would be claiming that he had a nuclear weapon and New York was his hostage.[48]

Then, on September 5, 1972, during the Olympic Games in Munich, seven members of the Black September organization, a secret branch of the PLO, seized eleven Israeli athletes in the Olympic Village, killing two in the process. They then demanded that Israel free 234 of their colleagues from prison in exchange for the nine surviving hostages.[49]

German authorities agreed to the terrorists' demand that a plane be provided to transport them and their hostages to Cairo, although the intention was to have German snipers "take out" the kidnappers at the airport. Zvi Zamir, the chief of the Mossad, Israel's secret intelligence service, watched as the Germans botched the operation. While some of the Black September terrorists were hit by the first wave of shots, several were able to kill the handcuffed hostages as they sat in the helicopters that had brought them to the airport.[50]

In Israel, Prime Minister Golda Meir and her chief advisors reacted by establishing a series of hit teams to hunt down and kill those involved in planning and carrying out the massacre, an operation designated Wrath of God. In the United States, James Schlesinger, a prominent defense intellectual and future director of central intelligence and secretary of defense, was serving as chairman of the AEC. He began to worry about terrorists arming themselves with weapons far more potent than the ones that Black September used in Munich. What if terrorists, he wondered, sought to go beyond guns and grenades all the way to nuclear weapons? A series of meetings that followed explored whether terrorists could steal plutonium and fashion it into a bomb, whether they could simply steal a bomb, and whether the United States would be able to find it before it turned an American city into a smoking, radiating ruin.[51]

Possibly Schlesinger's concern was stimulated by hearing of the Nth Country Experiment, conducted by the AEC several years earlier. In April 1964 two young physicists, David Dobson and David Pipkorn (soon replaced by Robert W. Selden), were hired by Livermore Radiation Laboratory (later Lawrence Livermore National Laboratory) and given the job of designing an atomic bomb from scratch—with access to a good university library, a few competent machinists to shape uranium or plutonium, and an explosives team, to provide some technical assistance. By December 1965, they had designed a plutonium bomb, and nine months after that they had a final design. The hypothetical test of their device, in April 1967, proved a success.[52]

While the AEC was beginning to think seriously about nuclear terrorism, it was already enhancing its capability to respond to Broken Arrow incidents. On December 8, 1973, it established the Accident Response Group (ARG), employing personnel from laboratories such as Los Alamos and Lawrence Livermore to operate the Surveillance Accident and Nuclear Detection System (SANDS). Among the contractors entrusted with helping to operate the system was EG&G, which in addition to operating the ARMS aircraft had photographed atomic explosions for the Manhattan Project during World War II and developed an expertise in weapons system design and analysis.[53]

That same day, the AEC Nevada Operations Office conducted an unannounced exercise, a "snap quiz," to test EG&G's capability to respond to a nuclear accident. It began with a phone call from Mahlon E. Gates to the Nevada headquarters rear guard station. Gates, a retired Army brigadier general, was the manager of the Nevada Operations Office. His nuclear experience began in early 1945 when he returned from service in the India-Burma theater and was assigned to the Manhattan Project as a special assistant to the district engineer in Oak Ridge, Tennessee. Then, in September 1948, after obtaining a master of science from the University of Illinois, he joined the Armed Forces Special Weapons Projects in Washington, where he remained until September 1952.[54]

His message began:

> This is Mahlon E. Gates, Manager, Nevada Operations Office. An Official NV/SANDS Emergency Response Exercise is now being initiated involving a hypothetical situation.
>
> An emergency situation involving nuclear explosive has occurred in the general vicinity of Vik, Iceland. The EG&G SANDS Team should initiate plans to deploy equipment and personnel.[55]

The exercise focused on two areas: testing the SANDS Emergency Response Notification Procedures and the ability of EG&G to mobilize, pack, and transport the SANDS equipment—the gear for detecting and evaluating radiation as well as limiting its impact—from Las Vegas to Nellis Air Force Base so that it could be picked up and deployed to the accident site. While some minor deficiencies were noted, they were not considered significant.[56]

About nine weeks after that exercise, President Richard Nixon received a report produced by an ad hoc group that had been established in February 1971 when national security advisor Henry Kissinger signed National Security Study Memorandum (NSSM) 120, "United States Policy on Peaceful Applications of Atomic Energy." In reading the report, Nixon was particularly struck by several conclusions, including the need to "weigh the possibilities of sabotage, plutonium contamination threats, and armed attacks (for example, by terrorists) along with the nuclear device threat," and the requirement for "a continuing process of threat assessment and establishment of appropriate countermeasures."[57]

At the time that Kissinger signed the directive, experts were particularly worried about the theft of, if not a bomb, then nuclear material that might be used by terrorists to build one. But for many years it would be extortionists, sometimes very young ones, rather than terrorists who would issue threats of nuclear destruction if the U.S. government did not comply with their demands.[58]

Even before Richard Nixon directed parts of the federal government to prepare for the threat of nuclear terrorism, several cities had been threatened with nuclear destruction. The city of Orlando, Florida, was the first, having received a letter promising to detonate a hydrogen bomb if the author's demands were not met. What the letter writer wanted was not a change in U.S. foreign policy or the removal of American troops from his homeland, but money.

In October 1970, the Police Department of Orlando received a letter informing them that the writer was in possession of a hydrogen bomb and demanded, in exchange for not unleashing its deadly force, $1 million and safe passage out of the country. The letter also provided instructions on how to communicate. The Orlando police proceeded to do just that, but rather than accepting the demands, they challenged the author to provide some evidence that he was capable of more than writing threatening letters, that he actually had a working nuclear device at his disposal. City officials of Orlando were not about to shell out $1 million when all they really knew was that the author had good penmanship and had gained access to a piece of paper, a pen, an envelope, and a six-cent postage stamp.[59]

The extortionist complied. The letter the police received was postmarked October 28, 1970, and mailed from Orlando. The envelope and one-page letter were handwritten. Its first paragraph informed the police, "We will not call you so that you may trace the call" and "You can reply to this letter by writing to us at 1603 Mosher Drive, Orlando, which is a vacant house." It also warned the police not to try to "catch us there" for if "one of our men gets stopped the deal is off."[60]

The second paragraph repeated what was demanded and what would happen if the authorities failed to comply: "We will not settle for less than we stated in our first letter, one million in cash and safe passage out of the country. If we do not get this Orlando will be in ruins."[61]

The final paragraph responded to the police department's challenge: "Just to clear any doubts you may have about us having a hydrogen bomb, there is a drawing of it with this letter. You will need an expert in nuclear weapons to tell you if it is genuine, but believe me, it is." The enclosed drawing showed a missile-shaped object—a rectangle tapering to a nose at the top—inside a missile-shaped object. The outer object was labeled "cobalt casing," while the nose of the inner object was labeled "fuse." In a short compartment below the fuse was a circular object with lines perpendicular to its edge, and a series of starlike objects inside, with a dark center. Lines were drawn and annotated: "TNT," "U^{235}," "U^{238} tamper," and "detonator." The second, much longer, compartment in the inner object was labeled "lithium hydride."[62]

The police rushed the sketch to McCoy Air Force Base, where an armaments officer took a look at it and proclaimed that "it would probably work"—a reaction apparently shared by Stanislaw Ulam, the co-developer of the hydrogen bomb, when the diagram was described to him. In the end though, the extortion scheme did not work. The police were ordered to deliver the requested $1 million to the vacant house. But eventually a fourteen-year-old high school science student, who had been observed mowing the lawn there, was arrested and confessed. Among the items discovered in his belongings was a small uranium souvenir that he had purchased at Oak Ridge, Tennessee, the home of Oak Ridge National Laboratory, first established as part of the Manhattan Project.[63]

Despite his attempt at extortion, the diversion of resources to address it, and the nature of the threat, the teenager escaped without jail time. After sentencing, the judge suspended the sentence and placed him under the supervision of two scientists so that his talent would hopefully be channeled in a positive direction rather than in a negative one, which might well happen if he were sent to jail.[64]

The AEC was never consulted because news of the threat did not make it into AEC channels until after the event was resolved. And there were other threats. In July 1971, Manhattan was threatened with a 20- to 25-kiloton nuclear device—possibly the genesis of the AEC official's discussion of a "hypothetical" threat to New York at the 1971 symposium. Then, in October 1972, the nation's capital was threatened with an "atomic device." In March 1973, somebody threatened to destroy both Chicago and Brussels.[65]

But none of those threats had produced federal action. It was a nuclear extortion threat issued well over three years after the Orlando incident that served as the catalyst to mobilize the United States to deal with such nuclear threats. Richard Nixon had approved a national security decision memorandum on domestic safeguards in April 1974, raising James Schlesinger's concerns to the presidential level. Some of the language from the 1971 study memorandum made it into the decision memorandum. It again reported that Nixon had noted the need "to weigh the possibilities of sabotage, plutonium contamination threats, and armed attacks (for example, by terrorists) along with the nuclear device threat" and "to have a continuing process of threat assessment and establishment of appropriate countermeasures."[66]

One of those already studying the threat of nuclear terror and how to defeat it was William Chambers. After the prolonged search for the fourth bomb at Palomares, Chambers wondered how much more difficult it would be to find a bomb that terrorists had hidden in a city. Probably it would be much more difficult, he thought. In the early 1970s, he helped establish an interagency working group—the Nuclear Material Detection Steering Committee—headquartered at the AEC, with representatives from the FBI, Nuclear Regulatory Commission (NRC), and several Defense Department units. Meanwhile, scientists tried to determine the capabilities and limitations of devices made to detect nuclear materials and the impact of urban conditions on the radioactive emissions for which they would be searching.[67]

The work of the committee, Chambers, others at Los Alamos, and EG&G—which had produced a proposal for the support of long-range search efforts whose objective was to detect nuclear materials at a distance—led to a field experiment in 1973 comparing alternative radiation detection techniques against assorted nuclear weapon sources at Nellis Air Force Base in Nevada.[68]

Then in May 1974, the U.S. government received its first serious nuclear threat. A letter demanding that $200,000 be left at a particular location arrived at the FBI. Failure to comply, it claimed, would result in the explosion of a nuclear bomb somewhere in Boston. Chambers soon heard of the threat from the Energy Research and Development Administration (ERDA), the successor to the AEC and the parent organization of Los Alamos. He was told, as if he was the head of Impossible Mission Force, to rush the best men and equipment east so they could search the city. Everyone was to assemble at Griffith Air Force Base in Rome, New York. Gathering everyone at such an obscure location, it was hoped, would keep both the press and the public in the dark.[69]

Just as Harold Agnew had called Chambers to ask him to pack a bag and head for Palomares, it was Chambers's turn to make some calls. On the receiving end of one of those calls was Carl Henry, who had arrived at Los Alamos in June 1961 with a master's in math and physics from the University of Wisconsin, planning to work there for the summer before returning to Wisconsin to earn his doctorate. Instead, he became a Los Alamos lifer.

Henry recalls being home with his family one evening in May 1974 when "good old Bill Chambers called." What Chambers wanted to know was could Henry "disappear for a few days." Henry said he could and became part of the Los Alamos contingent that headed for Boston.[70]

Most of the people selected to participate came from Los Alamos and EG&G. The company's Convair was loaded in Las Vegas and then stopped in Albuquerque to pick up the Los Alamos contingent. The plane next stopped in New York late in the evening on its way to Rome, apparently to pick up several people who had arrived on commercial airliners. Connections were missed so the personnel from Los Alamos went on to the air base by chartered bus to make early contact with the Air Force and FBI. The Convair arrived the next day.[71]

Reportedly, the following morning, after an FBI briefing, the search team hired a fleet of vans in which to hide their sophisticated detection equipment, which employed chemicals such as sodium iodide to signal the presence of neutrons or radioactive particles emitted by the uranium or plutonium in a nuclear device. They quickly discovered that they were missing the drills needed to install the detectors in the vans. "If they were counting on us to save the good folk of Boston," NEST field director Jack Doyle reportedly said, "well, it was bye-bye Boston."[72]

But according to William Chambers, the team never made it to Boston because the crisis was resolved before it was ready to go in. Carl Henry also recalls that they never made it past Rome Air Force Base and that he is "not sure that the FBI wanted scientists in lab coats wandering around until they needed them." Jack Doyle also disputes the claim that he was ever so flippant about the survival of the people of Boston.[73]

In any event, the threat to Boston was no more real than the threat to Orlando. It did not even lead the U.S. government to part with real money. FBI agents left a bag with $200,000 in phony bills and staked out the area. When no one came to pick it up, they concluded that it was all a hoax. But President Gerald Ford was undoubtedly concerned by the slap-dash, amateurish response to what could have been a very real threat. One result was a top-secret memo titled "Responsibility for Search and Detection Operations."[74]

The memo, addressed to Mahlon Gates, who was still the manager of the Nevada Operations Office, was signed by Maj. Gen. Ernest Graves, the AEC's assistant general manager for military application. Gates was "directed and authorized" to assume responsibility for the planning and execution of AEC field operations using AEC radiation detection systems for the "search and identification of lost or stolen nuclear weapons and special nuclear materials, bomb threats, and radiation dispersal threats"—a far more extensive mandate than simply cleaning up after a Broken Arrow.[75]

Graves further specified several actions Gates was to take in carrying out his new assignment. He was to develop plans for the deployment of search and identification capabilities, drawing on resources from the Nevada Operations Office as well as the Los Alamos, Sandia, and Lawrence Livermore laboratories. He also needed to be prepared to take control of AEC and AEC-contractor personnel at the site during search and identification operations, as well as to contact and support the FBI agent-in-charge at the site—since the Atomic Energy Act of 1954 had made the bureau the lead agency in dealing with nuclear theft and extortion. In addition, Gates was to keep an accurate catalog of AEC special radiation detection systems and related equipment that could be used in operations. He was also directed to coordinate with the AEC weapons program the availability of scientific advisors and technical staff to be used in deployments.[76]

The use of personnel from the labs, particularly their weapons programs, as well as key AEC contractors—not on a full-time basis but when events required—would be a notable aspect of the effort for decades to come. When they were called upon, they would be operating not as representatives of their full-time employers, but as members of a new team—the Nuclear Emergency Search Team or NEST.

Chapter 2

NUCLEAR EXTORTION

IN THE MID-1970S, NEST began to take form. Central direction would come from the Nevada Operations Office, in the persons of Mahlon Gates and his deputy, Troy Wade. Wade, described in one account as "a thin, athletic-looking man with a rather serene, narrow face trimmed by a small, black goatee," had joined the weapons test program at the Nevada Test Site in 1958 as an employee of Reynolds Electrical & Engineering. He went to work for Lawrence Radiation Laboratory in 1961 and the AEC in 1968. In 1974, Wade was the assistant manager of the Nevada Operations Office.[1]

NEST headquarters, or at least the repository of much of its equipment, was the Remote Sensing Laboratory at Nellis Air Force Base. For each laboratory or contractor that was part of the program, there was a senior representative to the search team. At Los Alamos it was William Chambers, while Bill Myre and Duane C. Sewell held those positions at Sandia and Lawrence Livermore, respectively. Sewell had entered the nuclear field in 1940 when, as a graduate student at the University of California at Berkeley, he began working for Ernest Lawrence. After the United States was dragged into World War II, Sewell went to work on uranium enrichment, separating U-235 from natural uranium. From Berkeley, he moved to Oak Ridge for the remainder of the war. At war's end Sewell headed back to Berkeley, where he was asked to manage the assembly and initial startup of the 184-inch cyclotron. In 1952 Lawrence requested that Sewell, Herbert York, and a small group of physicists start a branch laboratory at Livermore, California, which would eventually become Lawrence Livermore National Laboratory. While at Livermore, Sewell helped develop the capability to respond to nuclear accidents, such as Project Crested Ice in 1968.[2]

EG&G's senior representatives were Jack Doyle and Harold "Hap" Lamonds. Doyle, about thirty-five years old at the time, had left Texas for Las Vegas in 1964 to work on computer applications in an effort to employ nuclear power to propel American rockets to other planets. After that program was terminated, he moved over to EG&G, where he managed the company's emerging effort to utilize aerial measuring systems to map the natural radioactivity of the earth's surface. It was Doyle's aircraft that was used to locate the Athena missile in Mexico. Lamonds, the former head of the Nuclear Engineering Department at North Carolina State University, had designed and built most of the instrumentation for the nuclear reactor at N.C. State–the first reactor on a college campus. Of even more relevance for an organization such as NEST, he had designed and built a very advanced radiation counting device.[3]

Participating in NEST, for both the senior representatives and other personnel, did not mean giving up their day jobs. Those at the labs and EG&G who were asked and accepted the offer to become part of the team continued their daily work in weapons design, health physics, or some other discipline, knowing that they might be told to pack a bag and head off for some distant location from which they might never return.

But their first call-out would be relatively close to home, especially for those at Livermore, and involved no real risk. It was the first NEST exercise, held at San Francisco International Airport and designed to test the group's ability to operate in a real working environment without "letting anyone know you were there," recalls William Chambers. Care was taken to be sure that if a detection device was hidden in a tool box, the person carrying it had to look like a workman, whereas if the device was in a briefcase, it had to be in the hands of a "staff man."[4]

The suitably disguised NEST personnel patrolled the airport terminals and ramps. It was done with the knowledge of airport officials, because, as Chambers recalls, "even in those days you couldn't just wander around." What team members were looking for were actual radiation sources that had been placed in the airport, not the plutonium or enriched uranium that would be employed in a nuclear device but very weak sources that would not pose health and safety problems.[5]

In the mid-1970s, as NEST was just beginning to coalesce, the threats of nuclear extortion and nuclear terrorism were topics of concern to many in the U.S. government and the think tanks it funded. One issue was whether extortionists or terrorists could acquire a sufficient amount of plutonium or highly enriched uranium (HEU) and build a bomb. Potential material for a bomb could be acquired in a variety of ways.

Weapons-grade highly enriched uranium, consisting of at least 80 percent U-235, is the most likely fissile material to be used, or least desired, for building a homemade bomb. It allows for the simplest design—a gun-type weapon in which one subcritical mass of HEU is fired into a target mass, resulting in a nuclear detonation. Plutonium is an alternative but would require construction of a more sophisticated implosion weapon, since a gun-type weapon employing plutonium would likely set off only a messy fizzle, owing to the rate of spontaneous neutron emission from plutonium.[6]

Fissile material could be covertly siphoned off from reactors or overtly hijacked during transportation (which would increase the credibility of the threats that followed). As Robert Selden of Lawrence Livermore Laboratory, and one of the participants in the Nth Country Experiment, explained to the unpleasantly surprised representatives of several foreign atomic energy authorities in November 1976, reactor-grade plutonium would be highly useful in building a bomb.[7]

Of course, without the ability to build either a gun-type weapon or an implosion device, stolen fissile material could still be used in a far less dangerous dirty bomb. But some experts believed that a privately built atomic bomb was by no means impossible. The Special Safeguards Study, directed by David Rosenbaum for the Nuclear Regulatory Commission in 1974, noted the "slow but continuing movement of personnel in and out of the areas of weapons design and manufacturing" and that forced departures "can create very strong resentments in the people involved." And Ted Taylor, the former Los Alamos physicist who was the primary subject of John McPhee's *The Curve of Binding Energy*, believed that there was sufficient information in the public domain—works such as *The Los Alamos Primer* and the *Sourcebook on Atomic Energy*—that clandestine manufacture of a nuclear bomb was possible and a bigger threat than reactor accidents or nuclear war. Robert H. Kupperman, the Arms Control and Disarmament Agency's chief scientist, offered his opinion that "there is no doubt that mass annihilation is feasible, and resourceful, technically-oriented thugs are capable of doing it."[8]

In April 1976 the Energy Research and Development Administration (ERDA), which had replaced the Atomic Energy Commission that year, released a fact sheet on the results of a study it had conducted along with its weapon laboratories. The fact sheet reported that "the conclusion reached was that it would be *FOOLHARDY FOR ANY PERSON OR GROUP TO TRY TO MAKE A 'BASEMENT ATOMIC BOMB.'*" The fact sheet went on to state, "It is unlikely that an inexperienced group, however determined, could succeed in making a crude nuclear explosive device in a few weeks, or even in a few months" and "The more hurried the effort, the greater would be the risk of a fatal accident." The challenges faced by a group seeking to build a nuclear device would include obtaining the critical mass of fissionable material, the need for individuals with "more than elemental knowledge of physics, mechanical skills, and high explosives," and good machine shop facilities. The members of the group would also "be exposed to great danger" from the nuclear materials, the risk of a criticality accident, and the handling of high explosives. It was an attempt, recalls Victor Gilinsky, who at the time was an official at the NRC, "to scare bomb makers."[9]

Others wondered whether terrorists would bother, whether even if they could build a bomb it would suit their plans to build and use one. In 1975, one of those skeptics was Brian Jenkins, a thirty-three-year-old analyst with the RAND Corporation in Santa Monica, California. RAND could trace its origins back to 1946, when it grew out of Douglas Aircraft's Santa Monica research laboratories. Jenkins was four years old at the time, living in Chicago. By 1975 he was working at RAND, after graduating from high school at age fifteen, entering UCLA as a gifted student, and joining the Green Berets in 1965. Service in the special forces took him to the Dominican Republic and Vietnam.[10]

Jenkins would go on to become a well-known expert on terrorism, producing book chapters and reports for RAND and commercial publishers, appearing on television, working as an officer of the investigative firm Kroll Associates, as well as serving on or working for the White House Commission on Aviation Safety and Security and the National Commission on Terrorism and, eventually, consulting for NEST. His interest in terrorism began no later than January 25, 1968, when he started entering data on three-by five-inch index cards about an anti-Castro group's terrorist attack. Eventually, his data base would fill hard drives.[11]

By 1975 the threat of nuclear terrorism had attracted his attention. In November he testified before the California State Assembly and turned his testimony into a RAND paper: "Will Terrorists Go Nuclear?" Jenkins characterized potential nuclear terrorists as including extortionists, fanatical environmentalists, and disgruntled employees, and their actions as encompassing the spreading of radioactive material, attacks on nuclear reactors, as well as detonation of a nuclear device. However, part of his analysis focused on terrorists with a political agenda, and the possibility of their seeking to destroy large numbers of people via an atomic explosion. Jenkins concluded that this did not seem to be a very likely scenario.[12]

He argued that "terrorism for the most part is not mindless violence" but "a campaign of violence designed to inspire fear, to create an atmosphere of alarm which causes people to exaggerate the strength and importance of the terrorist movement." He went on to explain that "since most terrorist groups are small and have few resources, the violence they carry out must be deliberately shocking . . . Terrorism is violence for effect . . . Terrorism is theater."[13]

Jenkins argued that it would be relatively rare for terrorists to try to kill large numbers of people or cause widespread damage. "Terrorists," he wrote "want a lot of people watching, not a lot of people dead." That might explain, Jenkins thought, why, aside from potential technical difficulties, they had not already used chemical or biological weapons or even conventional explosives in a manner that would produce mass casualties: "mass casualties simply may not serve the terrorists' goals and could alienate the population." Therefore, Jenkins believed that "the assembly and detonation of a nuclear bomb appears to be the least likely terrorist threat."[14]

Jenkins also was skeptical that terrorists would be interested in the deliberate dispersal of radioactive material, by detonation of a dirty bomb or another device. Many of the consequences of such an attack—more serious and protracted illnesses, a statistical rise in the mortality rate, and, in the end, an increase in the number of birth defects—did not fit the pattern of terrorist attacks. Terrorists wanted immediate and dramatic effects from a handful of violent deaths, "not a population of terminally ill, vengeance-seeking victims."[15]

Jenkins's views were echoed, to a certain extent, by the authors of a study from the U.S. Congress's Office of Technology Assessment (OTA) in 1977. They noted that no single terrorist incident in the previous fifty years had killed more than 150 people, and that "incidents involving more than 20 deaths are rare." They also commented that "on the basis of the historical record and the theory of terrorism, it is not clear that causing mass casualties or widespread damage is attractive to a terrorist group."[16]

At the same time, the congressional authors noted that there was substantial disagreement among experts concerning the likelihood that terrorists would seek to acquire a nuclear capability. In addition, they commented that there was no assurance that terrorists would continue to behave in the future as they had in the past. With regard to nuclear terrorism, they concluded that if "non-state adversary groups with the will to threaten or carry out large-scale violence do appear, they may choose nuclear means, even if it is somewhat more difficult, because they understand the public fascination and fear, and know that the nuclear threat or act will have the greatest impact."[17]

But while experts were debating whether terrorists and extortionists could build a nuclear bomb and whether terrorists would use one, people continued to claim to have such weapons and be willing to employ them unless their demands were met. Ten months before Jenkins's testimony, Los Angeles received a threat in writing, including a drawing of a one-megaton hydrogen bomb (which Ted Taylor believed would be impossible for a non-government organization to build) supposedly from the radical Weather Underground. The letter accompanying the drawing claimed that bombs had been planted in three buildings. But nothing was found and nothing exploded.[18]

Six months later, in July 1975, there was another threat to kill a large number of people using a nuclear weapon. This one came not from politically motivated terrorists but from apparent extortionists. The letter claimed, "We have successfully designed and built an atomic bomb. It is somewhere on Manhattan Island," and offered proof in the form of an accompanying one-eighth-scale drawing. Then came the threat and the warning: "We have enough plutonium and explosives for the bomb to function. This device will be used at 6:00 P.M. July 10 unless our demands are met. Do not notify the public. This will result in hysteria and the use of the bomb."[19]

The fourteen-year-old who threatened Orlando wanted only $1 million, and those threatening Boston asked for a mere $200,000. Whoever was threatening New York seemed to be aiming for a far greater payoff: the price to avoid a nuclear detonation in Manhattan was $30 million. The money was to be paid in small, unmarked bills, out of sequence, drawn from twelve Federal Reserve banks.[20]

But it wasn't the amount of money that concerned federal officials — it was the drawing. It was "sophisticated, precise, and obviously made by someone who had more than a passing acquaintance with nuclear physics," according to one account of the episode. In compliance with instructions, the FBI placed an announcement about a truck accident in Vermont on the radio news to let the extortionists know that their demands would be met. A package large enough to contain the $30 million was placed at the drop site, in Northampton, Massachusetts, that had been specified in the note.[21]

As in Boston, a year earlier, the FBI did not use real money. The package was a dummy. And as in Boston, no one ever came to pick it up. Whether the letter represented a serious attempt to become rich through nuclear blackmail remains a mystery. The extortionists, or hoaxers, were never heard from again.[22]

During the very month that Jenkins appeared before the state assembly in Sacramento, a note threatening to detonate a nuclear bomb unless a large sum of money was given to the extortionist was delivered a few hundred miles to the south. The recipient was Fred L. Hartley, the chairman and president of Union Oil Company of California. Union Oil had been created in October 1890 from the mergers of three California oil companies: Sespe Oil, Torrey Canyon Oil, and Hardison & Stewart Oil. Hartley, a native of Vancouver, British Columbia, came on the scene in 1939, not as an executive but as a refinery maintenance worker with only $25 in his pocket, a "cast-iron will," and a knack for chemical engineering. By the 1950s he was moving the company into the business of geothermal power and the refining of oil from crushed shale. In 1964 he became president and chief executive officer, positions that he would hold for twenty-four years. During that time, he initiated a merger between Union Oil and Pure Oil of Illinois as well as expanded the company's operations to South Korea, Thailand, and the North Sea.[23]

In June 1974 the New York Times reported that Hartley's company had developed a new process for extracting oil and gas from shale, a process expected to increase the company's reserves by 15 percent. Later that year the paper also reported that California Attorney General Evelle Younger filed an antitrust suit against the company, which charged it with restraint of trade for allegedly threatening to cancel a franchise of two service station operators unless they stopped selling products not purchased from Union Oil.[24] But the threat from the state of California was nothing compared to the one in the letter that arrived in the fall of 1975.

On November 4, Hartley received a special delivery letter marked "PERSONAL," and subsequently determined to have been mailed from Long Beach, at the company's office on South Boylston Street in downtown Los Angeles. The typed letter, slightly less than a page in length and dated November 3, claimed, "There is a Nuclear Device with a potential of 20 kilotons concealed on one of your valuable properties, electronically controlled in Los Angeles County." It also told Hartley, "You will not call

Nov 3rd 1975

Mr Fred L. Hartley
Union Oil Co. of Calif
461 S. Boylston St
Los Angeles Calif.

Dear Mr Hartley:
There is A Nuclear Devise with A potential of 20 Kilotons concealed on
one of your valuable properties,electronicly controlled in Los Angeles
county, You will not call the authorities or use any electronic sur-
veilance e uiptment, You could trigger this bomb accidentally, and it
will be very DIRTY.
We are not A radical group and money is not our primary objective
however we are going to charge Union Oil for some of the advertising
they will receive from this project, When you follow our orders exactly
as we write them we will deactivate the devise and give you its location
you are then to call in the A.E.C. and let their technicians disect it.
We hope this will wake up some of our bureaucrats and they will prevent
one of these devises from falling into the wrong hands,.
                    This you will do.
1. Place One Million Dollars, Small bills (nothing over $I00.oo bill)
no markings numbers unregistered, numbers non-consective into two pieces
of aircraft luggage.
2. Rent two white Ford four door sedans from Avis, Place luggage into
rear seat of one, the car with luggage for.IO days.
3. On Nov. IO I975 place Add in Los Angeles Times Personal column
it will read"Fision, We do not want F.O. on L.A." then your 2I3 phone
number, No switch board, no bugs or taps.
4. On Nov. IO, I975 at 5.3O P.M. have both cars with one driver only
in each car parked at nearest telephone booth to Artesia Blvd And
Harbor Freeway, they will call you and wait for orders, We will call
you, there will be no Transmitters or recorders in this opperation.
5. You will not attempt to photograph, follow or apprehend our pickup
for the car(they will not know of us or contents of luggage)anyway.
6. you will not attempt to apprehend anyone spending this money,we are
going to give it anonymously to a group that unknowingly helped us with
this project.
If you fail to carry out all of these orders we will send copy of this
letter to the news media with instructions to evacuate So. Calif,We will
then trigger the devise,there will be Billions of dollars in damage and
Los Angeles will be sterile for a long time.

                                Fision

P.S.
Sorry for the typing we obviously could not have a secretary do this

Extortion Letter to Fred Hartley (Source: Federal Bureau of Investigation)

the authorities or use any electronic surveillance e[q]uipment, You could
trigger this bomb accidentally, and it will be very DIRTY."[25]

The author, who used the designation "Fision [sic]," went on to
explain: "We are not A radical group and money is not our primary objective" but "we are going to charge Union Oil for some of the advertising they
will receive from this project." The author promised that if Hartley's company followed orders precisely, "we will deactivate the devise [sic] and give
you its location." Union Oil was to then call the AEC and "let their technicians disect [sic] it." To add to the confusion, prior to the payoff instructions,
Fision wrote, "We hope this will wake up some of our bureaucrats and they
will prevent one of these devises from falling into the wrong hands."[26]

What followed were five-part instructions. Union Oil representatives
were ordered to place $1 million in small bills in two pieces of airport lug-

gage, rent two white Ford four-door sedans from Avis, and purchase an ad in the November 10 *Los Angeles Times* personal column reading, "Fision, We do not want F.O. on L.A." and providing a direct 213 phone number through which to reach Hartley. Then on November 10, the representatives were to drive the rental cars to a specific telephone booth to await instructions. The instructions included the usual boiler-plate language from extortionists and kidnappers about no use of surveillance equipment and no attempts to follow or apprehend.[27]

The author also instructed Hartley that no attempt should be made to arrest anyone spending the money, as "we are going to give it anonymously to a group that unknowingly helped us with this project." Fision warned that if the instructions were not followed, "we" would send a copy of the letter to the news media "with instructions to evacuate So. Calif" and "then trigger the devise [*sic*]." The results, the author warned, would be "billions of dollars of damage" and "Los Angeles will be sterile for a long time." In a postscript, Fision offered an apology of sorts for the poorly punctuated, frequently misspelled letter: "Sorry for the typing we obviously could not have a secretary do this."[28]

What Hartley's immediate response was is not known, but given that he was described as a "gruff-barrel-chested man" whose yacht was named "My Way" and who told reporters that his retirement plans were "none of your damn business," it was probably unprintable in the *New York Times* or any other family newspaper.[29]

Union Oil's security office alerted the FBI on November 4, which called NEST. Altogether, forty NEST members along with search equipment headed to Los Angeles. Dressed in business suits and carrying radiation detection devices in ordinary briefcases, some of the NEST personnel searched on the ground and from the air six major Union Oil installations—including oil plants and offices—in the Los Angeles area, beginning on November 6. Included were the Los Angeles Refinery, a 450-acre complex in Wilmington, California; the Los Angeles Terminal, a 30-acre site in Los Angeles; the 94-acre Torrance Tank Farm, also in Los Angeles; the 15-acre Harbor Tank Farm in San Pedro; and Union's home office building on South Boylston. They also checked Hartley's home. The searches took three days. They did turn up a small chunk of raw uranium that a company official kept in his desk as a souvenir.[30]

But there was a brief period when the team thought they might have located something that could cause serious harm. NEST official Jack Doyle recalled that "the guys were out there in their trucks listening to their earpieces. Suddenly one got an intensive reading, looked up and there, about 50 yards away, was a big bulky, unidentified wooden crate resting by a refinery fence. There was a moment of real panic." However, what the team found was not a nuclear device but a box some repairmen had left behind, sitting atop soil that was emitting natural radioactivity. Before they realized it was nothing threatening, "the searchers had plenty of time to think about the implications of their job," according to an early account of NEST's activities.[31]

Despite NEST personnel not having found any devices, or maybe because they did not, Union Oil placed the requested personal message in the *Los Angeles Times* on November 10. Rather than using the number in the ad, Fision phoned the pay phone specified in the November 4 letter sometime after 3:30 in the afternoon. Two bureau cars equipped with radios and containing dummy payoff packages were waiting. The FBI agents were ordered to another pay phone, where they received a second call. This one instructed that the vehicle with the payoff money be left in a parking lot at the California Yacht Anchorage in San Pedro, which was done at about 7:05 that evening. During the second call, the agents noted that an individual at a nearby phone booth concluded a phone call at the same time as Fision. Ignoring Fision's instructions, they trailed the suspect, who was driving a new car without license plates or a temporary operating permit, first to the Black Forest Restaurant on Pacific Coast Highway and then to the same parking lot where the bureau left the car with the dummy payoff. That car was then placed under "discreet surveillance."[32]

The driver, according to an FBI account, "disappeared into the boat storage area of the harbor" where he "was presumed to have boarded one of the hundreds of luxury boats stored in this area." The next morning the bureau was able to determine that the car was owned by a leasing company and used by one of its salesmen—Frank James, who was sixty-two years old at the time. When the agents, including one who had observed the driver of the license plate–free car and the one who had received both phone calls from Fision, confronted James on his boat, he denied any involvement. Both concluded he was lying.[33]

James did agree to let the agents search his boat and car, which yielded a typewriter, and turned over the clothes he claimed to be wearing the previous evening. He also agreed to have his fingerprints taken. A search of the clothes failed to reveal anything of interest to the agents. They also sent samples of two pages, typed by James on the typewriter, to the FBI laboratory. The lab tried but failed to match latent prints from the pay phone where agents believed Fision made his calls and from the extortion letter and envelope to those of James.[34]

While waiting to be fingerprinted at the local FBI office, James would tell the special agent-in-charge, Elmer F. Linberg, that he realized he was in serious trouble. And indeed he was—but not immediately. Although he denied that the voice on the tape made of Fision's February 10 phone calls to the FBI agents was his, the bureau found others who believed the voice did or might belong to Frank James. However, after reviewing the case against James in late January 1976, the Indictment Committee of the U.S. Attorney's Office in Los Angeles declined to prosecute.[35]

But the FBI effort to link James to the extortion attempt continued, including lining up more associates of James who believed that the voice of the extortionist sounded like that of James. One, after hearing the tape recordings, told the FBI, "It sounds like Frank James to me." Bureau interviews also began to reveal possible motivations for James's actions. A relative of James reported that the suspect was in financial difficulty and worried by his wife's medical problems.[36]

Eventually the bureau's efforts led to a three-count indictment of James, charging him with having sent the extortion letter and making the two telephone calls threatening nuclear destruction if the demand for $1 million was not met. Shortly after the indictment was issued, an official of the Union Oil security department provided the FBI a package of news articles and documents suggesting an additional motive: a conflict between Union Oil and the residents near the Union Oil tank farm on 22nd Street in San Pedro.[37]

On October 8, 1976, in U.S. District Court in Los Angeles, James was found guilty on all three counts of the indictment. On November 1, the presiding judge, William Gray, sentenced James to a remarkably light sentence: six months in jail, followed by three years of probation. In September 18, 1978, after Gray denied two motions on behalf of James, he ordered the convicted extortionist to report in one week to begin serving his sentence.[38]

In July 1976 the United States observed its bicentennial. Events commemorating the signing of the Declaration of Independence and the War of Independence actually started on April 18, 1975, when President Gerald Ford arrived in Boston to light a third lantern at the city's Old North

Church, to symbolize the beginning of America's third century. The following day he delivered a speech commemorating the 200th anniversary of the battles—of Lexington and Concord—that launched the American Revolution, and the Post Office issued a "US Bicentennial" postage stamp.[39]

But the major celebrations took place on Saturday and Sunday, July 3 and 4, 1976. Coverage, in the pre–cable news era, was limited to the three major networks and local stations, but it was extensive. CBS Evening News anchor Walter Cronkite hosted fourteen hours of coverage called "In Celebration of US," while NBC devoted ten hours to the "Glorious Fourth" along with other programs. Viewers could also watch the "Great American Birthday Party" on ABC. On July 4, a substantial fleet of tall-masted sailing ships gathered in New York City. The celebration also included fireworks in the skies over several major American cities, including the nation's capital. President Ford presided over the nationally televised Washington fireworks.[40]

The ceremonies went off without incident. But there had been concern inside the national security establishment that individuals or groups far less enthusiastic about America's history might be planning their own fireworks display, one that might involve a nuclear device and result in mass mourning rather than celebration. In an April 1976 assessment of nuclear terrorism, analysts at the Central Intelligence Agency (CIA) wrote, "The prospect of nuclear-armed terrorists can, in fact, no longer be dismissed." The same analysts also noted that there would be "major problems . . . involved in the acquisition, storage, transport, and employment of a nuclear device." Thus, the prospect of a dirty bomb was considered greater.[41]

There was no hard evidence that such a plan was in the works, but just to be on the safe side, NEST was called upon to provide some reassurance. During June 1976, team members conducted a survey of central Washington, D.C., to measure background radiation, since detecting threatening levels required knowledge of how much and what kind of natural radiation was present on an everyday basis—radiation that might come from Vermont granite, soil, or even a truckload of bananas. Their evaluation of several key facilities produced data that "would have been invaluable in the event of a nuclear extortion threat in the Washington area during the Bicentennial celebration," according to an official Department of Energy publication.[42]

If events followed the "Nest Operations Plan" for surveying Washington, D.C., three technicians arrived on June 3 to equip a rented utility van with power and communications systems for the operation. The van was to be used to obtain representative gamma and neutron background data. Any strong gamma signals obtained would be analyzed "to determine principal gamma contributors." The remaining crew and large detector equipment arrived on Sunday, June 6, on a Martin 404 aircraft.[43]

Altogether the NEST field detachment consisted of twelve people—the ERDA Nevada on-site manager; a scientific advisor; the NEST logistics officer (Jack Doyle); physicists from Los Alamos, Lawrence Livermore, and EG&G; as well as two pilots, two technical specialists, a communications engineer, and a logistics specialist.[44]

The drive around downtown Washington, which apparently began on June 8, covered areas around the city's monuments and memorials—the Washington Monument, Jefferson Memorial, and Lincoln Memorial. The unobtrusive van drove along the Potomac, along North Carolina Avenue, Highway 95, and along Pennsylvania Avenue. The next day, the van targeted New Hampshire, North Carolina, Pennsylvania, and Massachusetts avenues. On June 10, the focus was on "special areas" designated by the FBI's Washington field office, and the following day was devoted to "selected typical dwelling areas." On June 12, the NEST detachment was to pack up its equipment and return to Las Vegas on the Martin 404.[45]

The Energy Department had made the operation easier by its decision to establish a NEST presence closer to the nation's capital, and undoubtedly New York and Boston, a presence that could at least provide a quick reaction force in the event of any future nuclear threat to those cities. As a result, NEST-East had been established at Andrews Air Force Base in Maryland, best known as the site from which *Air Force One* departs and lands.[46]

Washington was not the only city where NEST deployed in 1976. It responded to another threat to Boston. A small NEST contingent also went to Spokane, Washington, after the police there received a message on November 23, 1976, threatening ten explosions, each one dispersing ten pounds of radioactive material, and demanding $560,000 in small bills. But there would be no arrests, no payoffs, and no damage.[47]

When members of NEST patrolled the streets of Washington in June 1976 to measure radiation levels, not only did they do it in secret, they did it as members of a secret organization, for NEST's very existence was classified. That changed in 1977. During a closed session of the House Armed

Services Committee, the panel's members were told of the team and, presumably, some of what it had done. That was followed by public disclosure in the form of a double-spaced, one-and-a-half-page fact sheet. According to one government official, it "was dropped quietly into a table in the press room at midnight on a Sunday night" in the hope no one would notice.[48]

However, according to William Chambers the announcement followed the conclusion that "we, the FBI would have to work with local government." It was apparent, Chambers recalls, that it would not be possible to keep NEST activities classified if the team was called out, since both the local government and police would have to be notified. NEST would have to do some of its work at the unclassified level, and thus they "succumbed to the obvious."[49]

The fact sheet announced that "a special group of scientists, engineers, and technicians has been formed by the Energy Research and Development Administration to provide technical assistance to the Federal Bureau of Investigation (FBI) in responding to nuclear threats" and that "the group is called the Nuclear Emergency Search Team (NEST)." It went on to inform any readers that the FBI had overall jurisdiction at the federal level, and the Department of Defense was responsible for explosive ordnance disposal.[50]

It also enumerated six missions for NEST personnel and equipment. They could evaluate the technical credibility of the threat, search for radioactive material, identify the isotope and quantity of radioactive material, assess the probability of nuclear yield or spread of radioactive material, assess the potential for personnel injury and property damage in the event that the device detonated, and assist in the render-safe and disposal operations.[51]

The fact sheet noted that in addition to ERDA, Los Alamos Scientific Laboratory, Lawrence Livermore Laboratory, Sandia Laboratories, and EG&G were "conducting continuing research and study projects to improve ERDA capabilities in this area."[52]

Among the contributions being made at Livermore, starting in 1977, was the Nuclear Assessment Program. Technical and behavioral experts at the lab would assess the nuclear threats—concerning stolen weapons, improvised nuclear devices (INDs), radiological dispersal devices (RDDs), and nuclear reactors—for the Energy Department, NRC, and FBI, and report their conclusions, their rationale, and recommendations. The information they were to provide would cover credibility of the threat, assessment of the device, technical and behavioral profiles, the hazards involved, the urgency of a response, and investigative leads. The assessors at Livermore would check to see if the threat was lifted from some novel or perhaps a work of nonfiction. They also would examine writing style, look for mis-spelled words, and check for references that would eliminate or enhance their credibility.[53]

This team was capable of deploying with other NEST personnel, bringing along all known data, critiquing disablement options, and provid-ing updates as the situation changed. It also relied on outside help, such as Dr. Murray Miron, a professor psychology at Syracuse University who specialized in psycholinguistics, specifically "in the language of those men who would use language to threaten others."[54]

Scientists at Los Alamos contributed by designing a portable suitcase that could be carried in a car or van and used to detect the neutrons emitted by radioactive material, which along with gamma rays are the only emis-sions from radioactive material detectable at a distance. The aluminum suitcase, with approximate dimensions of eighteen by twenty-six by twelve inches, and weighing seventy pounds, contained detectors, amplifiers, dis-criminators, power supplies, batteries, a battery charger, and detection logic circuitry. An alarm system, based on the amount of time between incoming neutron pulses, rather than the number of pulses within a given time period, would alert NEST technicians to the presence of nuclear material.[55]

In 1978 a second wave of lab and contractor personnel signed up for NEST. One of those was Alan V. Mode, who grew up just outside of Tacoma, Washington, a city of about 145,000 people, and traveled down-state, to attend Whitman College in Walla Walla. His 1962 degree from Whitman was followed by a doctorate in 1965 from the "infamous" chemis-try department at the University of Illinois, which turned out three hundred newly minted Ph.D.'s each year. Of the three graduate programs Mode had to choose from, Illinois offered him the most money. He joined Livermore in August 1965, specializing in organic and nuclear chemistry, and began over thirty years of work in nuclear weapons diagnostics. During the course of his nuclear chemistry work, he met NEST members, which eventually led to an invitation to join.[56]

In October 1978, a congressional office received a package containing a dry brown substance, with a note claiming that it was radioactive. NEST was called in and examined the material. It was dirt. That was only one of several NEST deployments for the year, which had included visits to Buffalo, New York, and Miamisburg, Ohio, in January, May, and August, respectively.[57]

During that year, the concern for nuclear terrorism reached the highest levels of the Intelligence Community and executive branch. In July, the national intelligence officer for nonproliferation was preparing a presidential briefing on nuclear terrorist threats, and in December the director of central intelligence issued the still-secret Special National Intelligence Estimate 6-78, *Likelihood of Attempted Acquisition of Nuclear Weapons or Materials by Foreign Terrorist Groups for Use Against the United States.*[58]

Wilmington, North Carolina, whose population even today is only about 100,000, was the childhood home to many who went on to become famous—most prominently, basketball superstar Michael Jordan. Others who merited the tag "famous" and called Wilmington home as children include the late journalists David Brinkley and Charles Kuralt, boxer Sugar Ray Leonard, Los Angeles Rams quarterback Roman Gabriel, and country music star Charlie Daniels.[59]

In contrast, among those who have lived or worked in Wilmington who would qualify for the description "infamous" is David Learned Dale, described as five feet ten inches tall, weighing about 180 pounds, with collar-length blond hair, a mustache, and a tan. Many of the one-time residents of Wilmington may have demanded a large sum of money (usually in exchange for their talents), but none, other than Dale, did so in exchange for the return of a hundred pounds of stolen uranium, an act that would result in a call asking for NEST's help.

On Friday, January 26, 1979, Dale was working as a temporary contractor employee at the General Electric low-enriched-uranium plant located about five miles north of Wilmington on approximately 800,000 square feet of land. The plant employed about sixteen hundred people and operated around the clock between 11:00 p.m. Sunday and midnight Friday. Unlike other days, Dale did more than work the day shift that Friday. At 10:50 that night he returned and entered the plant along with the night shift. Instead of showing his yellow contractor badge to gain admittance, he used his Florida driver's license, with its blue background. Dale believed that to gain access to the area of the plant he wanted to penetrate, he needed a picture badge with a blue background. His previous successful attempts to enter using his driver's license had established that plant security was less than the best.[60]

Once inside the plant, Dale ordinarily would have been guided by gates and fences into a parking area, except that one gate had been removed to allow the installation of truck scales. He was able to continue down the unprotected road to an area next to the building he wanted to penetrate. After entry, he continued on to his usual work area, the Chem Tech Lab, and used his own key to enter. Once in the lab he gathered his protective clothing, a two-wheel cart used to move 55-gallon drums, and a container for shipping chemicals. The container could hold two 5-gallon cans. He then headed for a door leading to a stairwell into the plant's radiation-controlled area.[61]

Although the door was normally locked, even though regulations did not require it to be, on the night of January 26 it was slightly open because the locking mechanism had malfunctioned. Once inside, Dale put on his protective clothing and climbed the stairs to the Blend Queue Area. He remove two 5-gallon cans of uranium oxide, carried them down the stairs, and placed them in the shipping container. He then removed his protective garments and retraced his steps back to the Chem Tech Lab. Once back in the lab, he opened a can and removed some of the material he intended to use for his extortion effort. With the two-wheel cart, he transported the remaining material to his car and loaded it in his trunk. He retraced his steps and left the plant just before midnight along with the departing shift, in time to avoid the requirement to sign out if leaving the plant after midnight.[62]

On Monday, January 29, Randall Alkema, the plant's general manager, arrived at work sometime after 8:00 a.m. Waiting for him in his office was a letter, marked "personal and private," that had been found outside by a cleaning woman, and a vial containing, it would subsequently be determined, 2.6 percent uranium oxide.[63]

The letter, hand-printed in capital letters, ran six pages long. It began by informing its reader that the "vial you are looking at contains a sample of uranium abstracted from your stock in Wilmington" and continued, "We are in possession of 66.350 kilograms. It consists of containers #2602 MO 1024 (35.350 KG) and #2602 MO 1017 (31.000 KG)." The writer went on to explain "Plan A": on February 1 similar vials would be sent to the NRC, the Union of Concerned Scientists (UCS), a variety of antinuclear groups, Ralph Nader, every major newspaper in the country, the White House, "and every Senator or Congressman who has ever expressed doubt about nuclear power." The result would be "a massive outcry from all quarters" that would force the NRC to order "an immediate shutdown of your plant." The author went on for another two pages, describing the specific reactions expected from groups such as the UCS and Clamshell Alliance, how the release would destroy the goodwill anticipated from the national conference on energy advocacy set to start on February 2 and would help turn the public against nuclear power. It would be "a resounding defeat for the industry, a disaster for GE in particular, and will destroy your career."[64]

But there was "one way and only one way that this can be avoided." That way involved GE assembling, within forty-eight hours, $100,000 in nonconsecutively numbered used bills—in ten-, twenty-, and fifty-dollar denominations. After the money was delivered, in compliance with the instructions that would follow, the uranium would be returned to Wilmington, the letter promised. The author also warned that the uranium had already been transported a thousand miles away from Wilmington and that "if you make even so much as an attempt to bring in the police . . . Plan B will be implemented automatically." Plan B involved everything threatened in Plan A, plus the contents of one can would be spread throughout the downtown area of a major city. In addition, the price of the remaining can would increase to $200,000.[65]

After checking that the containers identified by the extortionist were indeed missing, the general manager notified higher-level GE officials, who passed on the information to the NRC and the FBI's Atlanta office, which turned the case over to the bureau's Charlotte office on January 29. The special agent-in-charge in Charlotte requested that the bureau's Behavioral Science Unit prepare a personality profile, that the letter's writing style be compared with the writing in the anonymous question/suggestion forms that employees left for management as well as with the style of any previous extortion letters held by the FBI's laboratory, and that the letter be examined by the lab's Latent Fingerprint Section.[66]

A copy of the letter was also sent to Murray Miron, who would try to extract details about an anonymous author from what he or she had written. Miron apparently contacted the Energy Department's Nuclear Threat Credibility Assessment Group at Lawrence Livermore, the key element of the Nuclear Assessment Program, to obtain additional data to help in his evaluation.[67]

Miron provided a demographic profile of the "UNSUB" (unknown subject)—a college-educated Caucasian male, between twenty-five and thirty years old, with an interest in commercial activities, the stock market, and corporate affairs—and noted that he accurately assessed the commercial value of the stolen material, "which would not be generally known to the general public." Miron also concluded that his failure to provide data on the composition of the uranium hexafluoride or indication of its enrichment implied that he "is not trained in nuclear technology or engineering." He also concluded that "the consistent use of the GE acronym over that of the full name of the company and the absence of justification of choosing the Wilmington plant as the target indicates that UNSUB is employed at that facility" and that the motivational factors did not suggest that the UNSUB was "acting out of resentment or vengeful impulses" and that the "UNSUB is still employed in that facility with a good fitness record."[68]

Miron also concluded that despite the letter's claim that the theft was a group action, "the message content reflects content indicators which point to this as the act of a single perpetrator." In addition, he considered the assertion that the nuclear material was moved to a distant location improbable and "falsely designated to conceal the fact that the material is, in fact, close by." Indeed, Miron suggested that the material might be hidden in the plant, with the perpetrator having changed labels and serial numbers on the cans.[69]

The UNSUB, Miron believed, was above average in intelligence and dedication and "without a doubt a psychopath" who attributes "venal, solely commercial motivations to the officials of GE and the government." "There is not," Miron noted, "a single reference to principle or morality within the message." And there is "no indication that the scheme indicates political activism." Rather, the plan "is entirely motivated by instrumental monetary considerations." He doubted that the subject would dispose of the material in the way he threatened, although he might send one or two additional samples to one of the groups named.[70]

Miron was not the only individual charged with trying to assess the credibility of the threat and determine the identity of the perpetrator. According to one assessment, completed by a staff member of the Los Alamos Scientific Laboratory within an hour of the discovery of the note, the threat to distribute samples to Ralph Nader and others was feasible—particularly since the managing editor of the *Wilmington Star* had already received a plastic vial sealed with duct tape with a skull and crossbones and the word "poison" written in red. The assessment also concluded that the threat probably came from an employee at the plant who was working alone (because of the small amount of money being demanded) and motivated solely by financial gain.[71]

Several staffers from Lawrence Livermore also produced analyses between January 30 and February 1. A January 30 assessment reported the threat to have a high technical credibility owing to the accurate description of the missing containers and the isotopic assay of the sample. It also suggested that use of the phrase "the bomb to drop" in the extortion letter could imply the nuclear material might be dispersed via an airplane or from a high-rise building. An "operations practicality assessment," however, completed by an analyst that same day classified the threat as a moderate-confidence hoax because of the apparent flaws in the plan. It was not clear, according to the Livermore analyst, that distribution of samples would force a plant shutdown or result in damage to the industry. In addition, the analyst did not think much of the extortionist's demand that the money be paid in forty-eight hours or of the threatened consequences of bringing in the police.[72]

The judgment that the threat could well be a hoax, involving the theft of only a small amount of material, was echoed, to some extent, in the four-hour response by four other analysts from Livermore on January 30. They noted that while "the author of the threat appears to be disposed to carry out the threatened actions . . . his message also contains elements that are consistent with hoaxes—attempting to create a powerful threat from a weak position." Thus, they concluded that the author was willing to carry out the threat, but they also believed, "with moderate to high confidence," that "he does not have uranium oxide in more than gram quantities and therefore could not contaminate entire cities as threatened." The assessment's authors also agreed with Miron and the Los Alamos assessment that the threatener was probably a plant employee (since he could specify the missing containers, knew the name and phone number of the plant manager, and was able to slide his note under the manager's door) and was acting alone.[73]

Such analyses helped narrow the list of suspects—although a review of the credibility assessment effort by Livermore apparently contained a number of criticisms.* In any case, on February 1, the director of the FBI, informed the White House Situation Room that a number of possible suspects had been identified but that the "investigation was now focusing on one prime suspect." That suspect was David Learned Dale, whose handwriting was judged to match that of the extortion note. That, and other

---

*A letter from an official of the Energy Department's Office of Safeguards and Security to a special agent of the FBI's Criminal Intelligence Division noted that on page 65 of a Livermore report on the Wilmington, North Carolina, extortion incident, "the continuing problem of credibility assessment communications is identified," and that his office is "presently considering a proposal associated with improving upon the credibility assessment system." See Martin J. Dowd, Assistant Director for Security Affairs, Office of Safeguards and Security, Department of Energy, to Special Agent Robert Satkowski, Criminal Investigation Division, Federal Bureau of Investigation, March 2, 1979.

factors, led to his arrest at 3:30 that afternoon for violation of the Hobbs Act—for committing an act of extortion. Dale quickly admitted his guilt and told the FBI that the two missing containers were in a nearby field about three miles from the GE plant. On May 7, 1979, Dale was given a fifteen-year sentence, to be served at the Federal Correctional Center in Butler, North Carolina.[74]

NEST's involvement extended beyond helping Murray Miron analyze the content of the extortion letter. On January 31, 1979, NEST representatives were dispatched from NEST-East at the request of the FBI's Charlotte office. They traveled to North Carolina on their own plane, with a physicist serving as the head of the team. At about 7:30 that evening they arrived at the Wilmington General Electric plant to calibrate assorted radiation detection equipment as well as establish liaison with company personnel and representatives from the Atlanta region of the NRC.[75]

Starting about 8:00 a.m. on February 1, NEST personnel conducted a sweep of all parking areas at the GE plant, which produced no hits. In addition, they set up a discreet radiation detection checkpoint in the area of the gate controlling access to employees' vehicles. No unusual levels of radiation were detected. A helicopter equipped with radiation detection equipment arrived in Wilmington too but was not used because of the amount of background radiation present.[76]

NEST personnel also examined, for signs of radioactive contamination, Dale's residence and its immediate vicinity, the site where the containers were recovered, the personnel who recovered the containers, and the containers themselves. The containers were checked for alpha-beta contamination as well as gamma radiation.[77]

NEST's failure to find the missing uranium did not greatly concern its leaders, since they believed the team would have discovered the stash within forty-eight hours and that discovery was only preempted by the FBI's quick apprehension of Dale. What was disturbing to NEST officials such as Jack Doyle was that the incident was "a real step up the ladder," for never before had an extortionist actually possessed nuclear materials. "We began with paper threats that really had no basis in fact in them," Doyle observed in 1980. "Then we got into a generation of paper threats on which people had really done their homework and turned in some damn credible material. Next we had a couple of incidents where some hardware got out and some garbage men found a couple of homemade plutonium 239 containers—dead ringers for Government issue—in a garbage dump. Then Wilmington. What's the next step up the ladder? I hate to think."[78]

. . .

Less than two months after Dale was apprehended, NEST personnel returned to a middle Atlantic state to deal with a nuclear threat. However, the threat came from neither terrorists nor extortionists. Less than a minute after 4:00 a.m. on Wednesday, March 28, 1979, when about 50 to 60 of the plant's 525 employees were present, several water pumps in Unit 2 of the Three Mile Island nuclear power plant, ten miles southeast of Harrisburg, Pennsylvania, stopped working. In the days that followed, equipment failures, inappropriate procedures, human error, and ignorance produced what a presidential commission characterized as the "worst crisis yet experienced by the nation's nuclear power industry."[79]

At 6:30 a.m. that Wednesday, Mike Janowski, a radiation/chemistry technician, walked through the Unit 2 auxiliary building with a portable beta-gamma survey meter and detected rapidly rising radiation levels, the result of a partially uncovered reactor core. Soon he was running down the hall yelling, "Get the hell out!" Shortly before 7:00 a.m. a "site emergency" was declared and the process of notifying state and federal emergency agencies began. What the consequences would be were not clear. Would damage and radiation be confined to the plant or would threatening radiation spread to the surrounding area, putting citizens at risk and requiring evacuation?[80]

NEST resources had been committed to answering such questions even before the incident occurred. A March 8, 1977, agreement between the ERDA and the NRC called for NEST team personnel and equipment to respond to an emergency involving "NRC licensees," which included the nation's nuclear power plants. Before two o'clock on the afternoon of March 28, a Hughes H-500 helicopter, with sophisticated monitoring equipment, landed at the Capital City airport, the command post for emergency operations, with an advance NEST party.[81]

The particular element of NEST's capabilities that was needed at Three Mile Island was its aerial measurement system, which could determine how much radioactivity had been emitted into the atmosphere and where it was headed. About an hour later, team member Bob Shipman set out to find out some answers. After he took some background readings, his helicopter began a slow circle toward the plant. It was not long before Shipman's instruments began to go crazy, and the needles on the meters hit their limits. Shipman shouted to the copter's pilot to get out of the area.[82]

Shipman and his pilot began to fly in and out of the invisible plume emanating from the nuclear power plant, the boundaries of which they could identify by the change in readings. In addition, when the helicopter headed back to the airport and away from the plume, the instruments showed only background radiation, indicating the radiation came from noble gases such as xenon, and not the more dangerous fission products such as cesium, iodine, and strontium, which would have stuck to the helicopter.[83]

The initial NEST contingent would be supplemented with additional personnel flying in from Nevada and replacements for the advance party arriving from NEST-East. Over a dozen NEST personnel would continue to monitor the radiation levels in the vicinity of the power plant and would be able to provide the good news that there was little threat to public safety.[84]

In the summer of 1979, a NEST team traveled to Idaho—not in response to an extortion or terrorist threat but for one of the many exercises it would take part in over the years. It had been in Idaho two years earlier, at the Idaho National Engineering and Environmental Laboratory, which occupied about 890 square miles in the southeastern Idaho desert. The lab had been established in 1949 as the National Reactor Testing Station, and in 1975 it became the nation's second largest National Environmental Research Park.[85]

The Idaho laboratory had been the host for a NEST exercise in August 1977 designated NEST-77. The exercise had been conducted in cooperation with the FBI and Defense Department, which had the primary responsibility for explosive ordnance disposal, and involved about 150 individuals—either participants or observers—at a cost of about $200,000. All NEST would say about the exercise was that it was designed to "evaluate techniques and sensitive radiation detection and other special equipment." It was somewhat more specific in its "Observer Plan," which stated that the purpose of the exercise was to focus on "developing the technical aspects of improvised nuclear device (IND) diagnostics and rendering safe, and not serve as a full operational evaluation." In plainer language, the exercise focused on determining specifics of the device and disabling it.*

---

*William Chambers recalls it differently. He described it as the "first field exercise to test operationally all technical functions from search techniques to IND disablement in an integrated way with joint lab/EOD teams." William Chambers, "Summary: A Brief History of NEST," October 24, 1995, p. 2.

It was prepared to assure the press and public that "there is no danger to any of the participants, [lab] employees or the public." The actual exercise involved explosive ordnance personnel neutralizing booby traps and a NEST diagnostic team removing a nuclear source located in a van.[86]

Two years later, NEST had a new partner for the exercise, the 1st Special Forces Operational Detachment–Delta, better known as Delta Force. Delta had been created in 1977 to give the United States a dedicated counterterrorist unit. While NEST's scientists could detect the presence of a nuclear device and help disassemble it, they were not expected to forcibly recover it. That could be Delta's job. Eric L. Haney, a founding Delta Force member, recalls that the unit spent the week prior to the exercise in Idaho Falls, twenty-five miles east of the desert site, where the lab's Science and Technology Campus was located, "learning about reactors, nuclear materials, and atomic weapons."[87]

According to Haney, the exercise involved recovering a stolen nuclear device held by a group of terrorists who were also holding a group of American scientists. He also recalls that "working on this nuclear exercise, we got a bit of start. We found out that our normal rules of engagement didn't necessarily apply to nuclear materials." In contrast to Delta's philosophy that "we would go to any extremes to avoid harming a hostage . . . national policy dictated that when nuclear materials were involved, hostage lives were of secondary importance." But according to Haney, "we were confident that even in a nuclear incident, we could still save hostages."[88]

The decade ended in 1980 with an incident in Washington, D.C., that required NEST's attention. That event was the work of Tom Falvey and Patti Hutchinson of Greenpeace, the environmental and political organization created by a group of Canadian and expatriate American peace activists in Vancouver in 1970 and originally called the Don't Make a Wave Committee. In May 1972 it became the Greenpeace Foundation. From the beginning, the foundation's activities extended beyond protest, the dissemination of information, and peaceful political action. In 1978 and 1979, with a crew of twenty volunteers, the *Rainbow Warrior*, a ship purchased by Greenpeace in 1978, challenged Icelandic whaling in the north Atlantic. In September 1979, the ship was captured by an Icelandic gunboat. In early 1980 the ship was again detained, off the French port of Cherbourg, while trying to disrupt the transportation of nuclear waste to a reprocessing plant.[89]

According to a former Greenpeace official, Falvey and Hutchinson arranged to have uranium mine tailings picked up, he believes, from the side of Interstate 80 in South Dakota. Such tailings are by-products of uranium processing and can be obtained at abandoned mine sites. The radioactive material was placed inside a red 55-gallon drum packed in concrete. Also inside the concrete was the sensor from a single geiger counter, whose ticking was amplified through a sound system in the truck.[90]

During the afternoon of August 21, 1980, four representatives of Greenpeace held an antinuclear demonstration on the sidewalk in front of the White House. They left behind the drum, with its ticking geiger counter, to emphasize nuclear waste piles that it claimed were contaminating the western United States. U.S. Army explosive ordnance personnel carted the barrel off to Kingman Island, in the middle of the Anacostia River and near Washington's RFK Memorial Stadium. Meanwhile, the FBI called NEST, which dispatched a team to examine the barrel and dismantle it. At 6:45 that evening, NEST advised the FBI by phone that the "device was a hoax," according to an FBI memo, which also reported that "at no time did this device present a threat to the health of the individuals in the vicinity of the White House." Another memo reported that NEST advised that "no radioactive material or any other dangerous substance whatsoever was found."[91]

Somewhere along the way, possibly as early as the day of the demonstration, some officials apparently came to believe that Greenpeace had claimed to have placed a nuclear bomb in front of the White House — hence the reference to a "device." Further, several years later, Herb Hahn, program administrator of NEST at Andrews Air Force Base, was quoted in the *Washington Post* as saying, "They said it was a nuclear bomb, but it was really a recording device." According to former Greenpeace executive director Steve Sawyer, "We described it as what it was, i.e. radioactive waste. We sued the *Post* over that particular story, and by way of recompense they printed a very nice feature on us sometime later in their Sunday magazine."[92]

Chapter 3

MORNING LIGHT

In 1957, at Plesetsk, about five hundred miles north of Moscow, Soviet construction crews began digging out huge chunks of earth as part of their effort to build a secret military base. Its intended purpose was to serve as a launch site for the first Soviet intercontinental ballistic missile, the R-7. On December 15, 1959, the first R-7 was fired from the site, which was known only by the designation Leningrad-300. By the mid-1960s it had become a key site for launching Soviet satellites, including reconnaissance satellites, into high-inclination or polar orbits.[1]

About twenty years after construction began, on September 18, 1977, the Soviets launched a forty-six-foot-long, 7,700-pound Soviet reconnaissance satellite from Plesetsk. It went into an orbit with an inclination of 65 degrees and speed of 15,000 miles per hour, a speed that allowed it to complete one revolution of the earth every eighty-nine minutes.[2]

The spacecraft that blasted off that day comprised one part of the Soviet intelligence effort to keep tabs on the U.S. Navy—its submarines, aircraft, and surface ships, including destroyers, cruisers, and aircraft carriers. That effort, in addition to utilizing whatever traditional spies could be recruited, involved employment of the proverbial "fishing trawlers" loaded with eavesdropping equipment rather than fishing gear, land-based listening posts, photographic and electronic intelligence aircraft, and satellites. Heading up the effort was the chief of fleet intelligence, who reported to the chief of the Chief Intelligence Directorate of the Soviet General Staff—the GRU (Glavnoye Razvedyvatelnoye Upravleniye).[3]

The program that produced the satellite launched on September 18, the Space-Based Sea Reconnaissance and Detection System, began in 1959–1960. Its prime objective was to enhance the Soviet Navy's ability, particularly that of Soviet Naval Aviation, to target major U.S. and allied naval forces. It was given the technical designation "US"—the Russian abbreviation for "Controlled Satellite"—and subsequently the code name Morya-1 (Seas-1), which would be replaced by Legenda (Legend). The US program would evolve into two: US-P, spacecraft equipped to intercept the signals from surface ships, and US-A, spacecraft equipped with radar systems of sufficiently high resolution to detect and identify various classes of ships.[4]

The first US-A satellite, one of many test versions, had been launched on December 27, 1965, for an eighteen-day mission; it was identified only as Cosmos 102. Its purpose was as much an official secret as its launch site. The satellite orbited on September 18 was the twentieth in the series, and the seventh since the system had been declared operational by the Central Committee and Council of Ministers in October 1974. To the world it was identified only as Cosmos 954, and it followed another US-A satellite, Cosmos 952, that had been put into orbit two days earlier.[5]

The launch of the two Radar Ocean Reconnaissance Satellites, or RORSATs, as they were known by U.S. intelligence, within three days reflected the fact that they operated in pairs and had short lifetimes. With one following the other in twenty to thirty minutes, it would be possible for computers on the ground to estimate the speed and course of any ships that were detected. On their next pass over the region, ninety minutes later, the satellites could verify the estimates.[6]

Each satellite's primary payload was a semicircular X-band radar antenna, which extended out from the end of the cylindrical spacecraft to its full length. Apparently, there was also a secondary payload, a side-looking radar antenna. According to a 1975 U.S. interagency intelligence assessment, the radar could detect "medium-size and some small ships—such as cruisers and destroyers—under favorable conditions, and probably can detect large ships—such as aircraft carriers—even under adverse sea conditions." In addition to being able to transmit data to Moscow, the satellite was able to send it directly to Soviet naval units and possibly to Soviet Naval Aviation Backfire bombers.[7]

Radar images could be obtained even when clouds covered a target, because radio waves penetrate the same cloud cover that blocks the view of the cameras carried by photographic reconnaissance satellites. But it was not possible to produce images with the same clarity and precision as those produced by photographic satellites of the era. A radar antenna of sufficient size to produce such imagery would be far too immense to get into orbit and maintain in space. However, it was possible to place a radar about 155 miles above the earth and obtain images of sufficient resolution to detect and distinguish between large and medium-size vessels. But it would not be efficient to use the standard solar panels to power the spacecraft because of the atmospheric density at the altitude.[8]

The alternative was to use a nuclear reactor as a power source. Apparently, many test and operational models of the US-A satellites carried the

Bouk reactor—a predecessor of the Topaz model—with 66 pounds of more than 90 percent enriched uranium-235. The reactor, along with the fuel, weighed about 285 pounds. Because it was carrying radioactive material, the satellite, when its mission concluded, sometime between three and ten weeks, could not be allowed to reenter the earth's atmosphere as were photographic reconnaissance satellites powered by solar panels. Non-nuclear-powered satellites could be expected to burn up in the atmosphere, but a reactor and its core could well survive. Instead, the satellite's reactor and core would be boosted to an altitude of about 560 to 620 miles, which would keep the satellite orbiting the earth for approximately 500 to 1,000 years. By that time its radioactive fuel would have become less lethal and the reactor could be allowed to reenter the atmosphere.[9]

But Cosmos 954 did not follow the plan. According to Anatoliy Savin, the chief designer at the design bureau responsible for the development and production of the US-A satellites, a major malfunction occurred in the control system used for boosting the reactor and core into a higher orbit. As a result, the satellite would eventually reenter the atmosphere long before the radioactive material could decay. Keeping track of Cosmos 954's movements for the Soviet Union during the crisis were the controllers at the Soviet Air Defense Forces' Center for Monitoring Cosmic Space (TsKKP), a component of the System for Monitoring Cosmic Space (SKKP).[10]

Of course, the U.S. Intelligence Community also would have been closely watching the movements of Cosmos 954 starting from before the launch. U.S. spy satellites would have photographed Plesetsk during their repeated passes over the site, returning images of the launch vehicle waiting to be fired into space. One or two of the Defense Support Program (DSP) infrared launch detection satellites in geosynchronous orbit, 22,300 miles above the equator, would have detected the actual launch. Since DSP satellites could also monitor satellites in orbit, a use designated Fast Walker, they would have tracked Cosmos 954 as it circled the earth.[11]

But the bulk of intelligence on the movements of the Soviet satellite would have come from a variety of assets on the ground. In late 1977 those assets included, but were not limited to, a Navy "electronic fence" (the Navy Space Surveillance System, NAVSPUR) that detected satellites passing through it, a series of Baker-Nunn cameras at a variety of locations around the world, early-warning and ballistic missile radars that also could detect near-earth objects, and the Air Force Maui Optical System

(AMOS) telescope on the Hawaiian island of Maui, specifically on top of Mt. Haleakala, 10,000 feet above sea level. A Baker-Nunn camera was also located on Haleakala.[12]

One of the primary users of the data collected from America's assorted sensors was the Space Objects Identification Group of the Space Defense Center (subordinate to the Air Defense Command), which could determine a spacecraft's size and orientation; whether it was pointed toward the earth, the sun, or outer space; and whether it was tumbling, spinning, or rotating. Normally, the group would plot and analyze a satellite's orbit once a week—unless a problem was detected or a special request was made to examine a satellite's behavior.[13]

By November 17, intelligence information, possibly the result of NSA intercepts of TsKKP communications, indicated that Cosmos 954, whose reentry had been predicted for the following April by the Space Defense Center, was in trouble. The center's chief at the time, Lt. Col. William Yanchek, recalled that in late November or early December the "intelligence people came to us and asked us to run some predictions" on when the craft might decay.[14]

It was twenty-nine-year-old Capt. David R. Tohlen, a mathematician and the chief orbital analyst at the center, who spearheaded the effort to take a closer look at what Cosmos 954 was doing as it orbited the earth. Tohlen and his team soon discovered that the satellite, which had been circling the earth once every eighty-nine minutes, had slowed down by one-tenth of a minute and then by two-tenths of a minute. "It may not seem so, but that's a big change," Tohlen told the New York Times in early 1978.* "That was our biggest indication that something had occurred. The satellite had become unstable and this had increased the drag by six times." Tracking stations were instructed to monitor the ailing satellite on a daily basis.[15]

By early December, the Defense Intelligence Agency had taken an interest in Cosmos 954 and convened its own interagency group, which included representatives from the State and Energy departments and possibly the CIA and NSA. The group's members thought it likely that if the satellite remained stable in its orbit, it would reenter in the spring or summer of 1978. They also wondered whether the spy satellite had a fail-safe system that would sense the existence of a problem and automatically boost

---

*A change in speed of one-tenth of a minute would result in a difference of twenty-five miles in where the satellite would be expected to hit earth.

it into a higher orbit. Judgments differed and caution suggested they proceed without the assumption that such a system existed.[16]

The Defense Intelligence Agency panel concluded that there was a small chance that Cosmos 954's return to earth could pose a serious problem. By that time the State Department representative had drafted a letter to the NSC suggesting the issue be handled by the NSC staff, and the panel forwarded the letter to the council. At the same time, the Energy Department's representative was close to completing his statistical study of outcomes and probabilities. He ultimately concluded that there was only a 1-in-10,000 chance of any human being hurt by the satellite's return to earth.[17]

On December 8, the Energy Department's Nevada Operations Office began receiving data on the possible premature return of the Soviet spy satellite. Eleven days later, the NSC formed the Ad Hoc Committee on Space Debris, its membership representing the results of an "active recruiting" campaign by the committee's chairman and including individuals from the State, Defense, and Energy departments, CIA, NASA, and the Office of Science and Technology Policy. The NSC directed the preparation of precontingency plans, to ensure that tracking resources were available and that the proper agencies were receiving data from the systems monitoring the troubled Soviet satellite. The operation was designated Morning Light, a code name randomly generated by a computer in Washington.[18]

Early in the new year, on January 6, Captain Tohlen and his staff had concluded that Cosmos 954 had lost its attitude stabilization system, was out of control, and would crash-land within a day or two of January 23. Committee members soon received phone calls summoning them to the NSC. The council assigned responsibility for domestic contingencies to the Department of Energy, put the State Department on notice in the event the spacecraft landed on foreign soil, and instructed the Defense Department to provide the necessary support. The Joint Nuclear Accident Coordination Center (JNACC) was directed to coordinate logistical support between the Defense and Energy departments. Gus Weiss, an NSC staffer who was involved in the effort, recalled, "I found myself promising airplanes, reconnaissance, and all manner of gadgets to these agencies, should they be needed. At the time, I was not sure I had the authority to do this, but such was the sticky wicket of MORNING LIGHT members."[19]

Then, on January 12, U.S. national security advisor Zbigniew Brzezinski asked Soviet ambassador Anatoliy F. Dobrynin for details about the ailing satellite, explaining that U.S. tracking stations were reporting that it was behaving abnormally and U.S. officials were concerned that it carried a nuclear reactor. He wanted to know if the reactor was designed to disintegrate upon reentry or whether "there is a significant probability of impact of the nuclear fuel." "We were pretty sure that it was coming down and we wanted the Russians to provide some details about what was aboard," a presidential advisor told the New York Times. The next day, Dobrynin presented Brzezinski with some further details about the satellite, including its nuclear reactor. Additional contacts on the following day produced further disclosures.[20]

The Soviet reply of January 14 contained both good news and bad news. The good news was that the reactor "is explosive-proof because the accumulation of a critical mass is ruled out" and that "the design of the plant provides for its destruction and burning upon entering denser layers of the atmosphere." The bad news was that "in view of the accident aboard the satellite [depressurization], it cannot be ruled out that some destroyed parts of the plants still would reach the surface of the earth." "In that case," the Soviets claimed, "an insignificant local contamination may occur in the places of impact with earth which would require limited usual measures of cleaning up."[21]

A colleague of Weiss remarked that he wasn't really sure what the "usual measures of cleaning up" a reactor that slammed into the earth from outer space might be, and that there was some ambiguity about what was meant by "explosive-proof." Still, there was considerable relief at the news, or claim, that the reactor was designed to burn up during reentry.[22]

The committee had other issues to ponder too. Only the United States and Soviet Union were aware of the problems with Cosmos 954. One policy question was, Which other countries should the United States inform? The answer turned out to be "allies," including Great Britain, Canada, Australia, New Zealand, and Japan, and some other countries with which the United States shared special relationships, such as agreements to allow tracking facilities on their soil. But the nations warned by the United States were also asked not to make any public announcement, since there was no plan for the U.S. authorities to do so (even though the public was paying both their salaries and the bill for keeping track of what was in space and returning to earth).[23]

One White House security advisor would explain that the silence reflected the desire to "head off a recreation of Mercury Theater" — a reference to Orson Welles's "War of the Worlds" radio broadcast on Mercury Theatre on the Air in late October 1938, in which Martians were reported to have landed at Grover's Mill, New Jersey. Panic and hysteria followed among many listeners who did not realize, since the show was broadcast without station breaks or commercials, they were listening to a work of fiction.[24]

While the United States was communicating with assorted foreign governments, and various agencies were developing contingency plans in event that parts of the satellite, particularly the radioactive parts, landed on solid ground rather than in the two-thirds of the planet covered by water, others were busy monitoring the satellite's behavior.

Tracking stations were monitoring the satellite on a daily basis, and assorted groups, including several members of NEST at Lawrence Livermore National Laboratory, were trying to transform the raw data collected into reliable estimates of where the satellite would hit. One was Milo Bell, an engineer. The other was Ira Morrison, a mathematician. They were given exclusive use of a Control Data Corporation 7600 computer for as long as they needed to predict where Cosmos 954 would hit earth. At the time one of the world's most advance machines, the 7600 was C-shaped to save floor space, for it would have been about twenty-five feet long stretched out. It also cost several million dollars.[25]

Also providing support with his calculations at Livermore was Robert Kelley. After graduating from Harvey Mudd College in Claremont, California, in 1967, Kelley obtained a master's in nuclear engineering from the University of Missouri in 1968, a degree that led to a job offer from Lawrence Livermore and his spending the next five years, not in California, but at the Nevada Test Site. After that tour of duty Kelley was brought up to Livermore, where he specialized in plutonium isotope separation for weapons development. Morning Light proved to be his introduction to NEST, although it did not involve a trip to the harsh Canadian wilderness. In the much more pleasant environment of California, he tried to calculate when the Soviet satellite would burn up and the likely pattern of fallen debris.[26]

By January 17, the tracking data led to the conclusion that the satellite would crash into some part of North America. The following day, the Canadian government was notified of the unpleasant possibility that the satellite would be landing on its territory. During the final three or four days of the satellite's life, as its altitude dropped from 150 to 100 miles, the Space Defense Center's computers received and analyzed over five thousand observations from tracking stations around the world. As a result, on January 22, revised reentry projections led to the conclusion that the satellite would crash to earth in northern Canada.[27]

But eighteen hours before its eventual reentry on January 24, Captain Tohlen and his orbital analysts estimated that if the satellite reentered during its next revolution, it would splash down in the Pacific on the International Dateline, 30 degrees north of the equator. Six hours later they predicted a possible reentry off the coast of southwest Africa. After another six hours, with the satellite yet to reenter, Tohlen's attention turned to a possible splashdown in the Atlantic, at a location southeast of the Azores. Three hours later he alerted the consumers of his reports that the satellite would indeed come down over northern Canada. But an hour later, he had changed his mind, at least tentatively, and was focusing on an area in the Pacific north of Hawaii.[28]

Tohlen explained that "this satellite had high mass. The higher the mass, the lower the drag. Most other satellites would have had a higher drag and decayed at the Pacific target." But at 4:40 a.m., he received a message from the telescopic camera site on Maui reporting that Cosmos 954 was glowing with heat and on a trajectory that would take it to the vicinity of Canada's Queen Charlotte Islands. Tohlen picked up the phone and alerted the North American Aerospace Defense Command (NORAD).[29]

Back in Washington, the Defense Intelligence Agency's Current Operations Center had also been closely monitoring Cosmos 954. The center, Weiss recalled, had "its complements of maps, red and green telephones, TV monitors, and flashing lights." At 5:00 a.m. Eastern Standard Time on January 24, the center announced imminent reentry, within a window of time equal to one complete orbit—eighty-nine minutes. It took a little bit longer than predicted, but at 6:53 a.m., on revolution 2060, the Soviet spy satellite, or pieces of the spacecraft that had not burned up in the atmosphere, landed in Canada.[30]

While Cosmos 954 was doing its dance of death in space, the United States was able to provide tracking data to its Canadian ally. Once the satellite hit earth, President Jimmy Carter called Prime Minister Pierre Elliot Trudeau and offered U.S. assistance in locating the debris and in cleaning it up. In a return phone call, Trudeau accepted the offer. But knowing it had landed in Canada, even in a particular region in Canada, was a far cry from knowing exactly where it had landed, precisely where to send personnel to collect the debris and check for radiation contamination.[31]

One form of assistance involved employing the same overhead reconnaissance assets, the satellites and aircraft normally used to keep an eye on American adversaries, to help locate the debris. At the time, the United States had three active satellite reconnaissance programs, including the Gambit and Hexagon programs, whose satellites, KH-8 and KH-9, respectively, returned their imagery in film canisters. KH-8 images could have a resolution of under six inches, while KH-9 images, which covered much greater swaths of territory, had a resolution of between one and two feet. However, at the time of Cosmos 954's reentry and for a considerable time afterward, neither program had a spacecraft in orbit.[32]

An even more sensitive program was the Kennan program, which did have one of its satellites, a KH-11, in orbit. The first KH-11 had been launched less than a year earlier, on December 19, 1976, and would spend over two years in orbit. In contrast to the KH-8 and KH-9, the KH-11 could return its images in real time, as its optical system converted the varying light levels of the scene being viewed into numbers and relayed that data (via a satellite) to a ground station at Fort Belvoir, Virigina, where the image was re-created.[33]

A much older reconnaissance asset was the U-2, the spy plane that, in various versions, had been flying since the spring and summer of 1956, when U-2s began overflying Eastern Europe and the Soviet Union. In addition to carrying imagery and signal intelligence sensors, U-2s also gathered radioactive debris from atmospheric nuclear tests. The version being operated by the Strategic Air Command in 1977 was the U-2R, the latest variant of the spy plane, which flew at altitudes over 65,000 feet. The ones that flew missions over Canada in search of debris from Cosmos 954 after January 24, 1978, were equipped with high-altitude radiation air-sampling equipment in the hope that they could detect any radioactivity emitted from the crashed satellite.[34]

Eleven U-2 Morning Light missions, totaling 107 hours of flying time, were flown between January 24, 1978, and November 7, 1978. On the evening of January 24, one of those U-2Rs took off from its home at Beale Air Force Base, California, to fly a ten-hour sortie over northwestern Canada. Then, from late January through March, U-2s based at Beale flew six more air-sampling missions over the Pacific Ocean in an orbit that stretched from Beale to the Yukon. Another four missions followed: on April 10, May 11, August 8, and November 7.[35]

For those final four missions, the Air Force Technical Applications Center (AFTAC), whose primary mission was the detection of nuclear tests in the atmosphere or underground, asked SAC's Strategic Reconnaissance Center to have the U-2R fly a Pacific Ocean orbit that extended from Beale as far south as Baja, California. After having considered variables such as weather and seasonal wind patterns, AFTAC wanted the orbit moved southward in the unlikely event that a cloud of nuclear-contaminated air produced by Cosmos 954's January disintegration remained suspended and undetected in the stratosphere. As with the first seven missions, the final four missions produced negative results. There were no signs of radioactivity in the atmosphere as a result of Cosmos 954's reentry.[36]

In addition to the U-2, WC-135 aircraft, belonging to the Military Airlift Command but operated under AFTAC's directions, were also employed to search the atmosphere for signs of radioactivity. A WC-135 is 139 feet long, stands 42 feet tall, has a wingspan of almost 131 feet, and can take off with a load of personnel and cargo weighing about 300,000 pounds. WC-135s as well as KC-135s had been used for years to collect debris from atmospheric tests. The WC-135 missions also failed to find radioactivity in the atmosphere.[37]

Those findings provided convincing evidence that one feared consequence of the satellite's reentry with implications for public health — formation of a nuclear cloud from scattered radioactive debris that would float through the stratosphere for weeks or months — had not materialized.[38]

But that finding had no impact on the need and desire to search for whatever was left of the satellite. Radioactive pieces would be a hazard to the health of any Canadian citizen or wildlife that came in contact with them, and the debris had fallen in an area used by native people and other hunters and fishermen. It was also a part of the country across which caribou herds migrated. In addition, U.S. scientists, such as those working for the Air Force's Foreign Technology Division and Energy Department laboratories, might eventually learn a lot about Soviet space engineering and the satellite's capability from the remains of the spacecraft.[39]

As well as providing data from high-flying satellites and spy planes, the United States lent Canada the services of a contingent from NEST who would work in conjunction with Canadian radiation monitoring personnel. NEST planning meetings for a possible deployment began on December 6, before it was known where the malfunctioning satellite would land. On

January 12, as the reentry of Cosmos 954 came closer, NEST management and personnel were placed on alert.[40]

Ten days later, on Sunday, January 22, as reentry became imminent, two C-141 Starlifter aircraft arrived at McCarran International Airport in Las Vegas. Another two landed at Travis Air Force Base, located between San Francisco and Sacramento, while another put down at Andrews Air Force Base, about ten miles southeast of Washington, D.C. At each airfield, personnel began loading NEST equipment—some packed in shock-resistant containers—that originated at NEST's Las Vegas headquarters, Lawrence Livermore National Laboratory, and NEST-East headquarters at Andrews. The equipment included radiation detection devices, two small helicopters, a portable communications center, and a van that carried a small computer to analyze data produced by the detection devices. A commercial jet liner was also available to transport a large number of personnel if necessary.[41]

At the same time, sixty NEST personnel, including Jack Doyle of EG&G, remained on alert; they kept their "suitcases packed and were prepared to fly on 2 hours notice anywhere from Brazil to the Arctic." Where they might be headed if called was still up in the air, or more precisely, in low-earth orbit—despite the best efforts of America's satellite trackers and orbital analysts. "Upon until the last orbit, the guessing was anywhere in the world," Doyle remarked at the time. When he was called at 1:45 on the morning of January 24, he still did not know exactly where he would be headed. According to Quentin Bristow, a Canadian participant in Morning Light, the world was playing "Russian roulette with a vengeance."[42]

But once David Tohlen received the phone call from the Hawaiian space surveillance outpost and Pierre Trudeau accepted Jimmy Carter's offer of assistance, it became clear that NEST personnel and equipment would be headed north to search part of Canada's sparsely populated Northwest Territories. The territories had approximately the same northern and southern latitudes as Alaska and, despite occupying about 707,000 square miles, had a population of only forty thousand, with a quarter of that number residing in the territory's capital, Yellowknife. And there were eyewitness sightings: a night janitor in an office building in Yellowknife as well as a corporal serving with a Royal Canadian Mounted Police detachment at Hay River, 125 miles south of Yellowknife, reported a bright object descending to earth.* Tracking data indicated that they were seeing the

---

*In early February the chief of the CIA's Minneapolis office notified the chief of the CIA's Domestic Collection Division that an individual (whose identity has been redacted

remnants of Cosmos 954, that after a fifteen-minute reentry, the satellite, or what was left of it, had crashed somewhere between Yellowknife and Baker Lake, near Hudson Bay, about 500 miles to the northeast.[43]

Yellowknife is located on the north shore of Great Slave Lake, the second-largest lake in the Northwest Territories—298 miles long and 68 miles wide at maximum—and the ninth largest in the world. It is also the deepest lake in North America, at 2,015 feet. During the winter its ice is thick enough for semitrailer trucks to drive over. Baker Lake is about 500 miles to the northeast of Yellowknife. Until 1915, when a Royal Canadian Mounted Police outpost was established in the vicinity, a small community of Inuit comprised the only human presence in the area.[44]

Once it was known that the satellite landed in Canada, two C-141s carrying NEST personnel and equipment—one from Andrews and the other from Las Vegas—took off. A third, from Las Vegas, made the journey the next day, while the two Starlifters on standby at Travis were unloaded and released. When the aircraft began to touch down, at 4:45 p.m. local time (Mountain Standard Time) on January 24, it was not in Yellowknife but about 615 miles virtually due south at Canadian Forces Base (CFB) Edmonton, the Canadian military facility best suited to direct and support the search-and-recovery effort. At 8:30 MST that morning, Col. David F. Garland, the commander of CFB Edmonton, had been directed to assume control of Operation Morning Light.[45]

One of his first acts was to send the CFB Edmonton Nuclear Accident Support Team (NAST) to Yellowknife to check the city and smaller communities in the vicinity (including Fort Reliance) for radiation. The team left shortly after noon and arrived in time to conduct a detailed survey of the city that night, a survey that, since it involved troops dressed in yellow protective gear walking the streets while they examined radiation meters and took air samples, managed to cause some apprehension in the city's normally easygoing citizens until the results proved negative.[46]

Another one of Garland's first acts was to call Troy Wade in Nevada,

---

from the declassified document) "reported information that might relate to the Soviet satellite that fell in Canada on Tuesday, 24 January." The individual stated that while going to work on Friday, January 27, he observed "an odd object coming down in the sky." Presumably, the Minneapolis office thought the object might be some remnant of Cosmos 954. In any case, he forwarded the individual's name and phone numbers "in the event anyone is tracking UFO's." Chief, Minneapolis Office, To: Chief, Domestic Collection Division, Subject: Report of UFO at Time of Soviet Satellite Failure, February 9, 1978, available at www.foia.cia.gov.

still the assistant manager of the Nevada Operations Office and the person to talk to about how NEST could help Canada find what was left of Cosmos 954.[47]

In their talk, Garland laid out what help he hoped to get, at least initially, from NEST. Undoubtedly, Wade told him what assistance NEST would need on arrival, including arctic clothing suitable for severe weather conditions. The base prepared for "the onslaught of technicians and scientists." When the NEST aircraft touched down, technical assistance was

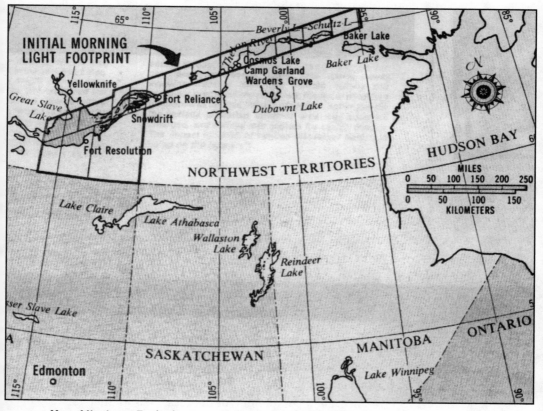

Map of Northwest Territories (Source: United States Department of Energy)

available to help mount the team's equipment into the Canadian aircraft and to check that the equipment and aircraft were compatible. Also nearby was Colonel Garland, who immediately conferred with Mahlon Gates, who was in charge of the contingent of seventy NEST personnel to arrive that day (and who would be joined by another fifty members before the operation concluded). Gates suggested that the team's members could use a good night's rest after the long journey before starting operations, but Garland told him that he was under orders to begin operations as soon as possible. NEST member Zolin Burson, who worked in EG&G's aerial measurements unit, and one of the NEST members who arrived that day recalled that they "were greeted by the commander and told to fly as soon as possible."[48]

Other NEST members who arrived to help Canada find the remains of Cosmos 954 were Joseph Tinney, the head of the National Resource Evaluation Program at Lawrence Livermore, and William Ayres, a health physicist who specialized in radiation fallout hazards. Russell Lease, head of the "Eastern Measurements Office" (NEST-East's cover title), and Richard Lynn of EG&G, a specialist in radiation detection, also experienced the Canadian winter. William Chambers was not among the contingent. He had participated in the planning stages but then tore up his leg in a skiing accident. William Nelson, who had succeeded Duane Sewell as the senior NEST representative at Livermore, replaced Chambers as one of the senior scientific NEST advisors to Morning Light.[49]

Nelson's path to Morning Light included graduation from an Oakland high school, a stint at the University of California at Berkeley as a major in forestry, a subject he lost interest in after a few years, and becoming a Navy aviation cadet in February 1953. The last led to a tour in the Far East and then a return to school, first at Oakland Junior College and then back at Berkeley. During his senior year at Berkeley he decided to pursue a master's degree, and as a result of looking for something to do over the summer, he wound up as an intern at Lawrence Radiation Laboratory with a high-level security clearance. After completing his master's, Nelson interviewed with a number of companies and "got many offers," but "none better than Livermore."[50]

Nelson's Morning Light job was one he shared with Richard L. Wagner, Livermore's assistant director for testing, who "attached himself" to the operation, Nelson recalls. While Nelson would serve as liaison to the Canadian military, Wagner would be responsible for the U.S. scientific personnel on the mission.[51]

By midnight, NEST detection equipment, including a gamma-ray spectrometer, which determines the energy and count rate of gamma rays emitted by radioactive substances, had been installed in two Canadian C-130 Hercules aircraft. The C-130 is a ninety-eight-foot-long plane that can carry up to 38,104 pounds of cargo and personnel and fly at about 340 miles per hour at an altitude of up to 35,317 feet, with a range between 2,455 and 6,070 miles. Two NEST helicopters with gamma-ray detection equipment were loaded directly onto the planes, to avoid the delay involved in disassembling and separating the equipment, since the range of the C-130s exceeds that of the Hughes H-500 helicopters. At about 12:30 a.m. local time on January 25, the first plane took off, followed by the second at 6:30 and a third at 12:55 p.m. Those flights marked the beginning of twelve-hour flight shifts for six crews. Flying to and returning from the search area consumed four hours of each flight. Since the effort took place in the far north during the dead of winter, much of the eight hours spent searching occurred in dark, with temperatures reaching –40°F (with a windchill of up to –105).[52]

The first NEST-equipped C-130 that flew on January 25 traveled along a straight line for the five hundred miles between Yellowknife and Baker Lake. The search area had been divided into eight sectors (eventually another six would be added), each thirty miles wide. During the rest of the day, the three NEST-equipped C-130s, with their gamma-ray detection equipment, would fly sixty-mile-long lines, back and forth, one nautical mile apart, at an altitude of 1,500 feet above ground in the western portion of the search area—covering half of the corridor's width in each shift. At 1,500 feet NEST's equipment could detect sources emitting enough radioactivity to represent a major danger, but not those emitting only low levels of radioactivity.[53]

The second search aircraft took off at about 6:30 that morning. On the ninth line a strong signal occurred, about three times greater than that for normal background radiation. The pilot was instructed to overfly the location two more times at an altitude of about 1,360 feet and once at a lower altitude. Each time, the signal was detected and seemed to be associated with a cliff. The location coordinates were determined, to allow for subsequent verification and analysis. Eventually, analysts concluded that the signal was probably from the many uranium deposits in the area, which could produce counts two to three times higher than normal background radiation.[54]

The third and last flight of January 25 took off at 12:55 in the afternoon, to cover sector 5. During the latter half of the flight, the equipment picked up a weak gamma signal. On the return trip a strong gamma signal

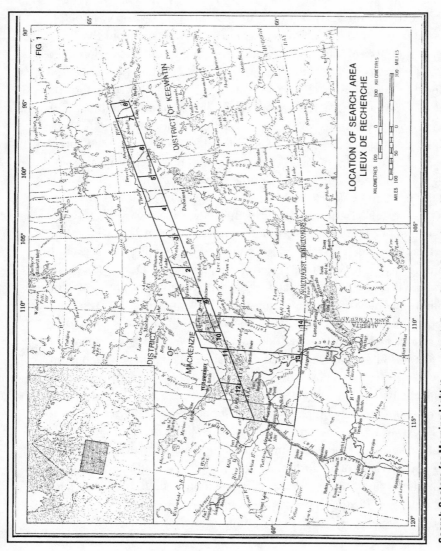

Search Sectors for Morning Light (Source: Atomic Energy Control Board, *Cosmos 954:*

The Occurrence and Nature of Recovered Debris, Ottawa, 1980)

was picked up and reconfirmed after several additional passes. Exactly where the signal originated from was difficult to determine because by that time it was dark and visual navigation was problematic. There was a strong possibility that the searchers had found a piece of Cosmos 954, for they were in a probable area of impact and one without geologic anomalies. However, the signal appeared too narrow for a point gamma source.[55]

The detection equipment provided by NEST, and carried on the flights, employed sodium iodide crystals, which produced a light flash when hit by a gamma ray. Photocells transformed the light into an electrical charge, whose intensity provided a measure of the gamma rays that hit the crystal. The radioactive substances that emit gamma rays do so in a unique pattern, which a computer can depict in the form of a graph resembling a fever chart, a chart that will look different for each radioactive substance.[56]

Three men would watch the radiation-monitoring console, looking for "a hit," an abrupt jump in gamma radiation levels above the background radiation that is emitted naturally from the terrain and received as normal cosmic radiation from space.[57]

Magnetic tapes of each survey—five radiation readings per second— were first processed in Edmonton, by computer on the van that arrived with the rest of the NEST equipment. The tapes were converted to a slow-scan video image and sent to Los Alamos and Livermore for further analysis, to filter out "background hits." The spent fuels from a nuclear reactor contain exotic products that can come only from the fission of uranium in a reactor. But the gamma rays emitted by natural uranium and thorium deposits in the Northwest Territories overlapped those of fission products, an overlap accentuated by the speed of the search planes. Computer analysis could help unscramble the puzzle, but there would still be instances when scientists would find themselves debating whether a hit was real or false. At Edmonton a "hit assessement group," chaired by a Canadian and including representatives of the Canadian Atomic Energy Control Board, Livermore, Los Alamos, and EG&G, wrestled with such issues.[58]

.   .   .

By late Thursday, January 26, the NEST contingent had reached over one hundred with the arrival of about twenty new people that day.* NEST personnel were on the ground as well as in the air. Ten members of the team (from the Department of Energy, EG&G, and Lawrence Livermore) had arrived at the Baker Lake area in the company of Canadian military personnel. That same day, Canadian radiation equipment arrived in Edmonton and was installed in a fourth C-130, which took off that night but only after Bob Grasty of the Geological Survey of Canada, who had arrived at the Edmonton base to take a look, discovered that no one there knew that his organization had been conducting gamma-ray spectrometry surveys for ten years.[59]

Up to twelve aircraft were involved in the search: four C-130 Hercules (three carrying NEST equipment), three CC-138 Twin Otter search-and-rescue planes (used to conduct visual searches), three CH-135 Huey helicopters, one CH-14 Chinook heavy-lift helicopter, and one plane belonging to NEST. Canadian helicopters deployed to Yellowknife also carried NEST detection equipment. The plane owned by NEST was a Convair 580T, which carried infrared radiation detection equipment.[60]

It was about 7:25 a.m. local time when the C-130 carrying Bob Grasty, *Toronto Star* reporter Sid Handelman, and the spectrometer system from the Geological Survey of Canada, developed by Quentin Bristow, took off from CFB Edmonton to complete the search of sector 1. On its seventeenth and final pass, at 8:00 p.m. that evening, while the plane was flying over the McLeod Bay area north of Fort Reliance, located on the northeast end of Great Slave Lake, Handelman leaned over the shoulder of Grasty, who was monitoring the spectrometer, and asked why the needle was moving so much. Grasty told him, "I think we've got a hit." Spectral analysis the following day by the NEST computer system verified levels of isotopes of lanthanum (used to strengthen alloys), zirconium (used in the cladding for nuclear fuel rods), and niobium (used in nuclear fuel) consistent with debris from Cosmos 954.[61]

On January 27, NEST and Canadian personnel were operational at Yellowknife, which put some of the territory to be searched within the

---

*One individual who would come and go very quickly was a representative of the Los Alamos laboratory's intelligence organization. He was "told to go home," according to William Nelson, who also recalls that there was a desire to be sure that the search effort was not perceived as an intelligence collection operation. Interview with William Nelson, Alamo, Calif., June 9, 2007.

range of helicopters. On February 6, a large NEST detection system would be mounted on one of those helicopters.[62]

Also, on January 27, eleven missions were flown from Edmonton, completing coverage of 60 percent of the original search area and resulting in the detection of several possible hits. In addition, NEST's Convair 580T overflew the site of the first hit. On January 28, one of the C-130s equipped with NEST detection gear would overfly the same area, a mission that succeeded in further verifying the hit. The following morning, search aircraft flying over McLeod Bay detected three hot spots, two of which were later confirmed as satellite debris.[63]

A discovery by people on the ground, one that "grabbed the headlines," according to one NEST member, took place on January 28—although it did not involve American NEST or Canadian NAST personnel. Late that afternoon, word reached Canadian authorities that two men had discovered and touched an object on the ice of the Thelon River that might have been part of Cosmos 954. The two, Mike Mobley and John Mordhorst, were, with four others, on a dogsled trip to the site where trapper and "hermit of the north" John Hornby and two colleagues had perished in 1927.* The six were camped at Warden's Grove, twelve miles from the site of their discovery and located in sector 4, about two hundred miles northeast of Fort Reliance.[64]

When Mobley and Mordhorst discovered the metal prongs and twisted struts embedded in a crater in the ice, they thought the metal pieces might be attached to a large dense object under the ice, which would lead Lawrence Livermore to begin work on a camera to photograph what, if anything, was beneath the surface. While the shape of the debris reminded the two of moose antlers, they assumed they were from a downed aircraft, and Mobley touched the metal with a gloved hand. When they returned to their base camp, they discovered that the rest of the group had heard a radio

---

*Hornby, forty-seven years old at the time of his death, was an explorer best known for his Arctic expeditions. His effort, in 1926, to spend a year on a spot by the Thelon River along with his cousin and another young man ended in tragedy when they missed the southward caribou migration and were unable to find enough food to survive the winter. "John Hornby," http://en.wikipedia.org/org/wiki/John_Hornby, accessed May 14, 2007; Department of Energy, Nevada Operations Office, *Operation Morning Light Canadian Northwest Territories/1978: A Non-Technical Summary of United States Participation,* NV-198, September 1978, p. 33.

broadcast about the satellite search. They called Fort Reliance with news of their discovery and were told, a little too late, "Don't go closer to that object than 1,000 feet." The next day Mobley and Mordhorst were flown by helicopter to Baker Lake, put on a C-130, and flown to Edmonton, where tests at the Cross Cancer Institute revealed their close encounter with the remains of the Soviet spy satellite had resulted in no ill effects. Their four colleagues were evacuated to Yellowknife.[65]

While the two explorers were on their way to Edmonton, a scientific team was sent out from Baker Lake to examine the discovery (which would turn out to be the only debris from Cosmos 954 in the area). Chopping though the ice with Inuit chisels, they found nothing under the ice and no signs of radioactivity. A subsequent analysis of the refrozen ice and snow indicated the presence of lithium, a substance commonly used as a neutron shield. The lithium had apparently produced a violent reaction with the snow and ice, resulting in enough heat to form the crater. C-130 radiation detection aircraft overflying the area quickly discovered more radioactive hot spots, which would prove to be due to geology rather than the wayward satellite.[66]

On the last day of January, the four NEST- and Canadian-equipped C-130 aircraft had finished their initial survey of all eight original sectors plus the two sectors (9 and 10) that had been added the day before to the west of sector 1, where so many hits had registered. A total of thirty-one flights had been conducted, on a twenty-four-hours-a-day, seven-days-a-week basis. The search results showed that all the radioactive fragments from Cosmos 954 had fallen within a six-mile-wide strip, extending partway along the center of the predicted reentry path. However, relocating the exact spot where the C-130s detected satellite pieces proved to be a major problem because of the navigation systems used in the original searches, which meant that the location of hits could only be determined to within plus or minus a mile. The addition of microwave ranging systems, along with photos and maps, on subsequent flights would make recovery far more precise.[67]

Also on January 31, the American-Canadian recovery team at Yellowknife was taken by helicopter over Great Slave Lake's ice to a site with radioactive debris. While flying eastward, the team received a message from a Canadian Forces Twin Otter that was in the vicinity. As a result, the helicopter landed and the team recovered a large, charred, stovepipe-shaped tube, lying in the snow with a large number of small pieces. The team's radiation detectors remained silent, but that did not mean the fragments were not from the wayward Soviet satellite—in fact, the markings on them indicated that they were. The objects were quickly gathered up and transported to Yellowknife.[68]

On February 1, based on the recognition that high levels of radioactive sources could have been easily missed on the initial flights, three C-130s equipped with gamma-ray detectors flew in formation, about 150 feet apart and at an altitude over 980 feet. The flight provided thorough coverage of any significant radiation sources over a path 4,590 feet wide, along the centerline of the non-wind-corrected track from sector 1 through sector 8 and back. A few additional probable hits were found in sectors 1 and 2. The flight was useful in that it ensured overlapping of the scanned terrain below and aided in interpreting possible hits by looking for coincident hits observed by different aircraft. It also provided reasonable assurance that a highly radioactive source did not exist along the centerline of the track.[69]

Other flights on that day and the days that followed also concentrated on the McLeod Bay and Fort Reliance areas. The effort now involved fourteen Canadian aircraft, including two CP-107 Argus planes equipped for aerial photography that had been added to the search effort on January 30 as well as NEST's Convair 580T, which also provided photographic and infrared coverage. Until February 4, the four C-130 Hercules aircraft carrying NEST and Canadian detection equipment worked around-the-clock.[70]

While the helicopters and aircraft continued to search for radioactive fragments from above, ground operations sought to investigate their findings and ultimately to haul away what they did find. On February 4, the Morning Light mission planning group at Edmonton decided to establish "Camp Garland" near where Mobley and Mordhorst had discovered satellite debris, after an expedition from Baker Lake the previous day found itself stranded overnight in survival conditions owing to a plane malfunction.[71]

A few days later, while NEST personnel continued to fly on C-130s and work side-by-side with Canadian scientists on ground search operations, there was one indication of decreasing NEST participation in Morning Light. The Convair 580T flew a mission from Edmonton and then headed back to the far warmer climate of Las Vegas. At the time, the NEST contingent had declined from its high of 120 personnel to 65.[72]

The size of the NEST contingent would increase temporarily after February 8 but begin to fall again on February 25. During that interval and beyond, with or without NEST help, Canadian aircraft, helicopters, and NAST personnel continued search-and-recovery operations—from Edmonton, Yellowknife, Baker Lake, and Warden's Grove—operations that produced hits and recovered various bits of Cosmos 954.

Thus, on February 10, near Snowdrift, a helicopter carrying detection equipment discovered several radioactive sources on the ice, sources that were too weak to be detected at the altitude at which the C-130s flew. Analysis of these small pieces revealed them to be part of the missing reactor core. Further helicopter flights, along the south shore of Great Slave Lake, produced more signs of radioactive debris, which also turned out to be reactor fragments. The reactor core apparently had disintegrated when it reentered the earth's atmosphere, and small pieces of the core had drifted southward, sprinkling over a large area south of the satellite's path—extending from Hay River in the west to a line from Fort Smith to Fort Reliance in the east.[73]

Also, on February 10, a CH-135 helicopter with radiation detection equipment checked out a crater in Great Slave Lake, with negative results. However, continuation of the mission resulted in discovery of seven new hits west of the town of Snowdrift. On February 11, all sources, of fingernail size or smaller, were recovered from the ice. Another low-level helicopter survey resulted in twenty-two additional new hits. It was the first indication that the majority of fission products from the reactor had broken up in "fallout"-size pieces and landed over a large area ranging from a trajectory path south of Fort Smith and beyond.[74]

During March, Canadian resources continued to replace NEST personnel and equipment, including at Edmonton beginning on March 3. On March 7, at Cosmos Lake (the landing strip for Camp Garland), Canadian-mounted helicopter detection equipment became operational, and U.S. personnel and equipment departed. On March 12, Canadian detection equipment became operational at Yellowknife. On March 19, U.S. aerial search operations from CFB Edmonton concluded, and the next day Canadian detection equipment was substituted for U.S. equipment on the aircraft flying from the base. That same day, U.S. participation in search-and-recovery operations from Yellowknife ended.[75]

On March 8, a C-141 returned NEST search and computer equipment and personnel to Andrews Air Force Base. Exactly fourteen days later, another Starlifter returned all remaining U.S. equipment to Las Vegas, although a small contingent of NEST personnel remained in Canada. Four days later, they were almost all gone. The final totals on AFTAC and NEST/Canadian airplane nuclear detection missions were 162 C-130 missions, five Convair 580T flights, five U-2 overflights, and eight WC-135 sorties.[76]

. . .

During the next month, Canadian search operations also wound down, with the Edmonton and Yellowknife operations ending on April 17. The following day, the last U.S. representatives left Edmonton, along with Canadian Atomic Energy Control Board personnel. On April 17, Edmonton and Yellowknife search operations were closed.[77]

Besides lending a hand to a close ally, the United States did ultimately obtain some intelligence benefits from the recovery effort—in part from the ability to determine the fuel for Cosmos 954's reactor. Identification of the fuel as a uranium-molybdenum alloy was based on a combination of simulation studies at Livermore, examination of fuel debris at Whiteshell Nuclear Research Establishment, and knowledge of reactor technology. Knowing about the fuel was key because it revealed much about the design of the reactor. One fuel would indicate a Topaz design, while another would suggest a Romashka design. The remains of the spacecraft apparently also proved useful for the Air Force's Foreign Technology Division, which produced a large number of reports on the satellite.[78]

Such knowledge did come at a cost, for while Canada may have appreciated U.S. help in locating the pieces of Cosmos 954, the Canadians left it to their ally to recover any costs associated with the operation. In late January 1979, the U.S. embassy in Ottawa reported that the Canadian government would ask the Soviet Union for $6,041,174.70 (in Canadian dollars) for damage caused by the uninvited intrusion of parts of the Soviet spy satellite into the Canadian northwest. That did not include costs incurred by the United States in connection with the incident. The U.S. government had left the decision up to Canada, which decided not to ask the Soviet Union to reimburse the United States for its search efforts.[79]

Chapter 4

A LOW-PROFILE DECADE

THE 1980s BEGAN with a rapid succession of nuclear threats, which undoubtedly meant a busy start to the year for the credibility assessment group at Livermore. On January 2, 1980, somebody threatened to detonate a low-yield nuclear bomb in San Francisco. The next two days brought nuclear threats to Buffalo, New York, and Indianapolis. The threat to the capital of Indiana was another one that Ted Taylor would have considered to be particularly implausible, since the author(s) of the threat claimed to have possession not just of a fission weapon but of a five-megaton thermonuclear device.[1]

Later that year, another threat would result in two members of NEST being called into action, although no one was claiming to have a nuclear device to detonate. The location was Stateline, Nevada, an "unincorporated town" on the eastern shore of the better-known Lake Tahoe. Stateline is known for its casinos, most of which qualify as resorts, and Nevada State Route 207, also known as Kingsbury Grade, which takes a driver up and over a mountain pass. In 1980, the town had at least three prominent resorts, including the Sahara Tahoe, where Elvis Presley performed from 1971 to 1976; Caesar's Tahoe, which had opened in 1978, with a 40,000-square-foot casino; and the eleven-story Harvey's Resort Hotel.[2]

The *Wikipedia* entry for Stateline lists five "notable" events associated with the town. One is the filming at the MontBleu Resort Casino and Spa, formerly Caesar's Tahoe, of the 2007 movie *Smokin' Aces*, described by the *New York Times* film critic as "a Viagra suppository for compulsive action fetishists and a movie that may not only be dumb in itself, but also the cause of dumbness in others." There was even less for the community to be proud of with regard to the remaining four events. They involved an accident and three criminal acts: the death of musician and politician Sonny Bono in 1998 while skiing, the mutilation and murder of a nine-year-old girl in 2000, and the shootout that resulted in the death of one man and injuries to two sheriff deputies in 2005.[3] But the most memorable of the notable events predated these, and it involved Harvey's.

At 5:30 a.m. on August 26, 1980, two musicians and their girlfriends were crossing the parking lot at Harvey's. In addition to seeing an apparently inebriated woman, they witnessed two men pushing a wheeled platform holding a large gray box with "IBM" stenciled, rather crudely, on its side. Still, despite the crude lettering, one of the musicians was impressed, commenting, "Wow, IBM delivers."[4]

Sometime shortly before 6:00 a.m., Bob Vinson, the slot shift supervisor at Harvey's, noticed what appeared to be a large gray metal box in the small anteroom on the second floor, next to the office for Harvey's internal PBX (private branch exchange) telephone system, which at the time was valuable for saving money on internal phone calls. There were actually two boxes: a larger one and a smaller one on top, with some switches. All the switches on the top box, except one, were flipped in the same direction. Vinson, along with a janitor who had wandered by, then noticed an envelope addressed to "Harvey's management."[5]

Vinson left to find the shift sergeant for Harvey's security detail, William Schonfeld, who would soon be ordering the other security guards to secure the second floor. The sergeant also called the hotel's security chief, directed that the Douglas County sheriff and fire departments be notified, and then went back to the anteroom to examine the box. He later estimated the larger box at about three feet high and wide and more than three feet long, and the smaller box at about a foot square with twenty to twenty-three switches. On each corner of the box was a jack and levels, which showed that it was placed on four pieces of plywood. "It was," Schonfeld would later remark, "a good piece of workmanship."[6]

It was not long before Simon Caban, the security supervisor, and Wayne Watt, a Douglas County police officer, were examining the box and the envelope. After concluding that it was not a letter bomb, they opened the envelope, pulled out a three-page letter, and began to read it. It was only a few seconds after they started that Watt pointed to the box and stated, "That's a bomb."[7]

The two men who had delivered the package were at the back of the building, where a white van was parked behind a construction trailer. They were met by a man in his late fifties, a man with gray hair, a month-old beard, a prominent nose, and a receding hairline who was wearing a cowboy hat, glasses, and a ski jacket. He slid in behind the wheel and asked his two passengers, "How did it go?"[8]

The men at the receiving end of the question were Willis Brown and Terry Hall, who had no idea that they had just delivered a bomb as part of an extortion plot. The questioner, who had hatched the plot, was John Birges, who had employed Brown and Hall when he ran a landscaping company. Birges, sixty-one years old at the time, had spent nearly nine years in a Soviet hard-labor camp for political prisoners. After being released, he and his wife, Elizabet, had sneaked across the Hungarian border into Austria. They arrived in New Jersey in 1957, but soon were living in California. Birges was also a gambler, having dropped at least $750,000 in Harvey's Casino. The bomb and extortion threat were his way of trying to recoup his losses and turn a nice profit in the process.[9]

The target of Birges's threat was the owner of Harvey's, seventy-five-year-old Harvey Gross, later characterized in his *New York Times* obituary as "a gambling pioneer who turned a tiny club into a multimillion-dollar casino empire." Gross had opened Harvey's Wagon Wheel in 1944 and then built the first high-rise hotel in Stateline in 1961. It became known as Harvey's Resort Hotel.[10]

The three-page letter, written by Birges's girlfriend, Ella Joan Williams, was a mixture of claims, promises, instructions, and threats—about what was in the large gray metal box, what to do, when to do it, and what not to do. It contained a "Stern warning to the management and bomb squads":

> Do not move or tilt the bomb, because the mechanism controlling the detonators in it will set it off at a movement of less than .01 of the open end of the Richter scale. Don't try to flood or gas the bomb. Do not try to take it apart . . . In other words, this bomb is so sensitive that the slightest movement either inside or outside will cause it to explode.
>
> This bomb can never be dismantled or disarmed without causing an explosion. Not even by the creator. Only by proper instruction can it be moved to a safe place where it can be deliberately exploded. Only if you comply with the instructions will you [learn] how to move the bomb to a place where it can be exploded safely.[11]

The letter also warned that the damage, if it were to detonate, would be very significant. "This bomb contains enough TNT to severely damage Harrah's across the street," it promised. "This should give you some idea of the amount of TNT contained within this box. It is full of TNT." The author also suggested that an area within 1,200 feet, almost a quarter of a mile, be evacuated.[12]

Despite the suggestion that a significant piece of business property be cleared of people, the letter demanded no publicity: "all news media, local or nationwide, will be kept ignorant of the transactions between us and the casino management until the bomb is removed from the building." What Birges did want was $3 million, and he wanted it within twenty-four hours—"there will be no extension or renegotiation," the letter stated. It also warned Harvey Gross that "if you do not comply we will not contact you again and we will not answer any attempts to contact us. In the event of a double-cross there will be another time sometime in the future when another attempt will be made. We have the ways and means to get another bomb in."[13]

The payoff, the letter directed, would be made by an unaccompanied helicopter pilot, who would receive his initial instructions at the Lake Tahoe Airport late that night—either from a cabdriver or by way of a call to a public telephone at the airport. He was to fly the route instructed and look for a strobe light, indicating where he was to land. There was also a promise if the casino paid the $3 million. The pledge was not to tell the bomb experts how to turn off the device, but how to safely move it to a remote area where it could be detonated without danger to life or property. There would be six sets of instructions, provided at different times: the first provided to the pilot, while the remaining sets could be picked up at the Kingsbury Post Office general delivery window.[14]

The battalion chief of the Tahoe Douglas Fire Protection District arrived at Harvey's at 6:30 that morning and was met at the front entrance by his two captains. After reading the extortion letter, they concluded that it contained portions written for the sole purpose of impressing bomb experts such as themselves. A "float switch" was mentioned, along with "an atmospheric switch set at 26.00 to 33.0." The letter also stated that there were three "automatic timers each set for three different explosion times."[15]

The men gathered their diagnostic equipment and carried it upstairs. It included X-ray equipment, a tripod, and sensitive listening devices, which they could use to visualize the inside of the bomb so they could think of a way to disable it. The bomb, resting on the four small plywood squares and the wheels it had been rolled in on, had been cranked up off the floor.[16]

While the local bomb experts tried to figure out what to do with the bomb, hotel security began an evacuation, which, as might be expected, led to speculation and rumor. Somebody claimed that there was a bomb and it might be radioactive, an assertion based on having heard that a nuclear response team had been spotted going into the hotel. Somebody else pinned the threat on the Iranians, who had been holding U.S. diplomatic personnel captive since the seizure of the U.S. embassy in Tehran the previous November. A third claim was that the bomb was the work of a disgruntled employee, which was a lot closer to the truth, since Birges could be considered a disgruntled customer.[17]

The fear that the device was far more deadly than one containing only TNT extended beyond random spectators. NEST veteran Alan Mode recalls that there was "at first a strong concern that it was nuclear." The initial feeling was, according to Mode, that a "NEST kind of response" was needed.[18]

The Nevada fire marshal was the catalyst in getting NEST involved. His subordinates contacted the Nevada Operations Office, informing its manager that they had what looked like a computer with an extortion note. The operations office told the fire marshal that they could provide X-ray devices that would be more effective than anything possessed by the fire marshal.[19]

The office also sent two members of NEST. William Nelson recalls that during the afternoon or early evening of August 26, he was informed that the fire marshal was interested in the use of NEST's advanced X-ray equipment. Nelson, who belonged to a flying club near Livermore, climbed into a Cessna, along with a radiographic technician, and flew to the South Tahoe Airport.[20]

The two were met by a van and driver, who, according to Nelson, drove "on the sidewalks" to Harvey's. When the van reached the front of the extortion target, the driver told Nelson and his colleague that the bomb was "right up the stairs" and that they should feel free to go take a look. Nelson, figuring that he had a reasonable chance of survival, took up the challenge. The technician and X-ray equipment followed. X-rays of the boxes showed circuits and relays, what might have been blasting caps, and what might have been a pressure switch. In addition, they showed wires running from the screws on the surface plate of the metal. If unscrewed by even a quarter of a turn, they would trigger the device. There were also trembler switches imbedded in the metal box that would produce a detonation if the bomb were tilted even slightly. Listening to the bomb with amplified stethoscopes revealed an "intermittent whirling noise." The X-rays also showed a toilet float, which kept the bomb from being defeated by flooding. There seemed to be no way to take it apart, or move it, or flood it. There was no simple way to clip the "red wire" and disable the bomb, Nelson recalled. And the whirring sound might represent a timing device. It was the type of bomb that would become known as a "sophisticated improvised explosive device," or SIED.[21]

That night, while experts were considering how to disarm the bomb without the extortionist's cooperation, Joe Cook—FBI agent and helicopter pilot—took off with a package that appeared, in weight and volume, to consist of $3 million in bills but really contained only $1,000 in actual currency. The FBI also failed to comply with Birges's demand in a second way: another of its agents was hidden on the helicopter to protect Cook. But there would be no payoff that night because Cook couldn't locate the strobe light, the result of Birges's belated acquisition of a battery to power the strobe—only one of several mishaps to befall Birges and the team he had assembled to help him collect his payoff. That team included Birges's girlfriend and his two sons, John Jr., age nineteen, and Jimmy, age twenty. John Jr. and Jimmy had helped him steal the dynamite for the bomb from a nearby hydroelectric project and had been promised $100,000 to help pick up the money. They also were supposed to drop the bomb off at Harvey's but backed out after an accident occurred while loading it into the van, forcing their father to recruit Brown and Hall as unwitting replacements.[22]

While the extortionists were frustrated by their failure to collect the $3 million payoff, the local authorities, Harvey's management, and nearby casinos were running out of patience. The unresolved threat was driving away customers, both locals and tourists. On August 27 the fire marshal proposed to tie a rope around the device and pull it over. Another idea, proposed by Leonard Wolfson of the Navy's Explosive Ordnance Disposal facility in Maryland, and which Nelson agreed to, was to build a linear-shaped charge, consisting of C-4 explosive taped to a two-by-four piece of lumber, which would be used to decapitate the bomb—virtually instantaneously separating the smaller box with all the switches from the actual explosive device.[23]

The C-4 was in stick form, so various technicians softened the material to make it sufficiently malleable to be placed in a shaped-charge liner, which was fabricated later in the morning in a Las Vegas plant. Wolfson and Army ordnance disposal personnel inserted the C-4 into the liner and taped the liner to the two-by-four. There was an inner liner, with an outer layer, made of brass material designed to generate a gas jet formation known as the "Munroe effect"—in which a hollow or void cut into a piece of explosive concentrates the explosive's energy. A computer and outside experts determined that the standoff area—the distance between the charge and target that is required to allow room for the gas jet to form before it reaches the target—was 8.5 inches. The two-by-four also had to be tilted 1.6 inches to ensure that the gas jet wouldn't slam into the lower box. The technicians calculated that they would amputate the top box of the bomb from the bottom box in .5 millisecond, cutting the trigger wires before an electrical charge could pass through to the explosives below.[24]

According to one account, Birges placed a couple of sticks of dynamite in the top box to wipe out any fingerprints he may have left behind while building the bomb. As a result, when the shaped charge was exploded at 3:43 that afternoon, the cumulative blast triggered the trembler switches and detonated the dynamite in the main box. (Nelson recalls that the firemen put the charge in backward.) In any case, the bomb exploded "with a thunderous blast . . . sending thick gray smoke streaming through the casino district and causing heavy damage to Harvey's." The explosion sent pieces of glass, concrete, and the casino's neon sign flying across the border into California, although that was only four blocks away.[25]

A security guard at the nearby Sahara Tahoe Hotel told the *New York Times* that the "whole front went out." The detonation gutted the second and third floors, blew out windows, and collapsed balconies. The damage came to $12 million.[26]

Once the bomb had gone off, the FBI's full attention turned to finding out who was responsible and putting them behind bars. Harvey's employees reported seeing the white van. Other witnesses came forward with memories of what they saw or might have seen that might be relevant to the investigation. Joseph Yablonsky, the FBI agent in charge of the investigation, told the press that an artist was compiling drawings of the three suspects— two men and a woman—with some of the descriptions provided as the result of hypnosis. Fingerprints were also reported to have been found on the bomb. In addition, the extortion letter was being studied, by NEST consultant Murray Miron among others, to produce a psychological profile of its author.[27]

In mid-September the FBI released sketches of two men, one said to be about five feet seven inches tall and twenty years old with sandy blond hair and a light mustache. The other was described as six feet tall, "a hayseed type with protruding ears," and in his mid twenties. A little over a year later, in September 1981, after a tip from the boyfriend of a girl whom John Jr. had broken up with, the two brothers would be in court pleading guilty. They had agreed to testify against their father, reportedly in retaliation for the beatings they had received in earlier years and his treatment of their mother, who had committed suicide in 1975. As a result they escaped time in prison.[28]

Their father did not. On the stand Birges claimed that a man named "Charlie" warned him that if he didn't bomb the hotel, he would cripple him. He further implied that the mastermind behind it all was Harvey Gross, who allegedly wanted to use the insurance money to renovate his hotel. He also apportioned some of the blame to his dead ex-wife for having given him $2,000 to gamble. It was a ploy to get him out of the house, he explained, so she could have sex with other men. The jury wasn't convinced, and Birges spent the rest of his days behind bars, dying from liver cancer in 1996 at the Southern Nevada Correctional Center. His girlfriend, Ella Joan Williams, was also convicted, but her conviction was overturned in 1984.[29]

Almost all the damage that Birges's bomb did was long ago swept up and either disposed of or used in the FBI's investigation. But a piece of bent aluminum from one of Harvey's windows is on a plaque in William Nelson's home office, near Livermore. The inscription on the plaque is "win some, lose some." This case was not a complete loss though. NEST did learn about how sophisticated homemade bombs could be, and about the booby traps one might contain. Nelson recalls that knowledge would have an impact on the program. It also led to an agreement between NEST and the FBI and the management of the national laboratories on how to respond to non-nuclear bomb threats.[30]

In 1981 there were three incidents. On January 9, Reno, Nevada, was threatened with plutonium dispersal. Seventeen days later, San Francisco was the target of a threat involving an alleged atomic device. On June 25, San Francisco was threatened again, but with even greater devastation. This time someone claimed to have a thermonuclear bomb ready to detonate in the city. A one-megaton device would level the city from downtown to Fisherman's Warf.[31]

On April 10, 1982, President Ronald Reagan signed National Security Decision Directive (NSDD) 30, titled "Managing Terrorist Incidents." Among its key provisions was its designation of the "lead agency"—the agency with the most direct operational role—in dealing with terrorist incidents. The Federal Aviation Administration was named the lead agency for "highjackings within the special jurisdiction of the United States," while the Department of Justice was to take the lead for terrorist incidents within U.S. territory. But for international terrorist events, the State Department was to take charge.[32]

The directive was not very specific about the types of terrorist incidents that could occur, or what the State Department would do in the event of an international terrorist incident. A month later, Richard L. Wagner, the veteran of Morning Light who was representing the Department of Defense, signed a memorandum of understanding, originally completed in January, that had already been signed by representatives of the State and Energy departments. With Wagner's signature, the memo took effect. It specified the role of the State as well as the Energy and Defense departments with regard to "malevolent nuclear incidents" outside the territory or possessions of the United States.[33]

By the time that memo was signed though, there had already been nuclear threats to several foreign nations, threats apparently conveyed to one or another component of the U.S. government and analyzed by the credibility assessment group at Livermore. On March 16, 1975, in addition to Washington, D.C., Beijing and Moscow were threatened with atomic destruction. During the first week of 1980, about two months after the U.S. embassy and staff in Tehran had been seized, Tehran was the target of a nuclear threat—the biggest and most implausible ever made, since it involved three 20- to 25-megaton bombs.[34] Of course, neither China, the Soviet Union, nor Iran was likely to ask for U.S. assistance in evaluating the credibility of a threat or locating a nuclear device hidden on their territory. But one day, a nation with closer ties might ask for just such assistance or the United States might offer it unsolicited.

In such an instance, the State Department's responsibilities would include obtaining the approvals necessary for U.S. aid, contacting other federal agencies, and requesting assistance from the Energy and Defense departments. Of course, many of the references to "Energy" in the memorandum were references to NEST. Thus, "Energy" would be expected to provide "scientific and technical support for assessment, search operations, identification, diagnostics, device access and deactivation, damage limitation," and so on—exactly what NEST would be asked to do for domestic malevolent nuclear incidents. In such an event, the State Department was required to provide NEST with exact copies of any threat messages, drawings, and other relevant intelligence as well "as all available information pertinent to an assessment of a threat perpetrator's technical capabilities to carry out a threat."[35] Thus, one day NEST personnel might find themselves boarding a plane to Ottawa, Sydney, Tokyo, Tel Aviv, or elsewhere in response to a credible threat to unleash atomic destruction.

While the memo concerned hypothetical nuclear threats, in 1982 there were real threats to a number of U.S. cities—"real" in the sense that some-one communicated a threat by phone or letter. On May 16, twelve uniden-tified U.S. cities were threatened with nuclear warheads. On June 14, in a case of déjà vu, Boston was threatened with a nuclear detonation. Less than a month later, in very early July, Washington, D.C., was threatened with a radioactive device. The year's threats concluded with two in October, on the other side of the country: Las Vegas on October 8 and Los Angeles on October 19. While Las Vegas faced only a ten-kiloton device, Los Ange-les faced a thermonuclear detonation, according to the threatener. But, as usual, all the threats proved to be empty.[36]

Between the beginning of 1980 and the end of 1982, two significant exercises were carried out. The first one, Sundog, took place in the des-ert near Stallion Gate, the northern entrance to the White Sands Missile Range in New Mexico. In addition to the Delta special operations unit, this full field exercise involved NEST and included a "tactical air insertion of NEST assets." It also entailed an assault on terrorist forces by Delta person-nel, with the work of diagnosing and disabling a simulated nuclear device assigned to NEST personnel.[37]

The second exercise, designated Prince Sky, also involved NEST and Delta and took place not on some remote facility in the desert but in down-town Los Angeles. Local law enforcement participated, and, Chambers recalls, the exercise "was carried out without public or media attention."[38]

At the very end of 1982, the State Department announced that NEST had been placed on alert, and it looked like NEST personnel might well be headed for some foreign business travel. But it wouldn't be the result of any threat to detonate a nuclear weapon. Rather, the Soviet Union was having trouble with yet another of its nuclear-powered ocean surveillance satellites. This time it was Cosmos 1402, which was forty-six feet long, weighed 11,000 pounds, and had a thirty-foot radar antenna, and a nuclear reactor located in the satellite's twenty-three-foot rear section.[39]

The problem with Cosmos 954 did not prevent eventual resumption of the Soviet Union's RORSAT program. Launch activities resumed in late April 1980 with Cosmos 1176. In 1981, three of the nuclear-powered satellites were orbited. And in May and June 1982, RORSAT's Cosmos 1365 and Cosmos 1372 were launched from Plesetsk to monitor naval developments during the short Falklands War between Britain and Argentina. They were followed by Cosmos 1402.[40]

Like Cosmos 954, Cosmos 1402 orbited at an inclination of 65 degrees, so that in the course of its revolutions around the earth it passed over all points between 65 degrees north latitude and 65 degrees south latitude, and thus could come down anywhere in between the Arctic and Antarctic circles. All the land in the Southern Hemisphere and the land in the Northern Hemisphere up to mid-Alaska and Scandinavia were included in that range. But almost 70 percent of what was under Cosmos 1402 was water.[41]

After it was launched in August 1982, Cosmos 1402 began orbiting at a maximum altitude (its apogee) of 173 miles and a minimum altitude (its perigee) of 157 miles. The satellite apparently operated normally until December 28. By early January 1983, the satellite trackers at the North American Aerospace Defense Command were tracking two objects associated with Cosmos 1402—the satellite with its reactor, and a fragment—and reporting that the satellite's orbit had dipped to an apogee of 153 miles and a perigee of 145 miles. In addition to reporting that it was losing altitude, NORAD was telling its customers that the satellite was behaving erratically. Department of Defense analysts reportedly suspected a rocket-system malfunction, a faulty separation of satellite and reactor, or some combination of those problems.[42]

Rather than try to keep the possible demise of the Soviet spy satellite a secret, as with Cosmos 954, the Defense Department issued a statement revealing the apparent malfunction and predicting a probable return to earth in late January. Soviet spokesmen, at least initially, claimed that nothing was wrong. At a Moscow news conference, Vladimir A. Kotelnikov, a vice president of the Soviet Academy of Sciences, claimed that the changes in the satellite's orbit were part of a "preplanned operation" and that "we have no worries about the fate of this Sputnik."[43]

Some space experts suggested that such claims might mean that Moscow believed it would be able to command the satellite to lift its orbit to a higher, safer altitude or it would be able to guide the satellite's reentry into the earth's atmosphere so that any surviving fragments would fall into a remote ocean area. But Kotelnikov's comments were not enough to convince the Defense and State departments that they were worrying needlessly. Spokesman Benjamin Welles responded, "We have no way of knowing if the Soviets have it under control. We hope so." State Department spokesman John Hughes was even more skeptical, telling reporters, "Our information is different, and we want to talk about that with them, and, of course, we want to make known our concern."[44]

In the meantime, NEST was placed on alert, in case it was needed anywhere in the United States. State Department spokesman Hughes also told the press that the United States was offering NEST's services to other nations that might be hit with debris. Ira Morrison, a veteran of Operation Morning Light, carried a pager, as did all other NEST members, so that he could be called into action without delay. Morrison, whose day job was as a computer analyst with Lawrence Livermore's Z Division, which analyzed sensitive intelligence about foreign nuclear weapons programs, was skeptical that the team would get any help from the Soviets. He recalled, while waiting for the Soviet satellite to come down to earth, that when Cosmos 954 was in trouble in 1978, "they really didn't tell us anything that was useful."[45]

In addition to placing people on alert, the Energy Department, around January 18, began loading three C-141 Starlifter cargo planes with equipment for NEST operations, including lead-lined containers for storing radioactive debris and the same type of equipment used in Operation Morning Light to detect radioactive satellite fragments from the air.[46]

By the time NEST had begun loading equipment onto the C-141s, the Soviet Union had acknowledged that all was not as it should be with Cosmos 1402. On January 15, Oleg M. Belotserkovsky, the longtime rector of the Moscow Institute of Physics and Technology, often referred to as the "Russian M.I.T.," spoke on Soviet national television for ten minutes. Belotserkovsky, an expert in mathematics and mechanics, told his audience that the satellite's fuel core would reenter the earth's atmosphere in mid-February, burn up, and be dispersed into "finely divided particles." Any fallout, he reassured his listeners, would pose no health risks. He also acknowledged, unlike previous Soviet spokesmen, that the reactor and spent nuclear fuel should have been boosted to a higher, longer-lasting orbit.[47]

American experts were skeptical of Belotserkovsky's claims that there were no health risks associated with the level of radioactive fallout expected from the satellite's reentry. The State Department also questioned his prediction of a mid-February reentry for the fuel core. A spokeswoman said she had no reason to question earlier U.S. predictions that both the satellite and the reactor of Cosmos 1402 would return to earth in late January.[48]

Those predictions proved accurate, for at 5:21 p.m. Eastern Standard Time on January 24—almost exactly five years after Cosmos 954 reentered the earth's atmosphere—Cosmos 1402 returned to earth. Members of the American military, serving on Diego Garcia, saw the burning satellite for forty seconds as it cut across the sky, while astronomers at the Royal Green-wich Observatory near London saw an object that looked like "a bright fast-moving star." In contrast to 1978, the latest wayward Soviet spy satellite fell, without incident, into the Indian Ocean, in a part of the ocean far south of the Indian subcontinent and far west of Australia, where there was not even an island on which to scatter debris.[49]

The United States alerted facilities, including stations operated by the Air Force Technical Applications Center, used to monitor nuclear fallout to check for any increase in atmospheric radiation due to the satellite reentry. In addition, U.S. aircraft and ships patrolled the Indian Ocean, looking for any signs of radiation. Meanwhile, U.S. space trackers continued to watch the fragment of Cosmos 1402, weighing less than 1,000 pounds, that had remained in orbit.[50]

That fragment was the fuel core, which, on January 24, the Soviet space monitoring organization predicted would burn up in the atmosphere between February 3 and 8. At 6:10 a.m. on the morning of February 8, the final piece of Cosmos 1402 "vanished in a fiery plunge over the South Atlantic Ocean 1,100 miles east of Brazil." According to a Pentagon spokes-man, the 110-pound enriched-uranium core appeared to have "burned harmlessly."[51] On this occasion, the services of Ira Morrison and other members of NEST would not be needed.*

On February 2, about a week before the final piece of Cosmos 1402 reen-tered the atmosphere, the United States faced another nuclear threat, from someone claiming to have dispersed radioactive material in Tampa. Much later in the year, another threat occurred, and this one called for a signifi-cant federal response. At 2:00 a.m. on an October morning in 1983, the

---

*Cosmos 1402 would not be the last encounter with a troubled Soviet nuclear-powered ocean surveillance satellite. In 1988, the Soviets lost control over Cosmos 1700 but were able to fire its reactor into a safe orbit. See William Harwood, "Crippled Soviet Satellite Fires Reactor into 'Graveyard Orbit,'" *Washington Post*, October 2, 1988, p. A6.

FBI's new Hostage Rescue Team (HRT)—fifty agents who had been chosen out of the bureau's pool of investigators—and a local SWAT team snuck into position. A few days earlier, a terrorist group with a nuclear weapon had promised to destroy Albuquerque, New Mexico, home of many members of NEST, if its demands were not met. In response, an HRT advance team soon arrived, established a tactical operations center, and began collecting intelligence on the suspected group. Not long afterward, the main HRT arrived in a C-130, which also carried vehicles and weapons.[52]

While negotiations dragged on for several days, the FBI believed it had located the nuclear weapons. A NEST helicopter, with a gamma-ray sensor, provided the confirmation. As the FBI suspected, the bomb was hidden in a building in downtown Albuquerque. The terrorists were hiding in a different location, not far away. Earlier surveillance work identified the terrorists and revealed all the booby traps at the terrorist hideout. Meanwhile, in the desert outside the city, the HRT constructed a duplicate of the hideaway and practiced for a possible raid.[53]

That night the HRT clandestinely approached the terrorist facility, while the local SWAT team gathered outside the building containing the nuclear weapon. The two commando units had arranged for a simultaneous attack. The terrorists had a remote detonator, but the FBI rescue team planned to block the terrorists' signal by electronic jamming. Members of the HRT placed charges in two different locations and stormed the building, throwing flashbangs as they entered. Within thirty seconds, the terrorists were dead, and Albuquerque was still standing. NEST's work had allowed the FBI and SWAT team to conduct the raid with confidence that they had located the nuclear device. Of course, it was only an exercise—one designated Equus Red.[54]

That exercise was "the first and last time," according to William Chambers, that a major urban search was attempted employing local emergency service personnel who were recruited and trained in the midst of the exercise. The difficulty of turning firemen and paramedics into a NEST auxiliary force on the fly proved too much, leading to the idea of a periodically trained group of reserve searchers.[55]

The multitude of nuclear threats in 1984 did not appear to produce NEST deployments—but threats there were. In February, Hill Air Force Base in Utah was threatened with an atomic bomb. In October, Detroit was the target, and the instrument of destruction was a nuclear device. On November

7, as the nation went to the polls to choose between presidential candidates Ronald Reagan and Walter Mondale, someone claimed to have hidden a hydrogen bomb at an unspecified location. Then, nine days later, Fairfax County, Virginia, was threatened with a "small nuclear device."[56]

There were also two threats to targets in California that year. On July 29 someone claimed to have a nuclear device and a willingness to detonate it in Covina. The following day, Los Angeles was threatened yet again, with an atomic bomb, but this time the city was in the midst of hosting the 1984 Summer Olympics—which the Soviet Union and thirteen other Eastern Bloc nations were boycotting in retaliation for the U.S. boycott of the 1980 Olympics in Moscow, a maneuver that meant more gold medals for the United States. President Reagan had mandated security preparations for the Olympics by his approval of NSDD 135, "Counterintelligence and Security Precautions for the Summer Olympic Games," on March 30, 1984. Whether the directive directed a NEST deployment as a precaution is not clear, since almost all of the top-secret directive had been redacted prior to its public release.[57]

According to William Chambers, NEST did deploy to Los Angeles as a precaution, part of what would become ongoing cooperation with the FBI in dealing with what would years later be designated a National Special Security Event (NSSE).[58]

In the first four months of 1985 there were two threats. On March 14, Chicago was threatened with a five-kiloton bomb. Then, in April, a small contingent of NEST personnel descended on New York, the catalyst for their journey, strangely, being a subway shooting that had taken place late the previous year. On December 22, 1984, four young African-American men boarded a downtown No. 2 express train intent on stealing money from video arcade machines in Manhattan. It was their bad luck that Bernhard Goetz entered the same subway car at the 14th Street station and took a seat nearby. Almost immediately, one of the four, Troy Canty, age nineteen, told Goetz to give him five dollars, a demand that he repeated when Goetz asked him, "What did you say?"[59]

Goetz, who had turned twenty-seven the month before, held a bachelor's degree in electrical engineering from New York University and had already been mugged twice. In a moment similar to what millions had viewed in movie theaters when they attended screenings of the 1978 Charles Bronson film *Death Wish*, Goetz stood and fast-drew a .38 caliber

Smith & Wesson and emptied its five-shot load into Canty and his three friends. Goetz would later tell the police that he had "snapped" and that his intention was to "murder them."[60]

All four survived, but only because Goetz ran out of bullets. As a result Goetz was tried for attempted murder and assault, rather than murder. But while some considered him a racist, others considered him both a vigilante and a hero. His act came at a time when New York reported a crime rate that was 70 percent higher than the rest of the country. On an average day, the subways hosted thirty-eight crimes.[61] And at least one or more of his admirers did not plan to sit idly by and wait to see how a jury of Goetz's peers would judge him.

On April 4, 1985, while Goetz was still awaiting trial, Mayor Edward Koch received a hand-printed letter. It began, "UNLESS ALL CHARGES AGAINST BERHARD GOETZ [sic] ARE DISMISSED BY 1700 HOURS, 11 APRIL— AND TOTALLY DISMISSED—A SUBSTANTIAL QUANTITY OF PLUTONIUM TRICHLORIDE . . . WILL BE INTRODUCED AT SEVERAL LOCATIONS INTO THE WATER SUPPLY OF NEW YORK CITY." The writer also warned the mayor not to make the contents of the note public.[62]

The NEST team that arrived in New York shortly after Koch received the letter was part of a two-fold NEST response to the threat. Back at Livermore, analysts with the credibility assessment program examined the brief letter both to judge its technical accuracy and to search for any clues it might yield about the author's willingness to carry out the threat. Meanwhile, the small contingent would check the water in New York's reservoirs up to April 11 for any sign that it had been contaminated, and would survey areas in the city at four-hour intervals for signs of radioactivity.[63]

At first the team found nothing dangerous. Tests of the water indicated plutonium levels of 0.1 to 0.6 femtocurie per liter.* Tests on April 17 showed levels of 21 femtocuries per liter in a single sample—still well below the federal guidelines of 5,000 femtocuries per liter as the maximum level of plutonium safe for drinking water. The tests could not determine whether the plutonium had been introduced as part of a trichloride compound or had come from another source, but experts did rule out nuclear power plants or the fallout from atmospheric nuclear tests as causes. They could not rule out the possibility that the containers used to hold the water samples were contaminated with plutonium.[64]

---

*A femtocurie is one-millionth of one-billionth of a curie (Ci), where $Ci = 3.7 \times 10^{10}$ decays per second.

Another incident occurred before the year was out. On November 22, someone claimed to have hidden three nuclear devices in Albuquerque. It is not known whether the threat was considered sufficiently credible to result in a deployment of NEST personnel.[65]

William Chambers recalls that in 1986 NEST "took an inward look at its progress over the prior decade through an independent review panel and found some reasons for both pride and despair."[66]

In early December 1986 a large group of NEST personnel arrived at Camp Atterbury, Indiana. It was the base Chambers had traveled to be discharged from the military at the end of World War II. But the NEST contingent was there for an exercise that they certainly hoped would alleviate some of the despair. By that time there had been six nuclear threats for the year. In April, it was New York and Murmansk (atomic devices); in May, Reno (nuclear device); in September, Wisconsin (nuclear device); in October, Westminster, California (thermonuclear device), and Concord, California (six-megaton device); and in November, Bethlehem, Pennsylvania (americium-241 dispersal).[67]

Construction on the camp had begun shortly after the Japanese attack on Pearl Harbor on December 7, 1941. During the war it was home to a number of Army divisions; the Wakeman General and Convalescent Hospital, the largest of its kind in the United States during the 1940s; and a prisoner-of-war camp for German and Italian soldiers. The Indiana National Guard established an air-to-ground gunnery range in 1958. The camp stretched about seven miles wide and twelve miles from north to south. Members of NEST were there for an exercise designated "Mighty Derringer." The Pentagon—which sponsored the exercise—had generated the name, and, whether intentional or not, it was appropriate for an exercise concerning nuclear terrorism, since it conjured up an image of a small device with a deadly impact.[68]

While Camp Atterbury was the local command post for Mighty Derringer, the city of Indianapolis was the main site of the exercise, nuclear sources having been deposited in several locations. One objective was to determine if NEST could deploy, get to a target city, do its search, and detect hidden nuclear weapons.[69]

A more important objective was testing the ability of the multiple organizations involved in managing a nuclear extortion or terrorist incident to work together, including the FBI's Hostage Rescue Team and the Federal

SITES OF MAJOR
SEARCH TEAM INVESTIGATIONS

1.	Los Angeles, Calif.	November 1975
2.	Boston, Mass.	January 1976
3.	Washington, D.C.	June 1976
4.	Spokane, Wash.	November 1976
5.	Buffalo, N.Y.	January 1978
6.	Pittsburg, Pa.	January 1978
7.	New York, N.Y.	May 1978
8.	Miamisburg, Ohio	August 1978
9.	U.S. Congress, Wash. D.C.	October 1978
10.	Wilmington, N.C.	January 1979
11.	Three Mile Island, Penn.	March 1979
12.	Sacramento, Calif.	April 1979
13.	Erwin, Tenn.	September 1979
14.	Washington, D.C.	August 1980
15.	Stateline, Nev.	August 1980
16.	Reno, Nev.	January 1981
17.	New York, N.Y.	April 1985
18.	Indianapolis, Ind.	November 1987

NEST Deployments 1975–1989 (Source: Judith Valente, "Secretive Federal Program Combats Terrorism," *Washington Post*, June 21, 1983)

Emergency Management Agency (FEMA). The exercise was, according to former NEST official Alan Mode, "really, really big" with "all of the agencies and organizations involved" so that "hundreds and hundreds of people" participated.[70]

Part of the exercise also took place at the Nevada Test Site, where it was possible to "have real explosions," according to former NEST official William Nelson. Participating along with NEST personnel were members of the Defense Department special operations forces.[71]

The exercise attracted high-level interest and involved high-level players. The State Department directed it from its Operations Center in Washington. William Nelson stressed its value in getting people and organizations, including the CIA and FBI, together so that if there was a real incident, they would have experience working together. But Alan Mode noted that NEST had some "difficulty with the exercise" and that it was too big, that everyone wanted to participate, and everyone wanted to use their "own gadget."[72] It was a problem that would recur a decade later.

In 1987 NEST returned to Indianapolis, although in much smaller numbers. And this time it was not an exercise. On November 27, a telephone caller made two claims: first, that he represented a Cuban political movement and second, that a nuclear device he had produced would detonate that night inside a bank building. NEST searched but found nothing.[73]

And, as might be expected, the threateners were not through for the decade. In June 1988 they claimed to have atom bombs in Washington, D.C., and Moscow. In January 1989, someone or some group claimed to have three nuclear bombs "somewhere in the USA," and in April, Washington, D.C., was threatened yet again with another, apparently imaginary, atomic bomb.[74]

Chapter 5

TARNISHED GOLD

THE EARLY 1990S were no more immune to nuclear threats than the early 1980s. Five locations were targets in 1990 alone: Denver, Colorado; El Paso, Texas; Sunnyvale, California (the headquarters of the Air Force Satellite Control Network); Washington, D.C.; and an undisclosed site in the United States. The threats included, respectively, a nuclear device, a nuclear weapon, an atomic bomb, a nuclear device, and two atomic bombs. Then there was Bethesda, Maryland, which merely had to face the specter of being threatened with plutonium dispersal.[1]

In 1991, New York and Washington, D.C., were threatened with nuclear bombs. In March 1992, nine U.S. cities were targets. That September, several cities, unidentified by those making the threats, were also threatened with nuclear devices. Then a few days short of Christmas, the targets moved overseas, although the United States was apparently informed by the threateners. Someone claimed to have two atomic bombs ready to destroy Tel Aviv and West Jerusalem. In April 1993, three atomic bombs were reported to be ready to cause devastation in Germany and the Vatican City.[2]

During the 1990s, the biggest deployment of NEST personnel and equipment took place in Louisiana. When the citizens of New Orleans and its suburbs woke up on Sunday, October 16, 1994, most were probably thinking of how they would spend their day or, possibly, about what the week ahead had in store for them. It is unlikely that more than a few, if any at all, had the danger posed by nuclear terrorists on their mind. The city was in the midst of Jeff Fest '94, held at Lafreniere Park, a 155-acre site with seven sports fields (five soccer and two baseball), other multipurpose fields, and a two-mile walking track. The festival included food, craft, music, and games and attracted a crowd of ten thousand on its opening day, Saturday. Among the crowd was a couple from Pittsburgh, who planned their annual vacation around the festival. When interviewed by a local reporter, one gushed, "The music's great. The food's great . . . we'll keep coming every year."[3]

Of course, they had no idea that at 7:55 a.m. the same day, the FBI received word that one of its informants was being held hostage by a domestic terrorist group, the Patriots for National Unity, in a New Orleans safe house. The next morning, after electronic surveillance revealed plans to kill the hostage, a raid by the FBI's Hostage Rescue Team freed the informant. During the debriefing that followed, the informant reported that members of the terrorist group were looking to obtain nuclear material and assemble several nuclear devices, and not just as an intellectual exercise. Ultimately, they wanted to kill a lot of people. In response to the possible nuclear threat, the FBI alerted a variety of government organizations, including NEST.[4]

The FBI's target, the Patriots for National Unity, called to mind other groups the FBI had tangled with in the past. It would be six months before the bureau would hear of Timothy McVeigh and witness the destruction that he unleashed in Oklahoma City. But, in the 1980s the FBI confronted the Covenant, Sword, and Arm of the Lord—a white hate group run by an Illinois-born ironworker and itinerant preacher named Jim Ellison. Former FBI agent Danny Coulson, who had helped arrange Ellison's eventual surrender, described him as a "cross between John the Baptist and James Dean," as "egocentric, insecure, and status-starved," and as "the General Patton of the Christian Identity movement." He preached that the Second Coming of Christ prophesied in the Book of Revelation was imminent. When it came, according to Ellison, 90 percent of the world's population would fail to make God's cut and perish in the Tribulation, a prophecy from the New Testament that promises fire and brimstone, rather than tolerance, for non-Christians.[5]

While waiting for the end to arrive, Ellison had established a heavily fortified compound on a 244-acre plot of land in the Ozarks, near Mountain Home, Arkansas. Activities at the compound included daily visits to the optimistically named Endtime Overcomer Survival Training School, in a mock village called Silhouette City. Inside, Ellison's devotees could spend part of their day shooting at figures given the characteristics of Ellison's pet hates. The figures were of policemen with a Star of David painted over their hearts.[6]

In addition to encouraging his followers to kill cardboard cutouts that couldn't shoot back, Ellison had some very real death and destruction in mind. Sometime during 1983 and 1984, Ellison tried but failed to blow up the Red River natural-gas pipeline at Fulton, Arkansas—a town so small (occupying two-tenths of a square mile and with a population of around

250) as to be nearly nonexistent. The explosive fizzled. He also dispatched a senior lieutenant with a briefcase filled with explosives and instructions to bomb a homosexual church in Kansas City. That plot also failed when the lieutenant could not bring himself to complete his mission. When FBI agents searched the compound after Ellison's surrender, they found a thirty-gallon drum of cyanide, which, Ellison told them, had been destined for the New York and Washington, D.C., water supplies.[7]

Unlike the Covenant, the Patriots for National Unity and their plans were just a figment of the imagination of NEST's Scenario Working Group (which included William Chambers) and NEST chief planner Lewis Newby, a former Navy pilot who was head of the NEST contingent at Sandia National Laboratories in Albuquerque. They were part of the scenario for Mirage Gold, the search team's first full field exercise since Mighty Derringer eight years earlier. Its purpose was to test how successfully various agencies could respond to such a threat and if they could work together effectively.[8]

Mirage Gold was the final exercise in a series designated Mile Shakedown. Planning had started by the summer of 1992. The series included a tabletop exercise designated Mica Dig (in the fall of 1993), with participants sitting at their desks and attempting to work through the problems they would face and the decisions they would have to make in the scenario given to them. The Defense and Energy departments would be represented by assistant secretaries and deputy assistant secretaries, respectively. That was to be followed by a field site communications exercise called Mild Cover (planned for the spring of 1994 but actually carried out in September) to test communications systems and procedures, including the voice and data transmission systems, radios, telephone systems, and video displays that would be used to communicate within and between participant organizations. One point of the exercise was to strain the archival databases of the organizations, to identify the point at which they started to break down. Finally, there would be a command post exercise (CPX), in which senior officials or substitutes would manage the crisis from Washington, and a full field exercise in the fall of 1994 (Mirage Gold) to test the ability of NEST, the FBI, and other agencies (including assorted military units and the Federal Emergency Management Agency) to find and disable the hidden weapons. By the time the series of exercises concluded, they had involved over 1,000 people, with 850 participating in Mirage Gold alone.[9]

A tabletop exercise like Mica Dig did not require any extensive deployment of personnel, but other exercises did. For example, in June a "no notice" Emergency Deployment Readiness Evaluation had already been conducted to determine exactly how many hours it would take to get NEST personnel and equipment airborne from Travis, Nellis, Andrews, and Kirtland air force bases. Mild Cover required 120 controllers, evaluators, and players to spend four days in September at New Orleans Naval Air Station (also known as Alvin Callender Field) in Belle Chasse, a part of the New Orleans metropolitan area with a population of around nine thousand. They checked the secure voice and data transmission systems to be used in the exercise, each agency's radios, microwave links, telephone systems, compressed video displays, and the tactical satellite installation at the Forrestal Operations Center.[10]

Among the organizations invited to participate in Mirage Gold were one or more "special mission units" of the Joint Special Operations Command (JSOC), which included the Navy's Seal Team 6 and the Army's Delta Force. While the JSOC did initially agree to take part, with its anticipated role being designated Errant Knight, the command eventually limited its participation to the command post exercise.[11]

In October 1992, FBI official W. Douglas Gow did accept the Energy Department's invitation to the FBI to participate in the exercise, which would give the bureau a chance to test the adequacy of the *FBI Nuclear Emergency Contingency Plan* and the memoranda of agreement between the FBI, Energy, and other agencies concerning the response to nuclear extortion or terrorist incidents. Another FBI document, produced at about the same time, characterized Mirage Gold as a "5-day, 24 hour a day scenario" that would "include a maritime/site assault, one mobile target, and two stationary targets." It also claimed that the variety of sites would provide the players "with a complex set of problems to resolve."[12]

Among those problems was the potential hostage/barricade situation at the safe house that the FBI office in New Orleans anticipated, which led the office to request deployment, as envisioned by the Scenario Working Group, of almost a hundred members of the bureau's HRT, one of a number of FBI units that participated in the exercise. While the HRT was being deployed, additional information about the house was collected and planning for an assault on the house began. In the early-morning hours of October 17, FBI eavesdroppers overheard instructions to kill the informant.

Predictably, authorization for the HRT to storm the safe house followed. The elite FBI unit "killed" six terrorists, rescued the informant, and gathered up whatever evidence was to be found in the house.[13]

One of the FBI's informants had revealed that the Patriots group was planning a series of bombings, involving conventional and high explosives. But the evidence gathered by the FBI's raiders at the scene as well as interviews of the rescued informant indicated that the Patriots organization had much grander plans. It intended to obtain fissile material from foreign sources, assemble several nuclear devices, and search for a "prime target." The evidence also provided some possible leads to a maritime vessel through a charter boat operator at Lake Michoud, located to the southeast of the intersection of Interstates 10 and 510. As FBI agents continued to investigate, their confidence grew that the authors of the scenario had included an "immediate and serious" nuclear threat to New Orleans as part of the exercise. Late in the afternoon, the bureau requested assistance from NEST, military explosive ordnance disposal units, and FEMA. Louisiana state officials were notified that a FEMA regional operations center had been established. The New Orleans Police Department, under investigation by the FBI for corruption, did not get a call.[14]

By early morning on October 18, participating military ordnance disposal units, representatives of FEMA, and the first wave of NEST search and support elements had arrived in the city and established their separate staging areas and command posts in an industrial complex across the Intercoastal Waterway from the New Orleans Naval Air Station. Located about twenty-seven miles southeast of New Orleans International Airport, the complex was owned by Brown and Root, a Texas-based company and subsidiary of Halliburton, which had built naval air stations and warships for decades. The complex had been unoccupied for several years but had been cleaned up for the exercise. The FBI's Joint Operations Center was established in the same complex. The communications equipment, including secure voice, data, and video display systems, was already there, having been installed during the Mild Cover exercise the previous month. By the middle of the day, the airlift of NEST personnel and equipment had been completed, although not without incident as one NEST team member suffered a heart attack.[15]

NEST equipment included briefcases, rental vans, and aircraft packed with radiation detection equipment and other sensors. NEST personnel were divided into a number of working groups, reflecting the many tasks NEST would be expected to carry out during such an event: support, plans and operations, search and diagnostics, access (to the device), disablement, and containment and effects. Although disablement was actually the responsibility of military EOD personnel, NEST personnel would serve, at least, as advisors when it came to trying to cripple the device before it detonated.[16]*

Intelligence gathered by the FBI was the basis for initiating searches in a variety of locations, including the first one, conducted by NEST personnel, in the Federal Aviation Administration noise abatement area near the New Orleans International Airport. By late afternoon of October 18, the maritime target was located, anchored at Lake Michoud, and placed under surveillance. FBI investigators, possibly through electronic surveillance, also learned that there were four hostages aboard the vessel along with another homemade nuclear device.[17]

Early on October 19, additional information drew attention to a small flying service on an airstrip off Magazine Drive in the Belle Chasse area, several miles southwest of Lake Michoud and near the naval air base. NEST searchers were directed to the area and got a "hit" during a drive-by, detecting a mock nuclear device in an airport shed. The FBI established surveillance on the flying service, which was supplemented by NEST radiation monitoring of a nearby road. The HRT started planning for an emergency assault based on the activities under observation.[18]

At about noon, three men were spotted leaving the flying service carrying a small but heavy bag containing nuclear components, which they loaded into a closed van parked nearby. The NEST monitors were activated as the van left the area, and the FBI initiated mobile surveillance. The van was observed entering a property at 797 Walker Road in Belle Chasse, also south of the naval air station and off Belle Chasse Highway, and owned by the same individual who owned the house assaulted by the FBI's rescue team on October 17.[19]

By midafternoon on October 19, the bureau had determined that there was no one left at the flying service after the van's departure. The explosive ordnance personnel had initiated access to the buildings. An improvised nuclear device was found in a shed, along with information indicating it was armed and set to detonate on October 20 at noon. NEST and military explosive ordnance disposal personnel attempted to determine the specific characteristics of the device and develop a render-safe plan.[20]

---

*In NEST exercises, a "nuclear device" might actually consist of several devices, for safety purposes (so that radioactive material and explosives are not included in the same device) and to facilitate the participation of different groups involved in the disablement effort. William Chambers, e-mail, February 26, 2008.

The device to be disabled, recalls Peter Zimmerman, the physicist behind *Gadget*, had been built by personnel from the Navy Explosive Ordnance Detachment Technical Division. And while they had never built such a bomb before, their device was "frighteningly plausible." When Zimmerman asked a former weapons designer to give him an estimate of the yield of such a device, the answer he got back was not reassuring—a considerable number of kilotons.[21]

Authority to disable the device was obtained during the morning of October 20. NEST personnel constructed a thirty-five-foot cone-shaped tent around the shed and pumped in thick aqueous foam to limit the blast's effects and absorb radioactive particles that would be emitted after the team destroyed the device with conventional explosives. The conventional explosives would turn the foam into billions of bubbles, which would dissipate. Unfortunately, after the foam was pumped in, it was decided to perform a "surgical disrupt"—cutting the proper wires and firing a shaped charge. Not only did this technique not require foam to mitigate the blast and absorb radioactive particles, but it also did not get rid of the foam. Since there was no way to get rid of the foam, early reentry for forensic purposes—to study the bomb's design—became impossible.[22]

Surveillance was maintained at the Walker Road site and plans were made to assault that site and the maritime target simultaneously to maintain the element of surprise, possibly with the help of Department of Defense "tactical resources." The terrorists at the two locations were in contact and known to be uncertain about the cause of the apparent failure of the device at the flying service. The group's leader, who was on board the boat, instructed some subordinates to return to the device and determine what went wrong. Neither they nor the group's leader would escape, and the exercise wrapped up at 1:38 a.m. on October 21, the boat having been raided and the nuclear device on board having been disabled.[23]

There was an initial "hot wash" of participants during the morning of October 21, where they gave their impressions of the exercise.[24] As with preceding exercises, Mirage Gold was also followed, in subsequent months, by a series of "after-action" reports by the agencies who were major participants. Such reports usually described the exercise, identified successes and failures, and offered recommendations to improve the chances of a successful response to a real nuclear crisis.

The FBI's after-action report characterized Mirage Gold as an "effective exercise" and evaluated seven different aspects of the operation: the scenario, interagency coordination of forensic objectives, controller training, operation of the exercise control cells, interagency coordination of media issues, information management, and technical support. It also contained twenty-six recommendations.[25]

In addition to its description of the background of the exercise and its planning, the FEMA report noted five exercise objectives, each followed by a discussion and evaluation. The summary that followed stated that "FEMA's opportunity to participate in Exercise MIRAGE GOLD proved to be a valuable experience in several respects. The exercise clearly demonstrated the lack of understanding that exists in agencies not familiar with the FRP [Federal Response Plan] regarding the concept of consequence management in an environment where a catastrophic emergency/event is possible but has not yet occurred." It also argued that "corrective actions that can be taken to address the problems noted . . . are generally straightforward."[26]

Of more relevance for NEST was the report prepared for the Nevada Operations Office by William Chambers, the former original NEST member, and Joel Carlson. Carlson was a former FBI agent who had joined Sandia laboratory after his FBI career and worked on NEST matters.[27] Their report was packed with discussions of the problems they identified and recommendations on how to rectify those shortcomings.

They noted problems with interagency agreements. The various directives for the federal response to a domestic nuclear terrorist incident were described as "fragmented, incomplete, or non-existent"—one of the consequences, according to Chambers and Carlson, being that the Defense Department expected to be involved in predicting the effects of the blast, which the authors asserted was the "sole responsibility" of the NEST Containment and Effects Team.* The Energy Department's policies slowed the

---

*This view was not shared by military explosive ordnance personnel. An after-action report prepared for the commander of the U.S. Army Forces Command, stated that "DOE [Department of Energy] and DOD [Department of Defense] organizations are tasked with developing estimates of the radiation dose from both dispersal and nuclear detonation. These estimates are important for evacuation decisions and estimates for casualty predictions. Estimates for fallout, dispersal, and initial radiation were provided by NEST and FRMAC [Federal Radiation Monitoring and Assessment Center]. During this exercise, operationally significant differences in fallout, dispersal, and initial radiation were noted. These differences significantly affected both evacuation decisions and casualty prediction estimates. Some of these differences were resolvable and some were not. It is important that the hazard predictions presented to decision makers present a

ability to respond to a threat, the authors found, because they required some communications to proceed in a series rather than simultaneously. Not surprisingly, they recommended a critical review of those procedures.[28]

Chambers and Carlson mentioned deployment problems too, which had been evident in the emergency deployment readiness evaluation test prior to Mirage Gold. The problems extended across the board and concerned activation, notification, transportation, and deployment of NEST elements. As a result, personnel and resources had been artificially prepositioned in anticipation of the exercise.[29]

There were also technical problems, including an "ineffective technical response" due to "unrealistic scenarios and timelines," as well as "inefficient acquisition and distribution of critical IND [Improvised Nuclear Device] data" to NEST field and management personnel. An additional problem was the "inability to detonate disablement explosive charges on the New Orleans (Belle Chasse) Naval Air Station," charges that would have dispersed the troublesome foam. The search was also flawed owing to the scarcity of escorting FBI agents, along with the agents' lack of knowledge of search techniques as well as safety and security requirements.[30]*

In addition, information management left much to be desired. The authors found the FBI's intelligence collection effort deficient. The bureau "was narrowly focused on . . . learning what was necessary to identify and capture the terrorists, not how the device was constructed or configured," which is "key to DOD and DOE efforts to diagnose the device, predict its effects, disable it, etc"—a complaint echoed in an after-action report prepared for the commander of the U.S. Army Forces Command, whose 52nd Ordnance Group provided disablement personnel. FBI agents either missed, or did not recognize as important to other elements of NEST, diagrams of the device's firing system that had been located in an area the agents had searched during the raid of October 17. Such data was "critical to the Disablement Team; the lack thereof could have meant the difference between success or failure in the deployment of disablement tools."[31]

---

consistent clear picture," and went on to recommend formation of a Joint Radiological Hazard Assessment Cell. See Maj. Gen. Joseph W. Kineer, Deputy Commanding General, Fifth U.S. Army, Memorandum for: Commanding General, FORSCOM, Subject: Exercise MirageGold After Action Report, November 15, 1994.

*One additional problem, according to a Mirage Gold participant, was that the FBI agents who were serving as drivers for NEST search personnel would respond to fictional reports of gunfire (as part of the exercise) rather than continue the search effort. Telephone interview with Robert Kelley, November 20, 2007.

In addition to the failure to collect vital information, Chambers and Nelson noted, there was a problem in sharing information among agencies owing to the security procedures for protecting classified information. The lack of equivalency of security classification levels among the participants "unnecessarily hampered interagency cooperation and the flow of vital information." Not surprisingly, the authors concluded that all major NEST organizations needed to "develop procedures to reduce or eliminate institutional barriers affecting the flow of information."[32]

Another problem was the difficulty NEST personnel "at all levels" had in obtaining "accurate, timely information regarding the developing situation." The authors noted that while the NEST mission, responsibilities, and number of deployed personnel had "grown dramatically," available tools for information transfer had "not been used to maximum advantage."[33]

There was some additional displeasure with the FBI, which, according to the after-action report, "conducted Exercise operation in 'Imperial fashion,' failing to communicate or coordinate with other agencies," a criticism that echoed from earlier exercises. And, according to the report, the FBI persisted in handling NEST situations on a case-by-case basis. (Participants would also tell congressional investigators that the FBI excluded non-FBI personnel from the Joint Operations Center, which was intended to include leaders from the different agencies).[34]

Chambers and Carlson attributed some of the problems experienced in the exercise to the five-year lapse since the last major interagency exercise. As a result, many personnel "at all player levels" had never been involved in such an event. The deficiency was particularly noticeable with respect to participants in the command, control, and management areas, in contrast to those in the scientific and technical fields. The authors recommended that a major interagency NEST exercise be held in the United States once every three years, as required by the 1991 Department of Energy order specifying the mission and responsibilities of NEST.[35]

Despite the many problems they identified, their conclusions looked at what they considered to be the positives of the exercise. Thus, they commented that in Mirage Gold, "four major agencies of the federal government melded their respective resources into developing a solution for a major criminal threat to a United States population center that had potential catastrophic consequences." In addition, the authors believed that the smaller-scale exercises in the series (Mild Cover, Mica Dig) provided "efficient and controllable experiences" for establishing the activities, training needs, logistical requirements, and liaison relationships that would exist in the full-scale exercise."[36]

But the optimism felt by those who wrote the FEMA and Nevada Operations Office after-action reports was decidedly not shared by Rear Adm. Charles J. Beers Jr., whose professional title required thirteen words: Deputy Assistant Secretary of Energy for Military Application and Stockpile Support, Defense Programs. Beers, the son of a naval officer, recalls that he had been a "submariner all my life," which included a stint as commanding officer of the USS *Minneapolis–Saint Paul* in the mid-1980s. He had held the post of deputy assistant secretary since August 1993 (and would depart in September 1995). It was a job that had traditionally been held by Air Force or Army generals. But Secretary of Energy James Watkins, a former admiral and submariner himself, wanted a submariner in the position. Navy regulations required that an admiral's first position be a "joint" one—that is, outside of the Navy alone. So Beers, who had just attained admiral status, found himself replacing Admiral Jerry Ellis as a deputy assistant secretary of energy.[37]

Beers recalled that at the time he took over the position, there was a great deal of infighting over NEST, and there was an attempt to move it under the department's Office of Intelligence. The problem was, according to Beers, that the individuals who made up NEST worked for laboratories such as Livermore and Los Alamos, and "lab people belong[ed] to me." Ultimately, NEST remained his responsibility.[38]

As a result, Beers had the authority to express his views in the type of memo that media accounts almost inevitably refer to as "brutal" or "scathing." In the memo he informed the manager of the Nevada Operations Office,

> Over the past several weeks, I have directed my staff to review the overall status of the readiness capabilities of NEST, focusing specifically on the recent full field exercise series, Mile Shakedown. The initial indications of this review are not promising, having indications that our overall stated capabilities are not as refined as they are required to be. Alleged shortcomings in the program focus on time lines, deployment, logistics, and overall integration of resources within DOE and the interagency community. I also have concerns about the integrity of the exercises we have conducted.[39]

Beers went on to enumerate several areas of concern. One was that a real threat situation would move faster than the one in the Mirage

Gold exercise, requiring "expedited procedures" that were "not consistent with actual practices." In addition, Beers was concerned that "the huge NEST structure" inhibited rapid decision making and action. He also charged that information—including device location and type of nuclear source—"was inappropriately leaked to the players" during both Mirage Gold and the Emergency Deployment Readiness Evaluation. Another problem Beers identified was the "erroneous information/data" given to disablement teams.[40]

Those four complaints did not exhaust the list of the admiral's concerns. "The disablement procedure for the device was not appropriate," he wrote and objected that "the NEST community has neglected to incorporate shortcomings which were brought out at past exercises." There was also the predeployment of communications capabilities, which "created optimistic and unrealistic results" owing to the availability of equipment before it could have realistically arrived. Airlift resource expectations, the memo claimed, were unreasonable and appeared to be extremely out-of-date. There also needed to be considerable improvement in the arrangements made for the safety of the search team in a hostile environment. Finally, "interactions with and communications between our other emergency response assets and Federal agencies require improvement."[41]

NEST veteran Alan Mode, who believed that the provision of advanced information compromised the ability to assess how NEST would respond in a real crisis, recalls that the Beers memo received a very negative reception at the labs. "Nobody wanted to hear criticism of NEST at the time." The memo also resulted in a "lot of finger pointing," Mode recalls.[42]

Other NEST veterans believed Beer's criticism to be less than fair. Some noted that limited funding required some prepositioning of equipment that would not actually be immediately available in the event of a crisis. Both William Chambers and William Nelson noted that the military had a very different view of the purpose of exercises than did the civilian leadership of NEST. They believed, from their experience with military participants, that for the military, which exercised repeatedly, the whole point of an exercise was to prove that the mission could be accomplished. In contrast, according to Chambers, the labs viewed exercises as an occasional means of getting all those who would be participating in a nuclear threat scenario together and taking them "over the edge"—identifying problems that would arise, which would lead to actions to correct those problems.[43]

Beers's reaction to those views was a laugh and the comment, "You could look at it that way"—although he clearly didn't and doesn't. In his view, a successful exercise would involve finding devices and disarming them.[44]

Thus, while key participants from the labs did not consider the exercise a failure, Beers did. And he was in a position to order a review of the exercise and the NEST enterprise. In his memo to the Nevada Operations Office manager, in addition to voicing his disquiet about Mirage Gold, he "requested" a general assessment of NEST with respect to the concerns described in the memo.[45]

To conduct that assessment, the Nevada Operations Office manager tapped Duane C. Sewell, one of NEST's founders. In 1978, Sewell had left Livermore, where he was deputy director, to serve as assistant secretary for defense programs in the newly created Department of Energy. In 1981 he left government to run a consulting business. From 1989 to 1993 he again served as Livermore's deputy director. In 1993 he retired from the laboratory and returned to his own consulting business.[46]

In addition to Sewell, who served as chairman, the "Nuclear Emergency Search Team Assessment Team" included Delbert N. Dilbeck of the FBI, Deputy Manager Ray D. Duncan of the Nevada Operations Office, William F. Hartman of Sandia National Laboratories, and Ronald T. Stearns of the Nevada Operations Office.[47]

Sewell and his colleagues studied existing policies and procedures as well as background documentation. In addition, the assessment team conducted 120 hours of interviews with sixty-five individuals representing a cross section of management, technical, and logistical support functions associated with the NEST program, as well as other participating organizations and agencies. Individuals from the Department of Energy headquarters, the Nevada Operations Office, Lawrence Livermore National Laboratory, Los Alamos National Laboratory, Sandia National Laboratories, EG&G Energy Measurements, the FBI, the Department of State Office of Counterterrorism, and the Department of Defense were questioned by the assessment team.[48]

The team's report, which Mode characterizes as "a benchmark in NEST history," was completed in time to be in print on July 12, 1995, although it was available only to a very select audience. The main body of the report, consisting of sixty-one single-spaced pages, discussed NEST's mission, management and organization, technical response capabilities, logistical and technical support, deployment readiness posture, deployment command and decision authorities, research and development, training, field exercises, interagency participation, intelligence, policies and procedures, and, finally, funding, budgeting, and planning.[49]

The assessment team observed that during its formative years, NEST focused on developing a capability to search for an improvised nuclear device or special nuclear materials that had been lost or stolen. During that time, the most likely event was expected to be an extortion attempt using a device or dirty bomb. While the team noted that the potential for such an event still existed, it also observed that terrorists, at both the national and international level, had the will and intent to employ WMD "with little regard for human lives or property."[50]

With respect to management and organization, Sewell's team reported that historically the Energy Department (and its predecessors) did not take an active role in the management and direction of the NEST effort but that the current Energy Department director had taken a more proactive role. Whereas the department's Office of Emergency Response had once had a staff of three, in 1995 it had twenty-three people, including seven staff members and advisors who were directly involved in the NEST program on a full-time basis.[51]

That proactive role, Sewell and his colleagues reported, had caused tension between Energy Department headquarters, the Nevada Operations Office, and the NEST groups working at the laboratories and for contractors, as well as declining morale among NEST personnel. Subsequently, Dr. Victor H. Reis, assistant secretary of defense programs in the Energy Department, argued that along with the headquarters' more proactive role came some significant changes that created tension, including the frequency and depth of exercises, the focus on long-standing technical issues, and an emphasis on dealing with the threat of nuclear terrorism rather than nuclear extortion.[52]

The team also reported that under the present method of operation, there simply were not enough bodies to accomplish many of the tasks associated with the overall field management and direction of "a complex multi-faceted operation." As a result, the Nevada Operations Office had to rely on other organizations or committees to provide support in areas such as the development of field policies and procedures as well as the planning, directing, and controlling of remedial actions.[53]

The panel suggested that the Nevada Operations Office and the laboratories consider escalating NEST to full program status and allocating the manpower and management attention needed to ensure that the system was fully ready to deploy and able to respond effectively to potential terrorist incidents. At the same time, it recommended that the Nevada Operations Office "exercise assertive leadership and establish a prompt and authoritative policy and decision making process in order to ensure that level of response capability is achieved and sustained."[54]

In evaluating NEST's technical response capabilities, Sewell's group examined eight different aspects: search, access, diagnostics, device assessment, disablement, containment, effects prediction, and consequence management. Highlights of the report include the group's findings on search, device assessment, containment, and effects prediction.

After examining search capabilities, the assessment group concluded that "the current suite of detection hardware and software are on the leading edge of the technology and, unless a breakthrough should occur which would increase sensitivity and detection ranges, any additional development will be limited to miniaturization, improvements in existing techniques and methods or the design and production of so called 'smart instruments' which can be utilized by untrained personnel in a search mode."[55]

The primary mission of the Device Assessment Team, the report stated, was to determine if the device, as constructed, could produce a nuclear yield and, if so, how large a yield and how various disablement options would affect the performance of the device. The expertise of the team's personnel constituted "the most unique as well as greatest strength that the laboratories bring to the NEST program."[56]

Sewell, Dilbeck, and their colleagues reported that with regard to containment, aqueous foam had proved "to be a very practical and effective material for containment and mitigation purposes," explaining that "aqueous foam possesses the capabilities required to rapidly attenuate blast pressures, and . . . is highly effective in capturing much of the radioactive material that might be associated with a high explosives detonation . . . Systems have been developed to contain the foam in place which can be erected quickly and have proven to be effective in field trials." However, "additional engineering efforts are required to develop more effective methods of adapting these containment structures to unconventional locations or sites where an IND or RDD might be emplaced." In addition, "effective techniques for the rapid dissipation of residual foam have yet to be developed. Such a capability could be useful in providing for immediate reentry to evaluate the effectiveness of the disablement efforts and to recover forensic evidence."[57]

The Containment and Effects Team included, the report informed its readers, a field-deployable component capable of processing and analyzing calculational models using the data gathered in the field. The models would take into account the effect of containment systems as well as climatological conditions in the immediate area. The team possessed computer-assisted techniques to provide decision makers with a complete description of all of the consequences that might be expected from such an event.[58]

With respect to research and development, the report noted that the majority of systems then in use for detection were by-products of the U.S. nuclear weapons program and that "only limited research" had been conducted to design equipment specifically for the NEST program. The problem was that the "Weapons Program has now been curtailed to such an extent that the remaining research programs have very little potential to contribute anything of substance to the continuing needs of the NEST program." Technical limitations of NEST could only be resolved, the panel wrote, by "the establishment and continued support of a steady state research and experimental program over an extended period."[59]

The panel continued on that theme, noting that Energy Department officials had never before been faced with a decision as to whether or not the department should sponsor a research and experimentation program specifically directed at NEST requirements. "As a result of changing circumstances," the Energy Department "has now arrived at the crossroads where management must decide if they are willing to accept the risks associated with those known limitations and continue with the 'status-quo' or seek the resources required to improve this situation." There were, however, "no guarantees that even a fully funded research program would resolve all of the current limitations."[60]

Its section with regard to field exercises, beginning on page 43, was the first time the panel explicitly referred to the Mirage Gold exercises that had led to its creation—only to dismiss the issue. The panel wrote that the "problems and concerns which resulted from the recent MIRAGE GOLD Exercise seem to have been adequately identified and described in the draft After Action Report as well as a number of other independent evaluations." As a result, the assessment team did not examine Mirage Gold and other field exercises in detail except to determine if there were any systemic problems that needed to be investigated. The panel continued, observing, in defense of the Mirage Gold planners, that "many of the concerns were related to the design and conduct of that specific exercise including many of the artificialities and simulations which will always be reflected to some degree in any field exercise. Most of the artificialities and simulations were driven by efforts on the part of the design staff to minimize costs."[61]

At the same time, the assessment team found that most organizations were in agreement that the next major field exercise should be strictly on a "no notice" basis in order to test the true response capabilities of NEST.

Selected elements of NEST assets, such as communications, would not be predeployed to the exercise site. In addition, the group concluded that at the Washington level, there should be direct participation by appropriate members serving in their designated roles—in contrast to surrogates or a simulated response group.[62]

Further, the team noted that most field personnel agreed that one of the next set of exercises should be conducted in a closed environment such as the Nevada Test Site to permit more realism in the design and conduct of the technical elements of the deployment. In addition, the exercises should be conducted on a "no fault, no recrimination basis." Problems with detection systems or errors in judgment "should be used as the basis for remedial actions."[63]

The assessment team's findings reflected those in the after-action report with regard to the issue of interagency participation. The team stated that the memorandum of understanding between the FBI, Defense Department, and Energy Department, which had last been amended in June 1982, was outdated and did not reflect several changes that had been agreed to by participating agencies. Meanwhile, the agreement between the State, Defense, and Energy departments relating to deployments overseas had lapsed, although the parties to the agreement had agreed to continue to honor the provisions.[64]

The "continued absence of current agreements" between NEST and other participating agencies had created a hardship on the field organizations, since they had not been able to finalize many of their deployment operating procedures or command and control systems or develop training programs incorporating the provisions of the most recent agreements. "The consequences of the prolonged absence of formal agreements which clearly delineate roles, responsibilities and authorities were reflected in the recent MIRAGE GOLD field exercise," Sewell and his colleagues wrote.[65]

The assessment team reached at least three other conclusions of importance. A comparison of the Mirage Gold after-action reports with the reports from earlier field exercises revealed many similarities in the problems identified, particularly those involving command and control. That suggested to Sewell and the rest of the team that there was no system for assembling a comprehensive list of problems and assigning responsibility for resolving them.[66]

Also, the team expressed concern that in the event of an actual nuclear terrorist threat, there was an inadequate process for obtaining review and approval of action plans from higher authority on short notice. It also questioned whether many of the officials in the chain of approval fully understood the kinds of decisions they would be asked to make or the potential consequences of such decisions.[67]

In addition, the group reported a number of significant technological constraints that limited NEST's ability to effectively respond to the full range of nuclear devices that a terrorist organization might use. Those constraints had been well known for many years, but Energy Department "management has not made a decision as to whether they are willing to continue to accept those limitations or seek the necessary resources to sponsor an appropriate level of research programs to address those limitations."[68]

Admiral Charles Beers, the man who was the catalyst for the Sewell report, recalls being pleased with it, characterizing it as a "good report," which led to NEST becoming "a lot more realistic" in its planning and exercises and "a lot more professional."[69]

Some of the history of Mirage Gold, Beers's criticism, the Sewell report, and the response of NEST management became the subject of hearings before the Permanent Subcommittee of Investigations of the Senate Committee on Governmental Affairs, whose members included Ohio's John Glenn and Georgia's Sam Nunn, two senators for whom proliferation and nuclear terrorism were priority issues. The hearings began on the last day of October 1995, continued the next day, and concluded with four days of testimony the following March, with a substantial portion of the hearings on March 27 focusing on NEST and Mirage Gold.

The news reported by congressional investigators undoubtedly helped alleviate the bad feelings that followed the Beers memo. A staff statement presented to the committee reported "that NEST is clearly a national asset which could not be duplicated by other organizations because of the unique scientific capabilities and field operational experience of the nuclear weapons laboratories that directly support it with volunteers and [research and development]." John F. Sopko, the deputy chief counsel to the Democratic minority, testified that since Mirage Gold, NEST had "successfully completed its first truly no-notice full-field exercise overseas," that "that had never been done before," and that NEST had "deployed all of its resources within established timelines"—apparent references to an exercise held in Jordan. That was a truer test, Beers recalls, than previous ones that entailed picking up NEST members and "flying them around the West" before landing at the U.S. exercise site.[70]

At the same hearings, Victor H. Reis, from the Energy Department, explained the change in philosophy, initiated at the department's headquarters. Reis told the senators that "NEST was originally designed to respond to incidents of nuclear extortion in support of the FBI" and that "the extortion scenarios allowed planning and operations to be conducted over a period of several days because the intelligence and law enforcement communities believed that the extortionist would allow time for negotiations."[71]

In addition, "the idea that a nuclear device would fall into the hands of terrorists and be detonated without notice" was not believed to be credible. As a result, "NEST capabilities were developed and based on large-scale deployments" and the "process was slow but very thorough." According to Reis, the "NEST organization continued to believe that time was on their side when responding to nuclear threats," although it is clear from the Sewell report and Reis's testimony that the officials in Washington responsible for oversight of NEST did not.[72]

One problem with the view of the NEST organization, Reis continued, was that it led to "an exercise program with large-scale deployments of personnel and equipment," exercises that were "cost prohibitive and digressed from field exercises with challenging scenarios to grand scale training." He was, however, "pleased to report that things have changed for the better." Reis explained that in early 1992, as a result of intelligence estimates, Department of Energy officials reevaluated the nuclear incident scenarios that guided NEST planning and exercises, and decided to place more emphasis on scenarios involving nuclear terrorism. Since "we now know that terrorists are willing and able to use large explosive devices . . . without warning," it was necessary to "assume that nuclear terrorist devices could be placed and detonated without warning."[73]

Therefore, according to Reis, NEST teams were practicing using a "wide variety of deployment scenarios from table top exercises to long range deployments to remote locations" in conjunction with the FBI and State and Defense departments. In addition, they conducted frequent, "smaller and more focused" terrorism-related exercises than in the past. The emphasis was on "rapid and customized deployment to a wide range of nuclear threats."[74]

NEST also had received praise a few months before the congressional hearings, from a representative of the Energy Department's inspector general. Lawrence R. Ackerly, regional manager of the department's Western Regional Audit Office, reported the findings of his audit of NEST and commented that in response to the Sewell report, NEST program management formed a strategic realignment committee and instructed it to begin addressing the report's recommendations.[75]

But the praise directed toward NEST and the Nevada Operations Office could not change the fact, illustrated by the Beers memo and Reis's testimony, that the key officials involved in supervising and providing direction to NEST's operations were now at Energy Department headquarters in Washington, D.C., not at the Nevada Operations Office in Las Vegas. In particular, a former health physicist with Lawrence Livermore now held the reins to the nation's nuclear emergency response team.

Chapter 6

PEOPLE, PAPER, AND MACHINES

MIRAGE GOLD and its aftermath solidified the transfer of power over NEST from the Nevada Operations Office to Department of Energy headquarters. One manifestation of that shift in power was the elimination of the NEST Executive Planning Board. Consisting of senior NEST representatives from the Nevada Operations Office, the laboratories, and key contractors, the planning board had decided NEST policy and supervised its operations.[1]

The individual who became the single most important person in determining how NEST operated was the head of the Energy Department's Office of Emergency Response, Lisa E. Gordon-Hagerty. Gordon-Hagerty had joined the Energy Department in 1992, after a stint on the House Committee on Energy and Commerce, where she had been a technical advisor to the minority staff. Prior to her move to Washington, she had worked at Livermore, following her acquisition of an undergraduate degree in psychology and a master's in health physics, both from the University of Michigan.[2]

By 1993 Gordon-Hagerty became the public face of NEST, which was somewhat ironic since she would subsequently tell one writer that she "was always aware of my surroundings because it's conceivable that I might be a target." And in 1993, when NBC wanted to do an "Insider's Report" on the organization, she was "very reticent," according to NBC producer Robert Windrem. One problem was that she believed the team was not ready, that prior to her arrival "the team had been a mess" and was living off its press clippings. But then she realized, Windrem recalls, that a television segment offered an opportunity to galvanize the team.[3]

He also recalls that when he and the NBC crew arrived in Las Vegas in August 1993, "we were stunned at the level of cooperation . . . Not only did we get a complete dog and pony show, with the latest technology laid out in the NEST hangar, we got up close looks at the choppers, interviews with key players, and a raft of video. They also let us go out on two missions with them."[4] And when *NBC Nightly News* filmed its story on NEST, Gordon-Hagerty was featured in an interview. She told her interviewer that NEST preferred to work in a low-profile manner, "so that we don't . . . unduly scare the general public. And we certainly don't want to give away our presence to the terrorists . . . We will search . . . using vans, that look just like . . . regular side panel vans that anyone else would have in a local area."[5]

She also reported, "We have briefcases and backpacks that look like anyone's briefcase that they'd be carrying to work. And inside that—inside that briefcase is a detector that can look for the radiation that's emanating from the nuclear device." Asked how the people who carry such briefcases look, she went on to explain, "They certainly are dressed like you and I . . . they don't unduly startle the public or make their presence known."[6]

In a 1995 *Insight on the News* article titled "Your Life May Depend on the Woman from NEST," reporter Anthony L. Kimery wrote, "In the event that anti-American terrorists should obtain such a weapon, there's only one person to call. And it's not the Man from U.N.C.L.E. nor James Bond. It's the woman from NEST . . . America's first line of defense against nuclear terrorism." The woman he was referring to, "the beautiful blonde who is chief of an agency so secret that even its name has been classified," was Gordon-Hagerty—even though, strictly speaking, she was not a member of NEST.[7]

She told Kimery that she considered her job to be "the most important in the country." It was a job Gordon-Hagerty would hold until 1998, when she joined the National Security Council staff as director of weapons of mass destruction preparedness, a position created when President Bill Clinton signed a presidential decision directive that May, "Protection Against Unconventional Threats to the Homeland and Americans Overseas." She would hold that job for another five years, till she left in 2003 to become executive vice president and chief operating officer of the United States Enrichment Corporation (USEC), a leading supplier of enriched uranium fuel for commercial nuclear power plants. In subsequent years she would be named to *Fortune* magazine's list of most powerful women.[8]

But it was the power she possessed over NEST before she left government, particularly her tenure in the Department of Energy, that had distressed some NEST veterans, who were, undoubtedly, glad to see her depart. It is also probable that a NEST veteran such as William Nelson spoke for others when he asserted, and not in praise, that Gordon-Hagerty "killed [NEST] in the form it was" and eliminated the oversight role of the Nevada Operations Office for NEST. Similarly, William Chambers believes she "began to think like the military" when she evaluated an exercise such as Mirage Gold, and he "wouldn't be surprised if some of the words [of the Beers memo] weren't hers."[9]

A very different view of Gordon-Hagerty comes from NEST veteran Robert Kelley, now on the staff of the International Atomic Energy Agency (IAEA). Kelley credits her with understanding that NEST would have to operate in an environment in which communicated threats by extortionists were a thing of the past, and the new era involved the perpetual threat of nuclear attacks by terrorists, attacks that were likely to come without warning. She was "strong enough to resist" the opposition that she faced and willing to "make enemies in the process."[10]

Her boss, Charles Beers, also praised her performance, calling it "very positive" and crediting her with "vision." In addition, he said, she enabled NEST to get attention, to be recognized, among the multitude of federal agencies that "would like to get their name in lights."[11]

Of course, much did not change. The controlling guidance for the FBI and NEST continued to reside in several key documents. The Atomic Energy Act of 1954 made the malevolent use or threatened use of special nuclear material a felony and assigned the FBI responsibility to investigate such threats. President Ronald Reagan also signed, in November 1988, Executive Order 12656, "Assignment of Emergency Preparedness Responsibilities," updating an earlier executive order. The order directed the Department of Energy, in consultation with the secretaries of state and defense, the director of the Federal Emergency Management Agency, and the Nuclear Regulatory Commission, to "develop plans and capabilities for identification, analysis, damage assessment, and mitigation of hazards from nuclear weapons, materials, and devices."[12]

In January 1986, Reagan signed a national security decision directive, "The National Program for Combatting Terrorism." The nine-page, single-spaced directive both set forth U.S. policy on terrorism—"firm opposition to terrorism in all its forms whether it is domestic terrorism perpetrated within U.S. territory, or international terrorism conducted inside or outside U.S. territory by foreign nationals or groups"—and assigned responsibilities across the government for carrying out the program.[13]

In June 1995, it was Bill Clinton's turn to sign a secret presidential directive outlining U.S. policy on counterterrorism, replacing Reagan's directive. The document reaffirmed the State Department's responsibility for managing the U.S. response to overseas terrorist incidents and the FBI's designation as lead agency in responding to domestic threats. It informed its select audience that "the United States shall give the highest priority to developing effective capabilities to detect, prevent, defeat and manage the consequences of nuclear, biological, or chemical (NBC) materials or weapons use by terrorists." The remainder of the directive, with regard to the U.S. response to weapons of mass destruction incidents, was deleted before its public release.[14]

But an unclassified Energy Department directive, issued in September 1991, "Nuclear Emergency Search Team," was still in force—and would remain so for more than another decade. The directive specified that the first request for NEST's services would be handled by the department's Emergency Operations Center in Germantown, Maryland. The center would then notify the duty officer for the deputy assistant secretary for military application (DP-20), the Nevada Operations Office, and the department's Office of Threat Assessment. The deputy assistant secretary was to then, if it was deemed necessary, activate an Operational Emergency Management Team while the Nevada field office was to mobilize and deploy the appropriate NEST personnel. Full deployment of NEST assets would require the approval of the deputy assistant secretary.[15]

The order also laid out the responsibilities and authorities of individuals from the secretary of energy down to contracting officers, with most of the key responsibilities for managing and operating NEST belonging to the deputy assistant secretary (and the Office of Emergency Response below him) and the Nevada Operations Office. In addition, the Office of Threat Assessment was given several jobs related to NEST: funding and operating the Communicated Threat Credibility Assessment Program at Livermore, participating in the Special Technologies Program research efforts designed to satisfy NEST requirements, and serving as liaison with the Intelligence Community in obtaining intelligence to support NEST operations. The director of the Albuquerque Operations Office was to ensure that assets belonging to the department's Accident Response Group (ARG) would be available to NEST if needed.[16]

The order included guidance to the Department of Defense, directed to the secretaries of the three largest military services—Army, Navy, and Air Force. They were to provide trained explosive ordnance disposal personnel for responding to Improvised Nuclear Device incidents in the continental United States. Each was to guarantee that there were service personnel who could respond to IND threats on services facilities, with the Navy also responsible for threats to Marine installations and "other areas as directed" by the president and secretary of defense.[17]

If NEST did deploy, a senior Energy Department official, normally the manager of the Nevada Operations Office, would be appointed as the Energy Senior Official (ESO) and assigned responsibility for the NEST response to the event. To help him carry out his job, he could turn to another piece of paper, actually several hundred pieces of paper—the two-hundred-page *NEST Energy Senior Official's Reference Manual*. The manual, printed in 1993 but still in force today, describes the various authorities under which NEST operates, interagency agreements, NEST operations policy, NEST response, predeployment considerations, on-scene resources and actions (including search, access, diagnostics, and health physics), support resources, legal and public affairs, security, and standard operating procedures.[18]

The basic mission of the NEST program, in contrast to the expected targets, had also not changed, at least not "appreciably" since 1974, according to the NEST assessment team. The primary mission, the team wrote, was "to assist the Federal Bureau of Investigation (FBI) in the conduct, direction, and coordination of search and recovery operations for nuclear materials, weapons, or devices; to assist in the identification of an Improvised Nuclear Device (IND), or a Radiological Dispersal Device (RDD), and to render advice on radiation and damage probabilities in the event of a detonation of such a device."[19]

The mission had, however, been expanded in two ways. NEST was to support the FBI and the Defense Department when dealing with a Sophisticated Improvised Explosive Device, the consequence of the episode at Harvey's Resort Hotel. In addition, it was to provide the same level of technical support to the State Department as it did to the FBI, for incidents outside the United States.[20]

Carrying out the mission still required resources spread across the country. The center of decision making concerning NEST was in the Washington area: the Department of Energy Office of Energy Response and the NEST-East contingent at Andrews Air Force Base, with about fifty people, two helicopters, and one fixed-wing aircraft. The NEST program manager continued to reside at the Nevada Operations Office. Out at Nellis Air Force Base, also in Nevada, was the NEST program headquarters—still the

Remote Sensing Laboratory, one tenant among many on the 11,300-acre base, which was home to assorted fighter wings and training centers. The laboratory was the repository of instruments—the attache cases packed with nuclear detection equipment, the detection and analysis equipment and the vans that transported it, as well as helicopters and fixed-wing aircraft that also carried detection and analysis equipment. In addition, it housed research testing and fabrication laboratories and shops.[21]

Lawrence Livermore, Los Alamos, and Sandia labs remained prime contributors of personnel. In addition, Livermore continued to host the Communicated Threat Credibility Assessment Program, staffed by the behavioral scientists, physicists, and other technical personnel who would evaluate three aspects of any threat: behavioral, technical, and operational. They would provide the results of their assessment to the FBI, indicating the credibility of the threat and including as much information as available that would allow law enforcement officials to identify and apprehend the threateners. Because of their work, about 90 percent of the nuclear threats from 1970 to 1995 did not require a NEST deployment.[22]

Contractors who could be counted on to provide members to the NEST team were EG&G (specifically, its Energy Measurements unit); Reynolds Electrical & Engineering Corporation (REECo), an EG&G subsidiary that was responsible for operation, maintenance, and support work at the Nevada Test Site; and Raytheon Services of Nevada, which also provided support to the Nevada Test Site (and prepared the NEST Energy Senior Official's Reference Manual).[23]

The personnel from those organizations who were at NEST's call had a multitude of specialties. They were atmospheric physicists, chemists, communication specialists, data analysts, engineers, health physicists, infrared physicists, logistic experts, management personnel, mathematicians, nuclear physicists, photographers, physicians, public information specialists, flight crews, and tracking and reentry analysts.[24]

If NEST personnel were to deploy, the ESO would select a senior scientific advisor (SSA) from one of the three nuclear weapons design laboratories. In some cases, a small advance party would be dispatched to the scene of the incident to work with the local authorities and to prepare for a full NEST deployment. Feedback from the advance party would determine the size and composition of the main party to be sent to the incident scene. If no time were available for an advance party, portions of NEST teams would depart as soon as possible.[25] In that case, a maximum of up to forty-five people would be expected to resolve the incident, but NEST could deploy a force of four hundred.[26]

Other organizations could also be involved in NEST deployments. The FBI continued to be the lead agency for domestic terrorist threats, with NEST providing support, whereas the Department of State remained the lead agency for overseas nuclear threats. If force were needed to subdue those threatening nuclear destruction, the FBI's Hostage Rescue Team, the Army's Delta Force, or the Navy's Seal Team 6 could be called on. Meanwhile, after the bomb is secured, NEST personnel would be advising explosive ordnance disposal personnel from the Army Forces Command 52nd Ordnance Group and from the Naval Explosive Ordnance Disposal Technology Division on how to neutralize the bomb before it detonates. EOD teams would also help counter booby traps, to allow NEST diagnostic personnel access to the possible nuclear or radiological device.[27]

In the mid-1990s, it could be said that people comprised the foundation on which NEST was built. Paper, in the forms of presidential and departmental directives, as well as manuals, provided the authority and guidelines for NEST operations. But a vital element of NEST's capabilities and operations was the multitude of machines available. They allowed NEST personnel to travel halfway across the world if necessary, search for nuclear devices or dirty bombs, disable them, and contain the effects of their work.

To move tons of equipment, along with personnel, NEST relied on Air Force C-141 Starlifters, which could virtually pull up to the front door of the Remote Sensing Laboratory, or at least land on the nearby runway. While not as large or as spacious as the C-5 Galaxy, which stands 65 feet tall and is 247 feet long, the C-141 has the capability of transporting substantial combinations of men and equipment in addition to its crew of six. The C-141, which first began operations in 1964, is 39 feet high and 168 feet long and has a wingspan of 160 feet. As long as the plane and its human and mechanical cargo weigh less than 323,101 pounds, it can get off the ground and travel up to 2,500 miles. In the air it can reach an altitude of 41,000 feet and fly at 500 miles per hour.[28]

Aside from having the space and power to transport a large volume of men and equipment, the C-141 has a number of features that make it more than a plane with a lot of available space. Its "material handling system" allows for the off-loading of 68,000 pounds of cargo, as well as refueling and reloading, in less than an hour. In addition, its cargo compartment can be modified to accommodate about thirty different missions and can hold two hundred people. Rollers in the aircraft's floor permit "quick and easy" pallet loading, according to one account. When the rollers are not needed, they can be turned over, leaving a flat surface for loading vehicles.[29]

Among the smallest items likely to be loaded on the Starlifter were handheld detector systems, which were maintained in the NEST inventory to meet various needs and blend in during covert searches. Each was equipped with electronics for the suppression of background radiation, which greatly enhanced the ability of the system to detect a small source. These systems were also capable of providing a signal only to the operator, using an earphone.[30]

One of the handheld items would look like an ordinary attache case. But rather than being filled with the books, documents, and electronic devices a businessman or professor might carry, the case would be packed with nuclear detection equipment, processing equipment, and a means of sending a signal to the person carrying it.

Such an attache case might be a smaller version of the aluminum neutron detector suitcase developed by Carl Henry and his colleagues in the 1970s, or its successors. The dimension of Henry's suitcase was approximately eighteen inches high, twenty-six inches long, and twelve inches deep. When packed with equipment, it weighed seventy pounds. That weight was from the detectors, amplifiers, discriminators, power supplies, batteries, battery charger, and detection logic circuitry packed into the case.[31]

The neutron detectors occupied the outer section of Henry's suitcase, which was designed to be carried in a vehicle in normal traffic, when the radiation source being sought was expected to be enclosed and located at a distance. An alarm in the suitcase would emit an audible signal if the data collected by the detectors, after processing, reached the "trip level." A three-position switch on the control panel gave a NEST member the option of resetting the alarm at the end of a sampling run, inhibiting the alarm, or leaving the alarm ready to go off until it was reset.[32]

Occupying more space on the C-141 would be NEST's large, sensitive detectors, which could be mounted in rented vans and used for area sweeps along streets and roads. Of course, the C-141 could also accommodate NEST-owned vans already loaded with detection and processing equipment. If the source of radiation were an automobile or a building near the street, the detector would be able to get a positive signal even while the van is moving.[33]

There was also room on the Starlifter for some of NEST's aerial detection equipment—its helicopters. The BO-105 is a lightweight twin-engine military helicopter produced in Germany. About ten feet tall and eight feet wide, with a twenty-nine-foot-long fuselage, it has a range of between 344 and 596 miles, depending on whether it carries auxiliary fuel. It can cruise at 127 miles per hour and can reach a maximum speed of 150 miles per hour.[34]

In addition, NEST had access to Hughes H-500 helicopters, which weigh a maximum of 2,550 pounds and can fly at 130 knots. The radiation detection capabilities of both the BO-105 and the H-500 were demonstrated during radiological surveys over Areas 18 and 20 of the Nevada Test Site during October and November 1980, during which they detected the presence of cesium-137 and cobalt-60.[35]

NEST has several varieties of aircraft that fly themselves, with the aid of a pilot, to work. The King Air B-200, almost forty-four feet long and fifteen feet high, with a wingspan of fifty-four feet, six inches, can be employed as an executive jet. With 8,233 pounds as its basic takeoff weight, it can transport about 4,250 pounds of equipment and personnel. It can seat between seven and fifteen people, in addition to the pilot, and fly at an altitude of 35,000 feet and up to 333 miles per hour when it is in its high-speed cruise mode.[36]

The Citation II, produced by Cessna, is a twin-engine jet aircraft, just over forty-seven feet long. In its standard configuration it includes space for two pilots, two to four equipment operators, and a scientific equipment package. It can reach an altitude of 43,000 feet, cruise at 350 knots (403 miles per hour), and carry up to 6,800 pounds of fuel, personnel, and cargo.[37]

Then there is the Convair 580T, used in Operation Morning Light. The first Convair 580 flew in January 1960, and more than a hundred have been produced. Each was almost eighty-two feet long, stood just over twenty-nine feet high, and had a wingspan a few inches more than 105 feet. It could reach an altitude of 25,000 feet and had a normal cruising speed of 325 miles per hour. Its maximum takeoff weight was over 58,000 pounds. The aircraft has been employed on a variety of civilian and military missions, carrying packages or passengers, and performing Air Force and Navy missions for both the United States and Canada. NEST's single Convair 580T carries infrared radiation detection equipment.[38]

Once the radiation detection systems carried on the Starlifter, or on any of the other planes that made up NEST's air force, discovered a radiation source judged to be a possible improvised device or dirty bomb, then other equipment delivered by the C-141 would come into use. Crucial to deciding what to do about a nuclear device or dirty bomb is the equipment that reveals the details about the bomb's construction, and its physics package. One type of diagnostic equipment is passive. It makes use of the radiation emanating from the material—X-rays, alpha rays, gamma rays, neutrons—to gather data from the device. Other equipment is active. It irradiates the device, looking for specific feedback that provides information on the nuclear and conventional explosive material it contains.[39]

Both X-ray and eavesdropping equipment, such as that used during the incident at Harvey's Resort Hotel, can help evaluate the internal structure of the device, including its fuzing and firing mechanisms. The X-rays from a diagnostic tool such as the Portac can disclose the status of a weapon's high explosives, which, if cracked, require stabilization with injections of a vulcanizing rubber before the weapon is moved.[40]

For many years, including the mid-1990s, NEST's equipment also included the Automated Tether-Operated Manipulator (ATOM), a robot with wheels and a remote-control arm. A long umbilical cord permitted ATOM to be manipulated from three miles away. The feed from stereo video cameras allowed the operator to view the area in front of the robot, while a third camera would provide a close-up of the arm's gripping mechanism.[41]

A Starlifter might also bring to a NEST deployment site a variety of equipment used in disabling a bomb. Of course, which particular type of equipment would heavily depend on what NEST's diagnostics revealed about the bomb's construction and physics package.[42]

If NEST personnel wanted to slice into a suspected bomb, they could employ a high-speed liquid abrasive cutter, a remotely operated instrument that uses high-pressure water and an abrasive medium to do the job. The cutter represents an alternative to a metallic saw whose sparks might set off a detonation. Or the cutter might be used to gain access to the bomb, as the Accident Response Group did in a 2007 exercise when it employed the cutter to gain entry to a van containing the warhead before the group could x-ray the warhead. The cutter can cut through aluminum, stainless steel, titanium, bulletproof glass, and armor.[43]

Also on board might be a supply of liquid nitrogen and its delivery system. Liquid nitrogen, at temperatures between −384°F and −410°F, could be used to freeze the electronics of a detonator, although an even more dramatic method of cooling would be to plunge the device into a slush of liquid and solid nitrogen. When properly insulated, in containers such as Dewar flasks, liquid nitrogen can be transported without significant loss caused by evaporation.[44]

More violent means of destroying a device might involve the use of explosives. A shaped charge such as the one used in Harvey's Resort Hotel is one alternative. Even more drastic would be the use of a thirty-millimeter cannon to blow the bomb apart. In contrast to twenty-five-millimeter rounds, which are typically for antipersonnel weapons, thirty-millimeter rounds are generally used against armored vehicles or fortified bunkers. Such ammunition is fired by a variety of U.S. military platforms, including the A-10 Thunderbolt aircraft, the AH-64 Apache helicopter, and the Marine Corps Expeditionary Fighting Vehicle, an amphibious vehicle intended for deployment in 2015.[45]

Another option is a .50 caliber rifle set on a tripod. The rifle was designed to attack parked or landing aircraft, armored personnel carriers, concrete bunkers, and bulk fuel storage facilities. Powerful enough to puncture armored limousines, it has an effective range of up to 2,000 yards in the hands of a skilled marksman. The ammunition for the rifle is the largest round available to civilians.[46]

If a thirty-millimeter cannon or .50 caliber rifle is used to destroy a device, deployment of aqueous (that is, watery) foam, such as that developed by Sandia and used during the Mirage Gold exercise, might be necessary. Technically, that foam is just one type of aqueous foam, beer and shaving cream being other examples. What all have in common is that they are "impermanent forms of matter" in which a gas, often air, is distributed in a mass of bubbles, each bubble separated from other bubbles by a liquid film that is almost, but not completely water.[47]

The foam placed inside the tent used to hold it during Mirage Gold was primarily engineered to absorb the radioactive material associated with dirty bombs as well as reduce pressures from a high-explosive blast. According to a Sandia fact sheet, "the resulting decrease in exposure to the population and contamination to downwind property can be dramatic." That same fact sheet reported that fabric enclosures, such as a tent, have been designed in variety of sizes to mitigate the effects of up to several hundred pounds of high explosives. The equipment for generating the foam, which can produce 60 to 300 cubic feet with a cubic foot of water, along with the tent can be packaged for deployment.[48]

Sandia also noted several "deployment considerations." One is that it can take labor and time to implement, and "therefore, people are at substantial risk of death or injury during the implementation." In addition, it warns that "compromises to the render-safe and re-entry procedures should be considered."[49]

While NEST's leadership, personnel, and equipment were poised to deal with nuclear terrorism or extortion in 1996, late in that year it looked like they would be deploying to deal with another nuclear threat—revisiting the experience of Operation Morning Light in 1978 and the near deployment in 1982 when Cosmos 1402's nuclear reactor threatened to return to earth. This time the problem was not a Soviet spacecraft, but only because there was no longer a Soviet Union. Rather, it was a Russian probe, Mars 96.

The probe was one of several missions to Mars launched that year. On November 7, the National Aeronautics and Space Administration (NASA) sent the one-ton Mars Global Surveyor on what would be a nine-year mission once it began orbiting Mars, which it started doing the following September. The probe's camera and other instruments would find evidence that water had once flowed on Mars, produce a global topographic map of Mars, and discover evidence that the planet once had a global magnetic field similar to Earth's. It would be the first American success with respect to Mars since the landing of two Viking spacecraft in 1976.[50]

On December 4, a Delta II rocket blasted off, carrying NASA's Mars Pathfinder on the first leg of its journey to the red planet. The spacecraft landed on July 4, 1997, and released its key passenger, Sojourner, a rover equipped with scientific instruments to investigate the planet's atmosphere, climate, geology, and composition of its rocks and soil. From its landing to its final transmission in September 1997, Pathfinder would return 2.3 billion bits of information, including more than 16,500 images from the lander and 550 images from the rover.[51]

In between the launches of Mars Global Surveyor and Mars Pathfinder, Russia sent up its Mars 96 probe, which it "was counting on . . . to give [its space program] a new lease on life." It carried over twenty instruments, from the United States and twenty European nations, to study the Martian surface and atmosphere, to study plasma, and to conduct astrophysical studies. At twelve minutes before midnight local time on Saturday, November 16, a four-stage Proton rocket carrying the Russian probe blasted off from the Baikonur Cosmodrome in Kazakhstan.[52]

The Russian spacecraft, weighing seven tons, consisted of five distinct vehicles. The largest section, at five tons, was to orbit the red planet. Then the two landers, each about 110 pounds, were supposed to enter the Martian atmosphere and transmit data from the surface. Finally, there were two "penetrators," in the shape of golf tees, each weighing 143 pounds and designed to withstand impact with the Martian surface.[53]

But none of the components of Mars 96 would get close to the Martian surface. By the following morning, Russia's military space forces were reporting that the mission had failed. The fourth stage of the Proton, which was to take the probe out of Earth's orbit, after which the probe would fire its own small engine to complete the escape from Earth, failed. The Russian NTV network called it a "black day" for Russian space research. Media reports indicated that it was expected to fall to earth. Unlike Cosmos 954 and Cosmos 1402, Mars 96 did not have a nuclear reactor aboard, but it did carry eighteen small energy generators or "batteries" powered by plutonium-238 that were to provide power to the four landing craft. The plutonium consisted of about two hundred grams of pellets the size of pencil erasers, held in heatproof metal containers the size of thirty-five-millimeter film canisters.[54]

The batteries contained "a very modest amount of plutonium," a Russian space official told CNN. "Nevertheless," an NSC official told CNN, "in what is considered to be the extremely unlikely event that one or more of the batteries break open the United States is prepared to offer all necessary assistance to any nation to deal with any resulting problems." And it appeared for a while that the nation that might need America's assistance was one of its closest allies and the host of key U.S. intelligence and military facilities.[55]

Robert Bell, an NSC official, reported that the probe was expected to hit central or eastern Australia, after it reentered the Earth's atmosphere about noon Australian time. To monitor the Russian probe, the U.S. Space Command and its subsidiary, the Air Force Space Command, employed the same sort of resources used during Morning Light. Bell also said that "SPACECOM believes the size of the probe is large enough to give pieces of it a chance of surviving re-entry, though most of the spacecraft will burn up in the atmosphere before [impact]."[56]

President Bill Clinton, vacationing in Hawaii before a planned state visit to Australia, spoke to Australian Prime Minister John Howard. Whether or not they specifically discussed NEST, the organization received orders on Sunday, November 17, to prepare for a possible mission to locate any radioactive material that might land Down Under. But just as Cosmos 954 did not crash where it was first expected, neither did Mars 96.[57]

Further analysis of the space probe's orbit led the U.S. Space Command to revise its estimates. Now the most likely unlucky country was Bolivia or Chile. That produced, at higher levels of the Department of Energy, a change in thinking about deploying NEST, although not without some dissent. It was thought that deploying NEST to either of those nations might not be in the best interests of the United States. Australia was one of America's closest military and intelligence allies. It was a key member of a decades-old signals intelligence alliance with the United States, Britain, and Canada and the host to key facilities employed by the United States to operate signals intelligence and missile detection satellites.[58]

Bolivia and Chile were not in that class. They were considered "not very important," according to a former NEST member. And aside from any hostility that a U.S. presence might produce, there was concern that the operating environment was simply too harsh. The Chilean landscape, with its extremely high altitudes, would make it difficult for a NEST helicopter, with its 13,000-foot ceiling, to operate effectively. Also mitigating against deployment was the minimal threat from the plutonium-238. If the batteries had not actually broken up, the whole operation would be unnecessary.[59]

But Robert Kelley, head of the Remote Sensing Laboratory at the time, was one of those who believed there would be value in sending NEST, that such a deployment would stretch the team and provide experiences that couldn't be gotten in planned exercises. The whole argument became moot when Bolivia and Chile appeared to escape unscathed, for initial reports indicated that the probe reentered the atmosphere above the southern Pacific Ocean west of South America around 8:30 p.m. Eastern Standard Time, with any debris, if it survived reentry, apparently landing in the ocean.[60]

Subsequently, Moscow admitted that the object tracked on Sunday, which had been the subject of such concern, was only the plutonium-free fourth stage and not the probe itself. Further analysis of data from U.S. tracking resources, including DSP satellites, led the U.S. Space Command to conclude that debris from the probe that survived reentry "would have fallen over a 200-mile portion of the Pacific Ocean, Chile, and Bolivia."[61] But that change in conclusion as to the fate of Mars 96 did not change the plans for NEST personnel. They still remained home.

COSMOS 954–TYPE SATELLITE
A Soviet ocean surveillance satellite. *Courtesy of Asiq Siddiqi*

NEST PERSONNEL EN ROUTE TO EDMONTON
NEST personnel en route to Edmonton to participate in Operation
Morning Light. *U.S. Department of Energy: National Nuclear Security
Administration, Nevada Site Office (DOE–NNSA/NSO)*

MEETING WADE, GARLAND, AND GATES
Troy Wade and Mahlon Gates of the Nevada Operations Office discuss
NEST participation with Col. David Garland, Canadian commander
of Morning Light. *U.S. Department of Energy: National Nuclear Security
Administration, Nevada Site Office (DOE–NNSA/NSO)*

NEST ANALYSIS
NEST personnel analyzing airborne data collected during Operation
Morning Light. *U.S. Department of Energy: National Nuclear Security
Administration, Nevada Site Office (DOE–NNSA/NSO)*

MIGHTY DERRINGER CUP
The coffee cup provided to participants of the 1986 Mighty Derringer exercise. *Courtesy of Carl Henry*

REMOTE SENSING LABORATORY
The Remote Sensing Laboratory at Nellis Air Force base, Nevada—NEST
headquarters. *Courtesy Robert Windrem*

LOADING OF NEST EQUIPMENT
NEST equipment being loaded on van. *Courtesy Robert Windrem*

NEST HELICOPTER
A NEST helicopter with radiation detection equipment. *Courtesy Robert Windrem*

MEETING WITH LISA GORDON-HAGERTY
A meeting of key Energy Department emergency response officials, including Lisa Gordon-Hagerty. *Courtesy Robert Windrem*

LISA GORDON-HAGERTY
A recent photo of Lisa Gordon-Hagerty. *Washington Life Magazine*

BIN LADEN
The Defense Intelligence Agency's "wanted" card for
Osama bin Laden. *Defense Intelligence Agency (DIA)*

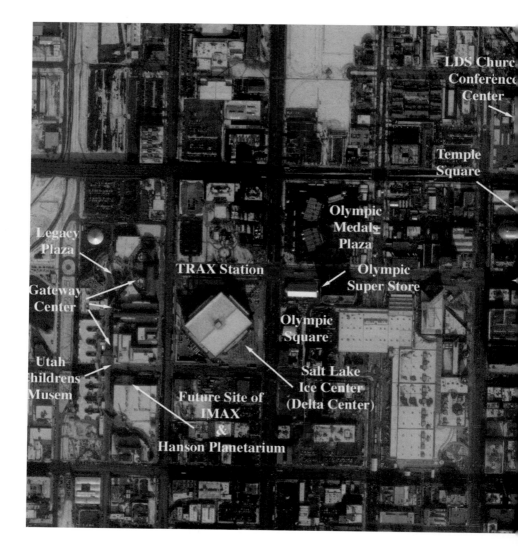

OLYMPIC VILLAGE
An overhead view of the Olympic Village for the
2002 Salt Lake City Olympics. *Courtesy of GeoEye*

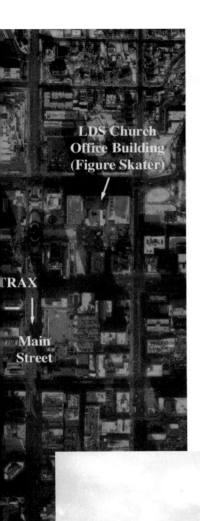

LDS Church Office Building (Figure Skater)

TRAX

Main Street

NATANZ
Iran's Natanz uranium enrichment facility.
Courtesy of Robert Windrem

SARGODHA
Pakistan's Sargodha ammunition depot, one of the suspected sites for the storage of the nation's nuclear weapons. *Courtesy of GeoEye*

TOPOFF-4

The command post for the 2007 Topoff-4 exercise. *Department of Homeland Security (DHS)*

LARGE AREA IMAGER
The large area imager, developed at Lawrence Livermore National
Laboratory, can be carried in a van and used to detect nuclear materials.
Lawrence Livermore National Laboratory, Department of Energy

Chapter 7

NEW ENEMIES

JUST AFTER 11:00 P.M. on May 28, 1993, a shock wave spread out across several hundred miles of the Australian outback. The Mundaring Seismic Observatory near Perth in southwestern Australia, registered a 3.6 magnitude reading. Truck drivers crossing the region, as well as aboriginal gold prospectors camping in the vicinity, witnessed bright flashes that lit up the night sky. Miners and engineers in the region also heard the rumble of loud explosions in the distance.[1]

That shock wave would lead a subcommittee of the Senate Committee on Governmental Affairs to investigate whether a terrorist group had actually acquired or built a nuclear device. But that investigation would not be launched until almost two years later, following the terrorist group's implication in a March 20, 1995, attack that killed twelve people and caused physical or mental trauma to another six thousand. The targets of the attack were the riders of Tokyo's subway system. The means of attack was not a nuclear device or dirty bomb but sarin, a colorless, odorless poisonous gas. Discovered in Germany in 1938, sarin is estimated to be five hundred times more toxic than cyanide, and capable of killing within a minute. Had it been dispersed as planned, casualties could have reached ten thousand.[2]

It was not the group's first venture into terrorism. In June 1994, in Matsumoto, Japan, it also used sarin, spraying it from a truck, killing seven and injuring two hundred people. Early in March 1995, the group had attempted to assassinate the chief of Japan's National Police. The group had also released anthrax in Tokyo on two occasions, although the attacks failed to produce any casualties.[3]

Known as Aum Shinrikyo (Supreme Truth), the group had been established in 1987 with the initially modest objective of assuming control of Japan. Approved as a religious organization in 1989, it ran a slate of candidates in the Japanese parliamentary election in 1990, which resulted in a humiliating defeat. Subsequently, the group began to preach that the world's end was imminent, that the United States would initiate Armageddon by starting World War III with an attack on Japan using fission or hydrogen bombs, and that salvation would come only to those who adopted the Aum faith. The cult's founder, Shoko Asahara, blind in his left eye from a young age and only partially sighted in his right, graduated from a school for the blind in 1977 and joined Agononshu, a Buddhist religious group, in the early 1980s. Despite offerings to the Buddhist group for a thousand consecutive days, the enlightenment promised never arrived, although Asahara did manage to attract a few disciples of his own. After returning, in 1987, from a trip to India, he told his followers that he had attained enlightenment, which now allowed him to take the money they offered.[4]

By the time of the Tokyo attack, the cult had grown from a single office in Japan to thirty offices in six different countries, with a worldwide membership of about 50,000—including about 10,000 in Japan and 30,000 in Russia. All together Aum recruited more than three hundred scientists with degrees in medicine, biochemistry, biology, and genetic engineering who were promised unlimited funding, although many were second-raters given a second chance by the cult. Included were a former researcher from the Japanese National Space Development Agency, an expert on chemical weapons who had majored in organic physics, a researcher who had studied particle physics, and a physicist from Osaka University. The savings that they and other members had turned over to Aum gave the group assets exceeding $1 billion.[5]

One connection between Aum and the seismic event in the Australian outback was the arrival of a delegation from the cult in April 1993, headed by "Minister of Construction" Kiyohide Hayakawa. The visit was followed by the purchase of a 500,000-acre sheep farm in Banjawam, Australia, about four hundred miles north of Perth. In addition to mining uranium from a nearby site, and then enriching it, the group also planned to test chemical weapons. That the group had something beyond raising sheep in mind was indicated by the equipment it brought to the farm: chemicals, gas masks and respirators, as well as picks, shovels, mining equipment, and a mechanical ditch digger. It also established a laboratory equipped with computers, glass tubing, glass evaporators, beakers, Bunsen burners, mixing bowls, and a rock-crushing machine. Details of its activities in Australia, and elsewhere, were derived from documents seized from Hayakawa after the Tokyo attack.[6]

Presumably, the seismic signals that rippled across the Australian outback in May 1983 were detected at Woomera, also in the outback, by Project Oak Tree—also known as Detachment 421 of the Air Force Technical Applications Center, which operated the U.S. Atomic Energy Detection System (AEDS). But if the Senate investigations subcommittee asked AFTAC for its assessment of the event, it has gone unreported.[7]

The subcommittee did turn to the Incorporated Research Institutions for Seismology (IRIS). Based in Arlington, Virginia, and supported by the National Science Foundation, IRIS had more than eighty member institutions as well as more than one hundred seismometers across the world. A team of IRIS investigators—Gregory van der Vink, the institute's director of planning, Danny Harvey of the University of Colorado, and Christopher Chyba of Princeton University—calculated that the force of the event was equal to the explosion of 2,000 tons of TNT, or about 170 times larger than the largest mining explosion in the Australian region.[8]

The estimated force of the event was consistent with a very small nuclear detonation of two kilotons (in contrast to the fifteen kilotons of the Hiroshima bomb). An American geologist observed that a "nuke is a very real possibility." But the signature of the shock wave was closer to that of an earthquake or meteor strike than a nuclear explosion.* Ultimately, the IRIS trio reported that the signature was "inconsistent with an explosion" while "the meteorite impact scenario is consistent with the eyewitness observations and with the energy levels derived from seismic records for the event." They also noted that the meteorite scenario was "an intriguing but unconfirmed possibility."[9]

But there was more to Aum Shinrikyo's nuclear activities than the location of the ranch, its interest in uranium mining, and the seismic event of May 1993. In August 1993, it had contacted a Connecticut-based manufacturer of interferometers, hoping to purchase one for research. The laser-based optical measuring device can be employed to determine the velocity of high explosives to be used in an implosion device.[10]

The cult also tried to acquire a variety of weapons from Russian sources. In 1992 Asahara led a delegation to Russia to meet with senior government officials. Aum's construction minister, Hayakawa, would travel to Russia more than twenty times, visiting several former Soviet republics. In February 1994, Hayakawa, "Minister of Science and Technology" Hideo Murai (the physicist from Osaka University), and three other members arrived in Russia to acquire AK-74's, 7.62 millimeter Kalashnikovs that weighed over seven pounds and can fire 600 to 650 rounds per minute.[11]

But Aum's ambitions didn't end with the acquisition of rifles. It was also interested in bombs, rockets, napalm tanks, and radar-guided missiles.

---

*The seismic signals from a nuclear blast commence with a very distinct spike at the moment of the explosion. The highs and lows of the signals quickly taper down, and the signals then return to their preexplosion levels. In the case of an earthquake, the seismic signals build to their peak, as tectonic plates slip by each other, and then more gradually return to their preearthquake levels.

Hayakawa priced a MiG-29 in mint condition at $20 million and a used one at $12 to 14 million. Another piece of firepower that the cult had its eye on was the 195-foot SL-13 Proton rocket, which could propel satellites into geostationary orbit. Hayakawa also recorded in his notes the need to build a launch site in Japan for the Proton. What he wanted to put on top of the rocket was not a satellite. In 1993 Aum's branch in Moscow asked to meet with Viktor Mikhailov, the minister of nuclear energy. The request was denied, so Mikhailov never heard what Hayakawa wanted. But an entry in the construction minister's notebook read, "Nuclear warhead. How much?"[12]

Subsequent entries listed prices for a device, including $15 million. Whether Hayakawa had merely discussed the possibility of acquiring a nuclear weapon or actually had entered into negotiations to buy a nuke is not known. But Aum's nuclear activities in Russia did go beyond shopping. In 1992, it held talks with Nikolai Basov, a Nobel Prize winner in physics, in Moscow. And at least one of its devotees had infiltrated the I. V. Kurchatov Institute of Atomic Energy in Moscow, named after the father of the Soviet atomic bomb, and a repository of weapons-grade nuclear material. It was also the home of three research reactors.[13]

In the aftermath of the Senate subcommittee's investigation, Senate staffer John Sopko was skeptical that, whatever its goals, Aum was likely to have acquired a nuclear warhead or the skills needed to build one. It was more likely, he believed, that the group could acquire highly radioactive material for use in a dirty bomb. But, according to the Tokyo police, the group did acquire substantial classified information about Russian, Chinese, South Korean, and Ukrainian nuclear installations, including the safety system of the Chernboyl power plant in the Ukraine. It also obtained data on the routes and procedures for the movement of nuclear fuel in Japan. The means was not bribery but computer hacking.[14]

The sarin attack on the Tokyo subways further undermined the view that terrorists would not seek to kill large numbers of people. According to Daniel Benjamin and Steven Simon, who served as directors of counterterrorism on the National Security Council staff during the Clinton administration, the attack

> pulled the rug out from under one of the hallowed verities of
> counterterrorism—namely, that terrorist groups might want to
> acquire weapons of mass destruction for the sake of bargaining

leverage but would not actually use them. Because of the general abhorrence of chemical, biological, and nuclear weapons, it was believed that terrorists would be loath to alienate possible supporters by using them. That kind of mass killing would also harden government attitudes: the only conceivable response to those who would use those weapons would be the complete destruction of their group.[15]

The difference between Aum Shinrikyo and many other terrorist groups, RAND terrorism expert Bruce Hoffman explained in 1995, is the difference between "secular terror" and "holy terror," terror driven by a religious imperative. The "holy terrorist" has a radically different value system and worldview as well as different concepts of morality from the "secular terrorist." While secular terrorists "generally consider indiscriminate violence immoral and counterproductive, religious terrorists regard such violence not only as morally justified, but as a necessary expedient for the attainment of their goals," wrote Hoffman.[16]

Hoffman also found that religious terrorists have a different constituency than the secular variety. While the latter attempt to appeal to both actual and potential sympathizers, religious terrorists make a sharp distinction between their religious community and the rest of the world. They employ dehumanizing terms such as "infidels," "non-believers," and "children of Satan"—terms designed to erode any restraints on terrorist acts since its victims are portrayed as unworthy of living.[17]

Islamic terrorism is one type of holy terrorism. It differs from secular terrorism in that it rejects all other ideologies and views itself as a total outsider. Also, Islamic terrorism is conducted as a holy war, which can only end in total victory. Its third characteristic is that it forms "the basis of a whole theory both of individual conduct and state policy." Killing the enemies of Allah and offering infidels the choice between converting to Islam or being executed is seen as the duty of every individual follower. Thus, Ayatollah Baqer al-Sadr wrote, "The world as it is today is how others shaped it. We have two choices: either to accept it with submission, which means letting Islam die, or to destroy it, so that we can construct the world as Islam desires."[18]

A number of groups qualify for the label of "Islamic terrorist organization," including Hamas and Hezbollah. Hamas (the Islamic Resistance

Movement) is a Sunni Muslim Palestinian group that triumphed over Fatah in the Palestinian elections in 2005. Its terrorist activities have included the June 2001 bombing of a Tel Aviv discotheque, which killed twenty-one, and an August 2001 suicide bombing in a Jerusalem pizza restaurant that left eighteen dead. Reportedly, many of its senior members are well educated and have graduate degrees in engineering, chemistry, physics, and medicine.[19]

The Lebanese-based, Iranian-supported Hezbollah (Party of God) battled Israeli forces in Lebanon in 2006. It is known or suspected to have been involved in a number of major terrorist attacks over the last several decades, including the suicide truck bombings of the U.S. embassy in April 1983, the U.S. Marine barracks in October 1983, and the U.S. embassy annex in September 1984, all in Beirut. In March 1992, it was responsible for the bombing of the Israeli embassy in Buenos Aires. The group is also suspected of involvement in the June 1996 bombing of the Khobar Towers housing complex, near Dhahran, Saudi Arabia, which housed U.S. military personnel.[20] But the group that represents the greatest threat—in terms of its ability to recruit trained personnel and procure the raw materials needed—is Al-Qaeda.

Al-Qaeda's founder, Osama bin Laden, born in July 1957, is one of fifty-seven children of a Saudi construction magnate. The thin, six-foot-five-inch bin Laden appeared to be awkward but was apparently very athletic, showing prowess as a horseman, runner, climber, and soccer player. He attended King Abdul Aziz University in Saudi Arabia, which had been founded in 1967, to study civil engineering. According to some accounts, he also became interested in religious studies, inspired by the taped sermons of Abdullah Azzam, a disciple of Sayyid Qutb, the leading intellectual of the Egyptian Muslim Brotherhood in the 1950s and 1960s and disparager of almost everything American, including the "animal-like" mixing of the sexes at church dances.[21]

After the Soviet invasion of Afghanistan in December 1979, bin Laden became one of a legion of young Muslims from around the world who arrived to fight in a jihad, or "holy war," as part of the mujaheddin, the Afghan resistance forces. With some of those forces receiving substantial outside support from Pakistan and the United States, including Stinger missiles that could disrupt Soviet air operations, they managed to drive the Soviets from Afghanistan by the end of 1988, a departure the Soviets announced that April. Although bin Laden took part in a 1986 battle in Jalabad and a 1987 assault against Soviet armor, he became known primarily for his ability to use some of his family's wealth to support the anti-Soviet effort.[22]

He was instrumental in establishing a financial support network, relying on Saudi and Persian Gulf financiers, that came to be known as the Golden Chain. Donations passed through charities and other non-governmental organizations and were used to purchase arms and supplies for the holy warriors. Mosques and schools in the United States and other parts of the world doubled as recruiting stations. To channel recruits to Afghanistan, bin Laden and Islamic cleric Abdullah Azzam established a "Bureau of Services."[23]

Defeat of the Soviet forces was not the end of bin Laden's Islamic activism, but only the beginning. He and Azzam agreed that the organization they had established should not be permitted to disappear. The result was creation of a base or foundation—Al-Qaeda—as a general headquarters for future jihad. By August 1988 bin Laden was clearly in charge, and supervised an organization that included an intelligence unit and military, financial, political, media affairs, and propaganda committees.[24]

In the fall of 1989, bin Laden accepted an invitation from the Sudanese political leader Hassan al Turabi to move his organization to the Sudan. He also agreed to help Turabi in his war against African Christian separatists in southern Sudan as well as build some roads. While his representatives were searching for property, he moved back to Saudi Arabia. In the aftermath of the Iraqi invasion of Kuwait, bin Laden's public opposition to the presence of U.S. troops in Saudi Arabia led the government to seize his passport. After he managed to get out of the country in April 1991, he relocated to the Sudan.[25]

In his new home, he created an "Islamic Army Shura" as a coordinating body for the federation of terrorist groups with which he was establishing links. Groups from Saudi Arabia, Egypt, Jordan, Lebanon, Iraq, Oman, Algeria, Libya, Tunisia, Morocco, Somalia, and Eritrea were among the organizations that formed alliances with bin Laden's group. Less formal relationships were established with other extremist groups in Africa and Southeast Asia. Bin Laden also maintained a connection with the conflict in Bosnia.[26]

On several occasions in 1992, his organization called for jihad against the Western "occupation" of Islamic territory, including the U.S. forces that first arrived in Saudi Arabia after the Iraqi invasion of Kuwait and those that deployed to Somalia in late 1992. To help Somalia warlords in fighting U.S. forces, Al-Qaeda set up a cell in Nairobi and used it to provide weapons and training.[27]

In 1996, a brief CIA biography of bin Laden characterized him as an "Islamic Extremist Financier" and "one of the most significant financial sponsors of Islamic extremist activities in the world today." It went on to list a number of efforts funded by bin Ladin, including the attempted bombings of U.S. servicemen in Aden in December 1992, the operation of three terrorist training camps in northern Sudan, the Egyptian extremist group al-Jihad, and the Kunar terrorist camp in Afghanistan.[28]

But by the end of 2000, bin Laden would become America's public enemy number one—no longer just an Islamic extremist financier, but a terrorist mastermind who the highest authority in the country wanted to see dead, if the CIA could arrange it. The National Commission on Terrorist Attacks Upon the United States noted a number of terrorist attacks in the 1990s where bin Laden's involvement was cloudy, including the 1993 bombing of the World Trade Center, the 1995 Manila plot to bomb a dozen airliners over the Pacific, and the 1996 Dhahran bombing.[29]

But there was no ambiguity when it came to bin Laden and Al-Qaeda's bombing, in concert with Egyptian Islamic Jihad, of two U.S. embassies in Africa during the summer of 1998, after the public issuance of a fatwa that February for "Jihad against the Jews and Crusaders"—a fatwa that declared it was "an individual duty for every Muslim who is able" to "kill the Americans and their allies, both civil and military," until their armies "depart from all the lands of Islam." On the morning of August 7, two bomb-laden trucks drove into the U.S. embassies in Nairobi, Kenya, and Dar es Salaam, Tanzania, only minutes apart—about 10:35 in Nairobi and 10:39 in Dar es Salaam. The attack in Nairobi left 213 dead. Twelve were Americans while almost all of the remaining dead were Kenyans. The Dar es Salaam bombing was less deadly, killing eleven, none of whom were Americans, and injuring eighty-five.[30]

When asked about the death of the non-Americans, bin Laden responded that "when it becomes apparent that it would be impossible to repel these Americans without assaulting them, even if this involved the killing of Muslims, this is permissible under Islam." When questioned about whether he had been the mastermind behind the attacks, he answered that the World Islamic Front for jihad against "Jews and Crusaders" had released a fatwa that was "crystal clear." He added that if the instigation for jihad against the Jews and Americans to liberate the holy places "is considered a crime let history be a witness that I am a criminal."[31]

The attacks produced a tepid U.S. response—Operation Infinite Reach—on August 27, 1998. Despite its name, it involved only the launch of eighty cruise missiles against a terrorist training camp in Afghanistan (where it was believed bin Laden might be attending a conference) and a pharmaceutical plant in the Sudan, believed to be involved in the production of chemical weapons. The failure of those attacks to curb bin Laden's lust for American blood was demonstrated in the fall of 2000. On October 12, a small boat packed with explosives and driven by Al-Qaeda operatives attacked a U.S. Navy destroyer, the USS *Cole*. The blast tore a hole in the *Cole*'s side and, more importantly, killed seventeen members of the crew and injured at least forty others.[32]

Then on September 11, 2001, Al-Qaeda's status as a terrorist enemy of the United States took a quantum leap. The hijacking of four planes by nineteen of its operatives and the successful use of three as missiles packed with jet fuel — destroying the Twin Towers of the World Trade Center in New York, tearing a hole in the Pentagon, and killing three thousand people — required more intricate planning than did the group's other terrorist attacks and unequivocally demonstrated Al-Qaeda's willingness to kill en masse. It seemed clear that Al-Qaeda, bin Laden, and Khalid Sheikh Mohammed, the chief planner of 9/11, would have had no regrets had all the tens of thousands of people who worked in the Trade Center died that day.

Indeed, they have said so on several occasions. In May 1998, bin Laden issued a statement with the title "The Nuclear Bomb of Islam," which declared that "it is the duty of Muslims to prepare as much force as possible to terrorize the enemies of God." When the subject of his nuclear ambitions came up in a December 1998 interview with *Time* magazine, bin Laden told the magazine's reporter, "Acquiring weapons for the defense of Muslims is a religious duty. If I have indeed acquired these weapons, then I thank God for enabling me to do so." During an interview with ABC News, he had much the same response: "If I seek to acquire such weapons, this is a religious duty. How we use them is up to us."[33]

And documents found in a house in an upscale neighborhood of Kabul in late 2001 — a building apparently used by Al-Qaeda operatives — provided evidence of Al-Qaeda's interest in obtaining nuclear weapons. The house showed signs of a quick exit, and in the haste to leave, the resident left behind a number of documents — discovered not by the CIA but by CNN.[34]

One document labeled "Superbombs" appeared to be a plan for a nuclear device, judged to be unworkable by experts, but it indicated that its author understood the various methods for detonating such a device. It described a little-known shortcut to initiate a nuclear explosion. A third document concerned the mining of uranium inside Afghanistan.[35]

In June 2002, Al-Qaeda spokesman Suleiman Abu Gheith posted "In the Shadow of the Lances," a three-part article, on the web site of the Center for Islamic Research and Studies. After counting up all the alleged victims of the United States and Israel, he declared, "We have the right to kill 4 million Americans—2 million of them children—and to exile twice as many and wound and cripple hundreds of thousands." He also claimed, "It is our right to fight them with chemical and biological weapons."[36] Nuclear weapons are not mentioned, but given the desired death toll and the indiscriminate killing envisioned, they would go a long way to making it possible to achieve the desired level of devastation.

In May 2003, bin Laden's desire to obtain, and willingness to use, nuclear weapons was sanctioned by the prominent Saudi cleric Sheikh Nasir Bin Hamd al-Fahd. His twenty-two-page, single-spaced "A Treatise on the Legal Status of Using Weapons of Mass Destruction against Infidels" was a response to a request, posted over the Internet, for a legal ruling on the use of such weapons "by Muslims engaged in jihad." He answered, "If the infidels can be repelled from the Muslims only by using such weapons, their use is permissible, even if you kill them without exception and destroy their village and stock."[37]

But that answer was only the prelude for his treatise. In his first chapter, al-Fahd observed that terms such as "contrary to legitimate international authority," "in violation of the Charter of Human Rights," and "in violation of the Geneva Convention" "have no standing in Islamic law, because God Almighty has reserved judgment and legislation to Himself." Judgment of such weapons depends only, he wrote, on "the Koran, the Sunnah, and the statements of Muslim scholars."[38]

Before turning to the pronouncements of Muslim scholars, al-Fahd wrote of arguments for permissibility of using weapons of mass destruction. Not surprisingly he accepted a number of such arguments. The Koran, he reported, includes God's edict that "whoso commits aggression against you, do you commit aggression against him like as he has committed against you." In addition, he wrote, "If those engaged in jihad establish that the evil of the infidels can be repelled only by attacking them at night with weapons of mass destruction, they may be used even if they annihilate all the infidels." Not surprisingly, "setting fire to enemy territory is permissible if the fighting requires it." And using an analogy from much earlier times, al-

Fahd noted that scholars have agreed that it is permissible "to bombard the enemy with a catapult" and "a catapult stone does not distinguish between women, children, and other; it destroys anything that it hits."[39]

The scholars whose proclamations he examined include the Hanafis, Malikis, Shafi'is, Hanbalis, Zahiris, and "other jurists." Those arguments were made long before the advent of nuclear weapons and concerned killing through such older means as fire, scorpions, snakes, and flooding. While the scholars may come from different schools of Islam, their bottom line was similar: "if necessary, anything goes." It was permissible to use the weapons of mass destruction of the time to "kill the infidels and their children." One scholar whom al-Fahd quoted argued, "God has commanded that the polytheists should be killed. He did not specify the manner in which it should be done, nor did he obligate us to do it in a certain manner. Therefore there is nothing to prevent their being killed by every cause of death: shooting, piercing, drowning, razing, casting from a cliff, and so forth."[40] Presumably, if he were alive today, that "so forth" would include chemical, biological, and nuclear weapons.

More recently, Sheikh Abu Bakar Ba'asyir, the spiritual leader of Indonesia's Jemaah Islamiya, an Al-Qaeda–affiliated organization, said that Muslims must embrace nuclear weapons "if necessary" because places like London and New York should fear more than conventional attacks. He also observed, "In battle it is best to cause as many casualties as possible."[41]

Of course, fantasies of inflicting nuclear terror are not by themselves a problem. But they become one when a group actively seeks to acquire the means of inflicting such terror and they have even a remote chance of succeeding. A 1998 U.S. federal indictment charged that "at various times from at least early 1993, Osama bin Laden and others known and unknown, made efforts to obtain components of nuclear weapons."[42]

One step for a nation or group in obtaining nuclear weapons is finding someone to manage the nuclear program—terrorist versions of Leslie Groves and J. Robert Oppenheimer. But one person can't do it alone, even if a nuclear device were to be stolen and detonated, much less constructed from scratch. Building a dirty bomb also takes some knowledge of physics and explosives.

Since the early 1990s, bin Laden has charged a succession of military commanders with the responsibility for procuring or developing weapons of mass destruction—nuclear as well as chemical and biological.

The WMD hunt killed Abu-Ubaydah al-Banshiri, who drowned in Lake Victoria in Africa's Great Rift Valley in May 1996 while on a mission to procure radioactive material for a dirty bomb. His successor, Mohammed Atef, was killed in an air attack in November 2001, not specifically for his quest for WMD but for a multitude of sins. Atef would be replaced by Khalid Sheikh Mohammed and Abu Zubaydah, both now in U.S. custody. Presumably, today's military commander has picked up his predecessors' responsibilities.[43]

A senior member of Al-Qaeda who was reported to have been the operational head of its unconventional-weapons program, code-named al Zabadi ("curdled milk"), was Midhat Mursi al-Sayid Umar, better known by those who care—including jihadists and Western intelligence services— as Abu Khabab al-Masri. An engineer, born in April 1953, al-Masri was initially thought to have been killed in an airstrike on Damadola in Pakistan in January 2006. But in early 2008 he was believed by U.S. intelligence officials to be alive. Then, in August, Al-Qaeda announced that he had been killed.[44]

As far as is known publicly, al-Masri's efforts focused on chemical weapons, first coming to attention for his role in running Al-Qaeda's Darunta training camp in Afghanistan. Al-Qaeda videotapes, shown on CNN in 2002, showed al-Masri and several assistants killing three dogs in chemical weapons experiments, using what was believed to be hydrogen cyanide, previously used in Nazi gas chambers. In addition to his close supervision of work on chemical weapons, he may have had ambitions of helping to build a dirty bomb, at least according to a report in the *New York Post*. His successor may be Abu Bashir Yemeni, who was reported to have worked closely with al-Masri.[45]

Al-Qaeda has also received an unknown level of assistance from members of Pakistan's nuclear establishment. Two of the members who discussed nuclear matters with bin Laden and his key lieutenants are Sultan Bashiruddin Mahmood and Chaudhry Abdul Majeed. Mahmood and Majeed ostensibly were in Afghanistan in connection with the Ummah Tameer-e-Nau (UTN), Reconstruction of the Muslim Ummah, an Afghan-based private relief organization whose announced mission was development, educational reform, and feeding the Afghan population. It was an organization that Mahmood founded after he resigned from Pakistan's Atomic Energy Agency in 1999, reportedly to protest Pakistan's willingness to sign the Comprehensive Test Ban Treaty.[46]

But there was also pressure for his resignation, partly at the behest of the United States, which had learned of Mahmood's sympathy for Islamic militant groups. He publicly supported the Taliban and suggested, in speeches at Pakistani universities, that Pakistan should be ruled in the manner that the Taliban ruled Afghanistan. Pakistani officials were also concerned about his suggestion that other Islamic nations should be supplied with weapons-grade uranium and plutonium produced by Pakistan. Pakistan's nuclear capability was "the property of the whole Ummah [Muslim community]," he claimed.[47]

After studying nuclear engineering in Britain in the 1960s, he returned home. According to one report, he became prominent in the 1970s after developing a technique to detect heavy water leaks in steam pipes at a nuclear power reactor near Karachi. After India's 1974 nuclear test, he attended, as a junior scientist, a meeting called by President Zulfikar Ali Bhutto to discuss Pakistan's response, and argued for a Pakistani bomb. He subsequently worked on Pakistan's clandestine gas centrifuge program and has been credited with playing a key role in establishing Pakistan's uranium enrichment program. His design of the unsafeguarded Khushab reactor, which was heavily dependent on illicit foreign procurement, was his most prestigious accomplishment.[48]

He also published articles on a variety of topics—electric motors used in radiation environments, quality assurance, technology transfer, and project management. But other publications demonstrated his strange fascination with the occult. In 1987, he was the author of a 232-page treatise titled *Doomsday and Life after Death—The Ultimate Fate of the Universe as Seen through the Holy Quran*. Included was a chapter that purported to explain how the world would end. In 1998, he produced *Cosmology and Human Destiny*, in which he claimed that sunspots have influenced major events in world history, including the French and Russian revolutions and World War II.[49]

Majeed, in the 1960s, trained at a plutonium facility in Belgium and then spent part of the 1970s or early 1980s at the International Center for Theoretical Physics in Trieste. When he returned to Pakistan, he began a long, successful career in the Nuclear Materials Division of the Pakistan Institute of Nuclear Science and Technology (PINSTECH) at Rawalpindi, before retiring in 2000. He was also reported to have been associated with the New Labs at Rawalpindi, a facility where plutonium for the nation's nuclear weapons was separated. The U.S. government has described him as an expert in nuclear fuels.[50]

Like Mahmood, Majeed had an extensive publication record, but unlike his colleague his resume did not include digressions into the occult. In the 1980s and 1990s, his works focused on nuclear detectors and the use of X-ray diffraction, fluorescence, and crystallography.[51]

Over a period of two or three days in August 2001, the two met with bin Laden and his top deputy, Ayman al-Zawahiri, and two other Al-Qaeda officials on several occasions at a compound in Kabul. According to the pair, who were detained and interrogated that October at the insistence of U.S. intelligence, bin Laden was intensely interested in nuclear, chemical, and biological weapons, and according to Pakistani officials, the two "spoke extensively about weapons of mass destruction." Bin Laden, according to Mahmood and Majeed, wanted to know if some radioactive material that he had obtained or had access to could be made into a weapon or something that could be used—they told him it was not possible. They also insisted that they did not provide the Al-Qaeda chief with any material or specific plans but took part in wide-ranging "academic discussion."[52]

No evidence has emerged that they did provide bin Laden with anything beyond words to help him in the nuclear field. But the discovery, in the office they had occupied in Kabul, of documents describing ways to employ anthrax as a weapon and powdered chemicals and, according to one report, "large amounts of significant data on nuclear weapons" indicated they were willing to go beyond purely academic discussions. Some U.S. intelligence officials suggested that the two, despite their nuclear backgrounds, did not know enough to help build a nuclear weapon. One of those officials told the New York Times that "these two guys were nuclear scientists who didn't know how to build one themselves" and that "if you had to have guys go bad, these are the guys you'd want—they didn't know much"—assertions that some experts viewed with a degree of skepticism.[53]

Whatever their ability to aid Al-Qaeda's nuclear ambitions, Mahmood and Majeed were not the only Pakistani nuclear scientists whose possible affection for the Taliban and bin Laden worried the United States. After they were interrogated, U.S. and Pakistani officials received reports that other scientists—ones with actual experience in the production of nuclear weapons and related technology—had been in contact with Al-Qaeda. Among the scientists named were Suleiman Asad and Mohammed Ali Mukhtar, who had extensive experience at Pakistan's most sensitive nuclear installations. Neither could be found in Pakistan when U.S. representatives asked that they be interrogated. They were, the Pakistanis responded, in Burma, doing research with local scientists. One may have tried to sell weapon designs to "unsavory customers." The CIA also reportedly wanted to investigate another four scientists for suspected links to Al-Qaeda.[54]

. . .

But bin Laden and Al-Qaeda have done more than talk about nuclear weapons and try to enlist physicists and engineers in their cause. During his time in Sudan, he plotted, with the assistance of a small group of engineers and physicists, to build a nuclear device. A key to the plan, which was formulated in 1993, was to buy highly enriched uranium from the former Soviet Union or—as an alternative—purchase a complete nuclear missile.[55]

An Al-Qaeda official, Jamal Ahmed al-Fadl, told an American court, during the trial of four men charged with assisting Al-Qaeda's 1998 bombings of the U.S. embassies in Kenya and Tanzania, that in 1993 he was sent to meet an individual outside of Khartoum in an effort to purchase uranium, allegedly from South Africa, for $1.5 million. He also claimed that he did not know whether the deal was ever completed.[56]

One of bin Laden's senior aides is believed to have visited at least three Central Asian countries to meet officials reported as good contacts, possibly by bin Laden sympathizers in Pakistan's Inter-Services Intelligence Directorate. Over the following year, the aide traveled back and forth from bin Laden's Sudanese headquarters to a number of Middle Eastern capitals and Central Asian cities and towns. He found no intercontinental ballistic missiles for sale, but he met one gang who thought it knew a sucker when it saw one. He was offered, and possibly bought, what was represented as more than 220 pounds of enriched uranium, but the gang had only low-grade fuel from a nuclear reactor, material that could never be used for a fission bomb.[57]

Other Al-Qaeda representatives were sent to Kazakhstan on the same mission, causing Israel to dispatch a senior official to that nation to attempt to short-circuit any sale. The Israeli intervention apparently worked, although bin Laden "still secured a network of friends and paid accomplices in the former Soviet Central Asian states and the Ukraine."[58]

According to one account, intelligence analysts believed that at some point, criminals had sold Al-Qaeda irradiated canisters alleged to contain uranium from Russian military bases, but the actual contents had no value to rogue nuclear scientists interested in building a bomb. They may also have fallen victim to smugglers who claimed to have Red Mercury, a mythical form of nuclear material, in some cases being nothing more than radiological waste.[59]

The early setbacks did not halt bin Laden's quest for radioactive material for a dirty bomb, fissile material for a nuclear device, or an intact nuclear warhead. According to Ivan Ivanov, a Bulgarian businessman connected to a Dubai company that supplies Asian laborers to Middle Eastern construction firms, he was approached by a bin Laden emissary in April 2001. The immediate result, Ivanov claimed, was a trip to Pakistan. Upon arrival he realized that his hosts were enthusiastic bin Laden supporters and that they apparently viewed his political connections in Eastern Europe as useful. Ivanov was then taken to meet the Al-Qaeda chief at a secret location along Pakistan's border with China, and then to a Rawalpindi villa. At the villa, Ivanov was introduced to a Pakistani scientist who described himself as a chemical engineer.[60]

The scientist told his visitor that he was looking for a way to obtain spent nuclear fuel rods from the Kozlodui nuclear electricity plant in Bulgaria. What he wanted, according to Ivanov, was "a legitimate way of buying nuclear waste from the power plant," and he was ready to give Ivanov money in advance so he could find local companies that would help him export the fuel rods. The Bulgarian businessman was offered $200,000 to establish an environmental firm to purchase nuclear waste, and was asked if he would run the company. Instead, he declined and, after his return home, reported the offer to Bulgarian authorities.[61]

Yet another attempt may have been planned for early 2001, according to Gen. Col. Igor Valynkin, who at the time was head of the 12th Main Directorate of the Russian Ministry of Defense, the organization responsible for the storage, transportation, safety, and security of nuclear warheads, as well as for the oversight of nuclear warhead research, design, testing, and production. According to Valynkin, there were two attempts to reconnoiter the 12th Main Directorate's S-shelters, heavily fortified concrete bunkers where nuclear warheads, when not attached to delivery systems, are stored. Valynkin also reported that there had been dozens of attempts to steal enriched uranium or plutonium since 1990.[62]

It was also reported that in 2002, Adnan El Shukrijumah, who is still being sought by the FBI for his alleged connection with an Al-Qaeda dirty bomb plot, posed as a student at McMaster University in Hamilton, Ontario—a university with a five-megawatt research reactor. U.S. officials believed he was there to obtain radioactive material. El Shukrijumah lived in the same part of Florida and worshipped at the same mosque as the American-born Jose Padilla, who was originally charged with plotting to detonate a dirty bomb in the United States.[63]

Al-Qaeda's effort was ongoing in 2003, according to Vice Adm. Lowell E. Jacoby, the director of the Defense Intelligence Agency, who told the Senate Select Committee on Intelligence early in the year that "Al Qaeda and other terrorist groups are seeking to acquire chemical, biological, radiological, and nuclear [CBRN] capabilities." There was no argument from Director of Central Intelligence George J. Tenet, who told the same committee, "We continue to receive information indicating that [Al-Qaeda] still seeks chemical, biological, radiological, and nuclear weapons."[64]

Four years later, senior intelligence officials were saying much the same thing. Lowell Jacoby's successor at DIA, Lt. Gen. Michael D. Maples, told the Senate Armed Services Committee in late February 2007 that "reporting continues to indicate that non-state actors, specifically [Al-Qaeda], continue to pursue CBRN options . . . The recent press claim made by the al-Qaida in Iraq leader asking for nuclear scientists to make 'germ' and 'dirty' weapons reinforces [Al-Qaeda's] interest and desire to acquire CBRN materials." Five months later, Edward Gistaro, the national intelligence officer for transnational threats, and Michael Leiter, the principal deputy director of the National Counterterrorism Center, told two congressional committees, "We assess that [Al-Qaeda] will continue to try to acquire and employ chemical, biological, radiological, or nuclear material in attacks and would not hesitate to use them if it develops what it deems is sufficient capability."[65]

But according to some claims and reports, Al-Qaeda has done more than try to acquire nuclear material or nuclear weapons—it has succeeded. One of those claims came from Osama bin Laden himself. In early November 2001 he was interviewed by Pakistani newspaper editor Hamid Mir, who was blindfolded and driven in a jeep from Kabul to an undisclosed location. Once he arrived, bin Laden told him, "We have chemical and nuclear weapons as a deterrent and if America used them against us we reserve the right to use them."[66]

In April 2002, Abu Zubaydah, the senior Al-Qaeda official who served as director of military operations and had been apprehended in Pakistan, told CIA and FBI interrogators that the terrorist group was working on developing a radiological dispersal device and that Al-Qaeda personnel "know how to do it." He also claimed that the group might try to smuggle it into the United States. One U.S. official told the *New York Times* that the captured terrorist "is well positioned to know what Al Qaeda is up to and we have to take his information seriously." It was also reported that British authorities claimed to have unearthed documents indicating that the group had constructed such a dirty bomb at an unidentified site in Afgahnistan.[67]

In February 2004, a pan-Arab newspaper claimed that Al-Qaeda had purchased tactical nuclear weapons from the Ukraine in 1998 and was holding them in secure places for possible use. A little over a year later, an intelligence source reported that Abu Musab Zarqawi, the leader of Al-Qaeda in Iraq, had obtained a nuclear device or was preparing to detonate a dirty bomb.[68]

In July 2005, the online publication *World Net Daily* made even more alarming claims—allegedly based on captured Al-Qaeda documents—that the group had obtained at least *forty* nuclear weapons from the former Soviet Union, with the assistance of Chechen terrorists. According to an Arab magazine, about twenty of those warheads were obtained from the Chechens in exchange for $30 million in cash and two tons of opium. The weapons were reported to include nuclear mines, suitcase nukes, artillery shells, and even some missile warheads. That was not the end of the bad news, according to *World Net Daily*, which also claimed that several of the weapons had already been smuggled into the United States over the Mexican border with the help of the MS-13 street gang and were to be detonated as part of a plan designated "America's Hiroshima." Cities alleged to be on the target list include New York, Washington, Las Vegas, Boston, Miami, Chicago, and Los Angeles. In addition, some former Russian special forces personnel were said to have been paid to help locate nuclear weapons that had been concealed in the United States during the Cold War.[69]*

Many of the claims concerning Al-Qaeda's acquisition of nuclear weapons revolve around "suitcase nukes." During the 1960s, the United States had developed Atomic Demolition Munitions. Potential uses included closing a mountain pass to prevent Soviet tanks from reaching Western Europe. One version, the Mk-54, was to be fired from a Davy Crockett recoilless rifle and employed a plutonium warhead, with a yield anywhere from ten tons to one kiloton. Another version of this warhead was the Special Atomic Demolition Munition (SADM), which was sixteen inches in diameter and twenty-four inches long, with a warhead weighing about fifty

---

*MS-13 is mainly a Central American gang whose original members arrived in Los Angeles and Washington, D.C., in the 1980s. "MS" stands for "Mara Salvatrucha." The name is derived from the Spanish word for army ant, *marabunta*, and is the nickname Salvadorans use to refer to themselves. In February 2005, the U.S. Intelligence Community concluded that there was no grounds for believing there was a connection between MS-13 and Al-Qaeda or other Islamic extremist groups. See "FBI Targets MS-13 Street Gang," www.pbs.org, October 5, 2005; Danna Harman, "U.S. Steps Up Battle against Salvadoran Gang MS-13," *USA Today*, February 23, 2005, accessed from www.usatoday.com.

pounds (but with another hundred pounds of weight contributed by safety and arming devices).[70]

In May 1997, retired Russian general Alexander Lebed told a U.S. congressional delegation that since the demise of the Soviet Union, 84 of 132 suitcase-size nuclear weapons were missing. In September he suggested that 100 of 250 were missing. Lebed also specified they were designated RA-115 and RA-115-01 weapons, which weigh up to a hundred pounds and have up to one kiloton of explosive power. In addition, Lebed claimed that the weapons did not require special access codes to be transmitted by higher authority to be certain that any use was authorized.[71]

Lebed's knowledge came, he claimed, from an investigation he ordered while serving as secretary of Russian President Boris Yeltsin's security council, a position he had been fired from in October 1996 because of his "outspoken manner and open presidential aspirations." Lebed, who had a reputation for exaggeration, also had a history of insubordination. A 1994 Defense Intelligence Agency biographic sketch described him as "the fiery and controversial commander of Russian forces in the Transdnestr region of Modolva" who "continues to retain his post despite a public stance that regularly tests his superiors' tolerance for insubordination." He was also described as having a "penchant for controversy."[72]

Lebed's comments certainly produced controversy. There was a dispute about whether such weapons existed, their exact characteristics if they did, and whether any had been lost. In response to Lebed's charges, the Russian Ministry of Atomic Energy (MINATOM) first stated that "no such weapons exist" and then "never existed, and do not exist." The Chief Intelligence Directorate of the Russian General Staff (the GRU), whose special forces had been identified as one of the entities that might possess such devices, asserted that no suitcase nukes were ever produced. Similarly, a former head of the KGB, another suggested owner of such devices, claimed that the "KGB had no use for nuclear weapons," while the Federal Security Service, the KGB's successor, claimed it had no information on KGB possession of such nuclear devices. The Russian national security advisor asserted that there was "no record of such devices." In early January 2002, the head of the 12th Department, Igor Valynkin, told a press briefing that "nuclear suitcases have never been produced and are not now being produced."[73]

But Lebed's accusations were not without support. In September 1997, Alexei Yablokov, Boris Yeltsin's former environmental and health advisor, claimed that suitcase nukes were built for the KGB and that he had met the designers. In December 1997, the Russian minister of defense told Representative Curt Weldon, "Yes we did build them . . . they will be destroyed by 2000." Maxim Shingarkin, a former major in the 12th Department, said the Soviet Union had built about a hundred suitcase bombs, and Russia had not added to the arsenal. The bombs, he claimed, were stored near Moscow, where about thirty to fifty members of the GRU were trained to transport them abroad and detonate them. In 2002, the Russian minister of atomic energy claimed that "all of these [miniature nuclear devices] are registered . . . it is technically impossible for them to find their way into the hands of terrorists."[74]

Tangled up with, and not unrelated to, the controversy over their existence was the debate over the exact, or even approximate, characteristics of such weapons. In 1996, the Center for Nonproliferation Studies at the Monterey Institute of International Studies was informed by a "senior advisor to Boris Yeltsin" (a description that would apply to Yablokov) that in the late 1970s and early 1980s, the KGB had received small nuclear weapons weighing less than seventy-five pounds. In 2002, officials at the CIA believed that the Soviets might have developed small nuclear landmines, but not small enough to fit into a suitcase. "They were not that small," according to one official. "It would require several people to move them." But subsequent information led Center for Nonproliferation Studies staffer Nikolai Sokov to conclude that two versions of the devices were created for the Soviet special forces (Spetsnaz): the RA-155 for the army and RA-115-01 for the navy (for underwater use). One device weighed sixty-six pounds and could be armed by a lone operator in ten minutes. The weapons were referred to as "nuclear backpacks" and had a yield of between one-half and two kilotons.[75]

Most accounts asserted that they would not be viable weapons unless used within a short period of time after their acquisition. The weapons were designed in such a way that after six months some of their components would have to be replaced. Further, the plutonium in nuclear weapons has to be replaced every five to ten years, so any suitcase nukes acquired with or before the collapse of the Soviet Union, which employed plutonium, would not be able to produce a nuclear detonation.[76]

In any case, it appears that none of the small weapons escaped Soviet and Russian custody and all had electronic protection systems, at least according to Russian claims. One claim was that they were kept at two secret storage facilities and had never been distributed to troops. And according to retired Russian general Vladimir Dvorkin, former director of Research Institute No. 4, the research arm of the Strategic Rocket Forces, they were equipped with a variety of permissive action links (PALs), as well as being protected against attempts to forcibly remove their electronic locks. Such an attempt would automatically cause the device to switch into safety mode, and therefore it would not explode. Also providing reassurance was Vladimir Denisov, who in 2004 reported that the Lebed commission, after Lebed's departure, was able to match records to actual weapons.[77]

In January 2002, a CIA report stated, "We have no credible reporting on terrorists successfully acquiring nuclear weapons or sufficient material to make them." That conclusion was probably based in part on an analysis of suspect radioactive material seized in Afghanistan by U.S. intelligence officers and Special Forces personnel. "We didn't find any type of serious radiological material," a Pentagon official told the *New York Times*.[78]

That sentiment was echoed in September 2002, when the author of a *Strategic Insight* paper for the Center for Contemporary Conflict of the Naval Postgraduate School observed that "so far there is no evidence that [Al-Qaeda] acquired enough nuclear material to develop a nuclear weapon, nor does it appear that they were able to acquire whole nuclear weapon assemblies." In 2006, the chief of research for the Intelligence Branch (AMAN) of the Israeli Defense Forces, Gen. Yossi Cooperwasser, said, "We've checked out the reports and don't have any evidence to support concerns over lost, stolen, or misappropriated nuclear devices."[79]

But bin Laden's failure to acquire fissile material or nuclear weapons is not necessarily proof that it is impossible to do, or that the United States and its allies can afford to be complacent in their efforts to stop him or others.

Chapter 8

DANGER AND RESPONSE

NEST VETERAN Alan V. Mode believes an act of nuclear terrorism against the United States is a matter of "when, not if." Another NEST veteran, Robert Kelley, thinks "we are in terrible trouble." They are not alone in their pessimism. Warren Buffett, whose forecasting ability has made him a billionaire, told *Fortune* magazine that a nuclear terrorist attack "will happen. It's inevitable. I don't see any way that it won't happen." That view was partially seconded by Graham Allison, the political scientist best known for his 1971 book *Essence of Decision: Explaining the Cuban Missile Crisis*. In a 2004 book on nuclear terrorism, he offered an assessment which concluded that "on the current path, a nuclear terrorist attack on America in the decade ahead is more likely than not."[1]

The when might follow the theft of completed warheads that could be detonated.* Or it might involve terrorists actually constructing an atomic bomb with illicitly acquired fissile material. In early 2007, the Government Accountability Office estimated that terrorists seeking nuclear weapons could use as little as 55 pounds of highly enriched uranium or 17.6 pounds of plutonium to build one, although the office does not specify a yield associated with such an effort, which would be determined by the technical capabilities of those building the device. Private sources have suggested lower amounts of HEU and plutonium.[2] A third possibility would be a dirty bomb, a weapon of "mass disruption" if not of mass destruction.

J. Carson Mark, a former Manhattan Project physicist, and several colleagues, including Ted Taylor, wrote that "schematic drawings of fission explosive devices of the earliest types showing in a qualitative way the prin-

---

*Even if the device came with protection that made its immediate, or even eventual, use unlikely, the "unauthorized possession of a military nuclear device would be a matter of grave concern. No matter that the group possessing the device may not be able to make it function." And the theft would certainly produce an all-out deployment of NEST personnel. See Robert Mullen, "Nuclear Violence," in Paul Leventhal and Yonah Alexander, *Preventing Nuclear Terrorism: The Report and Papers of the International Task Force on Prevention of Nuclear Terrorism* (Lexington, Mass.: Lexington, 1987), pp. 231–47.

ciples used in achieving the first fission explosions are widely available."
However, "detailed design drawings that are essential before it is possible to
plan the fabrication of actual parts are not available," and preparing such
drawings "requires a large number of man-hours and direct participation
of individuals thoroughly informed in several quite distinct areas." Those
areas include, but are not limited to, the chemical and metallurgical properties of the materials to be employed, radiation effects, electrical circuitry,
and high-explosives technology. It would be "exceedingly unlikely," they
wrote, that one individual "even after years of assiduous preparation" would
be prepared to confidently proceed in each of those fields. They do conclude that a group of terrorists with sufficient funds, time, expertise, and the
necessary equipment and fissile material might be able to build a device
with a nuclear yield.[3]

The terrorist effort to build an improvised nuclear device, as described
by one author, would involve

> work carried out in secret and in some private shop perhaps no
> larger than a five-car garage. The shop would contain numerically
> controlled milling machines and lathes as well as other expen-
> sive manufacturing equipment, and would require a plausible
> explanation—a front company set up to manufacture say, industrial
> pumps or automotive transmission components . . . Construction
> of the bomb would take maybe four months. The size of the tech-
> nical team would depend on the form of HEU. At minimum it
> would consist of a nuclear physicist or engineer, a couple of skilled
> machinists, preferably with operational experience in shaping ura-
> nium, an explosive expert who can design and handle the propel-
> lant, and perhaps an electronics person for the trigger.[4]*

Peter Zimmerman and Jeffrey Lewis provide a hypothetical example of
a clandestine nuclear compound where terrorists might construct a bomb
employing highly enriched uranium. The compound would be surrounded
by a barbed-wire fence. Inside would be a farmhouse, which the terrorists

---

*As a Pugwash Council chairman suggested, such a device might not only be built in
a garage but also be detonated there, if it was near the center of the target city. A timer
would allow plenty of opportunity for the perpetrators to make their escape. It would also
solve the problem of transporting the device—eliminating both the chance of a mishap
as well as of detection and apprehension. See Francesco Calogero, "Letter to the Editor:
Nuclear Terrorism," *Bulletin of the Atomic Scientists*, May/June 2002, p. 5.

would use largely as their living quarters, although some electronics work might be conducted in the basement. A steel building on the compound's grounds would be used to test weapon assemblies and double-check calculations. There would also be two uranium sheds on the property, where the enriched uranium could be stored a safe distance from the farmhouse. A machine shop/foundry would also be necessary and equipped with a vacuum furnace so the team could cast the uranium metal. Finally, a barn, after being cleaned and outfitted with a concrete floor, would be the site for the team's gun tests.[5]

The two authors also provide a list of resources and prices needed to complete such a project. With between $4,433,000 and $6,433,000, a terrorist leader could expect to pay for the physics and computation work (performed by a senior physicist and two assistants); metallurgy and casting (three or four personnel, the vacuum furnace, crucibles, and other equipment); precision machining and construction (another three or four personnel, a precision lathe, supplies, and other tools); gun design, assembly, and testing (three or four personnel, a recoilless rifle, supplies, and expendables); electronics, safeing arming, fuzing, and firing (one or two technicians and equipment); facilities (150-acre ranch along with improvements and maintenance); fissile material (costing $3 to $5 million); and transportation (one or two personnel for procurement, transportation for the device, and travel).

In October 2000, in an exercise at Los Alamos National Laboratory, mock terrorists, with suitable technical backgrounds, in an update of the Nth Country Experiment, were able to construct an improvised nuclear device—which does not mean that such an effort would be easy or certain to succeed, although some have come close to making that claim. When testifying before Congress in 1996, Dr. Gordon Oehler, director of the director of central intelligence's Nonproliferation Center, told his audience that "if the terrorist state acquires the nuclear materials . . . it would still be quite a technical challenge to turn that into a weapon."[6]

A far less technically challenging and less threatening objective would be the construction of a dirty bomb. Terrorists might use highly enriched uranium or plutonium for a dirty bomb. Or they might seek to acquire more available nonfissionable nuclear materials such as cesium-137, strontium-90, and cobalt-60, materials that cannot be used to make a nuclear weapon but could be used to make a dirty bomb, as well as to contaminate water supplies, business centers, government facilities, and transportation networks.[7]

In 1994, the authors of a report for the Department of Defense asked the reader to "imagine the impact if terrorists who carried out the bombing of the World Trade Center had surrounded the bomb's explosive core with cobalt 60, which is widely used in medical applications, or even a mass of nuclear waste left over from a power reactor." The resulting contamination, they wrote, "might have left Manhattan's financial district uninhabitable for decades and the ensuing panic [would] not only have shook the American populace but world financial markets."[8]

If the enormous catastrophe of a terrorist nuclear detonation, or the lesser one of a dirty bomb detonation, were to take place, the perpetrators, whether Al-Qaeda or some other terrorist entity, would had to have acquired either warheads, fissile material to use in an improvised nuclear device, or radioactive material to wrap around conventional explosives. Unfortunately, there are a large number of possible answers to the questions of where and how terrorists might be able acquire such deadly material.

Pakistan might be the source. The country's nuclear complex includes several facilities that produce highly enriched uranium and therefore would be expected to have stocks of highly enriched and low-enriched uranium. The main enrichment facilities are at the Dr. A.Q. Khan Research Laboratories at Kahuta. There is also a newer enrichment facility at the Wah Cantonment Ordnance Complex, which the United States refers to as the Gadwal Uranium Enrichment Plant, as well as the smaller Sihala and Golra ultracentrifuge plants just southwest of Kahuta and about six miles west of Islamabad, respectively.[9]

There is also a reactor at Khushab, which is estimated to generate enough power each year to produce enough plutonium for a few nuclear weapons. Located near Islamabad are the New Labs at Rawalpindi, adjacent to the Pakistan Institute of Nuclear Science and Technology, which are capable of handling all the irradiated fuel produced at the Khushab reactor. How the separated plutonium is stored is not clear, but probably includes vaults and other security arrangements.[10]

Fissile material in several forms—liquid, powder, and solid—can also be found at sites involved in the manufacture of nuclear weapons, including the one at Wah. The facilities produce metallic fissile material and shape the metal into nuclear weapons components. Other installations, some located near Wah, work to produce non-nuclear components and assemble, at least partially, the nuclear weapons.[11]

It is possible that Pakistan has not deployed its weapons with military units that would be able to quickly mate them to missiles or aircraft in the event of war or crisis—just as, during the early days of the Cold War, the U.S. nuclear weapons were in the hands of the Atomic Energy Commission rather than the Air Force or Navy. In any case, Pakistan's warheads are kept in several storage facilities whose location the government goes to great lengths to keep secret. According to reports, some are believed to be kept at six military missile and air bases, where then-president Pervez Musharraf ordered them moved after the terrorist attacks of September 11, 2001. But others may be hidden in tunnels or mines. It has also been reported that the weapons are implosion-type devices and are stored with their fissile cores separated from the non-nuclear components.[12]

According to government officials and outside analysts, Pakistan does not have a sufficient number of troops to quickly and simultaneously "lock down" all of the nation's nuclear weapons sites in the event of a civil conflict, an attempted coup, or a terrorist attack. In the aftermath of 9/11, journalist Seymour Hersh reported that "some of the government's most experienced South Asia experts have doubts about Musharraf's ability to maintain control over the military and its nuclear arsenal in the event of a coup; there are also fears that a dissident group of fundamentalist officers might try to seize a warhead." The basis for that concern were long-standing religious and personal ties between Army and Inter-Service Intelligence officers and the leader of the Taliban, Mullah Omar, as well as sympathy for Osama bin Laden's cause.[13]

Such ties also create concern that a nuclear device might be smuggled out of its storage facility and into the arms of members of Al-Qaeda. But, according to Ashley J. Tellis, who served as White House director of strategic planning for South Asia and senior advisor to the U.S. ambassador to India, Pakistan's armed forces have tight control over the country's nuclear weapons, and it is "highly unlikely" that anything would undermine that control.[14]

But there is always a risk, and some believe that Pakistan's nuclear weapons are not "one-point" safe or equipped with permissive action links as defined by the United States, which require the entry of a code before the weapon can be armed and fired. Other forms of protection, such as boxes with a lock or control mechanisms over the electronic firing systems, can be circumvented without a great deal of trouble.[15]

Clearly, both fissile material and weapons need to be transported between installations. How weapons are stored during transit, what means of transportation are used, and what security precautions are taken to protect the nuclear cargo is information that is not on the public record in Pakistan or elsewhere.[16] Possibly a sympathetic insider might provide Al-

Qaeda with information on the transportation and protective measures, to help the group in any hijacking attempt.

But if radioactive or fissile material or nuclear weapons prove to be impossible to obtain from Pakistan, there are other possibilities.

There is the specter of Iran. It already operates a nuclear reactor at Bushehr, as well as uranium enrichment facilities at Isfahan and Natanz and a plutonium reactor at Arak. As noted earlier, its government has a long history of supporting terrorism, particularly the terrorist actions of the Lebanese-based Hezbollah. In addition, the apocalyptic vision of its current president, Mahmoud Ahmadinejad, and possibly of a future one, or other officials creates a fear that if Iran were to develop nuclear weapons, one or more might eventually be transferred to Hezbollah and detonated in New York or Tel Aviv. Such a transfer might be sanctioned by the highest levels of the Iranian regime or be an independent act by military officials who control the nation's nuclear weapons. It has been argued that the expected consequences of being caught providing such weaponry to a terrorist group would deter such a risky act. But regimes, on occasion, have undertaken what have proved to be suicidal actions with respect to the United States— from Japan's attack in December 1941 to the Taliban's refusal to turn over Osama bin Laden in 2001. One Middle East expert has argued that, for several reasons, "Iran is not likely to provide chemical, biological, radiological, or nuclear weapons to a terrorist group." But an expert on Iran argues, "While the threat that Iran might give nuclear weapons to terrorists tends to receive far too much attention . . . it cannot be dismissed."[17]

Another possible source is North Korea, where the motivation would be money rather than ideology. The regime has shown a willingness to engage in a variety of terrorist and aggressive acts over its lifetime, acts that a seemingly rational regime would be deterred from undertaking. It has also shown a desire to accumulate revenue to finance the lavish lifestyles of its leadership, particularly Kim Jong Il, by any means necessary, including the counterfeiting of U.S. currency and the sale of illegal drugs. Based on North Korea's past failures to keep its end of agreements, it would be far from shocking if, despite its 2007 nuclear disarmament pledge, the country were to squirrel away some of its nuclear arsenal, estimated to be between eight and thirteen bombs in 2006. At some future date, one or more of those weapons might be put up for sale, when the cash flow reached a crisis stage. Former NSC counterterrorism chief Richard Clarke has argued that given

"North Korea's well-known reputation for sponsoring organized crime and selling missile technology to anyone with hard currency, and Kim Jong-Il's hatred for the United States, the possibility that the country would provide terrorists with a nuclear capability is not unrealistic." Indeed, in April 2005 a North Korean official told a U.S. academic that it could transfer nuclear weapons to terrorists if driven into a corner.[18]

While the U.S. invasion of Iraq ended any chance that Saddam Hussein's regime would produce nuclear weapons, it opened the door for looting of nuclear sites whose material could, at least, provide radioactive material for a dirty bomb. At one after another site associated with Iraq's nuclear activities, U.S. troops and the Defense Threat Reduction Agency's Direct Support Team (DST), a special Pentagon unit of special operations soldiers and nuclear specialists responsible for identifying weapons of mass destruction at Iraqi facilities, found signs of extensive looting. Not surprisingly, the Government Accountability Office would conclude that the Defense Department "was not ready to collect and secure radiological sources when the war began in March 2003 and for about 6 months thereafter."[19]

Among the seven sites where looters had been busy were the Tuwaitha Yellowcake Storage Facility, also known as Tuwaitha Location C, and the Baghdad Nuclear Research Center. Location C consisted of three buildings and a wall of concrete barriers about twelve feet tall on three sides. Its holdings included approximately five hundred metric tons of uranium and nonfissile radioisotope sources. The five hundred tons included mostly yellowcake, along with some low-enriched uranium and depleted uranium.[20]

U.S. forces secured Location C by April 7, 2003. But the rest of the facility was apparently wide open. When Navy Commander David Beckett and his master sergeant arrived on May 3, they discovered that for two weeks scores of Tuwaitha employees had been roaming the facility, while up to four hundred looters had been scavenging each day. Daoud Awad, the head of the electrical design department at Tuwaitha, said, "[I] saw with my own eyes people carrying the containers we used to put radioactive materials in" but those people "didn't know what was inside." How much, if any, nuclear material had been removed was not clear because of a dispute between the United States and the IAEA as well as a dispute within the Bush administration about the extent of IAEA involvement in Iraq. The conflict kept U.S. forces out of Tuwaitha's nuclear storage areas, but a short outdoor inspection on April 10 by a small survey team revealed that the door to one of them had been penetrated.[21]

Less than a mile down the road was another potential source of nuclear material, the Baghdad Nuclear Research Center, a major Iraqi radioactive waste depository. In addition to the remains of the reactors bombed by Israel in 1981 and by the United States in 1991, the facility stored industrial and medical waste as well as spent reactor fuel that could be used in a radioactive dispersal device. There were also significant quantities of partially enriched uranium, cesium, strontium, and cobalt. Its sensitivity was highlighted by the sand berm, sixteen feet high and four miles around, surrounding the facility. On May 3, a U.S. Special Forces detachment and eight nuclear experts from the DST arrived, only to find the site badly looted and unable to determine if nuclear materials were missing.[22]

The Baghdad New Nuclear Design Center, a conspicuous yellow building, housed the personnel who managed the crash program designed to produce a nuclear bomb for Iraq in 1991. After the war, many of the key scientists involved in the nuclear program moved to the center to conduct electrical, mechanical, and chemical engineering research, all potentially valuable areas of research for a country wanting to develop nuclear weapons. When the DST showed up to examine the site in April, it found it had been looted and was able to gather little information that would reveal exactly what had been removed.[23]

Also among the looted facilities were the Ash Shaykhili Nuclear Facility and the Tahadi Nuclear Establishment. Ash Shaykhili, located ten miles southeast of Baghdad, was the authorized storage site for the heavy equipment used in Iraq's pre-1991 nuclear weapons program. It held centrifuges used to enrich uranium, disks and machinery employed in the electromagnetic isotope separation method of enrichment, key parts of bomb-damaged reactors, vacuum pumps and valves, and small radiation sources. Army Lt. Col. Charles Allison, who led the Ash Shaykhili survey team, said the "warehouses were completely destroyed" by ransacking and fire and that all the enrichment processing equipment was stored there "but it was all gone or badly burned."[24]

The Tahadi facility was the headquarters for magnetic research and development of high-voltage power supplies, which could be employed as parts of an enrichment program. Once again, when members of the DST arrived, they found very little besides damage. What might have been missing were some small radiation sources, but not in significant quantity.[25]

While some of the looting at those and other sites was spontaneous and unorganized, a highly organized operation focused on specific facilities in order to steal valuable equipment, including high-precision equipment that could be used to make parts for a nuclear device. In 2005 the Iraqi deputy minister of industry, Sami al-Araji, said the organized looters "came in with the cranes and the lorries, and they depleted the whole sites." Dr. Araji said he had no information on where the looted material went, but according to two New York Times reporters, "his account raises the possibility that the specialized machinery . . . had made its way to the black market or was in the hands of foreign governments."[26]

There was also the matter of radioactive sources. All together, reported in 2003, about 1,100 sources spread across the country were a cause for concern. Melissa Flemming, a spokeswoman for the IAEA, noted, "There are some large and dangerous sources among them" and "We are deeply concerned about the possibility that some of this material has been broken into." Some of those sources were used in radiotherapy, X-rays, welding, and oil surveying. One concern was the threat to the health of ordinary Iraqis who weren't aware of what they were taking, believing it was just scrap metal. But there was another concern. Joseph Cirincione, head of the nonproliferation project of the Carnegie Endowment for International Peace, was "less worried about the uranium that seems to have disappeared than the highly radioactive elements that would be perfect for enhancing an al-Qaeda truck bomb."[27]

Of course, Russia, now-independent countries that were formerly Soviet republics, and Eastern European countries, virtually from the moment of the Soviet Union's demise, have been of great concern, given the Soviet Union's immense arsenal, its stocks of fissile material, its nuclear reactors, and the rapid decline in living conditions for the military officers, scientists, and technicians, which led to a corresponding decline in morale.[28]

If Osama bin Laden and his closest advisors were being briefed on the nuclear weapons and nuclear material distributed across Russia, the former Soviet republics, and Eastern Europe, they might be told of the four distinct parts of that nuclear complex that were potential sources of material. One would be Russia's stockpile of strategic and tactical nuclear weapons, controlled by the Ministry of Defense. Another would be the vast amount of weapons-grade fissile material in the possession of the Federal Agency for Atomic Energy (formerly MINATOM)—material that it produces as well as extracts from dismantled warheads—or in reactors in

Uzbekistan or Kazakhstan. The Russian atomic energy ministry also controls an enormous stock of fissile material produced by Russian nuclear power-producing reactors. In addition, it shares custody, with the defense ministry and several other government agencies and ministries, of fissile material held by research institutes and facilities throughout Russia for use in nonstandard nuclear fuel cycles, such as the naval propulsion and space reactor programs.[29]

When the Soviet Union disappeared in late December 1991, it left behind its huge nuclear arsenal of over 11,000 strategic nuclear weapons and more than 15,000 tactical nuclear weapons—artillery shells, short-range missiles, nuclear air-defense and ballistic missile interceptors, nuclear torpedoes, sea-launched cruise missiles, and nuclear weapons for shorter-range aircraft. By early 2003, Russia still had approximately 5,500 strategic warheads and between 7,000 and 12,000 tactical warheads.[30]

It has generally been accepted that the strategic nuclear weapons in Russia's possession (which includes all the strategic warheads that had been on the territory of former Soviet republics) were well protected and safe not only from outside assault but also from insider theft—at least as long as they were emplaced on delivery systems or in storage. In 1995 or 1996, Gen. Evgeny Maslin, of the Ministry of Defense's 12th Main Directorate, responsible for the storage and security of Russian nuclear weapons, told staff members from the Senate Permanent Subcommittee on Investigations that while he believed it was impossible to steal warheads from the ministry's storage, he did not have the same confidence when they were in transit on railway cars. In December 2004, the National Intelligence Council reported that two Chechen sabotage and reconnaissance groups "showed a suspicious amount of interest in the transportation of nuclear munitions," having been spotted at several major railroad stations in the Moscow region, apparently observing a special train used for transporting nuclear warheads.[31]

There was even greater concern over the tactical nuclear weapons that the Soviet Union left behind, which were often described as being strewn across the length and breadth of Russia in poorly protected facilities. These are "the nuclear weapons most attractive to terrorists—even more valuable to them than fissile material and much more portable than strategic warheads," according to former U.S. senator Sam Nunn, whose post-political career has included spearheading programs designed to keep nuclear weapons and material out of the hands of terrorists and rogue nations. But according to Amy Woolf of the Congressional Research Service, in the early 1990s Russia withdrew most of its tactical warheads from deployment, placing them in secure storage areas. In addition, the number of storage facilities were reduced from several hundred to fewer than one hundred.[32]

In the late 1990s one weapons storage site was described as being about thirty-seven square miles, surrounded by physical barriers with a limited number of entrances. The whole area had a technical alarm system along with active and passive defense systems. The weapons were located in a concrete installation with armored doors. No one individual could unlock the storage facility. Every nuclear device was under continuous automated observation, and any attempt to remove it would immediately produce an alarm.[33]

But not all storage sites have been so invulnerable. There were the disquieting comments of a "knowledgeable Russian," who, according to CIA chief John Deutch, told the CIA in the mid-1990s that "accounting procedures are so inadequate that an officer with access could remove a warhead, replace it with a readily available training dummy, and authorities might not discover the switch for as long as six months." Indeed, one Russian nuclear policy expert reported that in November 1993, two employees of the Zlatoust-36 Instrument Building in the Urals, west of Chelyabinsk, which is where nuclear weapons are assembled, removed two nuclear warheads from one of the facility's industrial sites. The warheads were recovered from a garage in a residential site in the neighborhood, and the thieves arrested.[34]

While no other actual thefts of Russian warheads are known, since the collapse of the Soviet Union a multitude of incidents have occurred involving theft and smuggling of nuclear material from Russian facilities, made easy by the erosion of the Soviet-era security system, the failure to replace the system's methods with alternatives suitable to Russia, and inadequate material control. In 1992, chemical engineer Leonid Smirnov pilfered 3.7 pounds of highly enriched uranium (90 percent U-235) from the Luch Scientific Production Association at Podolsk, an effort that took over twenty visits and was inspired by an account he read in a Moscow newspaper about a group of people who stole 1,200 grams of uranium. Smirnov was arrested on October 9, 1992 and would serve two years in prison. In late November 1993 Russian naval captain Alexei Tikhomirov entered the Sevmorput shipyard, near Murmansk, through an unmanned gate, broke into the building housing unused nuclear submarine fuel, and stole three pieces of a reactor core. Those pieces contained about ten pounds of HEU, enriched to approximately 20 percent. While Tikhomirov was able to put the fuel in a bag and walk out, he had more problems selling it—being arrested in June 1994 while attempting to exchange the fuel for $500,000.[35]

In 1994 there were a number of examples of apparent leakage from Russia's nuclear complex. In May 1994 German police seized 5.6 grams of plutonium, which was 99.78 percent pure plutonium-239, from the garage of one Adolf Jackle in Tengen, Germany. The material was believed to have come from Arzamas-16 (now the Russian Federal Nuclear Center) at Sarov or perhaps from a centrifuge facility in ex-Soviet central Asia. The next month, Bavarian police in Landshut seized 0.8 gram of 87.5 percent enriched uranium—believed to have come from a Russian reactor or naval fuel assembly—as a result of a sting operation. Another, complex sting operation orchestrated by the German Federal Intelligence Service (BND) and Bavarian police yielded almost a pound of near-weapons-grade plutonium (87 percent plutonium-239). That August ten Bavarian criminal police officers seized it at Munich airport after it arrived in a black suitcase on a Lufthansa flight from Moscow. In December almost six pounds of highly enriched uranium (87.5 percent enriched) was seized in Prague, where it was found in two plastic metal-wrapped containers in the back seat of a car. Those arrested included a Czech nuclear scientist, a Russian, and a Belorussian. The uranium appeared to have come from the same cache as the HEU that had been seized in June.[36]

Incidents of nuclear smuggling continued throughout the decade and into the current one. In 1998 Russian Federal Security Bureau agents arrested nuclear workers who they claimed were planning to steal forty pounds of HEU from one of the formerly secret nuclear cities near Chelyabinsk, just east of the Urals. The National Intelligence Council reported that in 1999 approximately four grams of weapons-usable material, which probably had originated in Russia, was seized in Bulgaria. It also reported that in 2003 a Russian/Armenian citizen was arrested on Georgian territory in possession of approximately 160 grams of HEU, although it was not certain where the material originated. In August 2003, Russian authorities arrested Alexander Tyulyakov, the deputy director of Atomflot, a state-owned company that maintained the nation's nuclear-powered icebreakers. Tyulyakov had kept over six pounds of enriched uranium in his car, his garage, and his summer cottage in Murmansk. (He was convicted and sentenced to eighteen months in November 2003.) In January 2006, Georgian authorities seized approximately one hundred grams of HEU from a Russian national who was attempting to sell it on the black market. That August they also intercepted an illegal shipment of two pounds of yellowcake.[37]

Despite the repeated arrests, the National Intelligence Council, in April 2006, was still worried. It wrote, "Undetected smuggling of weapons-usable nuclear material has likely occurred, and we are concerned about the total amount of material that could have been diverted or stolen in the last 15 years. We find it highly unlikely that Russian or other authorities would have been able to recover all the material likely stolen."[38]

Material that could be used in a dirty bomb, specifically the warheads attached to almost forty Alazan rockets, also appears to have gone missing. Originally built for weather experiments, thirty-eight of the small, thin missiles had warheads loaded with radioactive material, "effectively creating the world's first surface-to-surface dirty bomb."[39]

Apparently missing too are a number of radioisotope thermoelectric generators (RTGs), simple electric generators powered by radioactive decay, with the heat released by the decay being converted into electric energy. The Soviets used RTGs to power navigational beacons and communications equipment at military bases and along shipping lanes on its arctic coast. In 2006, the Russian Federal Atomic Energy Agency reported that the 651 RTGs at various sites in the federation needed to be either shut down or replaced with alternative energy sources. The devices contain up to 40,000 curies of highly radioactive strontium or cesium, material that "can be just ghastly to clean up" if used in a dirty bomb, according to Henry Kelly, president of the Federation of American Scientists. The IAEA classified the RTGs as "orphaned" nuclear sources and called for a major international effort to locate them and lock them up.[40]

All the concern about the security of the Russian nuclear complex has not prevented either the U.S. government or outside analysts from focusing attention on vulnerabilities in U.S. nuclear facilities. In a 1997 exercise at Los Alamos Technical Area 18 (TA-18), a U.S. Army Special Forces unit revealed that hijacking nuclear material from the site where America's nuclear capability originated was not all that difficult. Members of the unit entered the area, located multiple canisters of "HEU," and used a Home Depot garden cart to move enough weapons-grade material for several nuclear weapons out of Los Alamos and into the Santa Fe woods. Guards who rushed to stop the intruders were mowed down, although, since it was only an exercise, they were hit by lasers rather than actual bullets.[41]

Richard Levernier, who led war games on behalf of the U.S. government, recalled, "In more than 50 percent of our tests at the Los Alamos facility, we got in, captured the plutonium, got out again, and in some cases didn't fire a shot because we didn't encounter any guards." In 1998, at Rocky Flats, Colorado, a team of Navy SEALs successfully penetrated the site through the perimeter fence, entered a nearby building, "stole" a significant quantity of plutonium, left the building, and escaped through a fence.[42]

Ten years later, in the spring of 2008, a commando team undertook a mock attack on Lawrence Livermore National Laboratory in search of weapons-grade material. Their specific target was Building 332, where approximately 2,000 pounds of plutonium and weapons-grade uranium were stored. Despite the obstacles of multistory mesh fencing, a no-man's-land, electronic security equipment, and armed guards and cables to prevent a helicopter from landing on the roof, the "terrorists" quickly overcame those obstacles to reach its objective—a mock payload of fissile material. A National Nuclear Security Administration press release reported that while NNSA inspectors "noted several very positive areas, there were other areas requiring corrective action."[43]

There is also concern that nuclear materials might leave the Y-12 National Security Complex at Oak Ridge, Tennessee, an 811-acre compound where the Department of Energy produces HEU components and maintains a repository of 400 metric tons of metallic HEU, the easiest material with which to make an improvised nuclear device. Public officials have complained that the plant has too many structures and too small a buffer zone to secure it properly, and tests conducted by security teams have demonstrated that in the midst of an attack, intruders could get through the plant's outside fence and penetrate one of the six HEU storage buildings "in the time it takes to microwave a cup of coffee."[44]

The vulnerability of U.S. nuclear weapons in transit is also an issue. The Energy Department's Transportation Division moves nuclear weapons as well as weapons-grade uranium and plutonium from site to site along the nation's public highways. According to one report, sources familiar with the testing program stated that in several mock attacks the division's security guards were "literally annihilated" within seconds after the attacks started.[45]

Sources of weapons-grade or radioactive material may be found in a variety of other locations around the world. In December 2002, in Quininde, Ecuador, a criminal gang stole five iridium-powered industrial devices from a private company. That same month, in Port Hartcourt, Nigeria, a powerful radioactive device used in oil field surveys was stolen. In June 2003, a sting by Thai police resulted in the arrest of a man seeking to sell radioactive cesium for $240,000. Then, in September, Warsaw police arrested six people involved in an alleged plot to exchange over a pound of radioactive cesium for $153,000. In October 2004, in the United States, a radioactive measuring device was stolen from a truck when its driver went shopping. It eventually turned up in a Virginia Beach pawn shop, whose owner, Mitchell Dunbar, told the Associated Press, "The last thing I expected coming through these doors was a radioactive measuring device. I'm more concerned about people bringing loaded guns into the store." It is far from the only stray piece of equipment containing radioactive isotopes that has gone missing in the United States. In 1998 nineteen vials of cesium-137 disappeared from a Greensboro, North Carolina, hospital, while from 1996 to September 2001, U.S. business and medical facilities lost track of nearly fifteen hundred items of equipment with radioactive parts, over 50 percent of which had not been recovered as of mid-2002. And there are over 130 operating research reactors, fueled by weapons-grade uranium, in over forty countries ranging from the United States to Ghana.[46]

While Al-Qaeda and possibly other terrorist groups have undoubtedly surveyed the field of potential targets—looking for points of vulnerability, for individuals who can be bought, or for those who are already offering material for sale—the United States has been actively seeking to close the gaps through which nuclear material might slip into the hands of terrorists. The U.S. government has employed direct action, diplomatic pressure, as well as financial and technical assistance, even before Al-Qaeda became a major concern in the late 1990s. Success would mean that NEST would never be faced with the unenviable task of frantically searching an American city for a nuclear device that could rip it apart.

After the seizure of plutonium in Munich in August 1994, Western nations exerted strong diplomatic pressure on Moscow to be "more cooperative" in countering nuclear smuggling. In late 2001, Russian police arrested seven men accused of trying to sell more than two pounds of HEU. The men were arrested in the town of Balashikha, just south of Moscow, and accused of trying to sell a capsule containing uranium-235 for $30,000. About two years later, in November 2003, a Czech police sting operation resulted in the arrest of two men who attempted to sell them almost seven pounds of radioactive material, including thorium and uranium. Police seized the suspects in a hotel in Brno, 125 miles southeast of Prague. They were arrested as they were counting the $700,000 they believed they had received for the sale.[47]

Less critical than recovering weapons-grade uranium or plutonium, but important in shutting down possible sources of radioactive material for a dirty bomb, is the recovery of a plethora of industrial and medical devices, known as "Greater than Class C sealed sources," containing radioactive material, typically americium-241, cesium-137, plutonium-238, plutonium-239, and strontium-90. These sealed sources include portable and fixed gauges used in commercial manufacturing, gauges used by the construction industry for testing the moisture content of soil, medical pacemakers, medical diagnostics and treatment equipment, as well as gauges used for petroleum exploration and government and private research and development.[48]

There are currently between 250,000 and 500,000 such sources in the United States. To recover such sources when they are no longer of use to an organization, the Department of Energy runs the Off-Site Source Recovery Project, which goes into action when the holder of a source alerts the project that it has no further use for it or when the NRC or state regulators notify the project that a source needs to be recovered because it might present a potential health or safety problem. The Energy Department has estimated that the project will recover about 14,300 unwanted Greater than Class C sealed sources by the end of September 2010.[49]

Recovered items have included 1,632 gauges that had been used by the construction industry for testing the moisture content of soil, 1,500 gauges used for petroleum exploration, 588 medical pacemakers from a manufacturer in Minnesota, 483 from a manufacturer in Pennsylvania, 233 from a manufacturer in Florida, and 219 from the Department of Energy's Oak Ridge research facility in Tennessee.[50]

In the fall of 1993 the U.S. government learned that approximately 1,320 pounds of highly enriched uranium, almost pure U-235, was sitting in a poorly protected facility in Kazakhstan. Kazakh officials had discovered the situation at the Ulba Metallurgical Plant in Ust'-Kamenogorsk in 1992, during an evaluation of the nuclear legacy that the Soviet regime had left behind.[51]

The Ulba facility was located in one of the many Soviet "closed cities" where sensitive nuclear work was carried out. After entering the plant, the officials found about 2,000 tons of radioactive material, including the 1,320 pounds of weapons-grade uranium, which was contained in a beryllium alloy. Soviet scientists had planned to use the material in a research reactor dedicated to a project that was abandoned when the Soviet Union dissolved: the development of new Soviet naval nuclear propulsion systems.[52]

Following their discovery, the Kazakhs did what they could to improve security at Ulba, using locks, gates, and militiamen with guard dogs. "But they knew it wasn't enough," Jeffrey M. Starr, the Pentagon's principal director for threat reduction policy, recalled in 1995. Such measures would not prevent an attack from a modern terrorist team or even well-armed members of organized crime. And the Kazakhs could not afford to do more.[53]

Making the situation even more troublesome were reports suggesting that Iran was aware of the Ulba plant. Some reports indicated that Iranian representatives tried to contact Kazakh officials about possibly purchasing some of the material. And, according to Starr, the Kazakhs "knew that the interest was not limited to just the Iranians." An urgent request for help in either protecting it or getting rid of it was made, quietly, to the U.S. ambassador, William H. Courtney, who transmitted the request to Washington.[54]

In response, a specialist from the Energy Department's Oak Ridge, Tennessee, nuclear storage and processing facility arrived on a covert mission, to examine the material and determine the precise situation. He returned to the United States in two weeks, along with protected samples of the HEU, carried in a diplomatic pouch to avoid detection by U.S. Customs officers and others without a "need to know."[55]

Based on his report, the National Security Council concluded that the Defense Department should lead a joint effort, with the departments of State and Energy, to secure the fissile material and, if required, move it to a safe storage site in the United States. The Pentagon first designated the effort Project Phoenix, but it was the State Department's code name, Sapphire, that stuck.[56]

The team that arrived at Ulba, headed by Starr, first considered keeping the material at the site and upgrading security, an option that was soon rejected because of the enormous cost that would be involved in both the initial upgrades and the upkeep activities. In addition, there would always be some uncertainty about the facility's actual security. Further, the storage facility at Oak Ridge could easily accommodate the Ulba uranium. As a result, the NSC decided the material should be removed from Kazakhstan, a judgment concurred in by Kazakhstan. There was also agreement to maintain secrecy about what was being planned, so no negotiating teams would travel between Washington and the Kazakh capital of Almaty.[57]

The project had advanced by February 1994 to the next step: consulting Russia, a necessity because Russia might claim that as the Soviet successor state, it owned the fissile material. In addition, any airlift to transfer the material would have to cross Russian airspace. According to Starr, trying to keep Russia in the dark "was out of the question," although there was a risk that corrupt elements in the government might sell information about the planned operation to Iran or some other organization that the United States wanted to keep in the dark.[58]

The resulting plan for the transfer required first putting the uranium in a transportable form. It was still in a "corrosive" wet form, stored in a thousand canisters and six thousand sample bottles. In order to be able to work with it, technicians needed to remove the uranium from the containers and bake and dry it to eliminate water and oils. The material then needed to be placed in special metal containers, about the size of spray-paint cans, and put into canisters the size of a fifty-gallon drum. Then the drums were to be transported to the local airport.[59]

To carry out the operation, the United States recruited thirty-two volunteers for the processing and repackaging effort: twenty-seven technicians from Oak Ridge, four Russian linguists from the On-Site Inspection Agency, and one physician. The team was led by Oak Ridge's Alex Riedy, who put together a transportable, collapsible processing facility the size of a three-car garage. In August, an assessment team arrived in Ust'-Kamenogorsk to determine if the local airfield could handle the Air Force C-5 Galaxy transports that would be used to move the necessary people to and from Kazakhstan.[60]

In September, U.S. national security officials drafted a top-secret presidential decision directive authorizing the commencement of Project Sapphire and entrance into Kazakhstan to bring out the half ton of highly enriched uranium. Clinton signed PDD 32 on October 7, 1994, and the project began in earnest. Three C-5Bs took off from Dover Air Force Base in Delaware on October 8. They carried support crews, off-loading equipment, and Air Force Security Police personnel, the Department of Energy processing plant, the Oak Ridge team, ovens for baking the uranium, and the 1,400 containers that would be needed to hold it.[61]

The runway at Ust'-Kamenogorsk, eight thousand feet long, was "like a bucking bronco," according to Lt. Mike Foster, the operations officer for the 9th Airlift Squadron, but it did not prevent the planes from landing without incident. What proved a problem was the slippage in the expected departure date from November 1 to late November, a result of the time it took technicians to process and pack the uranium. As a result, the C-5 group coming to pick up the personnel, equipment, and uranium had to turn back because of blizzard conditions. On another try, only one of the four aircraft made it to Kazakhstan, with the other three diverting to other bases.[62]

At 4:00 a.m., when the first plane landed, a convoy of trucks departed the Ulba facility for the eighteen-mile trip to the airport. The trucks carried the uranium-filled canisters, the Energy Department team, militiamen, police, and Kazakh Army special forces troops. All roads were closed along the route while all lights were turned on to light the way. Because the second plane had not been able to make it, the convoy of trucks was only half the size planned.[63]

Despite an airfield bombarded by sleet, ice, and rain, the C-5 managed to lift off, on what would be a twenty-hour, five-aerial-refueling flight. Foster recalled, "We were sitting there in the cockpit writing Tom Clancy novels in our head about what would happen if we had to go down." When the flight did arrive at the Dover air base, the material was placed on unmarked Department of Energy tractor-trailers and sent by varying routes to the Oak Ridge Y-12 facility, where it would be transformed into low-enriched uranium for use in commercial nuclear power plants.[64]

In the aftermath of the 2003 U.S. invasion of Iraq, the United States also sought to transport radioactive material from that country back to the states. In July 2004, Energy Secretary Spencer Abraham announced that almost two tons of low-enriched uranium and about a thousand radioactive samples used for research had been removed from Iraq's Tuwaitha Nuclear Research Center and airlifted to the United States for security reasons, an operation that had been completed in late June. The radioactive samples included isotopes of cobalt, cesium, and strontium.[65]

More problematic is the recovery of devices with radioactive material located in former Soviet territory. In February 2002, an international team of experts arrived in the former Soviet republic of Georgia hoping to retrieve two radio thermal generators that were discovered in early December 2001 near Abkhazia, a mountainous province in western Georgia controlled by Muslim rebels. Three men who claimed to be woodsmen noticed the objects because the snow around them was melting, and lugged the surprisingly heavy cylinders, which were not much bigger than cans of string beans, to their campsite for warmth. But they soon became dizzy and nauseated. A week later they were suffering from radiation burns. What they had discovered were two cores of the radiothermal generators, filled with strontium-90, used to provide power in remote regions.[66]

The remoteness of the region and the danger involved in recovering the cylinders made it less likely that terrorists could successfully obtain them. But the IAEA was not taking any chances. "The good news is that the place is so remote, so difficult to reach, even for us. So I believe it is not so easy to reach for terrorists," Abel J. Gonzalez, director of the IAEA division of radiation and waste safety, remarked at the time. If terrorists tried to carry the radioactive cylinders away, he added, "they will probably kill themselves."[67]

The search for abandoned RTGs continued. Another two abandoned devices were secured during the opening days of a summer 2006 effort to trace lost radioactive sources in Georgia. A team from the Georgian government and IAEA found a powerful one in a pile of dirt on the floor of an abandoned factory in the village of Iri. Another, smaller source was discovered inside a house, in a can of nuts and bolts above a workbench.[68]

In 2002, the IAEA was trying to locate radioactive devices that had been shipped to an assortment of locations in the Soviet countryside in the 1970s as part of a project code-named Gamma Kolos or Gamma Ears. The devices were used to expose plants to radiation and measure the effects. Some of the tests were intended to simulate farming conditions after a nuclear war. In eastern Georgia, Soviet researchers bombarded wheat seed with radiation to determine if the plants would grow better. The experiments used a lead-shielded canister packed with enough radioactive cesium-137 to contaminate a small city.[69]

In the aftermath of 9/11 and reports that Al-Qaeda was interested in developing a dirty bomb, there was a particular urgency to the recovery effort. With assistance from the Department of Energy the IAEA conducted a ten-month sweep of Georgia, which turned up five Gamma Kolos devices. One had drawn the interest of a local businessman who was hoping he would be able to sell it on the black market. Four more devices were located in Moldova. There was no information to indicate that any of the cesium devices had been stolen, but some Central Asian states had no records showing how many of the devices existed or where they were located. Nor was there any solid estimate of the number of devices, which according to one account, could be "anywhere from 100 to 1,000."[70]

One means of keeping terrorists from building a nuclear or radiological dispersion device is to keep them from acquiring highly enriched uranium from civilian nuclear reactors around the world. Some of it had been provided, along with nuclear technology, by the U.S. government under President Dwight Eisenhower's Atoms for Peace program. Originally, in return, the recipients were required to pledge to forego the development of nuclear weapons and send spent fuel to the United States for treatment and disposal. In 1964, the U.S. government dropped the requirement that recipients return the material.[71]

In May 1996, in an attempt to reduce the chance of nuclear weapons proliferation, the Energy Department initiated the Foreign Research Reactor Spent Nuclear Fuel Acceptance Program to recover spent fuel containing highly enriched uranium that had been produced in the United States and that met certain criteria. It represented about 30 percent of the HEU the United States had provided to foreign reactors. In August 2003, the program was expected to take back only about half of the approximately 11,440 pounds of HEU it covered, a consequence of twelve countries not fully participating in the effort.[72]

In September 1996, the United States retrieved seven pounds of bomb-grade uranium, which it had originally supplied, that was sitting unprotected in a reactor in Bogota, Colombia, a situation that caused Assistant Secretary of Energy Thomas Grumbly to become "extremely concerned that it was essentially unprotected," that "anybody could walk out the door with it."[73]

One option for getting that uranium to the United States was to put it on a truck and drive it five hundred miles over rugged roads, roads threatened by the Revolutionary Armed Forces of Colombia (FARC), to the port of Cartagena. Once there, it would be loaded onto a ship chartered by the Energy Department. But rather than risk the journey by land, Grumbly, after reading press reports of resurgent guerilla activity, had his department charter a giant Antonov-24 cargo plane. The plane's entire nose section can be opened up, permitting a truck with its cargo to drive right up into the cargo hold without the need for transferring the containers. Operated by a private Russian cargo company, the plane happened to be in Argentina. The Russian crew flew the plane without incident from Bogota to Cartagena.[74]

Its cargo was placed on a ship, along with a similar load of enriched uranium from Chile. That ship then joined up with a similar ship carrying fuel from reactors in Sweden, France, and Switzerland. Together they arrived at the Navy Yard in Charleston, South Carolina. After being unloaded, their cargos, which together Grumbly said could be used to build "two crude bombs," were trucked to the Savannah River, South Carolina, nuclear fuel plant.[75]

In other cases, the United States has played a key role by financing transfer of weapons-grade uranium from reactors in Eastern Europe to Russia, where the material was diluted so that it could not be used to produce a nuclear yield. Before daybreak on August 22, 2002, the U.S. and Russian governments executed an operation that had been planned in secrecy for over a year. Spirited away was a hundred pounds of highly enriched uranium, enough for two or three nuclear bombs, from Belgrade's Vinca Institute of Nuclear Sciences, which had been built in 1958 as the foundation of an ambitious program whose ultimate goal was the production of nuclear weapons.[76]

Concern over the nuclear material at Vinca, estimated to be about 4.4 pounds of HEU and 22 pounds of spent fuel from a research reactor, dated back to at least 1999, when NATO forces were conducting bombing missions against Belgrade targets. Part of the concern stemmed from the fact that satellite photographs showed the facility to be poorly protected, with only a single guard booth. The first stage of the operation, the removal of nearly six thousand ingots or highly enriched uranium "slugs," was carried out over seventeen hours by hundreds of people, predominantly Yugoslav scientists and government officials, who received technical support from the State and Energy departments, the Russian Ministry of Atomic Energy, and the IAEA.[77]

Just as U.S. officials feared that the uranium from the Bogota reactor could be hijacked, they also feared that the Vinca material was an attractive target. Thus, late on August 21, 2002, the reactor was locked down while the uranium was loaded onto a truck. Then, early the following morning, three trucks—two of them decoys—left the facility. As the trucks headed toward the city's international airport, they were escorted by Yugoslav army helicopters and twelve hundred heavily armed troops. Security measures did not stop there. Police sealed off several of the city's major highways for hours and placed sharpshooters on rooftops to guard against a possible assault.[78]

After the cargo arrived at the airport safely, Energy Department and Russian officials supervised the loading of the uranium onto a Russian plane. At 8:04 a.m. the aircraft took off for Dimitrovgrad, about 520 miles southeast of Moscow and home of a reprocessing facility that specializes in converting weapons-grade uranium into a less threatening blend that can be used in civilian nuclear power plants.[79]

The following September, in an operation financed by the United States, Russia retrieved thirty pounds of weapons-grade uranium from the Pitesti Institute for Nuclear Research, west of Bucharest, Romania, a poorly secured Soviet-era nuclear reactor facility. The 80 percent enriched uranium, contained in eight canisters, was of particular concern because of its amount and the ease with which it could be transported by terrorists. "You could throw it in the back of a truck and drive away with it," Paul Longsworth, the Energy Department's deputy administrator for defense nuclear nonproliferation, said at the time. Instead, it was driven to the Bucharest airport and loaded on a Russian IL-76 cargo plane while technical experts from the United States observed.[80]

Then on the day before Christmas 2003, according to an account in the *Washington Post*, an "international team of nuclear specialists backed by armed security units swooped into a shuttered Bulgarian reactor and recovered thirty-seven pounds of HEU in a secretive operation intended to forestall nuclear terrorism." A team from the IAEA, accompanied by nuclear engineers from the United States and Russia, removed the seals from the containers storing the 36 percent enriched uranium and verified the contents before the material was loaded into four special canisters provided by Russia. The $400,000 operation, financed by the United States, took forty-eight hours and ended with the uranium arriving in Russia on an AN-12 cargo plane and being transported to the Dimitrovgrad facility.[81]

Such recovery operations continued into 2005 and 2006. In September 2005, in another covert predawn operation, financed by $2 million of American taxpayers' money, a truck and its armed escorts transported thirty-one pounds of highly enriched uranium from the KV-2 Sparrow reactor at a Czech Technical University campus on the outskirts of Prague. The convoy traveled through deserted streets, coming to a halt near a runway at the city's airport. Not long afterward, a Russian cargo plane landed and took off, carrying the uranium to a more secure storage site in Russia.[82]

In April 2006, the Energy Department's National Nuclear Security

Administration (NNSA) announced that it had completed the removal of about 139 pounds of weapons-grade nuclear fuel from a small reactor in Uzbekistan and the transfer of the material to a secure storage site in Chelyabinsk, Russia. Four months later, the Energy Department transferred ninety pounds of HEU from a laboratory in Otwock-Swierk, Poland, to the Warsaw airport in a convoy guarded by Polish special forces. Once there, it was loaded onto a Russian plane, one step closer to its final destination.[83]

In September 2007, ten pounds of highly enriched uranium was moved from a reactor in Vietnam, at Dalat, about 150 miles northeast of Ho Chi Minh City, to Russia to be blended down into commercial reactor fuel. Vietnam surrendered thirty-five unused fuel rods containing the uranium in exchange for Russian-made low-enriched uranium fuel rods that would allow the reactor to continue to operate without bomb-grade material. The reactor, which had been built under the Eisenhower administration's Atoms for Peace program, began operating in 1963, using U.S. weapons-grade uranium. It was shut down during the final days of the Vietnam War, and the U.S. government removed its fuel in a secret two-aircraft operation carried out only hours before the city fell to North Vietnamese forces. In the mid-1980s, thanks to Russian assistance and a new supply of HEU, the reactor was operating again.[84]

The Dalat operation followed an agreement between President Bush and Vietnamese President Nguyen Minh Triet in November 2006. For the two individuals who managed the effort—Andrew Bieniawski, an immigrant from South Africa who works for the NNSA, and Igor Bolshinsky, a Ukrainian immigrant who works at the Idaho National Laboratory, it is only one of many spots they have traveled to to convince nations to give up their stocks of weapons-grade uranium so it can be transformed into something safer. The two are part of the NNSA's Global Threat Reduction Initiative, which has been credited with locking down more than 80 percent of bomb-grade uranium at former Soviet Union sites outside Russia and converting fifty civilian research reactors in twenty-eight countries to operate on the low-enriched uranium not used in nuclear weapons.[85]

While Russia has proved willing to reprocess HEU into a less threatening form, both its nuclear weapons sites and a variety of military and civilian sites still contain weapons-usable material. In 1995, the Energy Department established the Materials Protection, Control, and Accounting (MPC&A) program, administered by the NNSA. Under the program, the Energy Department provided Russian nuclear facilities with a variety of modern nuclear security systems intended to enhance the Russian ability to keep track of and control its nuclear materials.

Those security systems have included physical protection systems, such as fences around buildings containing nuclear materials; metal doors protecting rooms where nuclear materials are stored; and video surveillance systems to monitor storage rooms. Other security systems include electronic sensors, motion detectors, and central alarm stations. In addition, the United States has provided material control systems, including seals attached to nuclear material containers that reveal whether material has been stolen from the containers, as well as badge systems that are intended to permit only authorized personnel to enter areas containing nuclear material. Russia has also received material accounting systems, such as nuclear measurement equipment and computerized databases to inventory the amount and type of nuclear material contained in specific buildings and to monitor their location.[86]

In early 2007, the Government Accountability Office reported that while the Energy Department claimed it had "secured" 175 buildings containing three hundred metric tons of weapons-usable nuclear material, 51 of the buildings did not have complete MPC&A upgrades. In addition, 35 buildings, including 32 that were part of the weapons complex, had not been upgraded. Security upgrades were still planned for another 210 buildings. In early November 2007, the United States finished a security upgrade at a Russian nuclear missile base in the Ural Mountains, completing a program of improvements at twelve Russian bases, including the installation of alarm and motion detection systems, modern gates, guardhouses and fighting positions, and metal and radiation detectors.[87]

In 1995, the Defense Department began assisting the Russian Ministry of Defense with improving its transportation security for nuclear warheads and security at nuclear warhead sites. Together, since 1995, the Defense and Energy departments have spent about $920 million to upgrade security at sixty-two sites, and plan to help secure a total of ninety-seven nuclear warhead sites by the end of 2008. But the plan excluded two key locations involved in manufacturing Russian nuclear warheads, which contain buildings with hundreds of metric tons of weapons-usable nuclear material.[88]

.   .   .

By the late 1990s, in an effort to detect nuclear material after it has been stolen, the U.S. Customs Service, with assistance from the Energy Department, was training personnel in Belarus and Eastern Europe to detect nuclear-related material, equipment, and technology. In addition, the Customs Service was overseeing the transfer of radioactive monitoring devices to former Soviet republics. By late 1996, nuclear-capable X-ray vans were on patrol in Belarus, the Ukraine, and the Baltic states. A year earlier, the United States had given one hundred handheld radiation detectors, along with $700,000 worth of laboratory equipment, to Kazakhstan to help analyze nuclear material samples.[89]

When the United States began its efforts, subsequent to the demise of the Soviet Union, to keep nuclear materials out of the hands of terrorists and rogue states, Al-Qaeda was not yet a major concern. And while the attacks on U.S. embassies in Africa and on the USS *Cole* moved Al-Qaeda and bin Laden up the list of troublemakers whose activities the U.S. government needed to address, 9/11 put them at the top of the list—and had a significant impact on NEST's operations.

Chapter 9

A NEW URGENCY

FORMER DIRECTOR of central intelligence George Tenet recalls that on December 3, 1998, he sat at home "and furiously drafted in longhand the memo . . . titled 'We Are at War'" and told his staff that he "wanted no resources or people spared" in the effort to attack Al-Qaeda.[1] That was one indication within the U.S. Intelligence Community of the growing attention to the terrorist organization.

Before and after that time, NEST continued to conduct exercises against a variety of possible threats as well as deploy in response to the occasional plausible threat. In addition, a directive signed by President Bill Clinton would establish a class of events that seemed to mandate precautionary deployments by a wide array of U.S. law enforcement and counterterrorist units—from the FBI and Secret Service to those consisting of scientists with radiation detection equipment or secret soldiers equipped with a variety of lethal weaponry.

On May 22, 1998, Clinton resorted to a measure he used sparingly during his administration—he signed a presidential decision directive. In contrast to his most recent two-term predecessor, Ronald Reagan, who signed more than 325 national security decision directives during his eight years in office, Clinton would only issue seventy-five. The one he signed that day, a few months into the sixth year of his presidency, was PDD 62, "Protection Against Unconventional Threats to the Homeland and Americans Overseas," and the fifth that concerned nonproliferation or terrorism.[2]

The directive noted "that the destructive power available to terrorists is greater than ever. Adversaries may thus be tempted to use unconventional tools, such as weapons of mass destruction to target our cities and disrupt the operations of our government." It also continued the practice of designating the State Department, FBI, and other agencies as the "lead" agencies in responding to certain types of terrorist events. In addition, the directive established a special class of events, designated National Special Security Events (NSSEs). The designation followed nomination by the

National Security Council and certification by the attorney general and secretary of the treasury. An event could qualify as an NSSE based on at least one of several factors: anticipated attendance by U.S. officials or foreign dignitaries, its size, or its significance.[3]*

Senior officials believed such events warranted greater federal planning and protection than other special events, for the obvious reason that they were judged to be very attractive targets to terrorists. A successful attack would either kill a lot of people or kill some very important people, or both. The first national special security event would be the mid-September 1998 meeting of the World Energy Council in Houston, an event attended by more than eighty oil ministers and eight thousand officials and executives from at least eighty-two nations who were there to celebrate the council's seventy-fifth anniversary as well as bemoan falling oil prices. By early February 2007 there had been twenty-seven special events, including a variety of international meetings, national political conventions, inaugurations and state of union addresses, the 2002 Winter Olympic Games in Salt Lake City, and six Super Bowls.[4] One result of the creation of this new category of events was more work for NEST.

In the mid-1990s, before the signing of PDD 62, NEST personnel continued to participate in a variety of exercises, such as Mirrored Image in Atlanta in 1996 (which involved an improvised nuclear device), Jagged Wind in June 1996, Ellipse Charlie in September 1996, Action Warrior in December 1996, Patriot Pledge in January 1997, Patriot Finance in June 1997, Ellipse Foxtrot in June 1997, and Bright Victory in March 1998.[5]

The first post–PDD 62 exercise was Gauged Strength in June 1998. That was followed by Package Satyr, conducted between August 4 and 6 at Pease Air National Guard Base in Newington, New Hampshire. It involved seventy-five participants from the Justice, State, Defense, and Energy departments, with fifty-two from Energy. The exercise tested the ability of NEST and other government personnel who made up the Foreign Emergency Support Team (FEST) to promptly assemble and be deployed on

*Today, such events are designated by either the president or the Secretary of Homeland Security after consultation with the Homeland Security Council, an authority bestowed when President George W. Bush signed Homeland Security Presidential Directive (HSPD) 7, "Critical Infrastructure Identification, Prioritization, and Protection," December 17, 2003, available at www.fas.org.

a dedicated FEST aircraft to a "foreign" country, where they would assist the host government in searching for and locating missing special nuclear material.[6]

At the end of August, another exercise, Errant Foe, began. It kept some of NEST's members busy from Saturday, August 29, to Wednesday, September 9. As with Package Satyr, NEST personnel, among the thirty-seven Energy Department members who participated, were engaged in an exercise that took place in a "foreign" locale, and it involved representatives of the U.S. Special Forces, probably Delta Force, and the Army Forces Command's 52nd Ordnance Detachment.[7]

After participating in Lost Beacon in July 1999, NEST personnel could be found in Pennsylvania in September for yet another exercise—this one designated Vigilant Lion. The event was sponsored by the Pennsylvania Emergency Management Agency, in cooperation with the Energy Department. It was no small event, involving more than three hundred participants from forty local, state, and federal emergency response agencies whose missions included managing hazardous materials, explosive ordnance, emergency management, law enforcement, and emergency medical response.[8]

Initially, some of those agencies favored conducting the exercise in Hershey, an area with a population of nineteen thousand, with the state police academy and a major hospital nearby. But getting the necessary approvals would have proved difficult, and it was believed that a large-scale realistic exercise in public would have produced significant public concern, if not alarm. Instead, it was decided to approach the Fort Indiantown Gap Military Reservation, home of the Pennsylvania National Guard Civil Support Detachment, whose leadership agreed to host the exercise.[9]

The exercise began on the evening of September 27, when a disgruntled former employee placed a radiation dispersal device on the intake vent of the two-story "Fig County office building" (a vacant structure), where approximately 550 county and city employees worked. With a small fan connected to a timer, the device "spread" strontium-90, which is absorbed by the body as if it were calcium and can produce bone cancer, throughout the building. By the end of September 28, a multitude of federal and state agencies were on the scene: the Pennsylvania National Guard Civil Support Detachment, the Pennsylvania Department of Environmental Protection, the FBI, and several Department of Energy organizations, including the Aerial Measurement System (AMS) and NEST.[10]

The FBI and AMS proved able to locate additional radiological substances in a residential area. But NEST's more sensitive equipment proved vital in finding the precise location: a rundown two-story residence on Lazy

Eye street. A vehicle-based search was used to identify the specific house, where the former employee resided. In a follow-on search on foot, NEST equipment detected high levels of radiation from material outside the house. Local, state, and federal law enforcement officials then raided the home, discovering additional conventional explosive devices inside, along with guides for building further bombs. NEST personnel also determined that there was a second radiological dispersal device in the dwelling with a two-hour timer that had been activated.[11]

In April 2001, NEST personnel were involved in an exercise designated Wasatch Rings, sponsored by the FBI and Utah Olympic Public Safety Command with a future national special security event in mind — the 2002 Olympic Winter Games in Salt Lake City. Despite the growing concern with Al-Qaeda and foreign terrorist groups, the exercise, staged at various Winter Olympic sites, revolved around a fictional radical domestic terrorist group. Scenarios included a plot to detonate an improvised explosive device during the games, an overland manhunt, a kidnapping incident, a hostage barricade situation, the detonation of a radiation-laced bomb, a train derailment that involved hazardous materials, and interception of an aircraft suspected of carrying radiological material by an FBI SWAT team (after it was identified, presumably by NEST sensors).[12]

NEST participation in the exercises came in a variety of forms, as the group's varied responsibilities were divided among a number of different teams. Indeed, by the late 1990s NEST had become almost an umbrella term, particularly because some NEST elements had been established as a result of closer links between NEST and the military, particularly the secret warriors of the Joint Special Operations Command.

Some members from NEST might arrive in the form of an eight-man Nuclear/Radiological Advisory Team (NRAT), which supervises the activities of all Energy Department personnel deployed during an incident, and is prepared to gather nuclear/radiological data and provide technical advice and recommendations to the "Lead Federal Agency" — the FBI in domestic incidents and the State Department for foreign incidents. It also serves as the Department of Energy portion of the interagency advisory team, the Domestic Emergency Support Team (DEST).[13]

The two components of NEST most associated with the team — because they constitute the "S" activity — are those involved in actual search operations, employing handheld and vehicle-mounted detection equipment. The Search Response Team will be first on the scene in response to a nuclear threat. The seven-member team, whose members are on two-hour recall, provides a quick response and may arrive on commercial aircraft. Once it arrives, it can be set up and ready to go in three hours. It can also equip and train local personnel to become searchers.[14]

A larger contingent of searchers, thirty-one scientists and technicians, make up the Search Augmentation Team, which can be on site in twelve hours. The size of the group as well as the technical capability they bring with them, allows for a sustained, fully equipped search effort of larger areas. Both teams are based at the Remote Sensing Laboratory.[15]

Two additional teams made up of NEST personnel go into action when the searchers have located a nuclear device. The Joint Technical Operations Team (JTOT) supports Defense Department and FBI explosive ordnance personnel, possibly operating in a "non-permissive or hostile" environment. The team, consisting of twenty-one Energy Department and ten Defense Department representatives, provides the advanced technical capabilities needed to move or neutralize nuclear weapons. The team's activities include reducing the yield of the device, rendering the device explosively and electrically safe, as well as performing demilitarization and disassembly operations needed to make the device nuclear safe—missions complicated by a lack of immediate knowledge of the design of an improvised nuclear device. As a result, the team's first task is to determine how the weapon was put together and its capabilities, and its members include experts in developing, testing, and evaluating the tools crucial for that task. It all adds up to a "stimulating mental challenge," according to one Los Alamos scientist.[16]

A JTOT deployment has two phases. During JTOT-1, personnel provide technical advice to Defense Department explosive ordnance disposal personnel to help them render safe a nuclear device. During JTOT-2 a joint NEST/Defense EOD team prepares the weapon for safe transport for final disposition.[17]

In addition to those working in the field, a JTOT home team—consisting of Los Alamos and Energy Department volunteers—provides the teams with access to additional experts who can respond to requirements from the teams in the field. At the site, JTOT members, using their laptop computers and stored data on more than a thousand U.S. nuclear tests, can run simulations of a device's destructive capabilities. If more extensive simulations are required, they can transmit information back to the home team, which has access to the lab's entire computing capability.[18]

If explosive ordnance personnel from Defense Department special mission units—such as Delta Force or the Naval Special Warfare Develop-

ment Group (formerly Seal Team 6)—get involved, NEST personnel, acting as a five-man Lincoln Gold Augmentation Team (LGAT), can provide
assistance. The augmentation team can provide advice concerning diagnostics, render-safe procedures, weapons analysis, device modeling, and
effects prediction. Back at the labs, like the JTOT, the team is supported by
a "home team"—in this case, the Lincoln Gold Home Team.[19]

In addition, the members of the Nuclear Assessment Program (NAP)
may have been called upon to participate in various exercises in addition
to responding to external nuclear threats. The director of the Lawrence
Livermore laboratory described the members of the program as consisting
of "a small group of professionals who are collectively knowledgeable in
nuclear explosives design and fabrication, nuclear reactor operations and
safeguards, radioactive materials and hazards, linguistic analysis, behavioral analysis and profiling, as well as terrorist tactics and operations." He
explained that assessor teams were organized into specialty teams and
"operate in secure facilities" at three sites. The Assessment Coordinating Center at Livermore directs credibility assessment operations for the
Energy Department and "provides a single point of contact for federal crisis
managers during . . . emergency operations."[20]

Jagged Wind involved members from the Search Response Team,
Search Augmentation Team, and Nuclear/Radiological Advisory Team.
Personnel from the same three teams participated in Package Satyr. In
Vigilant Lion representatives of the Search Response Team helped locate
the nuclear material on Lazy Eye Street. In contrast, during the Errant Foe
exercise in late August and early September 1998, representatives of the
Search Response Team and the Search Augmentation Team were absent,
while members of the Lincoln Gold Augmentation, Lincoln Gold Home
Team, and the JTOT did participate.[21]

In the midst of all the exercises there was an occasional threat not invented
by the Scenario Working Group. In 1998, NEST member Darwin Morgan
received a page while he was at the movies with his wife. It was from NEST
and directed him to stop whatever he was doing and come to the office.
The team had just received a tip alleging that a nuclear device was hidden on a train that was rumbling across South Dakota. A Search Response
Team, with its suitcase radiation detectors, rushed to the site—and found
nothing, apparently having wasted their time and taxpayers' money checking out a hoax.[22]

.   .   .

NEST faced another threat about two years later, in May 2000, although it came not from a nuclear terrorist or extortionist but from the superintendent of the Bandelier National Monument in New Mexico. Superintendent Roy Weaver decided to start a fire on May 4 because he believed the conditions were just right for the park's annual brush burning, which is intended to prevent a potentially disastrous fire. But when the winds turned out to be higher than expected, gusting at over fifty miles an hour, and the humidity did not rise as much as hoped, the brush fire became a wildfire that burned out of control.[23]

Among the consequences were the destruction of more than two hundred houses in Los Alamos and the forced evacuation of 25,000 people. The laboratory suffered too: damages amounted to several hundred million dollars, eight thousand acres were burned, along with thirty-nine temporary structures including trailers and storage units.[24] The fire also led to what was feared for a while to be a serious compromise of some of the data needed by NEST personnel to help prevent the detonation of an improvised nuclear device.

On May 7, with the fire raging, two NEST members at the Los Alamos lab entered the high-security vault of X Division, the lab component responsible for nuclear weapons design. What they were looking for were two computer hard drives, each approximately the size of a pack of cards, that were supposed to be inside locked containers in the vault. The containers were there, but the drives were not. The drives were to be used in laptops of NEST personnel and contained the U.S. nuclear weapons design data, as well as data on Russian nuclear testing, that NEST would use if it ever located an improvised nuclear device. Members would enter the available information into classified software on the drives and would receive, in return, suggestions on how to disarm the weapon. In the hands of terrorists, it would help them defeat NEST efforts to disable a bomb. A terrorist group could put "an extra wire, or an extra bump, or an extra piece of metal where there isn't supposed to be one," a Pentagon official observed. The missing data could also help terrorists bypass the internal safety system of a stolen weapon, intended to prevent an unauthorized detonation.[25]

Rather than report that the drives were missing, the NEST members kept the information to themselves, hoping they could locate them quickly and avoid a public relations fiasco or, even worse, a criminal investigation. They also hoped that possibly in the chaotic situation created by the fire, the hard drives might be in the hands of authorized personnel and would be returned when the emergency concluded. But when the fire ended, there was still no sign of them and a search began. When that produced no results, on May 31, more than three weeks after the initial discovery that they were missing, lab director John C. Browne was alerted. The next day both the the FBI and the Energy Department received the bad news.[26]

The feared public relations nightmare soon followed. The missing hard drives made front-page news as well as provided grist for politicians, cartoonists, comedians, and writers of letters to the editor. Bart Stupak, a member of the Michigan congressional delegation, complained that "the Menominee [Michigan] public library has a more sophisticated tracking system for 'Winnie the Pooh' than Los Alamos has for highly classified nuclear weapons data." And the author of a letter to the *New York Times* complained, "I cannot enter the local bank and remove $20 from an automated teller machine without being taped," yet "more than two dozen people have unfettered access to a vault that holds this country's nuclear secrets."[27]

The FBI arrived on June 5 at X Division to look for the hard drives, and the ensuing investigation created growing tension. There were a number of NEST members to investigate, as eighty-six members of the team had access to the X Division vault. For twenty-six, the control was less strict than at the local public library. They could enter without an escort and remove the hard drives without signing them out. The physicists at the lab did not embrace the FBI's late-night interviews and polygraph tests, accusing the G-men of Gestapo tactics, a point of view occasionally delivered to the agents on site by a physicist who would stop and give the unamused agent a "Heil Hitler!" salute.[28] Whether they also clicked their heels together for effect has gone unreported.

Before the end of the month, part of the mystery would be solved. To the great relief of NEST and other government officials, the hard drives were not in the hands of a terrorist. Indeed, just as one Los Alamos employee discovered them missing, another discovered them behind an X Division copier on June 16. The discovery didn't answer the question of how the drives had gotten from the vault to their temporary resting place behind the computer. And nobody was talking. In mid-January 2001 the Energy Department announced that the FBI had been unable to determine who was responsible for their disappearance.[29]

Energy Secretary Bill Richardson's announcement also noted that the FBI had discovered no evidence that there was outside involvement in the disappearance of the hard drives or that the classified information on the drives had been compromised. He also informed the press that the

FBI would be taking no further action and the matter was being turned over to the department's Albuquerque Operations Office and the University of California (the contractor responsible for running the labs for the Energy Department).[30]

On September 10, 2001, elements of NEST were in the middle of another exercise, designated Jackal Cave, a U.S. Special Operations Command operation held at RAF Fairford, about one hundred miles west of London and forty miles south of Oxford, in the Cotswolds region of the United Kingdom—where John le Carré's fictional spy George Smiley envisioned buying a cottage in which to spend his final years. The field had served as base for U.S. Air Force B-52s during the 1991 Gulf War as well as ones used to attack targets in Yugoslavia in 1999. U-2 spy planes flew from Fairford in 1995 as part of operations over Yugoslavia. It is also the only TransOceanic Abort Landing site in the United Kingdom for the NASA Space Shuttle.[31]

The entire exercise involved more than five hundred personnel, sixty-two aircraft, and 420 short tons of cargo. It was NEST's first participation in an overseas exercise since 1998. Three NEST elements were involved: the Nuclear/Radiological Advisory Team, the Lincoln Gold Augmentation Team, and the Joint Technical Operations Team.[32]

The absence of representatives of the two search teams, the participation of LGAT and JTOT members, and the classification of the after-action report—Secret/Focal Point—indicate that the exercise also involved the CIA and a special missions unit such as Delta Force to kill terrorists and seize a mock nuclear device, which needed to be moved and/or disabled.* But on September 11, the European Command's commander-in-chief cancelled the exercise. By September 15, all NEST and Energy Department members had arrived back in the United States, via military airlift.[33]

While NEST had been exercising against a hypothetical terrorist threat, a very real attack had occurred back home.

·   ·   ·

*The cover page to the after-action report indicates the document was classified Secret/Focal Point. Focal Point refers to "JCS information compartment dealing with CIA support to the military, special technical operations (STOs), and military-CIA operations." See William Arkin, *CODE NAMES: Deciphering US Military Plans, Programs, and Operations in the 9/11 World* (Hanover, N.H.: Steerforth, 2005), p. 368.

In the hour between 1:45 and 2:45 in the afternoon in England, probably in the midst of another day of the NEST exercise, the terrorist attacks of September 11 occurred. Al-Qaeda struck New York and Washington. It was only twenty seconds shy of 8:47 a.m. in New York when American Airlines Flight 11, which had taken off from Boston and was headed to Los Angeles, was flown into the World Trade Center's North Tower. It was one of four planes hijacked by Al-Qaeda operatives that morning. When another hijacked aircraft, United Airlines Flight 175, also scheduled to fly from Boston to Los Angeles, crashed into the World Trade Center's South Tower a few minutes after 9:00, it was clear that the United States was under attack.[34]

And there was more to come. American Airlines Flight 77, from Washington, D.C., to Los Angeles, had also been seized, probably between 8:51 and 8:54 a.m., a little over thirty minutes after takeoff. At 8:54, the plane made an unauthorized turn to the south, and shortly before 9:38 it slammed into the Pentagon. That left one plane, United Airlines Flight 93, which had departed Newark for San Francisco at 8:42. Within an hour it had been hijacked, and shortly before 10:00 a passenger revolt began. As a result, rather than smashing into Congress, the White House, or the CIA, all aboard died a few minutes later when the plane crashed into a field in Shanksville, Pennsylvania.[35]

The attacks would produce another "We Are at War" memo from Tenet, in which he told his employees, "We must all be passionate and driven—but not breathless. We must stay cool. We must keep our heads."[36] That advice certainly applied to people and agencies outside the CIA—and certainly to NEST.

By the time the Jackal Cave participants landed in the United States, NEST was in the midst of its first alert of a new era. Shortly after the attacks on New York and Washington, members of the team were "alerted they could potentially be called out [for duty] . . . so they were asked to be on standby," according to Nevada Operations Office spokesman Kevin Rohrer. Indeed, one NEST member recalls, "I got my notification between the time the first tower fell and the second tower fell." While there had been no specific nuclear threat, the alert was ordered as a precaution.[37]

NEST personnel had made it to New York, to the site where the World Trade Center towers had stood. At first, the NEST team was stranded in Las Vegas, but then it received clearance to fly its specially equipped plane to New York the next day. Officially, the team was searching for industrial radioactive sources and hot spots, fires under the rubble. It may also have been looking for evidence of a dirty bomb detonation.[38]

But the simple precautionary alert following 9/11 preceded what was feared to be a real threat. A Defense Intelligence Agency source code-named Dragonfire reported that a far more devastating attack might be in the works. His claims, which appeared in the Top Secret/Codeword *Threat Matrix* that was delivered to President George W. Bush on October 5, involved two frightening "mights." Terrorists might have obtained a ten-kiloton nuclear weapon from the stockpile that survived the Soviet Union, and the device might be on its way to New York City. If it detonated at the intersection of Fifth Avenue and 42nd Street, it would destroy most buildings and kill every person within a third of a mile radius (from 34th Street to about 51st Street between Lexington Avenue and Seventh Avenue). Within three-quarters of a mile (stretching from 23rd Street to 59th Street between First and Ninth Avenues), people would be killed immediately or receive fatal radiation doses, and buildings would look like the Alfred P. Murrah building in Oklahoma City after the terrorist attack.[39]

The *Threat Matrix* questioned the credibility of the source, owing to errors in his reporting of technical details, and ultimately the report turned out to have no substance—the product of a U.S. citizen who claimed he had overhead some unidentified people discussing the possibility of a nuclear weapon in a Las Vegas casino. But it managed to "generate . . . weeks of terrifying uncertainty in the small circle of agencies that knew about it," including director of central intelligence George Tenet and the White House Counterterrorism Security Group, according to *Time* magazine, partly because it was consistent with an intelligence report from a Russian general that his forces seemed to have lost a ten-kiloton weapon.[40]

Among those spared the terrifying uncertainty, in an effort to prevent a leak that might trigger mass panic among the city's residents, were the mayor of New York, Rudolph Giuliani, his police commissioner and the rest of the New York Police Department, as well as senior FBI officials. After the media revealed the incident, Bernard Kerik, who was the police commissioner at the time, described the decision to withhold the information as "appalling." Michael Bloomberg, Giuliani's successor, commented, "I do believe that the New York City government should have been told."[41]

Opposite: Damage to New York City from Ten-Kiloton Weapon (Source: Belfer Center for Science and International Affairs/R7 Solutions)

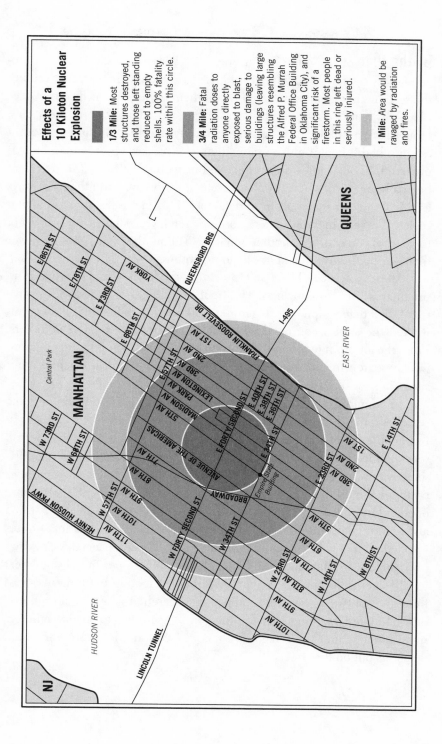

**Effects of a
10 Kiloton Nuclear
Explosion**

1/3 Mile: Most structures destroyed, and those left standing reduced to empty shells. 100% fatality rate within this circle.

3/4 Mile: Fatal radiation doses to anyone directly exposed to blast, serious damage to buildings (leaving large structures resembling the Alfred P. Murrah Federal Office Building in Oklahoma City), and significant risk of a firestorm. Most people in this ring left dead or seriously injured.

1 Mile: Area would be ravaged by radiation and fires.

.   .   .

By the time of Dragonfire's warning, NEST was already engaged in precautionary operations. Members of NEST's search teams were examining the readings of radiation detection equipment in helicopters hovering over New York City's docks and bridges and over the Capitol and the White House in Washington. There is no certainty that they would have found a bomb had it been hidden below them. As one law enforcement official observed, "I don't know how effective this would have been if there had been a bomb somewhere. You can't search everything, and there are ways to shield nuclear materials from detectors. That fact is, we're a wide-open society. We're vulnerable. There's only so much you can do, but you've got to do what you can." As another official said about the effort, "But it's better than having them sitting at home doing nothing."[42]

After September 11, NEST precautionary patrols also drove around urban areas in vans known as "Hot Spot Mobile Labs" armed with instruments that detect alpha, beta, gamma, and neutron radiation. Other teams walked the streets equipped with backpacks holding smaller detectors. From the air, from roads, and on the street, NEST was conducting random weekly search missions focusing on ports, warehouse districts, and other sites where a smuggled nuclear weapon might be concealed.[43]

In January 2002, the administration ordered NEST to begin periodic searches for a "dirty bomb" in Washington and other large U.S. cities, even in the absence of a threat. Almost every week the FBI randomly selected several cities for sweeps by NEST. A team of six or fewer NEST scientists secretly prowled areas, such as docks in a coastal town, that local authorities considered most likely to have hidden contraband. Some NEST personnel operated in unmarked moving vans loaded with the sophisticated gamma and neutron detectors that are sensitive to the emission of radiation. Others traveled on foot with detectors concealed in briefcases, backpacks, or even beer coolers. In Manhattan, in October 2001, NEST personnel stood next to FBI agents and police, waving handheld detection equipment across thousands of trucks that were stopped and searched—looking for either a dirty bomb or Dragonfire's ten-kiloton bomb. According to one law enforcement official, after the Dragonfire report, "we put a lot more hand-held detectors out on the streets."[44]

.   .   .

The attacks prompted a number of other changes. The Energy Department put additional equipment in the field "so it's much closer to the users," Energy official John Gordon told a congressional committee, and created two more regional bases from which to operate. In 2005, NEST had twenty-nine teams in ten locations.[45]

NEST deployments in Washington, starting in late 2001, were part of a secret Bush administration initiative: the erection of a provisional defense against nuclear terrorism around the nation's capital. Called the "Ring Around Washington," its objective was to detect a nuclear or radiological bomb before the weapon could be detonated. The ring consisted of a grid of radiation sensors in the district and at major points of approach by river and road. It was still under development at the time of the 9/11 attacks, and not without its problems. Under some conditions the neutron and gamma-ray detectors failed to identify dangerous radiation signatures. In other conditions they raised false alarms over low-grade medical waste and the ordinary background emissions of stone monuments. But the attacks meant there was no time to wait—the system was pressed into service as a large-scale operational trial.[46]

Along with the Ring and the NEST-equipped vans patrolling Washington, a Joint Special Operations Command special missions unit, probably Delta Force, with personnel already trained to render safe a nuclear weapon or its components, moved to heightened alert at a staging area near the capital—possibly Fort Belvoir, which houses another secret JSOC unit, the Intelligence Support Activity.[47]

Washington was not the sole focus of increased U.S. nuclear detection efforts. Advanced detection sensors were deployed at U.S. borders and overseas facilities. They were deployed at the sites of national special security events, including the 2002 Winter Olympics in Utah—as were personnel from NEST. In addition, the detection equipment carried by Customs Service officers was upgraded to NEST standards. The geiger counters that were worn on belt clips and resembled pagers were replaced by devices—gamma-ray and neutron flux detectors—that previously had been carried only by NEST personnel.[48]

Chapter 10

NEST AFTER 9/11

IN 2002, in the midst of the vastly increased concern over the threat of nuclear terrorism, the Nuclear Emergency Search Team ceased to exist, but only in the most trivial sense. During the first half of the year, the word "Search" was replaced by "Support" in the organization's title, so the acronym remained the same. The new name reflected NEST's role not only in searching for nuclear devices but also in helping to move and disable them, as well as the fact that the team's activities were conducted in support of the FBI or State Department. Those organizations continued as the lead federal agencies handling nuclear terrorist incidents, depending on whether the incident took place in the United States or overseas. The new name was also somewhat less dramatic, conveying less urgency—although that does not appear to have been a factor in the change.[1] In any case, the change was probably of consequence only to a select group of government officials.

Of far greater consequence that spring, to both government officials and the general public, were the intentions of a former Chicago gang member. Jose Padilla, thirty-one years old at the time, had converted to Islam and went by the name Abdullah al Mujahir. When Padilla arrived in Chicago on a flight from Zurich on May 8, 2002, FBI agents were waiting.[2]

It had been almost four years since Padilla had embarked on a series of travels that would eventually result in his arrest. On September 5, 1998, after a stretch in a Florida prison, he flew from Miami to Cairo, where he remained for the next eighteen months. Then, in mid-March 2000 he traveled to Saudi Arabia and attended the hajj, the pilgrimage to Mecca required of able-bodied Muslims who can afford it, at least once during their life. While in Saudi Arabia, he met an individual identified by the Justice Department as "The Recruiter," the type of designation one usually finds in a spy novel. When Padilla expressed interest in traveling to Afghanistan, where the Taliban ruled and hosted Osama bin Laden, his new friend invited him to go to Yemen first.[3]

Padilla accepted his offer, arriving in May 2000. The Recruiter helped him get to the Yemeni capital of Sanaa, where he was turned over to "The Sponsor," who was to help him with the next leg of his journey. On June 26, 2000, Padilla entered Pakistan and from there traveled to Qandahar in Afghanistan. Once in Qandahar he filled out an application form, as if he were applying for a job at a Wal-Mart. But he could have done that in Chicago. The information Padilla provided and the questions he answered were entered onto a "Mujahideen Identification Form/New Application Form" dated July 24, 2000, which the FBI would subsequently recover in Pakistan.[4]

In September and October of that year, the new recruit attended the Al-Qaeda–affiliated al Farouq training camp, the camp where more Guantánamo detainees trained than any other. There, according to Padilla, in addition to religious training he received instruction in a variety of skills needed for fighting rather than preaching. He trained in weapons, topography, communications, camouflage, clandestine surveillance, explosives, and physical fitness. Around April 2, 2001, he was back in Pakistan, in Karachi, and then left to return to Egypt. A little over two months later, on June 11, he reentered Pakistan on his way back to Afghanistan.[5]

But 9/11 would force Padilla back into Pakistan, at least temporarily. After the mid-November air attack that killed Al-Qaeda operations chief Mohammed Atef, a decision was made, presumably by bin Laden and his deputy, Ayman al-Zawahiri, to move Arab fighters out of Afghanistan. In the process, Padilla met senior Al-Qaeda official Abu Zubaydah, who was coordinating the exodus as well as sorting out those who would be sent back to Afghanistan from those who were to be permanently evacuated.[6]

After crossing into Pakistan, Padilla met Abu Zubaydah again, this time at a guesthouse in Lahore. Part of his time was spent conducting research on nuclear and dirty bombs. After remaining for a month, the former Chicago gang member headed for Faisalabad, where Abu Zubaydah joined Padilla and other jihadists again. But Zubaydah would soon find himself in American custody. On March 28, 2002, tracked through monitoring of his phone calls to the Faisalabad safehouse, he was shot three times during the operation to capture him. By that time Padilla had already departed. After arranging for medical attention, the CIA transferred Zubaydah to a secret prison in Thailand.[7]

At first Zubaydah was cooperative, at least partially. He revealed that Khalid Sheikh Mohammed was the mastermind behind 9/11 and used the name Mukhtar. But then he stopped cooperating. The CIA responded with tougher interrogation techniques, including waterboarding—placing its target on his back, with the head inclined downward, and pouring water on his face, forcing the target to inhale water. Death can appear to be imminent. Unlike Sheikh Mohammed, who required several "redippings" before cooperating, Abu Zubaydah had enough after one session. Along with what he revealed while under interrogation, the information found on his cell phone and computer and in documents in his possession consti- tuted a "motherlode," according to former director of central intelligence George Tenet.[8]

Sometime, either before or after the CIA turned up the pressure, Abu Zubaydah told his interrogators about a foreign recruit who, while in Fais- alabad, proposed an operation in which the fighter and his accomplice would travel to the United States and detonate a nuclear device, possibly in Washington, D.C. The two believed they could build such a device based on information available on the Internet. He did not tell the CIA that the foreign recruit was Jose Padilla, but provided "a generic descrip- tion of him . . . fairly sketchy information," according to one official. Abu Zubaydah had apparently been skeptical of the idea but told Padilla and his associate that he would send them to Karachi, where they could pitch the idea to Khalid Sheikh Mohammed, at the time still Al-Qaeda's opera- tions chief.[9]

Abu Zubaydah had followed through and arranged the meeting, after suggesting to Padilla that his ambition was simply not feasible and that it would make more sense to focus on a dirty bomb. (Later Abu Zubaydah would claim that he did not think that even that less ambitious idea would work, and warned Padilla that a dirty bomb was not as easy as he believed.) The optimistic Padilla was not discouraged, continuing to believe he could pull off such an attack.[10]

But Al-Qaeda's operations chief was, as Abu Zubaydah had predicted, skeptical of Padilla's plan. He suggested something less dramatic but more feasible — that Padilla and his accomplice undertake an operation origi- nally conceived by the deceased Atef. What Atef had in mind was a series of attacks on apartment buildings, using conventional explosives. Along with his associate, Padilla left Pakistan on April 5, headed first for Zurich and eventually the United States, where he landed on May 8.[11]

The information obtained during Abu Zubaydah's interrogation, along with information from other sources, had allowed the CIA and FBI to iden- tify exactly who their captive was talking about. That other information came from interrogations of other Al-Qaeda officials in U.S. custody as well as documents recovered in Afghanistan. "We had separate informa- tion from other sources, both human and documentary, that supported the notion that there was such a guy," according to a senior intelligence official.[12]

"We started trying to figure who he was and eventually did," added the official. "Then we tried to figure out where he was. Then we determined he was planning on coming to the U.S. So he was under surveillance." The surveillance went on for several weeks, while Padilla traveled from Pakistan to Zurich then to Egypt, followed by a return to Zurich. U.S. officials were then able to identify the flight that Padilla was taking back to the United States.[13]

On June 9 President George W. Bush designated Padilla an enemy combatant and ordered that he be transferred to the custody of the Department of Defense.[14]* Had Abu Zubaydah been less cooperative during his interrogations and Khalid Sheikh Mohammed more receptive to Padilla's dirty bomb plan, rather than the FBI waiting for Padilla, NEST might have found itself patrolling the streets of Washington, D.C., in search of his bomb.

Such patrols, starting in early 2003, would be conducted under the ultimate authority of a new government department: the Department of Homeland Security. Initially, in the aftermath of 9/11, the Bush administration argued that an Office of Homeland Security, operating out of the White House, would be sufficient to coordinate the myriad government departments and agencies central to protecting the homeland from future terrorist attacks. But in June 2002, under political pressure, the administration released a glossy brochure touting its proposal for a Department of Homeland Security.[15]

The brochure promised that the department "would unify authority over major federal security operations related to our borders, territorial waters, and transportation systems." By late November, the legislation, the Homeland Security Act of 2002, that would establish the new department was before Congress. And when former Pennsylvania governor Thomas Ridge took office as the first secretary of homeland security on January 24, 2003, he was in command of a department with more than 180,000 person-

---

*Ultimately Padilla would be sentenced to seventeen years and four months in prison for charges unrelated to his desire to detonate a dirty bomb, including a conspiracy to commit kidnapping and murder overseas. See Jess Bravin, "Padilla's Sentence Is Under the Minimum," *Wall Street Journal*, January 23, 2008, p. A4.

nel and many agencies that had been transferred from other departments, ranging from Agriculture to Defense.[16]

The new department absorbed, to name just a few organizations, the U.S. Customs Service from Treasury, part of the Immigration and Naturalization Service from Justice, the Transportation Security Administration from Transportation, the Plum Island Animal Disease Center from Agriculture, the Federal Emergency Management Agency, and the Strategic National Stockpile and National Disaster Medical System from Health and Human Services.[17] In addition, the legislation assigned Homeland Security a role in responding to nuclear emergencies, including searching for and disabling nuclear devices or dirty bombs in the hands of extortionists and terrorists.

The legislation established a directorate of emergency preparedness and response and an undersecretary as its chief. The new undersecretary's responsibilities included supervision of the department's Nuclear Incident Response Team, which could be activated at the direction of the secretary. That team would actually consist of units drawn from other departments that would be operating under the command of Homeland Security. For example, the Environmental Protection Agency's Radiological Emergency Response Team (RERT) as well as several components of the Department of Energy could be called on to form part of a response team. The Radiological Assistance Program (RAP), whose team members evaluate the extent of a radiological emergency and advise on minimizing its hazards, would be one, and in the right type of emergency, NEST would be another.[18]

But NEST (as well as RAP) remained a part of the Department of Energy. Since its personnel were drawn from Energy Department laboratories, they and the organization had to stay within the Energy Department. And the legislation creating the new department specified that nothing in it should be interpreted to limit the responsibility of the secretary of energy or the administrator of the Environmental Protection Agency for organizing, training, equipping, or employing their elements of the response team, or "exercising direction, authority, and control" over them when they were not operating on behalf of Homeland Security.[19]

In the wake of 9/11, measures to detect terrorist nuclear devices or dirty bombs before they detonated were not confined to NEST or even the federal government. The terrorist attacks promoted a diffusion of radiation detection technology that in earlier years might have largely been in the possession of NEST and other Energy Department organizations.

At the end of the same month that President Bush declared Jose Padilla an enemy combatant, partly because of his plans for a dirty bomb attack on the nation's capital, New York City's police commissioner, Raymond W. Kelly, announced that radiation detectors, which cost about $11,000 each, would be installed outside several city buildings. One had already been placed outside police headquarters in lower Manhattan, and officials said another would be set up outside the building's garage. The department's bomb squad and emergency services unit were to use two others, with City Hall a possible site for another.[20]

The detectors used were similar to the ones deployed in Washington, D.C., outside the White House and the Capitol. And by mid-2003, just in case detection and prevention failed, federal scientists had installed sensors to track wind currents in downtown Washington, Arlington, Virginia, and Silver Spring, Maryland—the first deployment of a high-tech network to help predict how chemical or biological agents or radioactivity would travel through the air—how urban "wind fields" might disperse fallout from a weapon of mass destruction.[21]

That network consisted of a half-dozen aluminum weather towers, each thirty feet tall, installed on top of government buildings and described by government officials as the most comprehensive wind analysis attempted in any U.S. city. The initial towers were placed near sensitive sites, including Capitol Hill, the White House, the Pentagon, the Mall, the National Zoo, and the National Arboretum, and on cellular relay towers within the Capital Beltway. The ultrasonic sensors sample the wind ten times a second, with the data being downloaded at fifteen-minute intervals and made accessible to emergency planners and scientists across the country. In addition, as part of a $3 million program called Sensor Net, the Energy Department added gamma radiation detectors to the towers, to test the feasibility of their use in neutralizing a radiological attack.[22]

Exactly one year after the 9/11 attacks, there was a brief concern that Al-Qaeda or some other terrorist group might have moved past Jose Padilla's vague plans to build a nuclear device or dirty bomb. One consequence of those attacks was the Maritime Security Act of 2002, which imposed new security requirements on the estimated eleven thousand ships entering the

Port of Newark each year, carrying three million shipping containers and close to thirty billion gallons of petroleum products. Ships were required to submit crew and passenger lists along with cargo manifests by radio ninety-six hours before entering the port.[23]

During the evening of September 11, 2002, a Coast Guard inspection team detected noises coming from containers in the cargo hold of a New York–bound German container ship, the ten-year-old, 708-foot-long *Palermo Senator*, the noises indicating there might be stowaways inside. But while the inspectors searched for stowaways (there were none), they detected low-level radiation emanating from the cargo hold. The Coast Guard then ordered the vessel back out to sea and guarded it in a special security zone six miles offshore, in anticipation of a more thorough inspection.[24]

With the cargo consisting of 1,200 forty-foot-long metal shipping containers stacked on top of each other both above and below deck, and with high winds and a choppy sea interfering, the inspection—supervised not by the Coast Guard but by the FBI—would wind up consuming more than two days. During that time, members of NEST, dispatched by the Energy Department, members of an FBI hazardous-devices response unit, which also operates nuclear detection equipment, and Coast Guard technicians searched the vessel, joined by Navy SEALs, whose special skills in dealing with nuclear-powered ships and maritime surroundings might have been needed.[25]

To the great relief of those involved in the inspection, NEST determined that the radioactive readings were coming not from a terrorist device but from naturally occurring radiation in the ceramic tiles among the cargo. On the afternoon of September 13, the *Palermo Senator* with its crew of twenty-one finally steamed into the Newark port after government officials concluded that it and its cargo "posed no danger or threat," or at least the probability was sufficiently low to allow the vessel to proceed.[26]

According to a Department of Justice audit report, the FBI hazardous-devices unit told the FBI special agent in charge of the Newark field office, who wanted to be certain there was not a nuclear device on board, that the unit could not provide absolute assurance based on the monitoring of radioactivity. In an answer that paraphrased J. Robert Oppenheimer's testimony over fifty years earlier, the unit told the special agent that the only path to certainty was to remove every container and to search each one individually, a process that would likely take weeks to complete.[27]

.   .   .

Federal officials were certain that an organization known as GLODO, in reality, posed no danger or threat to the citizens of Seattle or Chicago. But in the fictional world of the Topoff (Top Officials) 2 exercise, it had "a history of ruthlessness" and posed a very serious threat and an opportunity for NEST to once again test its ability to respond. At noon on a day in mid-May 2003, a hidden bomb exploded south of the central business district in Seattle, resulting in more than 150 people killed or injured. When significant levels of radiation were detected near the site of the explosion, it soon became clear to local officials that it was not an ordinary explosive device, but a dirty bomb. The next day Chicago was victimized by an equally fictional biological attack.[28]

The entire exercise unfolded over five days, starting on May 12, in what U.S. government officials described as the largest homeland security exercise in the history of the country, costing an estimated $16 million and involving more than one hundred federal, state, and local agencies, the American Red Cross, and Canadian government agencies and organizations. It also "turned a vacant lot next to a coffee roasting plant into what looked like the set of a low-budget action film."[29]

In addition to being a site for NEST search teams during the publicly acknowledged 2003 Topoff exercise, Chicago and Seattle were, at the same time, the targets of NEST teams that were part of a highly secret effort involving the FBI that had commenced early in 2002.[30]

At that time, the FBI and NEST began monitoring the air in the vicinity of more than a hundred Muslim sites in the Washington, D.C., metropolitan area. Monitoring targets included mosques, homes, warehouses, and businesses. While Washington was the primary focus of the effort, Muslim sites in Chicago and Seattle, along with Las Vegas, Detroit, and New York, were also targeted when threat levels increased.[31]

Mosques alone represented a significant set of potential targets. In Washington, probably the best known is the Islamic Center of Washington, D.C., on the Embassy Row section of Massachusetts Avenue. But one web site lists another twenty-three in the metropolitan D.C. area. Another web site lists forty-two mosques for Chicago and ten for Los Angeles.[32]

The Washington effort would involve, at its peak, three vehicles monitoring 120 sites each day, virtually all of which were Muslim sites designated by the FBI. Included were prominent mosques and office buildings in Washington, suburban Maryland, and Virginia. For the first ten months the reconnaissance was a daily event. Afterward, daily checks resumed during high-threat periods. Searchers were "tasked on a daily and nightly basis," and FBI and Energy Department officials met regularly to update the target list.[33]

Almost all of the targets were U.S. citizens, and up to 15 percent of the sites could be monitored accurately only by placing the monitoring equipment on the property under surveillance—including in mosque parking lots and private driveways. No search warrants or court orders were obtained, a practice that concerned some of those involved in the program. One participant told U.S. News & World Report, "A lot of us thought it was questionable, but people who complained nearly lost their jobs. We were told it was perfectly legal."[34]

Predictably, the Washington-based Council on American-Islamic Relations (CAIR) was also perturbed. When the program became public knowledge, CAIR spokesman Ibrahim Hooper objected that the program "comes as complete shock to us and everyone in the Muslim community," and "creates the appearance that Muslims are targeted simply for being Muslims. I don't think this is the message the government wants to send at this time." John Miller, the FBI's assistant director for public affairs, denied that the FBI targeted "any group based on ethnicity, political, or religious belief" while another official asserted, "Our investigations are intelligence driven and based on a criminal predicate."[35]

Officials also told reporters what they told participants concerning the program's legality, that warrants were not needed to drive into a mosque parking lot or onto a publicly accessible driveway or to monitor radiation in the vicinity. According to one official, "If a delivery man can access it, so can we." Another asserted, "A parking lot or a driveway is not necessarily private property and our equipment is not intrusive." But that wasn't the issue according to Georgetown University law professor David Cole, an expert in constitutional law. It might be permissible to conduct reconnaissance in public areas, such as mosques and public businesses, without a court order, he argued, but not surveillance of private offices and homes. "They don't need a warrant to drive onto the property—the issue isn't where they are, but whether they're using a tactic to intrude on privacy. It seems to me that they are, and they would need a warrant or probable cause."[36]

Cole pointed to a 2001 Supreme Court decision, in which the petitioner, Danny Lee Kyllo, asserted that his conviction for growing marijuana should be overturned on the grounds that the use of a thermal imaging device without a warrant constituted a search within the meaning of the Fourth Amendment.[37]

Danny Kyllo's troubles began in 1991 when William Elliott, an agent of the Department of the Interior, suspected that Kyllo was growing marijuana, which typically requires high-intensity lamps, in his Florence, Oregon, home. At 3:20 on the morning of January 16, 1992, Elliott and an associate employed a thermal imager, an Agema Thermovision 210 model, to scan Kyllo's home. The device converted radiation into images based on relative warmth, with black representing cool and white representing hot and shades of gray denoting relative differences.[38]

It took only a few minutes for the Thermovision unit, placed in the passenger seat of Elliott's car, to scan Kyllo's house from across the street behind the house. Elliott concluded, correctly, that Kyllo was using halide lights to grow marijuana in his house. A federal magistrate judge, when presented with the results of the thermal imaging, tips from informants, and utility bills, issued a warrant authorizing a search of Kyllo's home. When the warrant was executed, agents found an indoor growing operation involving more than a hundred plants, evidence that proved sufficient to convict Kyllo.[39]

The district court concluded that the Agema 210 "is a non-intrusive device which emits no rays or beams and shows a crude visual image of the heat being radiated from the outside of the house" and that there was no legal problem with the arrest. But the Supreme Court, by a 5-4 margin, disagreed. The majority opinion, delivered by Justice Antonin Scalia, noted that visual observation was not a "search," and that in a previous case, involving aerial photography of a Dow Chemical facility, the Court found "it important that this is *not* an area immediately adjacent to a private home, where privacy expectations are most heightened."[40]

And there was more than visual observation involved in the *Kyllo* case. The police were using a detection system that went beyond observation, and could be used to probe what was going on in the target's house. And citizens had, at the very least, Scalia believed, the right to expect that the police should not be free to conduct such probes without a warrant. He argued that "to withdraw protection of this minimum expectation would be to permit police technology to erode the privacy guaranteed by the Fourth Amendment" and that "obtaining by sense-enhancing technology any information regarding the interior of the home that could not otherwise have been obtained without physical 'intrusion into a constitutionally protected area' . . . constitutes a search—at least where (as here) the technology in question is not in general public use." A key point for the majority was that, in the case of a private house, "*all* details are intimate details, because the entire area is held safe from prying government eyes."[41]

Officials familiar with the FBI/NEST operation monitoring radiation at Muslim sites responded to the ruling by pointing out that the radiation sensors sampled the surrounding air. "This kind of program only detects particles in the air, it's non-directional," said one. "It's not a whole lot different from smelling marijuana." Another told the *New York Times*, "It's nothing intrusive. We're not searching into a particular building, just sniffing the air in the area."[42]

Officials also undoubtedly had in mind a Supreme Court case involving marijuana subsequent to the *Kyllo* decision. In that case, Roy Caballes was not as lucky as Danny Kyllo. The Supreme Court upheld his conviction in an Illinois court which found that a police dog had detected marijuana in the trunk of Caballes's car after he had been stopped for a traffic violation. A key factor in the Supreme Court decision was that the dog did "not expose noncontraband items that otherwise would remain hidden from public view . . . during a lawful traffic stop," which "generally does not implicate privacy interests." In the Court's view, critical to the *Kyllo* case "was the fact that the device was capable of detecting lawful activity" — in that case, intimate details in a home, such as "at what hour each night the lady of the house takes her daily sauna and bath."[43]

During mid-2003, some NEST members were not available for domestic operations or exercises because they were in Iraq. Before the Iraq Survey Group was established under David Kay, the task of hunting for Saddam's weapons of destruction was carried out by a number of military units, and at least in the weeks after the invasion, they had the assistance of members of NEST.[44]

This was not NEST's first contact with the problem of hunting for Saddam's nuclear programs. In the aftermath of the 1991 Gulf War, NEST was asked to prepare a search plan. It was, according to one former NEST member, "laughed out" of both Washington and Vienna, the home of the IAEA. The plan called for a deployment of a quantity of equipment and personnel that was "just completely out of balance" and represented "severe overkill."[45]

But while the IAEA may not have liked NEST's search strategy, the agency didn't mind having NEST along. William Nelson and several members of NEST would go to Iraq to assist in the search for Saddam's nuclear weapons activities.[46]

Toward the end of 2003, U.S. officials became concerned that Al-Qaeda was planning another major attack on the country. By December 19, analysts assembled what they considered to be extremely specific intelligence, including intercepts of telephone calls or e-mails of Al-Qaeda operatives. One concern was that Al-Qaeda had a 9/11 encore in mind: hijacking an overseas flight and crashing the plane into a U.S. city or the ocean. The concern was sufficient to lead the U.S. government to cancel fifteen commercial flights that were to arrive in the country from Paris, London, and Mexico as well as to provide jet fighter escorts for airliners as they approached Los Angeles International and Dulles airports. A second fear was that the terrorist group would use a shoulder-fired missile, such as a Stinger, to shoot down a jetliner. U.S. officials also worried that one of the large open-air New Year's Eve celebrations or college football bowl games might be a target, possibly of a dirty bomb.[47]

The concern over a dirty bomb stemmed not from specific intelligence but the continued belief that detonating one was a high Al-Qaeda priority. So, on December 21, the same day that he raised the nation's alert level from Elevated (Yellow) to High (Orange), Secretary of Homeland Security Thomas Ridge had his department send out large fixed radiation detectors and hundreds of pager-size radiation monitors to be used by local police in Washington, New York, Los Angeles, Las Vegas, Chicago, Houston, San Diego, San Francisco, Seattle, and Detroit.[48]

But Ridge did more than that. Using the authority given to him by the legislation creating his department, he ordered NEST searchers into action—to cities planning large public events. On December 22, they began their covert searches, taking measurements around the clock, presumably unnoticed by the general population. A Department of Energy official noted what officials in earlier years had also observed: "Our guys can fit in a sports stadium, or a construction site or on Fifth Avenue . . . Their equipment is configured to look like anybody else's luggage or briefcase."[49]

One of their targets was Baltimore, which was planning a New Year's party at its Inner Harbor, one of the city's prominent sites with attractions including the Maryland Science Center, the National Aquarium in Baltimore, World Trade Center, and the Baltimore Maritime Museum. Coast Guard and NEST personnel walked the waterfront with radiation detection equipment in search of nuclear signatures.[50]

Dozens of other searchers spread out across Manhattan, days away from its New Year's Eve celebration in Times Square, which up to a million people were expected to attend. Other NEST members worked closer to home, in Las Vegas, the site of a huge annual New Year's Eve party on the strip. Still others patrolled Los Angeles and Pasadena, where the New Year's Day Rose Bowl parade draws as many as one million observers.[51]

Early on December 29, the Las Vegas searchers received their first and only radiation spike from a rented storage facility near downtown. That finding "sent a jolt of tension through the nation's security apparatus," according to one account. The White House was notified. Experts rechecked their result using a more precise machine, which revealed the presence of radium, a radioactive material used in medical equipment and on watch dials, inside the cinderblock unit. While an unusual snow fell on Las Vegas that day, FBI agents secured the industrial area surrounding the site, and a "small army" of agents, scientists, and technicians converged on the business.[52]

As the padlock to the storage unit was about to be cut, a homeless man, who also happened to be the unit's owner, arrived on the scene and asked the officers not to cut the lock—which proved unnecessary when he provided the key. The scientists sent in a robot, probably the ATOM, to retrieve a duffel bag in which the man had been storing a cigar-size radium pellet—used to treat uterine cancer—since he found the shiny stainless-steel object three years earlier. Unaware of what he had found, he had wrapped it up in his nighttime pillow. Five tense hours after their radiation detectors had spiked, NEST personnel concluded the contents of the storage locker presented no threat.[53]

On Wednesday, January 19, 2005, a claim from an anonymous Mexican informant to the California Highway Patrol could have triggered a return engagement for NEST in Boston. The tipster said that the city was the target for an upcoming dirty bomb attack. The information was initially fielded the FBI's Joint Terrorism Task Force in San Diego, which passed it on to its Boston counterpart. The Boston unit shared it with local officials. The FBI also notified two offices in the Department of Homeland Security. The timing of the tip, just before a presidential inaugural, a national security special event that already would have NEST patrolling Washington, led to speculation that an attack was scheduled to coincide with the beginning of President Bush's second term.[54]

The information received by the FBI identified four Chinese nationals and two Iraqi nationals, who allegedly had illegally entered the United States from Mexico and were headed for New York and then Boston, as being involved in the dirty bomb effort. The two women and two of the men were also reported to be scientists. The information made its way into the media that same day, and officials called for calm. Officials also met in a bunker in suburban Boston to work out strategy before an evening briefing from Thomas M. Menino, the mayor of Boston. That evening, the office of U.S. attorney Michael Sullivan provided the names and photographs of four of the suspects—two Chinese men and two women—to the press, information that was immediately displayed across television screens.[55]

By Thursday, January 20, the FBI and Massachusetts officials had obtained more information on the six, which neither increased their concern or confirmed the informant's claim, and named another ten individuals "as persons of interest." But there was a significant degree of skepticism—undoubtedly in part because the informant claimed that the six he identified were waiting for a shipment of "nuclear oxide," a substance that does not exist. Governor Mitt Romney, in response to a reporter's question, noted, "There are some who would say that the information has a degree of unreliability to it" and later added, "Could this be a hoax? Why, of course." Officials in Washington were also skeptical, largely discounting, if not ruling out, the idea that Boston was about to be attacked. It was a skepticism that Homeland Security intelligence chief Patrick M. Hughes, former director of the Defense Intelligence Agency, explained, in a series of phone calls, to homeland security directors around the country.[56]

If there was anything that made such a claim plausible, it would have been the information from earlier years that Al-Qaeda cell leader Adnan El Shukrijumah had been spotted in Mexico and was actively involved in an effort to obtain radioactive materials for a dirty bomb to be smuggled into the United States. But ultimately, well before the end of January 2005, the FBI concluded that the tip from the anonymous Mexican was a false alarm, possibly the result of a suspected smuggler inventing the story to retaliate against people who failed to pay him. The bureau issued a statement that was unequivocal: "There were in fact no terrorist plans or activity under way."[57] And no need to call NEST.

.   .   .

NEST could also have received a call, not as a result of an informant's tip or an extortion note, but because of a spike in radiation detected by one of a number of networks in the country, such as the network that was being planned for a mid-size city in Colorado.

Colorado Springs is far from being among the most populous communities in the United States. The 186-square-mile city had a population of 369,815 in 2005, making it the second biggest city in Colorado. It also hosts the United States Olympic Training Center and is home of the Colorado Springs Sky Sox, the Triple A affiliate of the Colorado Rockies. None of those facts were likely to make it an attractive target to terrorists.

But the Colorado Springs area is also home to several major military bases. The city's largest military base, although not necessarily the most significant, is Fort Carson. At Peterson Air Force Base is the headquarters of the Air Force Space Command, responsible for a significant portion of America's military satellite and space surveillance systems as well as of the U.S. Northern Command, established in the aftermath of 9/11. In addition, it is the home of NORAD. Then, there is Schriever Air Force Base, where the 50th Space Wing controls a variety of warning, navigation, and communications satellites. As one Colorado Springs official observed, "We've got every military base in the world here." He added, "We're on the list of top 70 potential terrorist targets."[58]

As a result, in December 2005, the city was in the early stages of spending a substantial amount of money on a system that would warn that a dirty bomb or some other form of radiological attack had occurred—yet another example of how, after 9/11, the task of detecting radiological attacks was no longer the sole responsibility of a highly secretive unit in the federal government, but now included local community organizations.[59]

John C. Merritt was the focal point of the city's effort. The city had obtained four sensors, costing $30,000 each, for a test run, before applying for a grant to buy more—up to one to two million dollars' worth. Merritt was not a nuclear physicist but the city's principal traffic engineer—a reflection of the city's plan to place the sensors on traffic lights, the sensors then triggering an alarm at headquarters if they detected significant radiation. Traffic-light cameras where radiation was registered automatically would photograph the landscape in all four directions.[60]

.   .   .

The wider utilization of such technology increased the chance that NEST, in addition to precautionary deployments and responses to emergency calls originating from the federal government, might get an emergency call from a mayor whose city's detection system began blinking red, particularly if the city represented an attractive target to terrorists. There is also the chance that the call for NEST services might come from overseas.

Chapter 11

FOREIGN TRAVEL

ON OCCASION, threats against foreign cities or nations have been communicated directly to the U.S. government, including the threats against Tel Aviv, Moscow, and Murmansk mentioned earlier. But in other instances terrorists or extortionists have not bothered to "cc" the United States.

Between 1993 and 1995 alone, the German federal criminal police, the Bundeskriminalamt (BKA), recorded sixteen threats to spread radioactive materials for political or financial objectives. In one instance, an extortionist threatened to destroy four German cities by detonating "thermonuclear warheads" unless the State Lottery Administration paid him 100 million deutsche marks (about $62 million during that period). Then there was the letter signed "The Russian Mafia." It demanded a mere 250,000 deutsche marks from a German casino and threatened to detonate a nuclear device in its neighborhood unless the casino paid up. In addition, a caller, who understandably declined to give his name, claimed there was a Serbian plan to launch a grenade filled with radioactive waste in Munich if German troops were deployed to Bosnia.[1]

A group calling itself the "German People's Liberation Army" also issued a threat. The previously unheard-of group demanded that Poland evacuate former German territories that it had held since the end of World War I. Failure to comply, the liberation army warned, would result in Poland's president and parliament being exposed to more than two pounds of plutonium allegedly concealed somewhere in Warsaw. In a fifth instance, an anonymous caller warned a German government department that six nuclear warheads were buried in eastern Germany, and offered, for one million deutsche marks, to reveal their location. In a second call he threatened to detonate one device by satellite. Eventually, the extortionist was identified and arrested in Italy. But he never went to trial, hanging himself while he was in detention.[2]

Subsequent to the arrest in Prague in December 1994 of a Czech nuclear scientist, a Russian, and a Belorussian—apparently while they were waiting in their car to meet a prospective buyer of the nuclear material in their possession—the investigating officer in the case received a threatening letter. The officer wasn't the target of the threat but only the channel through which it was passed. The writer warned that unless the three were released, a small nuclear device would be detonated somewhere in Prague.[3]

In November 1995, a bit farther to the east of Germany, Shamil Basayev, leader of the Chechen separatists, threatened the population of Moscow with a radiological attack. Before being killed in July 2006, Basayev would direct the sieges of a Moscow theater in 2002 (which resulted in the death of more than a hundred hostages when Russian forces raided the theater) and a Beslan school in 2005, as well as the assassination of the Russian-backed Chechen president, Akhmad Kadyrov, also in 2005. But he first became well known in June 1995 when he led a raid against a hospital in Budennovsk, Russia, seizing the hospital and 1,600 people inside for several days. Before the siege ended, at least 129 civilians died and 415 were wounded in the fighting.[4]

In November, Basayev claimed that four radioactive packages had been smuggled into Russia, that at least two were hidden in Moscow, and that they could be detonated at any time he wished. To prove that the packages were not simply a figment of his imagination, the terrorist leader told Russian reporters where at least one parcel could be found. And a thirty-pound box containing radioactive cesium was found buried under the snow near the entrance to Izmailovsky Park, one of Moscow's most popular recreation areas whose main attraction is Pokhorovoskiy Cathedral. Russian officials tried to reassure residents that there was nothing dangerous in the radioactive container, with one stating that "the first tests showed that beyond one meter from the package there was no threat to health. Initial tests show that the package does not pose a serious threat to the environment or health."[5]

In March 2006, seven men were on trial in Britain, accused of having links to Al-Qaeda and plotting to carry out bomb attacks there. According to prosecuting attorney David Waters, one of those men, Salahuddin Amin, age thirty, had inquired about purchasing an atomic bomb from Russian Mafia figures in Belgium. Amin had allegedly been asked by a man he met at a mosque in Luton, his hometown, to contact another individual, Abu Annis, about a "radioisotope bomb."[6]

More recently, in November 2006, British intelligence officials reportedly believed that Al-Qaeda was determined to detonate a nuclear weapon on British soil. At that time, Dhiren Barot, a senior Al-Qaeda member, was jailed for conspiring to kill hundreds of thousands of individuals in the United Kingdom and the United States. His plans included blowing up public buildings using gas cylinders in limousines, launching a gas attack on the Heathrow Express rail shuttle, and rupturing the walls under the

Thames that keep the river from swamping the train that travels underneath. In the notebooks they seized, the police found details concerning the construction of a chemical laboratory, along with poison recipes as well as plans to use radiation to generate illness, panic, and death.[7]

Barot, a Hindu who had converted to Islam, had been communicating with Al-Qaeda about detonating a dirty bomb in Britain. Part of his research involved close examination of an unclassified report written by Charles Ferguson, a former nuclear submarine officer with training in physics. After leaving the Navy, Ferguson entered the world of security studies, coauthoring a book on nuclear terrorism while with the Center for Nonproliferation Studies in Monterey, California, and then becoming a senior fellow at the Council on Foreign Relations. Ferguson's report, *Commercial Radioactive Sources: Surveying the Security Risks*, appeared in 2003, and a printout with various portions highlighted was among the materials seized from Barot. Influenced by the report, Barot told Al-Qaeda that he was contemplating purchasing ten thousand smoke detectors, some of which contain small amounts of americium-241, as raw material for his bomb.[8]

Also occurring overseas are events—including athletic competitions—comparable to national special security events in the United States. In December 2001, in the wake of 9/11 and the recognition of the attractiveness of such events to terrorist groups, which had been demonstrated almost three decades earlier in Munich, the United States established an interagency committee, the International Athletic Events Security Coordination Group, chaired by a representative of the State Department. Members come from the Intelligence Community and several departments, including Defense, Energy, Justice, Homeland Security, and Health and Human Services. The group's mission is to coordinate U.S. efforts in support of foreign government and U.S. embassy operations to protect international sporting events from terrorist attacks.[9]

The most prominent of international athletic events is, of course, the Olympics. The first post-9/11 Summer Olympics took place in Athens, Greece, starting on August 13, 2004. By the time of the closing ceremony on August 29, which was attended by 70,000 fans, 10,625 athletes from 202 nations had participated in 301 events in twenty-eight different sports. Also participating or attending were approximately 5,500 team officials, 45,000 volunteers, and 21,500 media, in addition to the huge number of people who showed up to watch the competition.[10]

. . .

The combination of explicit threats and attractive targets suggests an overseas role for NEST and other radiation-monitoring elements of the Department of Energy in searching for possible nuclear or radiological dispersal devices as well as assisting the nuclear detection efforts of foreign governments. Indeed, almost one week before the beginning of the Athens games, the State Department produced a document titled *Strategic Plan for Interagency Coordination of U.S. Government Nuclear Detection Assistance Overseas*, in cooperation with elements of the departments of Commerce, Defense, Energy, and Homeland Security.[11]

The plan envisions distributing four types of radiation detection equipment to a variety of nations. One type involves pedestrian, vehicle, and portal monitors. Another is handheld radiation detection devices, the kind that NEST members might use while covertly searching for nuclear material. Third are isotope identifiers. Also included is equipment needed to support the operation of portal monitors and collection of data from the detection efforts.[12]

The plan links distribution of the equipment to four goals, one being to permit nations receiving the equipment to possess a comprehensive capability to detect and intercept illicit special nuclear or radiological material. Two additional objectives focus on ensuring that the equipment would be used to maximum effect: getting senior government leaders in recipient countries to commit to a continuing and comprehensive detection effort, and helping those countries establish the legal authorities that will allow them to search traffickers and seize illicit material. The final goal is to get countries receiving detection equipment, in cooperation with international organizations such as the International Atomic Energy Agency and the governments providing the equipment, to establish effective radiation detection standards and deploy the equipment.[13]

Four departments—State, Defense, Homeland Security, and Energy—are responsible for implementing the plan. The Energy Department's Second Line of Defense (SLD) program places nuclear and radiological detection equipment at international border crossings. Since 2002, the Energy Department has also been responsible for maintaining the equipment provided to twenty-one countries. The plan further notes that the SLD program "can capitalize on [the Energy Department's] inherent technical expertise and recommend best specifications and manufacturers for radiation detection equipment."[14] Clearly, much of that technical expertise resides with NEST.

. . .

While the 2004 *Strategic Plan* did not explicitly refer to an overseas role for NEST, another, older document does. The October 1993 *NEST Energy Senior Official's Reference Manual* notes that "NEST capabilities are also available to foreign governments as arranged by the [Department of State] in conjunction with the [Department of Energy] and [Department of Defense]." It also includes a security plan for protecting classified material "during a Nuclear Emergency Search Team (NEST) International Deployment," which prohibits classified data from being left unattended.[15]

Some of NEST's capabilities might have been provided to Greece during the 2004 Olympics, although they might not have been acknowledged as coming from NEST. The Greek government had established an Olympic Games Security Division of its Ministry of Public Order. In an effort to protect the games from terrorists, the division developed a comprehensive plan to deal with the full range of WMD threats—nuclear, radiological, biological, and chemical—called the NRBC Threat National Emergency Plan. A critical organization in carrying out the nuclear portion of the plan was the Greek Atomic Energy Commission.[16]

The commission's capabilities included two 6-man teams—a Response Team and a Support Team—composed mainly of scientists available during eight-hour shifts around the clock for a three-month period. The Response Team's duties involved on-scene monitoring, identifying and measuring radiological contamination, and recovering radioactive sources. Another NEST-type activity carried out by "mobile expert support teams" of the Greek Atomic Energy Commission were radiation surveys of Olympic venues, including the Olympic village, conducted one to two days before the games started.[17]

For these surveys, the Greek teams employed a variety of equipment. Among the devices they used in their patrols were sensitive neutron search detectors, a highly portable gamma spectrometer, portable plastic scintillation detectors (scintillation is a disturbance in the atmosphere), radionuclide identification devices, and a scintillation detector carried on the roof of a vehicle. Such equipment was probably very familiar to members of NEST, which might even have provided some of it or given advice on its operation, at Olympic and other sites. Certainly, one organization providing assistance to the Greek detection effort was the Department of Energy, which signed a declaration of intent with the Greek Atomic Energy Commission and the Greek customs service. A study by the Government

Accountability Office reported that Department of Energy programs "provided expertise and equipment to enhance Greece's capability to detect nuclear devices and materials at certain land borders and a major port." It also informed its readers that a Foreign Emergency Support Team, the overall framework under which NEST provides support to foreign governments, was deployed to the Athens Olympics.[18]

In July 2008, the People's Republic of China spent $2.5 million to buy portable radiation sensors—ICx Technologies' identiFINDER radiosotope detectors—from an American firm to protect against a dirty bomb attack at the August Olympics. Help also came from the United States in the form of a contingent of NEST members, who first arrived in Beijing in June. Deployment was reportedly a response to Chinese intelligence "indicating that any attack likely would involve a radiological [dispersal] device."[19]

Members might also have been involved in a cooperative effort with Russian nuclear detection and response personnel. An early November 2007 press release from the National Nuclear Security Administration trumpeted a field training exercise held in St. Petersburg from October 29 to November 2. In the exercise, according to the release, "emergency responders from the NNSA teamed up with their counterparts from the Russian Atomic Energy Agency (RORSATOM) for the first-ever joint radiological emergency response field training." The exercise was the consequence of the 2005 Bratislava agreement on nuclear security, signed by Presidents George W. Bush and Vladimir Putin.[20]

The week included two small-scale exercises to test responses to the dispersal of radioactive material. It concluded with a day-long exercise that involved notification and alert procedures, mission planning, deployment of response personnel, field operations, and resolution of the crisis. The week also included discussions on the theory of radiation detection, detection equipment uses, and real-world responses to terrorism situations— topics in which NEST has a great deal of expertise.[21]

The nuclear security administration promised that such exercises and cooperation would continue—with regular joint training exercises to follow, including a second one in the United States to which a Russian team had already been invited.[22]

NEST's major foreign operation—Morning Light—took place three decades ago. And NEST has not been called into action since then to help other countries deal with actual nuclear threats, at least as far as is known. But recently it was called into action on the high seas.

The island of Sri Lanka, officially the Democratic Socialist Republic of Sri Lanka, is a bit larger than the state of West Virginia and is located southeast of India, between the Bay of Bengal and Gulf of Mannar. It has been the site of a long-running civil war between the government and the Liberation Tigers of Tamil Eelam, better known as the Tamil Tigers—a group whose objectives include the creation of a separate Tamil state in the northern and eastern provinces of Sri Lanka and the elimination of moderate Tamils.

In October 2005, a radiation sensor at the Port of Colombo in Sri Lanka indicated the presence of radioactive material in an outbound shipping container. But because the port's surveillance system, which was being funded by the NNSA, had not become operational, the container was loaded and at sea before it could be identified. As a result, American and Sri Lankan inspectors were forced to quickly examine the camera images at the port, which led them to conclude that the suspicious crate could be on any of five ships, two of which were headed toward New York.[23]

The container that set off the radiation sensor was, potentially, according to Vayl Oxford, director of the Department of Homeland Security's Domestic Nuclear Detection Office, on a "pariah ship." It was possible, even if unlikely, that the radiation came from a nuclear device loaded onto the ship by Al-Qaeda or rogue members of Pakistan's armed forces. That mandated that the U.S. Intelligence Community make a concerted effort to find each of the five ships that could be carrying the container. Within five days, probably relying on a combination of imagery satellites and electronic intelligence satellites used to track ships, and possibly underseas sensors, the Intelligence Community settled the question of location. While the search for the ships was on, intelligence analysts examined the ships' manifests.[24]

One ship, it was discovered, was bound for Canada, while another was headed for Hamburg, Germany. Following up on the intelligence provided by the spy satellites and analysts was a team at the National Security Council. The White House decided to call on NEST. One team, probably a Search Response Team, flew to Canada, while another headed to Europe. After the Hamburg-bound ship was intercepted, NEST personnel in Europe turned their radiation detection gear loose on the cargo—and found nothing.[25]

The two ships headed for New York were stopped by the U.S. Coast Guard in territorial waters, about ten miles off shore—far enough so that any nuclear explosion might wipe out some members of the Coast Guard and the NEST contingent but would at least leave the city of New York relatively unscathed. Members of NEST boarded the vessels, armed with their diagnostic equipment, and—no doubt to their great relief—found no indications that nuclear or radioactive cargo was on board.[26]

The ship that did carry the container turned out to be on an Asian route. And what it was carrying was nothing more than scrap metal mixed with radioactive materials that had been improperly dumped. The whole episode was over in two weeks, and its end result was the disposal of some radioactive waste.[27]

Helping a foreign government locate radioactive material, or find a nuclear device or dirty bomb in the hands of a terrorist or extortionist, and checking for radioactive material on a ship passing through a port with the government's consent, are operations in which members of NEST would be welcomed. But there is another scenario involving NEST in which its members could be flying into extreme danger.

On one occasion, when Pakistan and India appeared to be approaching war, the United States and Pakistan discussed the possibility of U.S. forces evacuating Pakistan's nuclear arsenal, which some analysts believe would be the only situation in which U.S. efforts to sequester or seize the arsenal would be anything "but impractical to the point of absurdity."[28] But if the country were plunged into internal chaos, the U.S. president and his senior advisors might decide to keep Pakistan's nuclear devices out of the hands of Al-Qaeda or a radical Islamist regime.

Indeed, in the 2006 *National Military Strategy to Combat Weapons of Mass Destruction*, the chairman of the Joint Chiefs of Staff discusses two types of operations in which U.S. military forces would seek to keep nuclear weapons out of the hands of Osama bin Laden and his lieutenants. One is designated "elimination operations," defined as "operations systematically to locate, characterize, secure, disable, and/or destroy a State or non-State actor's WMD programs and related capabilities." Finding, seizing, and disabling Pakistan's nuclear weapons to keep them out of Al-Qaeda's hands would seem to fit the description.[29]

The chairman also included "interdiction operations" as a means of keeping nuclear weapons out of Al-Qaeda's control. Specifically, he characterized such operations as being "designed to stop the proliferation of WMD, delivery systems, associated and dual-use technologies, materials, and expertise from transiting between States of concern and between State and non-State actors, whether undertaken by the military or by other agencies of government." In simpler terms, such operations would include finding and seizing nuclear devices or nuclear material after they have been removed from a nation's holdings but before they can be delivered to a terrorist group.[30]

Such operations were also envisioned in a briefing by the Office of the Assistant Secretary of Defense for Special Operations and Low-Intensity Conflict. One briefing slide refers to "clandestine or other low visibility special operations taken to: locate, seize, destroy, capture, recover, or render safe WMD." It suggests that such operations could take place on land or at sea. Those views were echoed by the Defense Science Board in an August 2002 briefing, which noted that a top priority for special operations forces was "Detecting, Identifying, and Localizing WMD."[31]

At least one strategic analyst has argued publicly that such operations might be necessary with respect to Pakistan's arsenal, which may consist of as many as 115 warheads: "To guard against the worst possibility—Pakistani weapons in the hands of our enemies—America should have plans ready to provide security without Pakistan's permission, if emergency circumstances dictate, and even to take Pakistan's weapons out of the country if the need arises. Special operations forces in the region should be kept on high alert for quick, covert incursions to disable or even relocate the weapons to prevent their capture by unauthorized people."[32]

The focus on Pakistan is the result of its being both the least stable of the nine nuclear weapons states and one where there has been significant support for Osama bin Laden and Al-Qaeda, not only among the general population but also within the military and intelligence services. Pakistan has experienced four military coups. The most recent perpetrator of a coup was Pervez Musharraf, who resigned as president in August 2008. Musharraf walked a fine line since 9/11, trying to satisfy the United States that he was doing enough in the war on terror, but not doing so much that extremists found his rule intolerable. Despite those efforts, in 2003 he was the target of two assassination attempts in one week, apparently engineered by military officers with links to Al-Qaeda.[33]

In early November 2007, when the Pakistani Supreme Court was in the process of ruling on the constitutionality of Musharraf's reelection while he still served as armed forces chief of staff, he declared a state of emergency, suspended the constitution, and ordered the arrest of hundreds of political opposition leaders, lawyers, and members of the media. Arrests extended across the political spectrum and included not only Aitzaz Ahsan, the president of Pakistan's Supreme Court Bar Association, but also Hamid Gul, a former director of the Inter-Services Intelligence Directorate and architect of the Taliban.[34]

The turmoil surrounding Musharraf's reelection was followed by the crisis triggered by the assassination of Benazir Bhutto on December 27, 2007, during her campaign to be elected prime minister. Just twelve days earlier Musharraf had lifted his emergency order. Ultimately, the prime minister's job went to Syed Yousaf Raza Gillani, setting the stage for potential future clashes between the prime minister and president.[35] And Musharraf's resignation certainly does not preclude future turmoil.

Such turmoil can be a threat to Pakistan's political stability as well as to the security of the nation's nuclear weapons and fissile material. Key elements of the U.S. Intelligence Community, including the CIA, the Defense Intelligence Agency, the eavesdroppers of the NSA, and the National Reconnaissance Office, which operates both imagery and communications intelligence satellites, devote significant attention to monitoring the sites known to be associated with Pakistan's nuclear program as well as to determining where the nuclear components that make up the nation's 80 to 115 nuclear weapons are stored. That scrutiny was stepped up after Musharraf's declaration of emergency rule. Admiral Mike Mullen, in a mid-November 2007 Pentagon news conference, said, "I don't see any indication right now that security of those weapons is in jeopardy, but clearly we are very watchful, as we should be."[36]

But despite that effort, the U.S. government doesn't know "with absolute certainty . . . where they all are," according to a former U.S. official. Pakistan's desire to keep the United States in the dark about the locations was illustrated by its refusal to allow U.S. experts direct access to the bunkers where the components were stored, even though the United States provided almost $100 million in aid since 2001 to enhance Pakistan's nuclear security. That money purchased helicopters, night vision goggles, nuclear detection equipment, the construction of a nuclear security training center, fencing, and surveillance systems. It also included intrusion detectors and identification systems. On its own, Pakistan may have developed some form of permissive action links. But rather than permitting U.S. experts to visit Pakistani nuclear sites to install the equipment and instruct the Pakistanis on its operation, Pakistan sent its technicians to the United States for training. Nor have the Pakistanis been willing to show the equipment in action for fear of revealing too much about the locations of weapons bunkers and

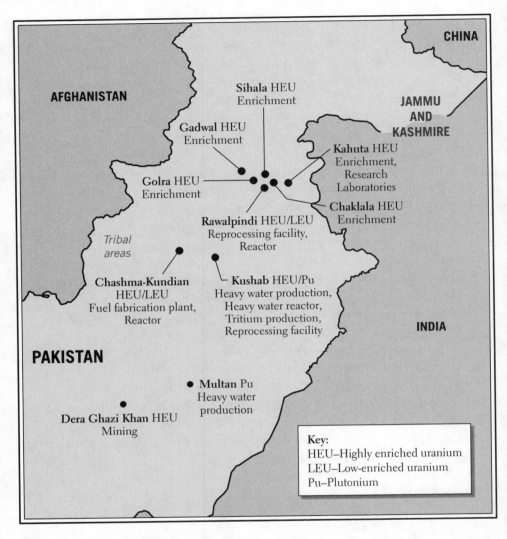

Pakistani Nuclear Sites (Sources: David E. Sanger, "So, What About Those Nukes?," *New York Times,* November 11, 2007, p. 8; Rodney W. Jones, Mark G. McDonough, with Toby F. Dalton, and Gregory D. Koblentz, *Tracking Nuclear Proliferation: A Guide in Maps and Charts* [Washington, D.C.: Carnegie Endowment for International Peace, 1998])

stored fissile material. To further complicate matters, the Pakistani military may have established phony bunkers that contain dummy warheads.[37]

Of course, Pakistani officials express confidence that the arsenal is secure. In a June 2007 briefing, Naeem Salik, an officer from the Strategic Plans Division, described security measures, including perimeter security (e.g., with closed-circuit TV cameras), transportation security, materiel control, and the Personnel Reliability Program. He also addressed the "perceptions and misperceptions" concerning Pakistan's arsenal such as worries about nuclear assets falling into the hands of "rogue generals" or "rogue scientists," an Islamist takeover, and the assassination or elimination of key leaders.[38]

Musharraf himself has claimed that the nation's arsenal is secure. In 2006, he appeared in a *New York Times* documentary, commenting that there was "no doubt" in his mind that Pakistan's nuclear weapons could "ever fall into the hands of extremists." He had previously claimed that his nation's nuclear protections "are already the best in the world." Those protections included restricting to a small group of senior officials—Musharraf and men he trusted—the authority to move or employ a nuclear device. In addition, he established within the National Command Authority the Strategic Plans Division, which is responsible for nuclear weapons operations and security.[39]

More recently, retired Lt. Gen. Khalid Kidwai, the division chief, stated that Pakistan's nuclear security apparatus is "second to none"—and includes a strictly controlled military chain of command, checks and balances, and the monitoring of scientists. He told foreign journalists, "There is no conceivable way Pakistan's military weapons are going to fall into the hands of extremists." Kidwai's position and that of the Strategic Plans Division were confirmed by an April 2008 announcement that the command-and-control system established under Musharraf would be maintained under the parliamentary coalition led by Syed Gillani.[40]

The division's senior officers are screened to eliminate candidates who are sympathetic to Islamic militants. Its Security Division is responsible for the Personnel Reliability Program, which monitors the activities of employees to uncover security risks. One employee was fired for passing out political pamphlets of an ultraconservative Islamic party and for encouraging colleagues to join him at a local mosque for party rallies. Kidwai is reported to have close ties to U.S. military officials. It was Kidwai who upgraded and expanded the Security Division. One American South Asia expert described him as "very impressive . . . Smart. Level-headed. Extremely competent in every respect" and in whom he had "a great deal of confidence in him as a wise custodian."[41]

In addition, Pakistan's practice of storing warheads, triggering devices, and delivery systems in different locales provides additional problems for those who might seek to seize them. Thieves, remarked Matthew Bunn of Harvard's Belfer Center for Science and International Affairs, would have to "knock over two buildings to get a complete bomb." He also noted that "theft would be more difficult to pull off, though presumably in a crisis that might change."[42]

Some U.S. officials have expressed confidence in Pakistan's ability to maintain control of its nuclear weapons. One U.S. officer told Reuters, a week after Musharaff's declaration that he had high confidence in the nation's military to maintain control, that "there has been no break." The *New York Times* reported that officials were relatively confident that even if Musharraf lost power or was killed, Pakistan still had reliable safeguards. Leonard Spector, a former Energy Department official and currently with the Monterey Institute of International Studies, believes that "only if there's a complete breakdown in society, would there be an issue," adding, "Even then, I think you'll find a cadre who protect the assets because it's the patrimony of the country." And according to Neil Joeck, an expert on Pakistan with the Lawrence Livermore National Laboratory, around 2000 "the military realized that they didn't have the sophisticated command and control they need." In addition, Joeck observed, the military's protections were strong and Pakistan's nuclear labs "very professional." John Brennan, a retired CIA official and former director of the National Counterterrorism Center, commented that Pakistan's nuclear safeguards are sufficient to resist "a fair amount of political commotion."[43]

Current government officials who appear to be satisfied with the state of Pakistan's nuclear security include State Department counterterrorism chief Dell Dailey and Deputy Director of National Intelligence for Analysis Thomas Fingar. Dailey told reporters that "the security of [Pakistan's] nuclear weapons has been first rate before, during and after the crisis the Pakistanis had." In congressional testimony he said that while "vulnerabilities exist," the Intelligence Community believed that "the ongoing political uncertainty in Pakistan has not seriously threatened the military's control of the nuclear arsenal."[44]

But others remain concerned, including David Albright, a physicist and former IAEA weapons inspector. "The control system is only as good as its weakest link," he observed. He also noted that "if there is [further] instability, Musharraf is going to have less ability to exercise control. . . . With tight controls and a strong leader you are OK. But if it becomes less stable, you could have fewer constraints and someone may grab an opportunity to steal something and sell it."[45]

He also commented that even if the military does not fragment and the components remain in their bunkers, there is a danger if the country is in chaos. "If stability doesn't return, you do have to worry about the thinking of the people with access to these things," he said. "As loyalties break down, they may look for an opportunity to make a quick buck. You may not be able to get the whole weapon, but maybe you can get the core."[46]

Matthew Bunn, who noted the difficulty of outside theft, still wonders about the reliability of some of the officers guarding the weapons. Referring to the 2003 assassination attempts, and the belief that there was inside support from Pakistani military officers, he wondered, "If that's what's going on with the military guarding the president, you have to wonder about what's going on with the military officers guarding the weapons."[47]

And Brennan himself noted that if the country goes beyond political commotion into civil war or anarchy, it would be impossible to reliably predict what would happen. "There are some scenarios in which the country slides into a situation of anarchy in which some of the more radical elements may be ascendant," he said. "If there is a collapse in the command-and-control structure—or if the armed forces fragment—that's a nightmare scenario. If there are different power centers within the army, they will each see the strategic arsenal as a real prize."[48]

Some analysts question whether there is anything the United States can do without Pakistani cooperation to secure those weapons. Pakistan, not surprisingly, has pledged to resist any attempt to seize its weapons. In December 2007, Gen. Tariq Majid, chairman of Pakistan's Joint Chiefs of Staff, objected to reports by "vested and hostile elements of the international media" about the security of the nation's nuclear weapons. "Suggestions have been made that our assets could either be neutralized or taken away towards [a] safer place to prevent them from falling into [the] wrong hands," reads a statement attributed to Majid. It also claimed that Pakistan's nuclear assets are very safe and secure, and the nation need not worry on that account. "There is a security system in place, which can ward off all threats, internal as well as external."[49]

Daniel Markey, a former State Department official who subsequently joined the Council on Foreign Relations, believes that "there is no good military option at all" and that any U.S. military operation to forcibly extract the weapons would lead to an "incredibly ugly scenario." A classified war game in 2006 revealed it to be an "unbelievably daunting problem," according to one participant.[50]

.   .   .

But U.S. officials may feel that it would be an even uglier scenario if Pakistan's nuclear weapons and fissile material fell into the hands of a government dominated by Islamic extremists sympathetic to Al-Qaeda or became vulnerable to seizure by the terrorist group. Two analysts have argued that the "United States could simply not stand by as a nuclear-armed Pakistan descended into the abyss." Danger would come in the event of "a complete collapse of Pakistani government control," with the vacuum being filled by Islamic extremist forces. One of those analysts also wrote that "were parts of Pakistan's arsenal to ever fall into the wrong hands, Al Qaeda could conceivably gain access to a nuclear device with terrifying results."[51]

There was, one official told NBC News, "a high degree of angst that the government would fall into the hands of bad guys and they would be in charge," who added that there were "some in the program who are sympathetic to the radicals." And former deputy director of central intelligence John McLaughlin noted, "I am confident of two things. That the Pakistanis are very serious about securing this material, but that someone in Pakistan is very intent on getting their hands on it." Thus, during her January 2005 confirmation hearings, Condoleezza Rice, when questioned about the issue, responded, "We have noted this problem, and we are prepared to try to deal with it. I would prefer not in open session to talk about this particular issue." Such contingency plans exist at the headquarters of the U.S. Central Command in Tampa, and such plans are "really, really black SAPs [Special Access Programs]," according to one expert on Pakistani terrorism—in a reference to "above top secret" programs.[52]

If U.S. officials do launch an operation to recover Pakistani nuclear weapons, without cooperation from that country's military, NEST may be a key component of that effort. Strategic analyst Bruce Blair wrote that "nuclear emergency search teams, which are trained in bomb detection and dismantling, should be ready to accompany such military operations. The teams, some from Nellis Air Force Base, in Nevada, know the basic design of Pakistani weapons from defectors' reports and could devise disabling procedures on the spot."[53]

Either scenario—one in which weapons wind up in the hands of Al-Qaeda or a takeover of the Pakistani government, the locations of nuclear devices not being known with certainty in both situations—could require NEST's search capabilities to locate them, and the capabilities of the Joint Technical Operations Team and Lincoln Gold Augmentation Team to help prepare the weapons for shipment to a safe location.

But if NEST personnel are sent into harm's way in Pakistan or elsewhere, they will need an escort. That escort may consist of a large-scale deployment of Army forces or a much smaller deployment involving one or more special units from the Joint Special Operations Command—Delta Force, the Naval Special Warfare Development Group (formerly Seal Team 6), the Intelligence Support Activity (Gray Fox). Also along might be members of the Army's 52nd Ordnance Group, whose insignia contains the words "Defusing Danger," or the Defense Technical Response Group, part of the Navy EOD Technical Division.

If U.S. Special Forces were to arrive as part of a cooperative operation with the Pakistanis to relocate or protect the arsenal, NEST might not be needed. Under other circumstances, such an operation would almost certainly be NEST's most dangerous deployment.

Chapter 12

CHALLENGES AHEAD

OCTOBER 22, 2006, was the final day in Mecca of Ramadan, the Islamic holy month. It was also, according to a message posted on the Internet on October 12, the day when seven National Football League (NFL) stadiums, including fields in New York, Seattle, Houston, and Miami, were to be hit with truck-delivered dirty bombs—attacks for which, the message predicted, Osama bin Laden would claim credit. The posting projected a death toll approaching a hundred thousand from the initial detonations. The author of the threats, who identified himself as "javness," promised that "in the aftermath civil wars will erupt across the world, both in the Middle East and within the United States. Global economies will screech to a halt. General chaos will result."[1]

The Department of Homeland Security notified local authorities, stadium owners, and the NFL, although from the beginning, it viewed the threat with "strong skepticism." A spokesman for the department revealed that there was no intelligence indicating that an attack was imminent, and explained that the alert was the result "of an abundance of caution." Within a week, FBI Special Agent Richard Kolko was able to tell the press, "This is a hoax."[2]

The FBI also knew that the hoaxer was Jake J. Brahm, a twenty-year-old grocery clerk from Wauwatosa, Wisconsin, whose threat was the result of a "writing duel" with a man from Texas who had the good sense, or good luck, not to post any threats. According to another bureau agent, "Brahm put out this threat thinking it was preposterous that no one would take it seriously. Unfortunately, he was wrong." As a result of that miscalculation, Brahm found himself facing a possible five-year prison sentence and $250,000 fine. In late February 2008, Brahm pleaded guilty in response to a one-count indictment which charged him with willfully conveying false information that the stadiums would be the targets of an attack by terrorists with radiological dispersal devices. Brahm was sentenced in June 2008 to six months in federal prison.[3]

.   .   .

For some, while the threat of nuclear terrorism may be more serious than a hoax from the imagination of a twenty-year-old grocery clerk, neither is it a looming catastrophe that requires a major national and international effort. John Mueller, a professor of political science at Ohio State University, dismisses as "fantasy" the fear that a new nuclear power will pass one or two bombs to friendly terrorists to deliver against some common enemy. He finds little reason to be concerned about the contacts between bin Laden and Pakistani scientists or the material recovered from Al-Qaeda facilities dealing with nuclear weapons. The prospect that a terrorist group will obtain an atomic bomb "seems to be vanishingly small," he observed in early 2008. Military analyst William Arkin poses the question, "Could terrorists really obtain sufficient materials and put together all of what would be needed to manufacture a nuclear weapon?" He also provides an answer: "not after 9/11."[4]

Also among the skeptics is Mark Fitzpatrick, a senior fellow for non-proliferation at the prestigious International Institute for Strategic Studies in London. Only about eighteen pounds of highly enriched uranium, not enough for even a single bomb, had leaked into the international black market, Fitzpatrick told reporters at an institute meeting in June 2007. Fitzpatrick's colleague, Robin Frost, argues that "the risk of nuclear terrorism, especially true nuclear terrorism employing bombs powered by nuclear fission, is overstated, and the popular wisdom on the topic is significantly flawed." Frost goes on to question that wisdom with regard to Russian nuclear weapons, the nuclear black market, improvised nuclear devices and dirty bombs, and potential state sponsors of nuclear terrorism.[5]

Others would argue that the threat is all too real and time is short. As noted earlier, Graham Allison, the director of Harvard's Belfer Center for Science and International Affairs, believes that "based on current trends, a nuclear terrorist attack on the United States is more likely than not in the decade ahead." Allison's colleague Matthew Bunn points to the November 8, 2007, attack on the South African nuclear facility at Pelindaba—where hundreds of pounds of weapons-grade highly enriched uranium are stored—as one among several causes for concern. Before the one group of intruders was chased off by a security force, another group disabled the detection systems at the site's perimeter, entered without setting off an alarm, and shot a worker in the emergency control center. After forty-five minutes inside the second perimeter, the intruders left via the hole they had cut in the fence. Another pessimist is Gen. Eugene E. Habiger, who is in the "not if, but when" camp. The main title of a November 2007 statement presented by an official of the Federal Emergency Management Agency to a Senate committee on the subject of dirty bombs was "Not a Matter of 'If', But of 'When.'" IAEA chief Mohammed ElBaradei characterized the nuclear material falling into the hands of extremists as an imminent threat.[6]

But while acts of nuclear terrorism may not be inevitable, or have a better than 50-50 chance of taking place, they may still be considered a serious threat and worth significant attention, because even if the probability of such an attack is low, the costs would be very high. A 2006 RAND study examined the likely costs in lives, property, dollars, and disruption following the detonation of a ten-kiloton device smuggled into the Port of Long Beach in a shipping container. Sixty thousand lives and six hundred thousand homes would be lost. One billion square feet of commercial property would be destroyed while three million people would be evacuated for three years. The financial costs associated with all those consequences, when added to the costs of the damage to the port and surrounding infrastructure and worker's compensation claims, would total about $1 trillion.[7]

It might indeed be possible for a terrorist group—whether it be Al-Qaeda, Aum Shinrikyo, or another organization—to raise the money, recruit the personnel, assemble the machinery, and acquire the HEU to build an improvised device. Or in some circumstances, efforts to deter a regime from passing on its nuclear weapons to a terrorist group might fail. Events that prevent deterrence from being effective could include the impending defeat and dismantlement of a nuclear-armed rogue regime or the complete collapse of a government's authority combined with a military sympathetic to terrorists' cause.[8]

And although the damage from a dirty bomb attack—the type threatened in Jake Brahm's hoax—would be significantly less than that from a nuclear detonation, it would still be significant. Indeed, according to one former NEST member, the issue of a dirty bomb has been considered "more sensitive" than the threat of a stolen or improvised nuclear device because a dirty bomb is so much more likely to occur. It requires material that is more plentiful and less securely held than weapons-grade plutonium or highly enriched uranium. Just as important, the task of building a dirty bomb is dramatically easier than constructing a device to produce a nuclear yield—the former being well within the ability of solitary individuals.[9]

· · ·

Certainly, it is the judgment of the U.S. Intelligence Community that Al-Qaeda remains interested in inflicting nuclear devastation on the United States. In February 2007, Lt. Gen. Michael D. Maples, director of the Defense Intelligence Agency, told the Senate Armed Services Committee that "reporting continues to indicate that non-state actors, specifically al-Qaida, continue to pursue CBRN options." In May, FBI chief Robert Mueller told an interviewer that bin Laden desperately wanted to obtain nuclear devices and explode them in American cities, especially New York and Washington. That July, the authors of a national intelligence estimate, *The Terrorist Threat to the US Homeland*, wrote that "al-Qa'ida will continue to acquire and employ, chemical, biological, radiological, or nuclear material in attacks and would not hesitate to use them if it develops what it deems is sufficient capability." Rolf Mowatt-Larssen, the head of the Energy Department's Office of Intelligence and Counterintelligence, is one of those convinced that Al-Qaeda is trying to acquire a nuclear bomb. In April 2008 he told a Senate committee, "Today, al-Qa'ida's nuclear intent remains clear."[10]

Seconding the U.S. assessment was a Russian security officer, who in October 2007 told an international conference of security experts that terrorists were increasing their efforts to obtain the raw materials to produce a dirty bomb.[11]

The assessment of American and Russian intelligence analysts that Al-Qaeda remains interested in weapons of mass destruction, including nuclear or radiological weapons, is backed up by the words and actions of the terrorist group's leadership and members. In a September 2006 audiotape, Abu Hamza al-Muhajir (aka Abu Ayyub al-Masri), the leader of Al-Qaeda in Iraq, called on experts in "chemistry, physics, electronics . . . and all other sciences—especially nuclear scientists and explosive experts"—to join his group's war against the West. "We are in dire need of you," he said. He also promised professional satisfaction. "The field of jihad can satisfy your scientific ambitions, and the large American bases [in Iraq] are good places to test your unconventional weapons, whether biological or dirty."[12]

In November 2007, an alleged Al-Qaeda operative and two supporters were put on trial in Germany. According to the German prosecutor, the thirty-two-year-old leader of the group trained in a camp in Afghanistan and fought against U.S. and allied troops during their post-9/11 invasion of Afghanistan. Subsequently, he moved to Germany on bin Laden's orders. Once there, the prosecutor charged, he searched for supporters to finance Al-Qaeda activities as well as obtain radioactive material for a dirty bomb.[13]

Preventing Al-Qaeda or some other terrorist group or nuclear extortionist from obtaining a nuclear weapon or producing a dirty bomb can be achieved by a variety of measures. In some instances, one approach might be sufficient. In other cases a combination of counterterrorist activities might prove successful in preventing a mushroom cloud from forming over Manhattan or the explosive dispersal of radioactivity across parts of Washington.

Officially, the "First Line of Defense" is the Materials Protection, Control, and Accounting (MPC&A) activity, the assistance given to Russia, Pakistan, and other nations to improve their ability to inventory and maintain control over their nuclear weapons as well as fissile and other nuclear material. Another component of the effort to prevent nuclear material from falling into the wrong hands is to assist nations to locate radioactive sources, such as the radioisotope thermoelectric generators distributed across Russia. Arranging the transfer of HEU or plutonium from insecure to secure locations and diluting it into a useless form are other elements of the effort. One manifestation of this continuing effort is the agreement signed in November 2007 by Secretary of Energy Samuel W. Bodman and the director of the Russian Federal Atomic Energy Agency. The agreement will result in thirty-four tons of surplus uranium from Russia's weapons program being converted into mixed oxide fuel, which would then be irradiated in a reactor at the Beloyarsk Nuclear Power Plant.[14]

In order to enhance the U.S. ability to conduct such programs, the Nuclear Materials Information Program (NMIP) was established on August 28, 2006, when President Bush signed NSPD 48/HSPD 17. The program is an interagency effort managed by the Energy Department's Office of Intelligence and Counterintelligence. Its goal is to consolidate information from all sources concerning worldwide holdings and security status of nuclear materials.[15]

The effort to establish radiation detectors and detection systems at foreign border crossings, airports, and port areas (under the Megaports Initiative) constitutes the Second Line of Defense Program. In December 2005, the United States and Israel signed an agreement to install detection equipment at the Israeli seaport of Haifa. Initial operations of radiation detection equipment began in January 2008. As of November 2007, the

United States and Russia agreed to equip all of Russia's border crossings, a total of 350 sites, with radiation detection systems by the end of 2011. Radiation detection equipment was also being installed in Greece, Slovakia, and a number of former Soviet republics. In December, the National Nuclear Security Administration agreed to provide the Cypriot Customs Service with an upgraded radiation-monitoring portal for the Port of Limassol. Two months later, in late February, the NNSA and Malaysia agreed to install radiation detection equipment at Port Klang and the Port of Tanjung Pelepas. Approximately seventy-five ports across the world are to be equipped with equipment to screen cargo containers for nuclear or radioactive material.[16]

Closer to home is the deployment of similar detection systems at U.S. ports, border crossings, and airports, reminiscent of the 1950s initiative that followed the Panofsky report. By May 2005, the Department of Homeland Security had installed more than 470 radiation portal monitors at sites throughout the United States. It had deployed 670 portal monitors by the end of that year and intended to install a total of 3,035 by September 2009—at twenty-three international mail and package handling facilities, 205 land border crossings, 106 seaport terminals, and international airports. The monitors in place by February 2006 gave the United States, according to Homeland Security's Customs and Border Protection directorate, the ability to screen about 32 percent of all seaborne shipments carried in containers, 90 percent of commercial trucks and 80 percent of private vehicles entering from Canada, and approximately 88 percent of all commercial trucks and 74 percent of all private vehicles entering from Mexico. In December 2007, the department reported that it had deployed more than a thousand radiation detection devices to U.S. land and sea ports of entry. In addition, according to a Homeland Security press release, 100 percent of cargo containers crossing the southern border are scanned for radiation, 91 percent of cargo at the northern border is scanned, and more than 97 percent of vehicles are scanned at U.S. seaports.[17*]

And Colorado Springs is not the only city to have radiation detectors placed at assorted locations within or around it. In early 2007, the New York Times reported that the federal government, as part of the Securing the Cities experiment, planned to install an elaborate network of radiation detec-

---

*According to two scientists with the Natural Resources Defense Council, the radiation monitors at U.S. ports (as well as ones planned for the future) are not a reliable means for detecting highly enriched uranium. See Thomas B. Cochran and Matthew G. McKinzie, "Detecting Nuclear Smuggling," Scientific American, April 2008, pp. 98–104.

tors on some of the bridges, tunnels, roadways, and waterways that carried traffic into New York City, creating a fifty-mile zone around the city.[18]

Meanwhile, in late 2007, the Homeland Security and Energy departments (almost certainly including NEST) were working with Chicago law enforcement officials to equip helicopters with gamma radiation detection equipment. The city would be able to use such helicopters to conduct aerial surveys to map current and legal sources of radiation, such as those employed in medical facilities. But they would also have another use, the deputy undersecretary for counterterrorism, Steven Aoki, told a Senate committee. They could give the Chicago police a NEST-like capability to support the hunt for an individual or group with a dirty bomb or other radioactive source. While the city's police could be assisting the FBI in their on-the-ground investigative efforts, the helicopters could be assisting NEST in its search for radioactive signatures.[19]

Two years earlier, the New York Police Department, which had a $30 million grant from the Department of Homeland Security to develop a regional radiological detection and monitoring system, had requested that the Department of Energy measure background radiation and locate hot spots in all five boroughs by helicopter. The effort, which consumed about four weeks and over a hundred flight-hours, was completed in the summer of 2005, at a cost of approximately $800,000. According to a Government Accountability Office report, NYPD officers, in the course of conducting the survey, were "accompanied by DOE scientists and technicians" (in other words, NEST members) and identified over eighty locations with unexplained radiological sources. Each of the hot spots, most of which turned out to be medical isotopes located at medical facilities, was investigated. Knowledge of the locations will allow the NYPD to separate real threats from false alarms—and reduce the chance of an unnecessary NEST deployment.[20]

A less publicized effort to keep terrorists from detonating a nuclear device in an American city was launched in June 2003, when President Bush signed NSPD 28, "Nuclear Weapons Command, Control, Safety, and Security." One component of the directive was the instruction to the nation's nuclear weapons laboratories to develop technology that would make any new U.S. nuclear weapon virtually impossible to use if it were to fall into terrorists' hands. In response, scientists are working on technology that would cause the destruction of every component inside—including the plutonium and uranium—if anyone tampered with the weapon.[21]

·   ·   ·

The man in charge of much of the effort to provide radiation detection capabilities, both overseas and in the United States, is Vayl Oxford, a graduate of West Point and the Air Force Institute of Technology who became a professor of aeronautics at the Air Force Academy. Oxford went on to become director for counterproliferation at the Defense Nuclear Agency and Defense Special Weapons Agency (1993–1998) and then the National Security Council. In between, he served as deputy director for technology development at the Defense Threat Reduction Agency.* Reportedly a protégé of Vice President Dick Cheney, who was unhappy with Homeland Security's progress in developing radiation detectors, Oxford, in September 2005, was handed the reins of a newly created office in Homeland Security, the Domestic Nuclear Detection Office or DNDO (pronounced "din-doe"), established by a presidential directive that April.[22]

The directive assigned the new office responsibility for developing and deploying nuclear and radiological capabilities and enhancing those capabilities through "an aggressive, expedited, evolutionary, and transformational program of research." DNDO's installation of state-of-the-art portals and distribution of handheld radiation detection equipment represented its attempt to fulfill the first part of that mandate.[23]

Three programs, if they are successful, would satisfy the second part of the mandate. The Advanced Spectroscopic Portals (ASP) program is one. Current detectors cannot distinguish between naturally occurring radioactive material, such as that in granite tiles, and materials associated with a nuclear device or dirty bomb. A successful ASP program would produce detectors that can distinguish between the two. The Cargo Advanced Automated Radiography System (CAARS) program is to produce an imaging system that can detect, within cargo, high-density material—providing a warning sign that something in the cargo might be shielding threatening materials from the ASP detectors. The third transformation program is the Mobile and Human Portable Radiation Detection Systems effort, intended to produce radiation detection systems capable of being held by hand (five pounds) or carried in a backpack (fifteen or twenty pounds) for law enforce-

---

*The Defense Nuclear Agency became the Defense Special Weapons Agency in 1996. In 1998, the newly created Defense Threat Reduction Agency absorbed the Defense Special Weapons Agency, the Defense Technology Administration, and the On-Site Inspection Agency. See Joseph P. Harahan and Robert J. Bennett, Defense Threat Reduction Agency, *Creating the Defense Threat Reduction Agency*, January 2002, pp. 9–10, 82.

ment. An improved capability for detection and identification of isotopes is an intended feature.[24]

The assorted efforts to keep nuclear material out of the hands of international criminals and terrorists, as well as to increase the chance of detecting nuclear smugglers who might try to move their contraband across international borders or ships containing nuclear cargo, have produced a number of successes and advances. Many Russian nuclear weapons sites are more secure than they were a decade ago, weapons-grade uranium or plutonium has been either blended into less dangerous substances or moved from vulnerable locations, and nuclear reactors have been converted so they employ low-enriched uranium fuel, which cannot be used to make nuclear bombs.[25]

But commentary and criticism, from outside experts as well as government auditors, suggest that the mission of creating an architecture that would eliminate the prospect of nuclear terrorism, or at least reduce the probability of such an event to the lowest level feasible, is far from accomplished. Thus, the congressional Government Accountability Office noted the progress made in enhancing security at Russian nuclear sites, but questioned whether the upgrades can be sustained in the long run. The office has also questioned the priorities assigned by the Department of Energy in securing radiological sources, particularly the emphasis on securing medical facilities rather than waste storage facilities and radio thermal generators, where "the most dangerous sources" are to be found.[26]

DNDO has been the subject of criticism in several GAO reports. In March 2007, the congressional office charged that the office's assessment of the advanced spectroscopic portals did not fully support the detection office's procurement decision and that DNDO had not made sufficient effort to understand the strengths and limitations of the current portals. Then in September, the accountability office issued a report alleging that federal program managers had rigged testing of the portals to certify that the equipment was reliable, noting that contractors had been allowed to collect data about the types of radioactive material to be used in the tests of the portals. The contractors were then able to set the portals' detection capabilities to maximize their ability to detect those specific types of materials. As a result of the allegations, the program was halted in late 2007. Outside experts questioned whether the objectives of Oxford and DNDO's transformational research are even theoretically feasible, and suggested that Oxford "is fighting the laws of physics."[27]*

A mid-2008 review by the Government Accountability Office concluded that while DNDO had taken positive steps to develop a global nuclear detection architecture, it lacked "an overarching strategic" plan to guide its path to a more comprehensive architecture. A review by the Congressional Research Service, published at the same time as the GAO report, noted a potential problem as a result of the office's heavy reliance on detailees or liaison personnel from other government agencies and contractors—a loss of institutional memory that could make long-term efforts difficult to sustain.[28]

False alarms, even with equipment that works as promised, can be a serious problem. One of those with firsthand experience is Glen Neilson, a Customs and Border Protection officer who was working at Pier A at the Port of Long Beach in 2007 when he heard his computer's voice announce, "Gamma Alert!" It was the fifth alert in the previous five minutes, one of about five hundred experienced at the Long Beach and Los Angeles ports each day, and was apparently triggered by a rusty yellow container. Neilson ordered the truck hauling the container to a secondary inspection station and checked the container's shipping manifest. The container was supposed to contain window shutters from China.[29]

At Neilson's orders, officers used a four-foot bolt cutter to open the

---

*The ASP Independent Review Team, chaired by an official of the Homeland Security Institute and whose members were drawn from a variety of the Energy Department's laboratories and former Defense Department operational test and evaluation officials, found that the "ASP could—if it performs in the field as intended . . . reduce some key uncertainties in the nation's ability to counter the threat of nuclear smuggling." In testimony before Congress, Vayl Oxford stated that the team concurred with the Government Accountability Office that some tests were "not designed to measure the range of ASP performance" but did not agree with the GAO that ASP testing had relied on "biased test methods that enhanced the performance of the ASPs." See George F. Thompson, Homeland Security Institute, "Nuclear Smuggling Detection: Recent Tests of Advanced Spectroscopic Portal (ASP) Monitors; Final Report of the ASP Independent Review Team (IRT)," Statement before House Committee on Homeland Security, March 5, 2008, p. 7; Vayl S. Oxford, Domestic Nuclear Detection Office, "Nuclear Smuggling Detection: Recent Tests of Advanced Spectroscopic Portal (ASP) Monitors," Statement before House Committee on Homeland Security, March 5, 2008, p. 8.

container. They then used a handheld isotope scanner to see if they could locate the source of the radiation. It took ten minutes before they discovered that the source was not a nuclear device, a dirty bomb, or an inanimate object of any kind. It was the big-rig driver, who had received a dose of medical radiation, leading him, he complained, to "[set] off radiation monitors all over the port."[30]

More than one observer has noted the ease with which narcotics, including large shipments of marijuana, are smuggled into the United States by land, sea, and air, as well as the ability of people to cross into the United States from its northern or southern neighbors. The ability to evade security systems has also been noted, along with the lapses of security personnel and equipment. In March 2006, the Associated Press revealed that a study conducted for the Department of Homeland Security found that lapses by private firms at foreign and American ports, aboard ships, and with respect to trains and trucks "would enable unmanifested materials or weapons of mass destruction to be introduced into the supply chain." Cargo containers, the study revealed, could be opened secretly while in transit to allow items to be inserted or removed.[31]

Even more dramatic and disturbing was another Government Accountability Office report in March 2006, which revealed that undercover investigators were able to slip radioactive material, sufficient for two dirty bombs, across U.S. borders in Texas and Washington State in December 2005. The good news was that alarms at the sites were triggered when the radiation detectors picked up the small quantities of cesium-137, a prime candidate for use in a dirty bomb, that the investigators were trying to bring into the country. The bad news was that customs agents allowed the investigators to enter the United States because the agents were duped by counterfeit Nuclear Regulatory Commission documents which authorized the individual named to receive, possess, and transfer radioactive material.[32]

While various measures to prevent nuclear terrorism can be visualized as successive layers, with the first (security of foreign nuclear facilities) being the most distant from the U.S. homeland, the second being closer (foreign border crossings), and the third still closer (U.S. points of entry), there are other measures that do not quite fit into such a sequential framework. One of those is intelligence.

In the wake of 9/11, preventing another terrorist attack on the United States, particularly a nuclear terrorist attack, is the primary objective of the sixteen-member U.S. Intelligence Community. Some of the members are more crucial to attaining that objective than others. There are the analysts responsible for sorting through and making sense of the voluminous data gathered by several agencies. Those analysts work for the National Counterterrorism Center (subordinate to the Office of the Director of National Intelligence), the CIA's Counterterrorism Center, the State Department's Bureau of Intelligence and Research, the Department of the Treasury, the Defense Intelligence Agency, the Office of Naval Intelligence, the Office of Intelligence and Counterintelligence in the Department of Energy, as well as Z Division of the Lawrence Livermore National Laboratory.

Key agencies providing them with data are the National Security Agency, which intercepts communications and other electronic signals; the National Reconnaissance Office, the developer and operator of the nation's spy satellites; the CIA, which recruits and runs spies as well as engaging in technical collection operations; and the Defense HUMINT Service, a part of the Defense Intelligence Agency that also recruits and runs spies. In addition, a multitude of foreign intelligence and security services, through liaison arrangements with the United States, share intelligence on a wide variety of targets, including terrorists' targets.

The intelligence they provide can be relevant to each aspect of preventing nuclear terrorists from building or stealing a nuclear device or dirty bomb and then detonating it at the location of their choice. Intelligence operations may identify foreign nuclear installations and provide data on the level of security, allow analysts to assess the effectiveness of border security for countries of interest, detect illicit nuclear trafficking, disclose transfers of terrorist funding, or provide information on the attempts by terrorist groups to build or buy a nuclear device or dirty bomb.

Thus, the CIA was eventually able to penetrate the nuclear trafficking operation of Pakistan's A. Q. Khan, a penetration that ultimately led to the unraveling of the network. The agency reportedly was able to recruit an employee of the Scomi Precision Engineering (SCOPE) corporation, a Malaysian-based company established by associates of Khan, ostensibly to produce high-tech components for use in the oil industry. The employee actually supervised production of centrifuge components, which were loaded on a ship, the BBC *China*, headed for Libya—information he apparently provided the CIA. The ship was intercepted by agents from the United States and the other countries. The interception led in part to Libya ending its nuclear program and providing the United States with intelligence about its nuclear suppliers, including Khan.[33]

Intelligence operations might also reveal terrorist plots in time to stop them. The interrogation of Abu Zubaydah led to the identification of would-be dirty bomber Jose Padilla. Communications intercepts have led to the disruption of a number of non-nuclear terrorist plots as well as the apprehension of key terrorists. Pre-9/11 successes due in whole or in part to communications intelligence include a planned Al-Qaeda attack on American overseas diplomatic or military establishments, including the Prince Sultan Air Base in Saudi Arabia (1998), a planned attack on U.S. military installations in Saudi Arabia (June 2001), and a planned attack on U.S. diplomatic facilities in Paris (about June 2001).[34]

Post-9/11 communications intelligence successes with regard to terrorism include the location and arrest of Abu Zubaydah, along with nineteen Al-Qaeda operatives (March 2002); the arrest of Sheikh Ahmed Salim, wanted for his role in the 1998 embassy bombings (July 2002); the arrest of Ramzi Binalshibh, one of the Al-Qaeda planners for 9/11 (September 2002); and the arrest of 9/11 mastermind Khalid Sheikh Mohammad (March 2003).[35]

An attempt to produce an improvised nuclear device might certainly be subject to detection by America's spies. According to Peter Zimmerman, if an IND plot is in motion, "you might see it when it sticks its nose above the parapet." Such a plot would require, as Zimmerman and Lewis noted, a supply organization, land (such as the Australian ranch purchased by Aum Shinrikyo), shipping and purchasing activity, and a contingent of people to build the device, conceivably as many as one hundred. And then there is the problem of moving money to pay suppliers, including the supplier of fissile material.[36]

Of course, not only can intelligence help prevent a nuclear terrorist attack, but also in the event one occurs, it may be able to identify the entity responsible for the attack (assuming that entity doesn't claim credit) and those who contributed, particularly by providing a bomb or components. The same can be said for nuclear forensics, an activity that might help scientists determine whose arsenal a bomb came from or where the nuclear material for an improvised device or a dirty bomb originated—a determination known as attribution. Attribution can provide the justification for retribution as well as the demand for restitution. It can thus serve to deter those who might wish to aid a terrorist attack but only if they can count on their role going unnoticed.

The U.S. nuclear forensics effort is mandated by NSPD 17, "National Strategy to Combat Weapons of Mass Destruction," signed by President Bush in 2002. The unclassified version of the directive states that "an effective response requires rapid attribution." With the intention of providing a means of centralizing planning and integrating nuclear attribution efforts that are spread across the federal government, DNDO established its National Technical Nuclear Forensics Center in 2006. Entities with nuclear forensics capabilities include Lawrence Livermore (its Forensic Science Center), other national labs, and the Defense Threat Reduction Agency.[37]

Nuclear forensic techniques used to determine the responsibility of a nuclear detonation on U.S. or allied territory overlap U.S. efforts to gather intelligence about the design, fissile material, and other characteristics of foreign nuclear weapons. In the unlikely event that a detonation were to occur in a remote part of the United States, its precise location could be determined by a number of U.S. satellites, including the Defense Support Program and Global Positioning System satellites, which are equipped with nuclear detonation detection packages. Any nuclear debris emitted into the atmosphere, a highly likely consequence of a terrorist detonation since the blast would almost certainly be above ground, would be key evidence to settling a variety of questions about the characteristics of the bomb. However, in all but one case (the 1979 Vela incident),* determining the entities (nations) that have detonated devices has never been an issue since they have been detonated within territories controlled by the state responsible for the detonation. Also, for detonations on its own or allied soil, the United States would have access to debris from the point of detonation and to the territory immediately around ground zero, access the U.S. government did not have when the Soviet Union or China detonated a device.[38]

---

*On September 22, 1979, an Air Force Vela nuclear detonation detection satellite registered a double light flash that seemed to indicate the detonation of a nuclear weapon somewhere in the South Atlantic. Despite suspicion that either South Africa or Israel (or both) had tested a nuclear device, the United States was unable to gather any nuclear debris, and the issue of whether a device was actually tested has not been determined definitively—at least as far as what is known publicly. See Jeffrey T. Richelson, *Spying on the Bomb: American Nuclear Intelligence from Nazi Germany to Iran and North Korea* (New York: W. W. Norton, 2006), pp. 283–316.

The possibility of attribution stems from the fact that every nuclear weapon has distinct signatures. These include physical, chemical, elemental, and isotopic properties that provide clues as to what material was in the weapon and its construction. The shape, size, and texture of the nuclear material would determine the bomb's physical signatures. The bomb's unique molecular components would determine the device's chemical signatures. Alternative reprocessing techniques leave behind trace amounts of specific organic compounds or elements that suggest certain technical approaches were employed. Isotopic signatures of the material can reveal whether it has been in a nuclear reactor, and serve as a fingerprint for the type and operating conditions of a given reactor. They can also assist in determining the age of the material, which would provide additional clues about its origins.[39]

The signatures detected can help analysts ascertain the type of reactor from which the plutonium came, or indicate the likely enrichment process that produced the uranium. By comparing the results of the initial analysis to a database of known reactor types or of samples of HEU produced by different enrichment processes, forensic workers might determine the origin of the material or at least narrow the field of viable suspects, eventually pinning the blame on the culprit with the assistance of additional intelligence and data.[40]

In addition, analysis of debris scooped out of the air by specially equipped aircraft might allow nuclear forensic analysts to estimate bomb efficiency. That information could reveal who built it. Current computer programs can assist in debris analysis by estimating the predetonation isotopic mixture, which when combined with data on the isotopic mixture after the detonation might make it possible to infer the efficiency of the bomb and its design. Knowledge of the bomb's design can narrow down the weapon's possible origins. As Ted Taylor argued, and it remains true today, it would be extremely unlikely for a terrorist group to build its own hydrogen or boosted implosion weapon (using tritium and deuterium) without state assistance. On the other hand, if the source of debris were determined to be a crude, gun-type uranium bomb, that would indicate the serious possibility that the device was made without assistance.[41]

A number of organizations can provide previously acquired data such as samples to be used as part of the attribution process. Included would be the CIA, the Defense Intelligence Agency, the Air Force Technical Applications Center, which operates the U.S. Atomic Energy Detection System, the national laboratories (including Los Alamos and Lawrence Livermore), Z Division, and NEST, with its database of known weapons designs.

But there is no guarantee that America's attribution capability would be sufficient to deter some groups, partly because attribution can be a prolonged process with no guarantee of success, especially if the samples that would match those from a device's debris might not be in the hands of the United States or any of its allies. Confidence that the United States does not have samples of a country's nuclear DNA might make that country willing to provide terrorists with a bomb or nuclear material. Thus, while a robust attribution capability might reduce the probability of a terrorist operation to detonate a bomb in the United States, it does not preclude such an operation.[42]

If efforts by the United States and other nations fail to safeguard nuclear weapons and material, to prevent illicit trafficking, and to prevent nuclear material or a complete weapon from entering the country, whether through radiation detection at foreign and U.S. borders or via satellites and spies, there is a last line of defense. It includes the secret soldiers of the Joint Special Operations Command, the military's explosive ordnance disposal units, the FBI, and NEST.

NEST faces a number of challenges in ensuring that it is prepared to deal with extortionists or nuclear terrorists. One is that NEST and its various elements, whether the Search Response Team or the Lincoln Gold Augmentation Team, stay in practice. Deployment for national special security events is one means of doing so. As noted earlier, twenty-seven such events occurred between 1998 and February 2007. Continued participation in exercises such as the yearly Topoff is another. The most recent version of Topoff, Topoff 4, which was conducted concurrently with the U.S. Northern Command's Vigilant Shield' 08 exercise, took place over five days in mid-October 2007 in Arizona, Oregon, and Guam—which fall in the Northern and Pacific Commands area of responsibility. The exercise, which involved fifteen thousand participants, centered around a series of dirty bomb threats and incidents, including the prevention of such an attack—the prime rationale for NEST's existence.[43]

Beyond practice, the exercises also provide an opportunity for NEST and the multitude of other government agencies involved in nuclear counterterrorist operations to learn to work with each other. In addition to the considerable number of organizations that have been involved in one or more aspect of such activities for several years—NEST, other elements of the Energy Department, components of the Department of Defense, and

NATIONAL SPECIAL SECURITY EVENTS 1998–2007

EVENT	LOCATION	DATE
World Energy Council Meeting	Houston, Texas	Sep. 13–17, 1998
NATO 50th Anniversary Celebration	Washington, D.C.	Apr. 23–25, 1999
World Trade Organization Meeting	Seattle, Wash.	Nov. 29–Dec. 3, 1999
State of the Union Address	Washington, D.C.	Jan. 27, 2000
International Monetary Fund Spring Meeting	Washington, D.C.	Apr. 14–17, 2000
International Naval Review (OpSail)	New York, N.Y.	July 3–9, 2000
Republican National Convention	Philadelphia, Pa.	July 29–Aug. 4, 2000
Democratic National Convention	Los Angeles, Calif.	Aug. 14–16, 2000
Presidential Inauguration	Washington, D.C.	Jan. 20, 2001
Presidential Address to Congress	Washington, D.C.	Feb. 27, 2001
United Nations General Assembly 56	New York, N.Y.	Nov. 10–16, 2001
State of the Union Address	Washington, D.C.	Jan. 29, 2002
Super Bowl XXXVI	New Orleans, La.	Feb. 3, 2002
Winter Olympic Games	Salt Lake City, Utah	Feb. 8–24, 2002
Super Bowl XXXVII	San Diego, Calif.	Jan. 26, 2003
State of the Union Address	Washington, D.C.	Jan. 20, 2004
Super Bowl XXXVIII	Houston, Texas	Feb. 1, 2004
Sea Island G8 Summit	Sea Island, Ga.	June 8–10, 2004
President Reagan State Funeral	Washington, D.C.	June 11, 2004
Democratic National Convention	Boston, Mass.	July 26–29, 2004
Republican National Convention	New York, N.Y.	Aug. 30–Sep. 2, 2004
Presidential Inauguration	Washington, D.C.	Jan. 20, 2005
State of the Union Address	Washington, D.C.	Feb. 2, 2005
Super Bowl XXXIX	Jacksonville, Fla.	Feb. 6, 2005
Super Bowl XL	Deetroit, Mich.	Feb. 5, 2006
President Ford State Funeral	Washington, D.C.	Jan. 3, 2007
Super Bowl XLI	Miami Gardens, Fla.	Feb. 4, 2007

Source: Shawn Reese, Congressional Research Service, *National Special Security Events*, November 6, 2007.

the Environmental Protection Agency—there are newcomers, such as the Department of Homeland Security and its nuclear detection office. Thus, even if existing organizations have established a smooth working relationship, new exercises can help integrate the newer organizations into the operational environment.

NEST also faces an environment in which radiation detection activities are far more diffused than in earlier years, even more than a decade ago. In addition to the federal government's monitoring, local governments such as Colorado Springs, Washington, New York, and Chicago, as mentioned earlier, have radiation detection capabilities. This diffusion presents both opportunities and problems for NEST. The multiple efforts can provide earlier warning than in the past, and NEST might be able to call on trained personnel from these localities to assist in searches. But there is also a greater chance of false alarms, which could cause completely unnecessary NEST deployments.

NEST faces other challenges as well, beyond patrolling the area near Super Bowls, participating in exercises, working in cooperation with other federal agencies, and possibly having to respond to locally generated false alarms. Many of those challenges were noted in the Sewell report a dozen years ago. One consistently mentioned by NEST veterans is the need to recruit qualified personnel, a challenge made more difficult by a lack of U.S. weapons design efforts. The veterans worry that it will be impossible to maintain a cadre of individuals who are technically equipped to deal with the challenges NEST faces, from understanding the design of weapons to figuring out how to dismantle them. NEST veteran Alan Mode commented that as a result, the younger generation at the labs "wouldn't have a clue what a bomb looked like" and people with real experience are aging. As far back as 1996, the Energy Department was warned of a growing talent shortage because nuclear scientists were retiring. Congress's cancellation of a new nuclear warhead program in December 2007, however justified it might be on other grounds, certainly doesn't help.[44]

It is also important to maintain qualified personnel who can evaluate the credibility of any communicated nuclear threats, whether they be issued by a twenty-year-old grocery clerk or a group or individual more likely to be serious. Today, the central authority for the assessment of such threats is the NAP Communications and Coordination Center, the successor to the Department of Energy's Communicated Threat Credibility Center at Lawrence Livermore. Assessments are performed by personnel at Livermore and Los Alamos as well as by behavioral scientists on the East Coast.[45]

Another challenge facing NEST is to maintain a sufficiently large arsenal of detection equipment—handheld devices, attache cases equipped with detectors, vans, and aircraft—so that it can carry out its mission, possibly in multiple locations, when called upon. But as of mid-2003, NEST had only four helicopters and three fixed-wing aircraft at Nellis and Andrews air bases. The Energy Department's inspector general warned that the team's top aircraft sometimes were unavailable to carry out missions, and contingency plans were lacking.[46]

At the same time, various national laboratories have been working on extending NEST's capabilities in a variety of ways. Over the last several years, scientists at Los Alamos, to assist NEST in understanding and disabling such weapons, have developed a catalog of crude designs that a terrorist group might use to build a nuclear weapon.[47]

The labs have also been working on extending detection capabilities. Scientists at Argonne National Laboratory developed a small portable detector whose heart is a small wafer of gallium arsenide, which when coated with boron or lithium can detect the neutrons emitted by fissile material. Raymond Klann, head of the group at Argonne that produced the new detector, noted that "the working portion of the wafer is about the diameter of a collar button, but thinner."[48]

Then there is the handheld Cryo3 detector, developed in a collaborative effort between Lawrence Berkeley, Los Alamos, and Lawrence Livermore laboratories. The device, based on the radiation-sensitive element germanium, detects the gamma-ray "fingerprints" of radioactive materials. In addition, Los Alamos scientists developed a detector that can see through lead and other heavy shielding in truck trailers and cargo containers to detect uranium, plutonium, and other dense materials. The technique, muon radiography, is far more sensitive than X-rays, with none of the radiation hazards of the X-ray or gamma-ray detectors in use at U.S. borders.[49]

Another handheld device is the RadNet detector. It combines a cellular telephone, a personal digital assistant with Internet access, and a global positioning system locator with a radiation sensor. Data collected by the units can be transmitted and plotted to a geographic map, allowing NEST or other users to determine the exact location of high-radiation signals from possible clandestine nuclear materials or devices. The detector is also able to eliminate false alarms due to background radiation emitted by food, medical devices, soil, or other nonthreatening radiation sources.[50]

In September 2007, *Scientific American* reported that Los Alamos had developed a method to search for heavy elements such as uranium via muons, subatomic particles from space formed from the collision of cosmic rays with molecules in the upper atmosphere. By 2008, "'muon tomography' might be guarding U.S. borders"—and be available to members of the NEST search teams. Each minute, approximately ten thousand muons reach each square meter of the earth's surface and can penetrate tens of meters into rocks and other matter before attenuating owing to absorption or deflection by other atoms. Such scattering is most extensive when they come in contact with dense substances such as uranium and plutonium.[51]

Another recent instrument that NEST might be able to put to good use is the large area imager developed by a trio of scientists at Livermore. The device, which can be carried on the back of a small truck or trailer, relies on gamma rays, produced through radioactive decay, to detect radiation sources, which can include uranium or bananas. The extreme penetrability of gamma rays makes it possible to detect radioactivity even if the radiation source is shielded by concrete, dirt, or a few centimeters of lead.[52]

In addition, in early 2008 the National Nuclear Security Administration reported that it planned to provide the FBI with a way to disrupt the detonation of an improvised nuclear device, a means developed by one of the national laboratories. The bureau would be able to employ the tool to put the device in a standby mode, giving more time for NEST's Joint Technical Operations Team and military explosive ordnance disposal teams to permanently disable the bomb.[53]

Hopefully, even if NEST successfully meets such challenges, its deployments will be limited to exercises, uneventful national special security events, and the search for the remnants of satellites that crash into remote regions of the world. For even with the best technology and most skilled personnel, NEST would face a difficult task.

Improved detection equipment may not be enough without good, indeed very good, intelligence—at least with regard to an improvised or stolen nuclear device. University of Maryland physicist Steven Fetter, who has examined the use of radiation detection capabilities in identifying bombs and warheads, observed that a dirty bomb made with cesium-137 or cobalt-60 would be "hot as gangbusters" and that a large detector carried on a low-flying helicopter would have a good chance of detecting the device.[54]

But when it comes to a nuclear device, he believes that to characterize the problem as one of finding a "needle in a haystack" understates the difficulty. He also notes that while people in the field talk about "transformational" research and development, such as detection relying on antineutrinos, "the laws of physics are what they are." Thomas Cochran, a nuclear physicist and nuclear weapons expert with the Natural Resources Defense Council, said, "It's probably largely a waste of money, unless they have good intelligence on a specific scenario." And the Mirage Gold after-action report acknowledges that "it is a drastic mistake to assume that

NEST technology and procedures will always succeed, resulting in zero nuclear yield."[55]

But like many forms of insurance or protection that may never be needed or may not protect against all threats, NEST is a capability that, had it not been established in 1974, would have been considered essential to create in 2001.

APPENDIX

U.S. NUCLEAR EXTORTION THREATS EVENT LIST: 1970–1993

	DATE	PLACE	THREAT
1.	Oct. 27, 1970	Orlando, Fla.	Hydrogen Bomb
2.	Sep. 14, 1971	Borough of Manhattan, N.Y.	Nuclear Device, 20–25 Kilotons
3.	Oct. 20, 1972	Washington, D.C.	"Atomic Device"
4.	Mar. 16, 1973	Chicago, Ill., and Brussels, Belgium	Atomic Bomb Threat
5.	Apr. 1974	United States	Seven Atom Bombs
6.	May 1, 1974	Boston, Mass.	Plutonium Bomb, 500 Kilotons
7.	May 1974	San Francisco, Calif.	Four Plutonium Dispersal Devices
8.	May 1974	Washington, D.C.	Nuclear Bomb
9.	Aug. 1974	Unidentified Big City	Nuclear Bomb, 10+ Kilotons
10.	Oct. 2, 1974	Lincoln, Neb.	Nuclear Bomb
11.	Dec. 19, 1974	Jacksonville, Fla.	Four Radioisotope Bombs
12.	Dec. 24, 1974	New Orleans, La.	H-Bomb
13.	Jan. 4, 1975	Dallas, Texas	Plutonium Bomb
14.	Jan. 31, 1975	Los Angeles, Calif.	Hydrogen Bombs, 5 Megatons
15.	Feb. 17, 1975	Chicago, Ill.	Nuclear Device (Atomic Bomb)
16.	Mar. 6, 1975	Philadelphia, Pa.	A-Bomb Castings
17.	Mar. 16, 1975	Moscow, Peking, and Washington, D.C.	Three Atomic Bombs
18.	Mar. 18, 1975	Washington, D.C.	Nuclear Device, 1 Megaton
19.	Apr. 8, 1975	Ohio	Plutomium Nuclear Devices
20.	Apr. 11, 1975	California	Nuclear Bomb; $300,000
21.	Apr. 28, 1975	Unidentified Big City	Atomic Bomb
22.	July 7, 1975	Unidentified Big City	Nuclear Bomb; No demand.
23.	July 10, 1975	Manhattan Island	Atomic Bomb
24.	Aug. 1975	Boston, Mass.	Atomic Bomb; No demand.
25.	Aug. 1975	Unidentified ERDA Site	Atomic Bomb; No demand.
26.	Oct. 10, 1975	Springfield, Mass.	Atomic Bomb (Plutonium)

DATE	PLACE	THREAT
27. Oct. 25, 1975	New York, N.Y.	Radioactive Dispersal Bomb
28. Nov. 4, 1975	Los Angeles, Calif.	Nuclear Device, 20 Kilotons
29. Nov. 17, 1975	Twelve Unidentified Cities	Twelve Atomic Bombs
30. Nov. 18, 1975	New York, N.Y.	Two Nuclear Bombs
31. Jan. 1, 1976	New York, N.Y.	Twenty-five Bombs Nuclear Radioactive
32. Jan. 4, 1976	Raleigh, N.C.	Bomb, 25 Megatons
33. Jan. 6, 1976	Washington, D.C.	Atomic Bomb
34. Jan. 30, 1976	Denver, Colo.	Nuclear Device
35. Feb. 3, 1976	Columbia, S.C.	Bomb, 100 Megatons
36. Mar. 10, 1976	Columbus, Ohio	Atomic Device
37. July 27, 1976	Unidentified	Atomic Bomb
38. Aug. 14, 1976	Eight Unidentified Cities	Bomb Threat
39. Aug. 16, 1976	Phoenix, Ariz.	Atomic Bomb
40. Aug. 26, 1976	Los Angeles, Calif.	Nuclear Device; $1,500,000
41. Nov. 1, 1976	Milford, Conn.	Thermonuclear Mines
42. Nov. 23, 1976	Spokane, Wash.	Ten Radioactive Dispersal Bombs
43. Feb. 7, 1977	Seattle, Wash.	Nuclear Device
44. Mar. 1977	St. Louis, Mo.	Atomic Bomb; No demand.
45. Mar. 21, 1977	Washington, D.C.	Nuclear Bomb (Small, Armed, and Ready to Fire)
46. Apr. 1, 1977	Five Unidentified Countries	Contaminate All Fresh
47. Apr. 15, 1977	Chicago, Ill.	Anti-Matter or H-Bomb
48. Apr. 28, 1977	Boulder, Colo.	Unconventional Low-Yield Device
49. Nov. 18, 1977	Galveston, Texas	Atomic Bomb; $500,000
50. Sep. 26, 1978	Manhattan, N.Y.	Radioactive Dispersal
51. Dec. 28, 1978	Albuquerque, N.M.	Implied Nuclear Threat
52. Jan. 30, 1979	Wilmington, N.C.	Uranium Threat
53. Mar. 2, 1979	Hilo, Hawaii	Nuclear Bomb
54. Mar. 12, 1979	Boston, Mass.	Radioactive Dispersal
55. Apr. 3, 1979	St. Louis, Mo.	Nuclear Bomb
56. Apr. 9, 1979	Sacramento, Calif.	Radioactive Dispersal
57. Apr. 24, 1979	Cedar Rapids, Iowa	Radioactive Dispersal
58. Jan. 2, 1980	San Francisco, Calif.	Low-Yield Nuclear Bomb
59. Jan. 3, 1980	Buffalo, N.Y.	Nuclear Bomb
60. Jan. 4, 1980	Indianapolis, Ind.	Nuclear Explostion, 5 Megatons
61. Jan. 7, 1980	Iran	Three Atomic Bombs, 20–25 Megatons
62. Jan. 11, 1980	Unidentified Location	Nuclear Bomb

	DATE	PLACE	THREAT
63.	July 16, 1980	Chicago, Ill., Plus Several Unidentified Cities	Nuclear Bombs
64.	Jan. 9, 1981	Reno, Nev.	Plutonium Dispersal
65.	Jan. 26, 1981	San Francisco, Calif.	Atomic Device
66.	June 26, 1981	San Francisco, Calif.	Nuclear Bomb
67.	May 16, 1982	Twelve Unidentified U.S. Cities	Nuclear Warheads
68.	June 14, 1982	Boston, Mass.	Nuclear Device
69.	July 2, 1982	Washington, D.C.	Radioactive Device
70.	Oct. 8, 1982	Las Vegas, Nev.	Atomic Device, 10 Kilotons
71.	Oct. 19, 1982	Los Angeles, Calif.	Thermonuclear Detonation
72.	Feb. 2, 1983	Tampa, Fla.	Radioactive Dispersal
73.	Feb. 13, 1984	Hill Air Force Base, Utah	Atomic Bomb
74.	July 29, 1984	Covina, Calif.	Nuclear Device
75.	July 30, 1984	Los Angeles, Calif.	Atomic Bomb
76.	Oct. 18, 1984	Detroit, Mich.	Nuclear Device
77.	Nov. 7, 1984	Unspecified Location	Hydrogen Bomb
78.	Nov. 16, 1984	Fairfax County, Va.	Small Nuclear Device
79.	Mar. 14, 1985	Chicago, Ill.	Nuclear Device, 5 Kilotons
80.	Apr. 4, 1985	New York, N.Y.	Plutonium Dispersal
81.	Nov. 22, 1985	Albuquerque, N.M.	Three Nuclear Devices
82.	Apr. 4, 1986	New York City–Murmansk	Two Atomic Devices
83.	May 6, 1986	Reno, Nev.	Nuclear Device
84.	Sep. 22, 1986	Wisconsin	Nuclear Device
85.	Oct. 8, 1986	Westminster, Calif.	Thermonuclear Device
86.	Oct. 17, 1986	Concord, Calif.	Nuclear Device, 6 Megatons
87.	Nov. 13, 1986	Bethlehem, Pa.	Americlum-241 Dispersal
88.	Jan. 30, 1987	Indiana	Nuclear Device
89.	Nov. 27, 1987	Indianapolis, Ind.	Nuclear Device
90.	June 4, 1988	Washington, D.C., and Moscow, USSR	Atom Bombs
91.	Jan. 28, 1989	Somewhere in the United States	Three Nuclear Bombs
92.	Apr. 20, 1989	Washington, D.C.	Atomic Bomb
93.	Jan. 27, 1990	Denver, Colo.	Nuclear Device
94.	Apr. 13, 1990	El Paso, Texas	Nuclear Weapon
95.	Oct. 5, 1990	Sunnyvale, Calif.	Atomic Bomb
96.	Oct. 19, 1990	Washington, D.C.	Nuclear Device
97.	Nov. 12, 1990	Bethesda, Md.	Plutonium Dispersal
98.	Nov. 28, 1990	Somewhere in the United States	Two Atomic Bombs
99.	June 14, 1991	New York and Washington, D.C.	Nuclear Bombs

DATE	PLACE	THREAT
100. Mar. 27, 1992	Nine U.S. Cities	Nuclear Weapons
101. Nov. 10, 1992	Unknown Cities	Nuclear Devices
102. Dec. 23, 1992	Tel Aviv and West Jerusalem	Two Atom Bombs
103. Apr. 9, 1993	Germany and Vatican City	Three A-Bombs

ABBREVIATIONS AND ACRONYMS

AEA	Atomic Energy Act
AEC	Atomic Energy Commission
AEDS	Atomic Energy Detection System
AFTAC	Air Force Technical Applications Center
AMAN	Intelligence Branch, Israeli Defense Forces
AMOS	Air Force Maui Optical System
AMS	Aerial Measurement System
ARG	Accident Response Group
ARMS	Aerial Radiation Measurement System
ARMS	Aerial Radiological Measuring System
ASP	Advanced Spectroscopic Portals
ATOM	Automated Tether-Operated Manipulator
BKA	Bundeskriminalamt
BMEWS	Ballistic Missile Early Warning System
BND	Bundesnachrichtendienst (German Federal Intelligence Service)
CAARS	Cargo Advanced Automated Radiography System
CAIR	Council on American-Islamic Relations
CBRN	Chemical, Biological, Radiological, Nuclear
CFB	Canadian Forces Base
CIA	Central Intelligence Agency
CIRG	Critical Incident Response Group
CPX	Command Post Exercise
CURV	Cable-Controlled Underwater Recovery Vehicle
DCI	Director of Central Intelligence
DEST	Domestic Emergency Support Team
DIA	Defense Intelligence Agency
DNDO	Domestic Nuclear Detection Office
DOD	Department of Defense
DOE	Department of Energy
DSP	Defense Support Program
DST	Direct Support Team

DTRA	Defense Threat Reduction Agency
EACT	Emergency Action Coordinating Team
EG&G	Edgerton, Germeshausen and Grier
EOD	Explosive Ordnance Disposal
ERDA	Energy Research and Development Administration
ESO	Energy Senior Officer
FBI	Federal Bureau of Investigation
FEMA	Federal Emergency Management Agency
FEST	Foreign Emergency Support Team
FIDLER	Field Instrument for Detection of Low Energy Radiations
FORSCOM	Forces Command
GAO	Government Accountability Office
GE	General Electric
GRU	Glavnoye Razvedyvatelnoye Upravleniye (Chief Intelligence Directorate, Soviet General Staff)
HEU	Highly Enriched Uranium
HRT	Hostage Rescue Team
HSPD	Homeland Security Presidential Directive
HUMINT	Human Intelligence
IAC	Intelligence Advisory Committee
IAEA	International Atomic Energy Agency
IDF	Israeli Defense Forces
IND	Improvised Nuclear Device
IRIS	Incorporated Research Institutions for Seismology
JCSM	Joint Chiefs of Staff Memorandum
JNACC	Joint Nuclear Accident Coordinating Center
JSOC	Joint Special Operations Command
JTOT	Joint Technical Operations Team
KGB	Komitet Gosudarstvennoy Bezopasnosti (Soviet Committee for State Security)
LGAT	Lincoln Gold Augmentation Team
LLL	Lawrence Livermore Laboratory
LLNL	Lawrence Livermore National Laboratory
MINATOM	Ministry of Atomic Energy (Russia)
MPC&A	Materials Protection, Control, and Accounting
MS	Mara Salvatrucha
NAA	North American Aviation
NAP	Nuclear Assessment Program
NASA	National Aeronautics and Space Administration
NAST	Nuclear Accident Support Team (Canada)

NATO	North Atlantic Treaty Organization
NAVSPUR	Naval Space Surveillance System
NDHQ	National Defence Headquarters (Canada)
NEST	Nuclear Emergency Search Team (1974–2002)
NEST	Nuclear Emergency Support Team (2002–present)
NIE	National Intelligence Estimate
NIO	National Intelligence Officer
NMIP	Nuclear Materials Information Program
NNSA	National Nuclear Security Administration
NORAD	North American Aerospace Defense Command
NRAT	Nuclear/Radiological Advisory Team
NRC	Nuclear Regulatory Commission
NSA	National Security Agency
NSAM	National Security Action Memorandum
NSC	National Security Council
NSDD	National Security Decision Directive
NSPD	National Security Presidential Directive
NSSE	National Special Security Event
NSSM	National Security Study Memorandum
OTA	Office of Technology Assessment
PAL	Permissive Action Link
PBX	Private Branch Exchange
PDD	Presidential Decision Directive
PINSTECH	Pakistan Institute of Nuclear Science and Technology
PLO	Palestine Liberation Organization
RAP	Radiological Assistance Program
RDD	Radiological Dispersal Device
REECo	Reynolds Electrical and Engineering Corporation
RERT	Radiological Emergency Response Team
RORSAT	Radar Ocean Reconnaissance Satellite
RORSATOM	Russian Atomic Energy Agency
RTG	Radioisotope Thermoelectric Generator
SA	Special Agent
SAC	Special Agent-in-Charge
SAC	Strategic Air Command
SADM	Special Atomic Demolition Munition
SANDS	Surveillance Accident and Nuclear Detection System
SCOPE	Scomi Precision Engineering
SIED	Sophisticated Improvised Explosive Device
SKKP	System for Monitoring Cosmic Space (Soviet Union)

SLD	Second Line of Defense
SNIE	Special National Intelligence Estimate
SSA	Senior Scientific Advisor
Topoff	Top Officials
TsKKP	Center for Monitoring Cosmic Space (Soviet Union)
UCS	Union of Concerned Scientists
UNSUB	Unknown Subject
UTN	Ummah Tameer-e-Nau (Reconstruction of the Muslim Ummah)
WMD	Weapons of Mass Destruction

TERMINOLOGY

alpha particles: a highly ionizing form of radiation emitted by radioactive nuclei such as uranium or radium.

attribution: the assignment of origin to nuclear material.

background radiation: radiation that comes from natural sources such as granite, soil, and bananas.

beta particles: high-energy, high-speed electrons emitted by certain types of radioactive substances.

cesium-137: a radioactive isotope formed mainly by nuclear fission that is extremely toxic, even in small amounts.

cobalt-60: a highly radioactive substance used for industrial, medical, and other commercial purposes.

gamma rays: radiation emitted by a nucleus when it transitions to a lower energy level.

highly enriched uranium: uranium that contains 20 percent or more of the uranium-235 isotope.

implosion weapon: a weapon that detonates when an arrangement of explosives rapidly compresses one or more pieces of fissile material into a supercritical mass.

Improvised Nuclear Device: a nuclear weapon assembled by a terrorist or criminal organization.

isotope: atoms of the same element that have the same number of protons but a different number of neutrons and thus different atomic masses, such as uranium-235 and uranium-238.

isotopic signature: the fingerprint of an element characterized by the types and amounts of isotopes it contains.

muon: a naturally occurring elementary particle produced when cosmic rays strike air molecules in the upper atmosphere.

muon radiography: the use of detectors to monitor the change in muon trajectory before and after muons interact with an object, thereby constructing a three-dimensional image of that object.

neutron: a subatomic particle with no net electric charge.

neutron radiography: a nondestructive detection technology that uses a neutron beam to penetrate an object and, by measuring how the neutrons are affected, produces information about its interior structure and composition.

nuclear forensics: methods that analyze radioactive debris or intercepted nuclear material to determine its origins, transportation route, and possible applications.

passive gamma-ray detection: a method that detects nuclear material by spotting its naturally emitted gamma radiation.

plutonium: a heavy, radioactive metallic element produced artificially in reactors by bombarding uranium with neutrons. Plutonium, in the form of the plutonium-239 isotope, is one of the two types of fissile material used to produce a nuclear detonation.

radioactivity: material which has an unstable nucleus that decays spontaneously and emits particles.

shielding: material that surrounds a radiation source and reduces the amount of radiation emitted.

uranium: a naturally occurring metal whose rare uranium-235 isotope is one of the two types of fissile material used to produce a nuclear detonation.

ACKNOWLEDGMENTS

This book is an extension, a rather large extension, of an article I wrote for the *Bulletin of Atomic Scientists* several years ago. The opportunity to write that article provided a base of knowledge for further research into the history and activities of the Nuclear Emergency Support Team.

That research has been augmented in several ways. A number of colleagues have provided information, documents, and photographs. Included are Robert Windrem of NBC News, William Burr of the National Security Archive, Asiq Siddiqi, William Arkin, and Dwayne Day.

In addition, a variety of valuable documents have been released in response to Freedom of Information Act (FOIA) requests to the Department of Energy and its components in the field, including the Lawrence Livermore and Los Alamos national laboratories and the Nevada Site Office. Other federal agencies that have provided documents in response to FOIA requests include the Central Intelligence Agency, Nuclear Regulatory Commission, the Defense Intelligence Agency, and the Departments of State, Energy, Defense, Justice, and Homeland Security. I appreciate the work of the FOIA officers of those organizations and those who reviewed materials for release.

Public affairs officers Steven Wampler of Lawrence Livermore and Kevin Rohrer of the Nevada Site Office provided assistance in obtaining photographs and information. Roger Strother of the National Security Archive provided research assistance, and the Archive provided support in a variety of ways.

My greatest debt is to those, including several NEST veterans and other knowledgeable individuals, who took the time to speak with me about the organization and the problems of nuclear detection. This group includes Adm. Charles Beers, Dino Brugioni, William Chambers, Steven Fetter, Victor Gilinsky, Carl Henry, Robert Kelley, Allen Mode, William Nelson, and Peter Zimmerman. Bill Chambers also read a number of chapters.

Thanks also go to my editor, Leo Wiegman, Jennifer Cantelmi, and the others at W. W. Norton who helped turn my manuscript into a book.

NOTES

PREFACE

1. Tony Shaw, *British Cinema and the Cold War: The State, Propaganda and Consensus* (London: I.B. Taurus, 2001), pp. 117–118; "Seven Days to Noon," http://en.wikipedia.org, accessed November 22, 2007.
2. "Broken Arrow (1996 film)," http://en.wikipedia.org, accessed November 22, 2007; "The Peacemaker (1997 film)," http://en.wikipedia.org, accessed November 22, 2007.
3. Nicolas Freeling, *Gadget* (New York: Coward, McCann & Geoghegan, 1977); Wolfgang Saxon, "Nicolas Freeling, 76, Dies; Set Novels in Modern Europe," *New York Times*, July 23, 2003, accessed from www.nytimes.com.
4. Larry Collins and Dominique Lapierre, *The Fifth Horseman* (New York: Simon & Schuster, 1980).
5. Tom Clancy, *The Sum of All Fears* (New York: G.P. Putnam's Sons, 1991). A number of changes were made for the film version. See "The Sum of All Fears (film)," http://en.wikipedia.org, accessed November 22, 2007.
6. Donald Hamilton, *The Removers* (Greenwich, Conn.: Fawcett, 1961), p. 168.
7. Michael Connelly, *The Overlook* (Boston: Little, Brown, 2007).
8. Department of Defense Directive 5230.16, Subject: Nuclear Accident and Public Affairs (PA) Guidance, December 20, 1993, pp. 10–11; DOE/NRC Interagency Working Group on Radiological Dispersal Devices, *Radiological Dispersal Devices: An Initial Study to Identify Radioactive Materials of Greatest Concern and Approaches to Their Tracking, Tagging, and Disposition*, May 2003.

CHAPTER ONE: "BYE-BYE BOSTON"

1. Kai Bird and Martin J. Sherwin, *American Prometheus: The Triumph and Tragedy of J. Robert Oppenheimer* (New York: Knopf, 2005), p. 349.
2. Ibid.
3. Gregg Herken, *Counsels of War* (New York: Oxford University Press, 1987), p. 179; Spurgeon M. Keeny Jr., "In Memoriam: Wolfgang K.H. Panofsky," *Arms Control Today*, November 2007, pp. 51–52.

4. Lindesay Parrott, "Korea Foe Delays Truck Talk Reply: Says Ridgway Lies," *New York Times*, August 30, 1951, pp. 1, 3.

5. On the capabilities and significant limitations of the Tu-4, see Stephen Zaloga, *Target America: The Soviet Union and the Strategic Arms Race, 1945–1964* (Novato, Calif.: Presidio, 1993), pp. 72–79.

6. Director of Central Intelligence, NIE-31, *Soviet Capabilities for Clandestine Attack against the US with Weapons of Mass Destruction and the Vulnerability of the US to Such Attack (mid-1951 to mid-1952)*, August 30, 1951.

7. Ibid., pp. 1, 4.

8. Ibid., p. 4.

9. Ibid., pp. 4–5. Also see "Customs Hunting Atom Smugglers," *New York Times*, February 16, 1954, p. 2.

10. Director of Central Intelligence, NIE-31, *Soviet Capabilities for Clandestine Attack against the US with Weapons of Mass Destruction and the Vulnerability of the US to Such Attack (mid-1951 to mid-1952)*, p. 6.

11. JCSM-3-68, Subject: Clandestine Introduction of Nuclear Weapons to the United States, January 2, 1968; John F. Kennedy, NSAM 161, "U.S. Internal Security Programs," June 9, 1962.

12. Timothy Naftali, *Blind Spot: The Secret History of American Counterterrorism* (New York: Basic Books, 2005), p. 17; Director of Central Intelligence, NIE 11-7-63, *The Clandestine Introduction of Weapons of Mass Destruction into the US*, March 1963, p. 4.

13. Director of Central Intelligence, NIE 11-7-63, *Clandestine Introduction of Weapons of Mass Destruction into the US*, p. 2n3; Director of Central Intelligence, SNIE 11-9-55, *Clandestine Introduction of Nuclear Weapons under Diplomatic Immunity*, June 28, 1955, p. 2. Other estimates on the subject are: Director of Central Intelligence, NIE 11-7-60, *Soviet Capabilities and Intentions with Respect to the Clandestine Introduction of Weapons of Mass Destruction into the US*, May 17, 1960; Director of Central Intelligence, NIE 4-68, *The Clandestine Introduction of Weapons of Mass Destruction into the US*, June 13, 1968; Director of Central Intelligence, NIE 4-70, *The Clandestine Introduction of Nuclear Weapons into the US*, July 7, 1970.

14. Director of Central Intelligence, NIE 11-7-60, *Soviet Capabilities and Intentions with Respect to the Clandestine Introduction of Weapons of Mass Destruction into the US*, p. 4; Joint Chiefs of Staff, Memorandum to Secretary of Defense Robert McNamara, "Clandestine Introduction of Weapons of Mass Destruction into the US," June 13, 1968, in U.S. State Department, *Foreign Relations of the United States, 1964–1968, Volume X: National Security Policy* (Washington, D.C.: U.S. Government Printing Office, 2002), pp. 653–655; NIE 4-68, *Clandestine Introduction of Weapons of Mass Destruction into the US*, pp. 2, 5; Director of Central Intelligence, NIE 4-70, *Clandestine Introduction of Nuclear Weapons into the US*, p.1. For a review of these estimates, see Micah Zenko, "Intelligence Estimates of

Nuclear Terrorism," *Annals, AAPSS* [*American Academy of Political and Social Science*], September 2006, pp. 87–102.

15. Clark Rumrill, "Lost: One H-Bomb Call Owner," *Washington Post*, April 17, 2005, pp. D1, D6; Air Force Nuclear Weapons and Counterproliferation Agency, *Air Force Search & Recovery Assessment of the 1958 Savannah, GA B-47 Accident*, April 12, 2001, p. 2; Boeing, "B-47 Stratojet," www.boeing.com, accessed March 7, 2007.

16. Rumrill, "Lost: One H-Bomb."

17. Ibid.; "North American F-86L Sabre Cockpit," www.mapsairmuseum.org/Sabre .htm, accessed March 7, 2007.

18. Rumrill, "Lost: One H-Bomb"; Air Force Nuclear Weapons and Counterproliferation Agency, *Air Force Search & Recovery Assessment of the 1958 Savannah, GA B-47 Accident*, p. 1. In 2001 the Air Force consulted several other government organizations, including the Navy and Department of Energy, to determine if a search-and-recovery operation should be undertaken, and concluded that "it is in the best interest of the public and the environment to leave the bomb in its resting-place and remain categorized as permanently lost." A search in 2005 found no trace of the weapon, and the Air Force again concluded that since the bomb could not explode it should be left at sea. See Air Force Nuclear Weapons and Counterproliferation Agency, *Air Force Search & Recovery Assessment of the 1958 Savannah, GA B-47 Accident*, p. 1; "Search Fails to Yield Missing Nuclear Bomb," *Washington Times*, June 18, 2005, p. A3.

19. On U.S. information policy concerning the accident, see David Stiles, "A Fusion Bomb over Andalucia: U.S. Information Policy and the 1966 Palomares Incident," *Journal of Cold War Studies*, 8, 1 (Winter 2006), pp. 49–67.

20. U.S. Air Force, "BROKEN ARROW: Palomares, Spain," *Nuclear Safety*, 51 (May–June 1966), pp. 4–8, 29–37; Tad Szulc, *The Bombs of Palomares* (New York: Viking, 1967), pp. 16–20; John W. Finney, "Radiation Found Where B-52 Fell," *New York Times*, January 24, 1968, pp. 1, 6; Scott D. Sagan, *The Limits of Safety: Organizations, Accidents, and Nuclear Weapons* (Princeton, N.J.: Princeton University Press, 1993), p. 185; U.S. Congress, House Committee on Appropriations, *Department of Defense Appropriations for 1967, Part 6* (Washington, D.C.: U.S. Government Printing Office, 1967), p. 40.

21. Szulc, *Bombs of Palomares*, pp. 20, 23–24.

22. Ibid., pp. 28–29.

23. Ibid., pp. 29–30; Flora Lewis, *One of Our H-Bombs Is Missing . . .* (New York: McGraw-Hill, 1967), pp. 5–8, 12–13, 25, 42–43; "B-52 and Tanker Collide over Spain; 5 Dead, 2 Missing," *New York Times*, January 18, 1966, p. 16; Systems Analysis Team, *Analysis of Ballistics of Four MK 28 FI Weapons Released as a Result of the Collision of a B-52 and KC-135 near Vera, Spain, on 17 January 1966*, February 7, 1966, p. 25; U.S. Congress, House Committee on Appropriations, *Department of Defense Appropriations for 1967, Part 6*, p. 40. The Systems Analysis Team was

an ad hoc group consisting of representatives from Sandia and the Air Force. The report is available at the Defense Department's Electronic Reading Room: www .dod.mil/pubs/foi/master_reading_list01.html (135.pdf).

24. Lewis, *One of Our H-Bombs Is Missing*, pp. 49–52.

25. Ibid., p. 53.

26. Ibid., p. 54.

27. Ibid., p. 58; Szulc, *Bombs of Palomares*, p. 159; Larry Collins, "Nuclear Terrorism," *New York Times Magazine*, December 14, 1980, pp. 36ff; Howard Simons, "U.S. Faces an Unending Cleanup Task," *Washington Post*, February 25, 1966, pp. A1, A9.

28. Collins, "Nuclear Terrorism"; "Physical Review Online Archive," http://prola.aps .org, accessed March 15, 2007; Interview with William Chambers, Los Alamos, N.M., July 10, 2007; William Chambers, e-mail, December 16, 2007.

29. Lewis, *One of Our H-Bombs Is Missing*, p. 78; U.S. Air Force, "BROKEN ARROW: Palomares, Spain."

30. Simons, "U.S. Faces an Unending Cleanup Task"; Jeffrey T. Richelson, *Spying on the Bomb: American Nuclear Intelligence from Nazi Germany to Iran and North Korea* (New York: W.W. Norton, 2006), p. 208.

31. History & Research Division, Strategic Air Command, SAC Historical Study 109, *Sixteenth Air Force Operation Recovery, 17 January–7 April 1966, Volume I*, April 1968, pp. 22–23; Lewis, *One of Our H-Bombs Is Missing*, pp. 78–79.

32. Lewis, *One of Our H-Bombs Is Missing*, pp. 84–85, 88; U.S. Congress, House Committee on Appropriations, *Department of Defense Appropriations for 1967, Part 6*, p. 43.

33. "U.S. Said to Hunt Lost Atom Device," *New York Times*, January 20, 1966, pp. 1, 9; History & Research Division, Strategic Air Command, SAC Historical Study 109, *Sixteenth Air Force Operation Recovery, 17 January–7 April 1966, Volume I*, pp. 106–107.

34. History & Research Division, Strategic Air Command, SAC Historical Study 109, *Sixteenth Air Force Operation Recovery, 17 January–7 April 1966, Volume I*, p. 108.

35. Ibid.; Systems Analysis Team, *Analysis of Ballistics of Four MK 28 FI Weapons Released as a Result of the Collision of a B-52 and KC-135 near Vera, Spain, on 17 January 1966*, p. 25.

36. Tad Szulc, "H-Bomb Is Recovered Intact after 80 Days," *New York Times*, April 8, 1966, pp. 1, 12; U.S. Air Force, "Broken Arrow Aftermath," *Nuclear Safety*, 52 (September–October 1966), pp. 2–7; Telephone interview with Dino Brugioni, March 13, 2007; U.S. Air Force, "BROKEN ARROW: Palomares, Spain"; "Cable-Controlled Underwater Recovery Vehicle," www.spawar.navy.mil, accessed April 3, 2007; U.S. Congress, House Committee on Appropriations, *Department of Defense Appropriations for 1967, Part 6*, p. 52.

37. History & Research Division, Strategic Air Command, SAC Historical Study 113,

Project Crested Ice: The Thule Nuclear Accident, Volume I, April 23, 1969, p. 1; Sagan, *Limits of Safety,* pp. 65, 157, 170–172.

38. Weapons Systems Division, Directorate of Nuclear Safety, "BROKEN ARROW–THULE," *Nuclear Safety,* July–August–September 1968, pp. 2–5; Neil Sheehan, "Pilot Says Fire Forced Crew to Quit B-52 in Arctic," *New York Times,* January 28, 1968, p. 3; Neil Sheehan, "Radiation Danger Doubted in Crash," *New York Times,* January 27, 1968, pp. 1, 10; Sagan, *Limits of Safety,* p. 156.

39. Weapons Systems Division, Directorate of Nuclear Safety, "BROKEN ARROW–THULE"; Defense Atomic Support Agency, *Project CRESTED ICE: USAF B-52 Accident at Thule, Greenland, 21 January 1968,* n.d., Annex B, p. 1; John W. Finney, "B-52 with H-Bombs Plunges into Ice in Greenland Bay," *New York Times,* January 23, 1968, pp. 1, 12; Neil Sheehan, "Parts of 4 Bombs Located in Arctic," *New York Times,* January 29, 1968, pp. 1, 2.

40. Finney, "B-52 with H-Bombs Plunges into Ice in Greenland Bay"; Sheehan, "Parts of 4 Bombs Located in Arctic"; History & Research Division, Strategic Air Command, SAC Historical Study 113, *Project Crested Ice,* pp. 3, 38.

41. Defense Atomic Support Agency, *Project CRESTED ICE,* p. 1; Grant Elliot, MIT Program in Science, Technology, and Society, "US Nuclear Weapon Safety and Control," December 12, 2005.

42. History & Research Division, Strategic Air Command, SAC Historical Study 113, *Project Crested Ice,* p. 28; Weapons Systems Division, Directorate of Nuclear Safety, "BROKEN ARROW–THULE"; Defense Atomic Support Agency, *Project CRESTED ICE,* pp. 35, 91; Leo Heaps, *Operation Morning Light: Terror in Our Skies, The True Story of Cosmos 954* (London: Paddington Press, 1978), p. 24.

43. Collins, "Nuclear Terrorism"; Jim Eckles, "The Athena That Got Away," www.wsmr.army.mil/pao/FactSheets/AthenatoMexico.htm, accessed April 28, 2007.

44. Collins, "Nuclear Terrorism"; Eckles, "Athena That Got Away."

45. Collins, "Nuclear Terrorism"; Eckles, "Athena That Got Away."

46. Collins, "Nuclear Terrorism"; Eckles, "Athena That Got Away"; L. Deal, J. Doyle, Z. G. Burson, and P. K. Boyns, "Locating the Lost Athena Missile in Mexico by the Aerial Radiological Measuring System (ARMS)," *Health Physics,* 23, 1 (July 1972), pp. 95–98.

47. Collins, "Nuclear Terrorism"; Eckles, "Athena That Got Away"; Deal, Doyle, Burson, and Boyns, "Locating the Lost Athena Missile in Mexico by the Aerial Radiological Measuring System (ARMS)."

48. Ralph E. Lapp, "The Ultimate Blackmail," *New York Times Magazine,* February 4, 1973, pp. 13ff.

49. Jeffrey T. Richelson, *A Century of Spies: Intelligence in the Twentieth Century* (New York: Oxford University Press, 1995), p. 353.

50. Ibid.

51. Ibid., pp. 353–354; Collins, "Nuclear Terrorism."

52. Dan Stober, "No Experience Necessary," *Bulletin of the Atomic Scientists,* March/

April 2003, pp. 57–63; Michael Levi, *On Nuclear Terrorism* (Cambridge, Mass.: Harvard University Press, 2007), pp. 74–75.

53. Traffic Management Officer, 87th Combat Support Group, Tactical Air Command to Atomic Energy Commission, Subject: Accident Response Group Exercise, December 11, 1973; Mahlon E. Gates, "NV Sands Exercise Report," January 2, 1974; "History, E&G Division, URS," www.urscorp.com/EGG_Division/history.php, accessed March 14, 2007.

54. U.S. Army, Biography, "Brigadier General Mahlon E. Gates," July 1969.

55. "Report: SANDS EXERCISE December 8, 1973," n.d., p. 7, enclosure to: Gates, "NV SANDS Exercise Report."

56. "Report: SANDS EXERCISE December 8, 1973," p. 1; Gates, "NV SANDS Exercise Report."

57. Henry A. Kissinger, National Security Study Memorandum 120, "United States Policy on Peaceful Applications of Atomic Energy," February 19, 1971; Henry A. Kissinger, National Security Decision Memorandum 254, "Domestic Safeguards," April 27, 1974.

58. Thomas O' Toole, "Fear of Nuclear Theft Stirs Experts, AEC," *Washington Post*, May 26, 1974, pp. A1, A16; Thomas O' Toole, "AEC Seeking to Cut Peril of Atom Theft," *Washington Post*, May 27, 1974, pp. A1, A22.

59. Lapp, "Ultimate Blackmail," pp. 13ff.

60. Ibid.

61. Ibid.

62. Ibid.; John McPhee, *The Curve of Binding Energy* (New York: Farrar, Straus & Giroux, 1980), pp. 118–119.

63. Lapp, "Ultimate Blackmail," pp. 13ff; McPhee, *Curve of Binding Energy*, p. 119.

64. McPhee, *Curve of Binding Energy*, p. 119.

65. "U.S. Nuclear Extortion Threats List," n.d. The list was provided to the author by a former member of NEST.

66. Kissinger, National Security Decision Memorandum 254, "Domestic Safeguards."

67. Collins, "Nuclear Terrorism"; Chambers interview; W. H. Chambers, "Summary: A Brief History of NEST," October 24, 1995.

68. Chambers interview; Chambers, "Summary: A Brief History of NEST."

69. Collins, "Nuclear Terrorism."

70. Telephone interview with Carl Henry, November 28, 2007.

71. Collins, "Nuclear Terrorism"; Chambers interview; Chambers e-mail.

72. Collins, "Nuclear Terrorism."

73. Chambers interview; Henry interview; Telephone conversation with John F. Doyle, July 23, 2007

74. Collins, "Nuclear Terrorism."

75. Major General Ernest Graves, Assistant General Manager for Military Application, Atomic Energy Commission, to M. E. Gates, Manager, Nevada Operations, "Responsibility for Search and Detection Operations," November 18, 1974.

76. Ibid.

CHAPTER TWO: NUCLEAR EXTORTION

1. "Personnel Profiles," *NTS News*, May 1978, p. 13.
2. Interview with William Chambers, Los Alamos, N.M., July 10, 2007; U.S. Congress, Senate Committee on Governmental Affairs, *Global Proliferation of Weapons of Mass Destruction, Part III* (Washington, D.C.: U.S. Government Printing Office, 1996), p. 70.
3. Chambers interview; James K. Ferrell, "History of the Chemical Engineering Department at North Carolina State University," n.d., ; "NC State University College of Engineering Timeline," n.d., accessed from www.che.nsu.edu/history/History of the ChEDepartment.pdf and www.engr.ncsu.edu/news/media/pdfs/timeline.pdf.; Larry Collins, "Nuclear Terrorism," *New York Times Magazine*, December 14, 1980, pp. 36ff.
4. Chambers interview.
5. Ibid.
6. Michael Levi, *On Nuclear Terrorism* (Cambridge, Mass.: Harvard University Press, 2007), pp. 65–97.
7. James R. Shea, Director of International Programs, Nuclear Regulatory Commission, Memorandum for: The Commissioners, Subject: ERDA Unclassified Briefing on Reactor Plutonium and Nuclear Explosives, December 3, 1976; Robert W. Selden, Lawrence Livermore Laboratory, "Reactor Plutonium and Nuclear Explosives," November 1976.
8. David M. Rosenbaum, *A Special Safeguards Study*, 1974, reprinted in U.S. Congress, Senate Committee on Governmental Operations, *Peaceful Nuclear Exports and Weapons Proliferation* (Washington, D.C.: U.S. Government Printing Office, 1975), pp. 469–483; John McPhee, *The Curve of Binding Energy* (New York: Farrar, Straus & Giroux, 1980), pp. 123, 126–127, 193; Richard Burt, "Pentagon Game Simulates a Nuclear Blackmail Case," *New York Times*, November 15, 1977, p. 10.
9. ERDA, "Hazards of Attempting to Fabricate a Nuclear Explosive," April 1976. Hoover Institution, Papers of Victor Gilinsky, Box 632, Folder: Weapons, 1976–1983; Interview with Victor Gilinsky, Santa Monica, Calif., March 28, 2007.
10. Merton E. Davies and William R. Harris, *RAND's Role in the Evolution of Balloon and Satellite Observation Systems and Related Space Technology* (Santa Monica, Calif.: RAND, 1988), p. 6; Paul Bagne, "Interview with Brian Michael Jenkins," *Omni*, November 1994, accessed from www.accessmylibrary.com; "RAND Expert Biography: Brian Michael Jenkins," www.rand.org, accessed March 21, 2007.
11. "RAND Expert Biography: Brian Michael Jenkins"; Bagne, "Interview with Brian Michael Jenkins"; Chambers interview; Greg Kirkorian, "Calmly Taking Terror's Measure," *Los Angeles Times*, January 31, 2008, pp. A1, A23.
12. Brian Jenkins, RAND Paper P-5541, "Will Terrorists Go Nuclear?" November 1975, pp. 3, 7.
13. Ibid., p. 4.

14. Ibid., pp. 4–6.
15. Ibid., p. 6.
16. Office of Technology Assessment, *Nuclear Proliferation and Safeguards* (Washington, D.C.: Office of Technology Assessment, 1977), p. 121.
17. Ibid., pp. 122, 127.
18. Dan Stober, "Missing Nuclear Data Is Vital to Bomb Sleuths," *San Jose Mercury News*, June 15, 2000, p. 1A; McPhee, *Curve of Binding Energy*, p. 103.
19. Collins, "Nuclear Terrorism."
20. Ibid.
21. Ibid.
22. Ibid.
23. "Unocal Corporation," www.answers.com, accessed March 20, 2007; Thomas C. Hayes, "Unocals Chairman Digs In," *New York Times*, April 16, 1985, accessed from www.nytimes.com; "Unocal Names Chief Executive," *New York Times*, June 7, 1988, accessed from www.nytimes.com; Wolfgang Saxon, "Fred L. Hartley, 73, Built Unocal into Multibillion-Dollar Company," *New York Times*, October 21, 1990, accessed from www.nytimes.com; Richard J. Stegemeier, "A Century of Spirit: The History of Unocal," address to the Newcomen Society of the United States, Los Angeles, October 15, 1990, p. 17.
24. "Union Oil Develops New Shale Process," *New York Times*, June 11, 1974, p. 62; "Union Oil is Facing Antitrust Charges in California Suit," *New York Times*, December 27, 1974, p. 47.
25. Assistant Director in Charge, Los Angeles to Director, FBI, Subject: UNSUB, aka Fission; Fred L. Hartley, Chairman of the Board, Union Oil Company of California—Victim Extortion, November 5, 1975; Letter, Fision to Mr. Fred L. Hartley, November 3, 1975.
26. Letter, Fision to Mr. Fred L. Hartley.
27. Ibid.
28. Ibid.
29. Hayes, "Unocals Chairman Digs In"; Saxon, "Fred L. Hartley, 73, Built Unocal into Multibillion-Dollar Company."
30. Collins, "Nuclear Terrorism"; John R. Emshwiller, "In Atom-Bomb Scare, Federal NEST Team Flies to the Rescue," *Wall Street Journal*, October 21, 1980, pp. 1, 22; Judith Valente, "Secretive Federal Program Combats Terrorism," *Washington Post*, June 21, 1983, pp. C1, C7; Chris West, "Birds-eye View of NEST," *News & Views*, 10, 8 (September 1984), pp. 1, 4–6; Los Angeles to Director, Unsub; aka Fision, Fred L. Hartley, Chairman of the Board, Union Oil Company of California—Victim Extortion 00: LA, November 6, 1975; Untitled FBI document, November 10, 1975.
31. Collins, "Nuclear Terrorism."
32. Los Angeles (9-5766) (P) to Director, Unknown Subject: aka Fision, Fred L. Hartley, Chairman of the Board, Union Oil Company of California—Victim Extortion

00: Los Angeles, November 11, 1975; Untitled FBI statement of SA [Deleted], November 12, 1975.

33. Los Angeles (9-5766) (P) to Director, Unknown Subject: aka Fision, Fred L. Hartley, Chairman of the Board, Union Oil Company of California—Victim Extortion 00: Los Angeles, November 11, 1975.

34. Ibid.; ADIC, Los Angeles to Director, FBI, Subject: UNSUB, aka Fision; Fred L. Hartley, Chairman of the Board, Union Oil Company of California—Victim Extortion 00: Los Angeles, November 13, 1975; ADIC, Los Angeles to Director, FBI, Subject: UNSUB, aka Fision; Fred L. Hartley, Chairman of the Board Union Oil Company of California—Victim Extortion 00: Los Angeles, November 12, 1975; Statement by SA [Deleted], November 10, 1975; Identification Division, Latent Fingerprint Section, to: SAC, Los Angeles, Subject: UNSUB, aka Fision; Fred L. Hartley, Chairman of the Board, Union Oil Company of California—Victim Extortion, November 28, 1975; Identification Division, Latent Fingerprint Section, to: SAC, Los Angeles, Subject: UNSUB, aka Fision; Fred L. Hartley, Chairman of the Board, Union Oil Company of California—Victim Extortion, December 11, 1975.

35. Statement of SAC Elmer F. Linberg, SAs [Deleted], November 11, 1975; Statement of SA [Deleted] and SA [Deleted], November 13, 1975; Untitled, undated FBI document obtained under Freedom of Information Act.

36. FBI, Unknown Subject, aka Fision; Fred L. Hartley, Chairman of the Board, Union Oil Company of America—Victim, April 27, 1976; Statement of SAs [Deleted] and [Deleted], March 19, 1976; Statement of SA [Deleted], April 8, 1976.

37. Los Angeles to Director, Frank (NMI) James, aka Fision; Fred L. Hartley, Chairman of the Board, Union Oil Company California—Victim Extortion 00: LA, June 23, 1976.

38. Los Angeles to Director, Frank NMI James AKA Fision; Fred L. Hartley, Chairman of the Board, Union Oil Company of California—Victim Extortion 00: Los Angeles, October 8, 1976; SAC, Los Angeles to Director, FBI, Subject: Frank (NMI) James, aka Fision; Fred L. Hartley, Chairman of the Board, Union Oil Company of America—Victim Extortion; AR—Hobbs Act (Extortion) 00: LA, September 21, 1978.

39. "United States Bicentennial," http://en.wikipedia.org/wiki/United_States_Bicentennial, accessed March 20, 2007.

40. Ibid.

41. Central Intelligence Agency, *International and Transnational Terrorism: Diagnosis and Prognosis*, April 1976, pp. 4–5.

42. West, "Birds-eye View of NEST."

43. "Subject: Washington, D.C., Nest Operations Plan," undated NEST document obtained under the Freedom of Information Act.

44. Ibid.

45. Ibid.

46. Philip L. Cantelon and Robert C. Williams, *Crisis Contained: The Department of Energy at Three Mile Island: A History* (Washington, D.C.: Department of Energy, 1980), pp. 32–33; Chambers interview; W. H. Chambers, "Summary: A Brief History of NEST," October 24, 1995, p. 2.

47. Valente, "Secretive Federal Program Combats Terrorism"; Emshwiller, "In Atom-Bomb Scare, Federal NEST Team Flies to the Rescue"; Stober, "Missing Nuclear Data Is Vital to Bomb Sleuths."

48. Collins, "Nuclear Terrorism."

49. Chambers interview.

50. ERDA, Fact Sheet, "Nuclear Emergency Search Team (NEST)," 1977; Gerald R. Ford, Executive Order 11953, "Emergency Preparedness Functions," January 7, 1977.

51. ERDA, Fact Sheet, "Nuclear Emergency Search Team (NEST)."

52. Ibid.

53. Lawrence Livermore National Laboratory, Nonproliferation, Homeland and International Security, "Radiological and Nuclear Countermeasures," www.llnl.gov, accessed April 3, 2007; Untitled briefing slides provided by a former NEST member; Interview with Alan V. Mode, Pleasanton, Calif., April 9, 2007.

54. Lawrence Livermore National Laboratory, Nonproliferation, Homeland and International Security, "Radiological and Nuclear Countermeasures"; Eric Pace, "Murray Miron, 62, Psychologist Who Aided F.B.I.," *New York Times*, July 28, 1995, accessed via www.nytimes.com; Untitled briefing slides provided by a former NEST member.

55. E. Dowdy, C. N. Henry, and R. D. Hastings, Los Alamos Scientific Laboratory, LA-7108, *Neutron Detector Suitcase for the Nuclear Emergency Search Team*, February 1978; Telephone interview with Carl Henry, November 30, 2007.

56. Mode interview.

57. Valente, "Secretive Federal Program Combats Terrorism."

58. Presidential Briefing Coordinator, Memorandum for: All Office Directors and NIOs, Subject: Presidential Briefing Topics for 27 June and later, June 23, 1978, CIA Records Search Tool (CREST), National Archives and Records Administration.

59. "Wilmington, North Carolina," http://en.wikipedia.org, accessed March 27, 2007.

60. Nuclear Regulatory Commission, Office of Inspection and Enforcement Circular No. 79-08, "Attempted Extortion—Low Enriched Uranium," May 18, 1979; Collins, "Nuclear Terrorism"; SAC, Charlotte (117-42) (P), to Director, FBI, Subject: Unknown Subjects; Theft of 66 Kilograms of 2.6% Enriched Uranium from the General Electric Low Enriched Uranium Plant, Wilmington, N.C., 1/29/79, AEA-Extortion, 00: Charlotte, January 30, 1979.

61. Nuclear Regulatory Commission, IE Circular No. 79-08, "Attempted Extortion—Low Enriched Uranium"; Collins, "Nuclear Terrorism."

62. Nuclear Regulatory Commission, IE Circular No. 79-08, "Attempted Extortion—Low Enriched Uranium"; Collins, "Nuclear Terrorism."

63. "Sanitized Summary of G.E. Wilmington Incident," attachment to: Nuclear Regulatory Commission, IE Circular No. 79-08, "Attempted Extortion—Low Enriched Uranium"; From [Deleted] For [Deleted], Federal Bureau of Investigation, Subject: UNSUB, aka Extortion Involving the General Electric Low Enriched Uranium Plant, Wilmington, N.C., 1/29/79—Nuclear Extortion, January 29, 1979.

64. Copy of untitled extortion letter, received in response to Freedom of Information Act request to the FBI.

65. Ibid.

66. "Sanitized Summary of G.E. Wilmington Incident," attachment to: Nuclear Regulatory Commission, IE Circular No. 79-08, "Attempted Extortion—Low Enriched Uranium"; Nuclear Regulatory Commission, Information Notice No. 79-02, "Attempted Extortion—Low Enriched Uranium," February 2, 1979; SAC, Charlotte (117-42)(P), to Director, FBI, Subject: Unknown Subjects; Theft of 66 Kilograms of 2.6% Enriched Uranium from the General Electric Low Enriched Uranium Plant, Wilmington, N.C., 1/29/79, AEA-Extortion, 00: Charlotte, January 30, 1979.

67. Charlotte FBI Office, CE 117-42, Judicial Process, n.d.; FBI Director to White House Situation Room, Unknown Subjects; Theft of 66 Kilograms of 2.6% Enriched Uranium from General Electric Low Enriched Uranium Plant, Wilmington, North Carolina, January 29, 1979, Atomic Energy Act—Extortion, January 31, 1979; FBI, "Criminal Investigative Division," January 30, 1979.

68. FBI Director to White House Situation Room, Unknown Subjects; Theft of 66 Kilograms of 2.6% Enriched Uranium from General Electric Low Enriched Uranium Plant, Wilmington, North Carolina, January 29, 1979; Atomic Energy Act—Extortion, January 30, 1979.

69. Ibid.

70. Ibid.

71. Director EACT, USDOE, to FBI Headquarters, Wilmington Incident, January 30, 1979.

72. F. W. Jessen Livermore/Dir EACT/USDOE, Wash, DC, To: RHEGGTN/DOE HQS EACT, Nuclear Threat No. 46, January 30, 1979. Jessen is transmitting the assessments of F. Kloverstrom, R. Remillard, and George Moore.

73. F. W. Jessen, Univ. of Calif. Lawrence Livermore Laboratory, To: RHEGGTN/ Martin Dowd, EACT/HQ, Germantown, Md., Four Hour Response, 30 January 1979. Jessen is transmitting the analysis performed by J. Krofcheck, G. Gass, B. Jenkins, and P. Tropodies.

74. Director, FBI, to: White House Situation Room, Unknown Subjects; Theft of 66 Kilograms of 2.6 Percent Enrichment Uranium from General Electric Low Enriched Uranium Plant, Wilmington, North Carolina, January 29, 1979; Atomic Energy Act—Extortion, February 1, 1979; FBI, "Criminal Investigative Division," February 2, 1979; Charlotte to Director FBI, Changed: [Deleted]; Theft of 66 Kilograms of 2.6 Percent Enriched Uranium from General Electric (GE) Low-Enriched Uranium Plant, Wilmington, N.C., January 29, 1979, AEA-Extortion,

February 1, 1979; FBI, CE 117-42, Judicial Process; Untitled FBI memo, February 8, 1979.

75. Charlotte, CE 117-42, "Administrative," n.d.

76. Ibid.

77. Ibid.; FBI, CE 117-42, February 6, 1979, p. 82.

78. Charlotte, CE 117-42, "Administrative," n.d.; Collins, "Nuclear Terrorism."

79. Cantelon and Williams, *Crisis Contained*, p. 3; Richard Roberts, "Event Rated Serious," *Patriot*, March 29, 1979, www.threemileisland.org/downloads//49.htm.

80. Cantelon and Williams, *Crisis Contained*, p. 6.

81. Ibid., p. 21; Roberts, "Event Rated Serious."

82. Cantelon and Williams, *Crisis Contained*, p. 39.

83. Ibid., pp. 40-41.

84. Ibid., p. 42.

85. Idaho National Laboratory, "History," www.inl.gov/history/index.shtml, accessed April 2, 2007.

86. Maj. Gen. J. K. Bratton, ERDA, Untitled message, June 12, 1977; F. D. Koopman, "Observer Plan" (Draft), March 24, 1977.

87. Eric L. Haney, *Inside Delta Force: The Story of America's Elite Counterterrorist Unit* (New York: Delacorte, 2002), p. 180; Idaho National Laboratory, "History."

88. Haney, *Inside Delta Force*, p. 181.

89. "Greenpeace," http://en.wikipedia.org/wiki/Greenpeace; Sunday Times Insight Team, *Rainbow Warrior: The French Attempt to Sink Greenpeace* (London: Hutchinson, 1986) p. 11.

90. Steven Sawyer, e-mail, April 3, 2007; FBI, "Criminal Investigative Division," August 22, 1980, available in FBI Electronic Reading Room, Greenpeace file.

91. FBI, "Criminal Investigative Division"; Washington Field to Director FBI, "Atomic Energy Act—Information Concerning," August 21, 1980; Washington Field to Director FBI, "Greenpeace Foundation Demonstration, White House, Washington, D.C., August 21, 1980; Atomic Energy Act—Information Concerning," August 22, 1980.

92. Valente, "Secretive Federal Program Combats Terrorism"; Steven Sawyer, e-mail. The *Washington Post* published an article on Greenpeace in late 1984: Bob Reiss, "The Greening of Activism," *Washington Post Magazine*, December 2, 1984, pp. 20ff.

CHAPTER THREE: MORNING LIGHT

1. "Plesetsk Cosmodrome," http://en.wikipedia.org/wiki/Plesetsk_Cosmodrome; Steven J. Zaloga, *Target America: The Soviet Union and the Strategic Arms Race, 1945–1964* (Novato, Calif.: Presidio, 1993), pp. 150–151.

2. Nicholas L. Johnson, *The Soviet Year in Space 1986* (Colorado Springs, Colo.:

Teledyne-Brown Engineering, 1987), p. 41; "Cosmos 954: An Ugly Death," *Time*, February 6, 1978, accessed from www.time.com; Leo Heaps, *Operation Morning Light: Terror in Our Skies, The True Story of Cosmos 954* (New York: Paddington, 1978), p. 14.

3. Viktor Suvorov, *Soviet Military Intelligence* (London: Hamish Hamilton, 1984), p. 61; Desmond Ball, *Soviet Signals Intelligence (SIGINT)* (Canberra: Strategic and Defence Studies Centre, 1989), pp. 80–123.

4. Asif Siddiqi, "Staring at the Sea: The Soviet RORSAT and EORSAT Programmes," *Journal of the British Interplanetary Society*, 52 (1999), pp. 397–416.

5. Ibid.

6. Ibid.

7. Ibid.; Director of Central Intelligence, Interagency Intelligence Memorandum, *Soviet Dependence on Space Systems*, November 1975, p. 13; Jeffrey T. Richelson, *Sword and Shield: The Soviet Intelligence and Security Apparatus* (Cambridge, Mass.: Ballinger, 1986), p. 104.

8. Siddiqi, "Staring at the Sea."

9. Ibid.; Director of Central Intelligence, NIE 11-1-80, *Soviet Military Capabilities and Intentions in Space*, August 6, 1980; "Cosmos 954: An Ugly Death"; Sven Grahn, "The US—A Program (Radar Ocean Reconnaissance Satellites—RORSAT) and Radio Observations Thereof," www.svengrahn.pp.se/trackind/RORSAT/RORSAT .html, pp. 4–5, accessed October 30, 2006.

10. Siddiqi, "Staring at the Sea."

11. Jeffrey T. Richelson, *America's Space Sentinels: DSP Satellites and National Security* (Lawrence: University Press of Kansas, 1999), p. 107.

12. Craig Covault, "Maui Optical Station Photographs External Tank Reentry Breakup," *Aviation Week & Space Technology*, June 11, 1990, pp. 52–53; Andrew Pickles, "A Brief History of Astronomy in Hawaii since 1940," www.mkooc.org/ css-timeline.html, accessed May 8, 2007; John T. Jefferies, "Astronomy in Hawaii, 1964–1970," University of Hawaii Institute for Astronomy, www.ifa.hawaii.edu/ users/jefferies/Preface.htm, accessed May 8, 2007.

13. John Noble Wilford, "Trackers Describe Vigil," *New York Times*, January 29, 1978, pp. 1, 8.

14. Wilford, "Trackers Describe Vigil"; Department of Energy, Nevada Operations Office, *U.S. Participation in Operation Morning Light: A Technical Report*, March 1981, p. 41.

15. Wilford, "Trackers Describe Vigil."

16. Gus W. Weiss, "The Life and Death of Cosmos 954," *Studies in Intelligence*, 22, 1 (Spring 1978), pp. 1–7.

17. Ibid.

18. Ibid.; NDHQ to U.S. Department of Energy, Subj: Morning Light, November 20, 1978 (includes handwritten comments); Department of Energy, Nevada Operations Office, *U.S. Participation in Operation Morning Light*, p. 41.

19. Weiss, "Life and Death of Cosmos 954"; Wilford, "Trackers Describe Vigil"; Department of Energy, Nevada Operations Office, *U.S. Participation in Operation Morning Light*, p. 3.

20. Weiss, "Life and Death of Cosmos 954"; Richard D. Lyons, "Soviet Spy Satellite with Atomic Reactor Breaks Up in Canada," *New York Times*, January 25, 1978, pp. A1, A8.

21. Weiss, "Life and Death of Cosmos 954"; Department of Energy, Nevada Operations Office, *U.S. Participation in Operation Morning Light*, p. 42.

22. Weiss, "Life and Death of Cosmos 954."

23. Ibid.; Department of Energy, Nevada Operations Office, NV-198, *Operational Morning Light, Canadian Northwest Territories/1978: A Non-Technical Summary of United States Participation*, September 1978, p. 2.

24. Lyons, "Soviet Spy Satellite with Atomic Reactor Breaks Up in Canada."

25. Heaps, *Operation Morning Light*, p. 40; Gordon Bell, "A Seymour Cray Perspective," Seymour Cray Lecture Series, University of Minnesota, November 10, 1997, Slides 50, 52.

26. Telephone interview with Robert Kelley, November 20, 2007.

27. Ibid.; Wilford, "Trackers Describe Vigil"; Department of Energy, Nevada Operations Office, *U.S. Participation in Operation Morning Light*, p. 42.

28. Wilford, "Trackers Describe Vigil."

29. Ibid.; Major Bill Aikman, "Operation Morning Light," Sentinel, 2 (1978), pp. 4–16.

30. Weiss, "Life and Death of Cosmos 954"; Department of Energy, Nevada Operations Office, *Operation Morning Light, Canadian Northwest Territories/1978*, p. 8.

31. Weiss, "Life and Death of Cosmos 954."

32. Jeffrey T. Richelson, *America's Secret Eyes in Space: The US KEYHOLE Spy Satellite Program* (New York: Harper & Row, 1990), pp. 87–88, 360–361.

33. See Jeffrey T. Richelson, *The Wizards of Langley: Inside the CIA's Directorate of Science and Technology* (Boulder, Colo.: Westview, 2001), pp. 198–202.

34. Office of the Historian, Strategic Air Command, SAC Historical Study 187, *History of SAC Reconnaissance Operations*: 1978, 1979, and 1980, June 1, 1982, pp. 208, 210.

35. Ibid., p. 210.

36. Ibid.

37. Ibid., pp. 208, 210; Robert S. Hopkins III, *Boeing KC-135 Stratotanker* (Leicester, England: Aerofax, 1997), pp. 154–157; "WC-135 Constant Phoenix," www.af.mil/factsheets.

38. Office of the Historian, Strategic Air Command, SAC Historical Study 187, *History of SAC Reconnaissance Operations*, pp. 209–210.

39. "Cosmos 954: An Ugly Death"; W. K. Gummer, F. R. Campbell, G. B. Knight, and J. L. Ricard, *Cosmos 954: The Occurrence and Nature of Recovered Debris* (Ottawa: Atomic Energy Control Board, 1980), p.1.

40. Department of Energy, Nevada Operations Office, *U.S. Participation in Operation Morning Light*, p. 41.

41. Ibid., pp. 42, 89; Department of Energy, Nevada Operations Office, *Operation Morning Light, Canadian Northwest Territories/1978*, pp. 5, 7; Robert Gillette, "Cosmos Hunt Puts U.S. Teams to Test," *Los Angeles Times*, February 12, 1978, pp. A1, A12–A13.

42. Department of Energy, Nevada Operations Office, *Operation Morning Light, Canadian Northwest Territories/1978*, p. 5; Gillette, "Cosmos Hunt Puts U.S. Teams to Test"; Quentin Bristow, "Operation Morning Light—A Personal Account," 1995, http://gsc.nrcan.gc.ca/gamma/ml_e.php.

43. Aikman, "Operation Morning Light," p. 5; "Northwest Territories," http://en.wikipedia .org, accessed May 31, 2007; Department of Energy, Nevada Operations Office, *Operation Morning Light, Canadian Northwest Territories/1978*, p. 8.

44. "Yellowknife, Northwest Territories," "Great Slave Lake," both from http:// en.wikipedia.org, both accessed May 31, 2007; Aikman, "Operation Morning Light," p. 5; "Baker Lake," http://en.wikipedia.org, accessed June 2, 2007.

45. Department of Energy, Nevada Operations Office, *U.S. Participation in Operation Morning Light*, pp. 43, 90; Department of Energy, Nevada Operations Office, *Operation Morning Light, Canadian Northwest Territories/1978*, p. 9; Weiss, "Life and Death of Cosmos 954."

46. Aikman, "Operation Morning Light," pp. 5–6; Department of Energy, Nevada Operations Office, *U.S. Participation in Operation Morning Light*, p. 297.

47. "Personnel Profiles," *NTS News*, May 1978, p. 13; Department of Energy, Nevada Operations Office, *U.S. Participation in Operation Morning Light*, p. 43; Heaps, *Operation Morning Light*, p. 27.

48. Department of Energy, Nevada Operations Office, *Operation Morning Light, Canadian Northwest Territories/1978*, p. 9; Department of Energy, Nevada Operations Office, *U.S. Participation in Operation Morning Light*, pp. 43, 90; Aikman, "Operation Morning Light," p. 6; "12-Hour Flights in Darkness over Vast Frozen Corridor," *EG&G Focus*, March 1978, pp. 3–4, 6; R. L. Grasty, "The Search for Cosmos-954," in K. Brian Haley and Lawrence D. Stone (eds.), *Search Theory and Applications* (New York: Plenum, 1980), pp. 211–220 at p. 211.

49. Heaps, *Operation Morning Light*, pp. 33, 35, 47, 106; Interview with William Chambers, Los Alamos, N.M., July 10, 2007; Interview with William Nelson, Alamo, Calif., June 9, 2007; Richard Roberts, "Event Rated Serious," *Patriot*, March 29, 1979, accessed from www.threemileisland.org.

50. Nelson interview.

51. Ibid.

52. "12-Hour Flights in Darkness over Vast Frozen Corridor"; Department of Energy, Nevada Operations Office, *U.S. Participation in Operation Morning Light*, pp. 43, 188; "CC-130 Hercules," www.airforce.forces.gc.ca, accessed June 3, 2007; H. W. Taylor, E. A. Hutchinson, K. L. McInnes, and J. Svoboda, "Cosmos 954: Search for Airborne Radioactivity on Lichens in the Crash Area, Northwest Territories," *Science*, September 29, 1979, pp. 1383–1385; Aikman, "Operation Morning Light," p. 7.

53. Grasty, "Search for Cosmos-954," p. 211; "12-Hour Flights in Darkness over Vast Frozen Corridor"; Department of Energy, Nevada Operations Office, *Operation Morning Light, Canadian Northwest Territories/1978*, p. 14.

54. Department of Energy, Nevada Operations Office, *U.S. Participation in Operation Morning Light*, p. 189.

55. Ibid., pp. 190, 193.

56. Gillette, "Cosmos Hunt Puts U.S. Teams to Test"; Taylor, Hutchinson, McInnes, and Svoboda, "Cosmos 954.

57. "12-Hour Flights in Darkness over Vast Frozen Corridor."

58. Gillette, "Cosmos Hunt Puts U.S. Teams to Test"; "12-Hour Flights in Darkness over Vast Frozen Corridor"; Department of Energy, Nevada Operations Office, *U.S. Participation in Operation Morning Light*, p. 199.

59. Bristow, "Operation Morning Light—A Personal Account"; Department of Energy, Nevada Operations Office, *Operation Morning Light, Canadian Northwest Territories/1978*, pp. 15, 25, 61; Department of Energy, Nevada Operations Office, *U.S. Participation in Operation Morning Light*, pp. 43, 103.

60. Department of Energy, Nevada Operations Office, *Operation Morning Light, Canadian Northwest Territories/1978*, pp. 15, 25, 61; Department of Energy, Nevada Operations Office, *U.S. Participation in Operation Morning Light*, pp. 43, 103; "CC-138 Twin Otter," www.airforce.forces.gc.ca, accessed June 3, 2007.

61. Department of Energy, Nevada Operations Office, *Operation Morning Light, Canadian Northwest Territories/1978*, p. 25; Department of Energy, Nevada Operations Office, *U.S. Participation in Operation Morning Light*, pp. 194–195; Aikman, "Operation Morning Light," p. 8; Heaps, *Operation Morning Light*, p. 74.

62. Department of Energy, Nevada Operations Office, *U.S. Participation in Operation Morning Light*, p. 44.

63. Ibid.

64. Department of Energy, Nevada Operations Office, *Operation Morning Light, Canadian Northwest Territories/1978*, p. 25; "Scenes from Warden's Grove," *EG&G Focus*, March 1978, p. 10; "John Hornby," http://en.wikipedia.org/wiki/John_Hornby, accessed May 14, 2007; "12-Hour Flights in Darkness over Vast Frozen Corridor."

65. "Scenes from Warden's Grove"; Department of Energy, Nevada Operations Office, *Operation Morning Light, Canadian Northwest Territories/1978*, p. 36; Department of Energy, Nevada Operations Office, *U.S. Participation in Operation Morning Light*, p. 44; Aikman, "Operation Morning Light," p. 9.

66. Grasty, "Search for Cosmos-954," p. 213; Department of Energy, Nevada Operations Office, *U.S. Participation in Operation Morning Light*, pp. 44, 197; Aikman, "Operation Morning Light," p. 13.

67. Grasty, "Search for Cosmos-954," p. 213; Department of Energy, Nevada Operations Office, *U.S. Participation in Operation Morning Light*, pp. 44, 197, 198; Aikman, "Operation Morning Light," p. 13; "12-Hour Flights in Darkness over Vast Frozen Corridor."

68. Aikman, "Operation Morning Light," p. 12.
69. Department of Energy, Nevada Operations Office, *U.S. Participation in Operation Morning Light*, p. 199.
70. Department of Energy, Nevada Operations Office, *Operation Morning Light, Canadian Northwest Territories/1978*, p. 42.
71. Department of Energy, Nevada Operations Office, *U.S. Participation in Operation Morning Light*, pp. 45, 52.
72. Ibid., pp. 44, 47, 197; Department of Energy, Nevada Operations Office, *Operation Morning Light, Canadian Northwest Territories/1978*, pp. 61, 62.
73. Grasty, "Search for Cosmos-954," p. 213.
74. Department of Energy, Nevada Operations Office, *U.S. Participation in Operation Morning Light*, p. 212.
75. Ibid., p. 47.
76. Department of Energy, Nevada Operations Office, *Operation Morning Light, Canadian Northwest Territories/1978*, pp. 30, 61, 62, 197; Department of Energy, Nevada Operations Office, *U.S. Participation in Operation Morning Light*, pp. 47, 48; Gillette, "Cosmos Hunt Puts U.S. Teams to Test."
77. Department of Energy, Nevada Operations Office, *U.S. Participation in Operation Morning Light*, p. 48.
78. R. L. Landingham and A. W. Casey, Lawrence Livermore Laboratory, *MORNING LIGHT Cleanup and Recovery Operations: Simulation Studies of Possible Reactor Fuels*, August 31, 1978, p. 1.
79. "Canada-USSR," *National Intelligence Daily*, January 23, 1979, p. 19.

CHAPTER FOUR: A LOW-PROFILE DECADE

1. "U.S. Nuclear Extortion Threats Event List," n.d. The list was provided to the author by a former member of NEST.
2. "Stateline, Nevada," "Lake Tahoe Horizon Casino," "Mont Bleu Casino & Spa," all in http://en.wikipedia.org, accessed November 9, 2007; Jim Sloan, "Render Safe," *Reno Gazette-Journal*, August 21, 2005, accessed from www.rgj.com.
3. "Stateline, Nevada"; A. O. Scott, "Sometimes Pulp Fiction Emphasizes Pulp over Fiction," *New York Times*, January 26, 2007, accessed from www.nytimes.com.
4. Sloan, "Render Safe"; Jim Sloan, "Special Delivery for Harvey Gross," *Reno Gazette-Journal*, August 22, 2005, accessed from www.rgj.com.
5. Sloan, "Special Delivery for Harvey Gross."
6. Ibid.
7. Ibid.
8. Ibid.
9. Ibid.
10. "Harvey Gross, 78, a Pioneer in Lake Tahoe Gaming Clubs," *New York Times*, November 3, 1983, accessed from www.nytimes.com.; Tim Anderson and Jim

Sloan, "Where Are They Now?" *Reno Gazette-Journal*, August 28, 2005, accessed from www.rgj.com.

11. Jim Sloan, "A Stern Warning: 'It Is full of TNT,'" *Reno Gazette-Journal*, August 22, 2005, accessed from www.rgj.com.

12. Ibid.

13. Ibid.; Jim Sloan, "The Payoff: There Will Be No Extension or Renegotiation," *Reno Gazette-Journal*, August 25, 2005, accessed from www.rgj.com; "Bomb Extortionist's Letter Said Betrayal Would Bring Repetition," *New York Times*, August 31, 1980, p. 18.

14. Jim Sloan, "We Never Expected Them to Get the Bomb inside the Casino," *Reno Gazette-Journal*, August 24, 2005, accessed from www.rgj.com; Sloan, "Payoff."

15. Sloan, "Stern Warning."

16. Ibid.

17. Ibid.

18. Interview with Alan V. Mode, April 17, 2007, Pleasanton, Calif.

19. Interview with William Nelson, June 9, 2007, Alamo, Calif.

20. Ibid.

21. Ibid.; Sloan, "Stern Warning."

22. Sloan, "Payoff"; Sloan, "We Never Expected Them to Get the Bomb inside the Casino."

23. Nelson interview; Jim Sloan, "Once the Charge Was Set, There Was No Going Back," *Reno Gazette-Journal*, August 28, 2005, accessed from www.rgj.com; Jim Sloan, "In a Deserted Casino, Bomb Experts Flip the Switch," *Reno Gazette-Journal*, August 27, 2005, accessed from www.rgj.com.

24. Sloan, "In a Deserted Casino, Bomb Experts Flip the Switch."

25. Nelson interview; Robert Lindsey, "Bomb Set by Extortionists Goes Off after Nevada Casino Evacuated," *New York Times*, August 28, 1980, pp. A1, A12.

26. Lindsey, "Bomb Set by Extortionists Goes Off after Nevada Casino Evacuated"; Nelson interview.

27. Sloan, "Payoff"; "Bomb Extortionist's Letter Said Betrayal Would Bring Repetition"; "Clues Checked in Nevada Blast, Including Fingerprints on Bomb," *New York Times*, August 30, 1980, p. 10; Robert Lindsey, "F.B.I. Says Fingerprints Were Left on Bomb That Wrecked Casino-Hotel," *New York Times*, August 29, 1980, p. 12; Sloan, "In a Deserted Casino, Bomb Experts Flip the Switch."

28. "F.B.I. Releases Sketches of Casino Blast Suspects," *New York Times*, September 18, 1980, p. A27; "Around the Nation: Two in Casino Bombing Plead Guilty in Bargain," *New York Times*, September 9, 1981, accessed from www.rgj.com; Sloan, "Once the Charge Was Set, There Was No Going Back."

29. Jane Ann Morrison, "TV Special on 1980 Bombing Puts Focus on Old Memories, New Attitudes," www.reviewjournal.com, August 27, 2005, accessed October 26, 2006; "John Birges," http://en.wikipedia.org/wiki/John_Birges.

30. Nelson interview; W. H. Chambers, "Summary: A Brief History of NEST," October 24, 1995, p. 3.

31. "U.S. Nuclear Extortion Threats Event List."

32. Ronald Reagan, National Security Decision Directive 30, "Managing Terrorist Incidents," April 10, 1982.

33. *Department of State (State), Department of Energy (DOE), and Department of Defense (DOD) Memorandum of Understanding (MOU) for Responding to Malevolent Nuclear Incidents Outside U.S. Territory and Possessions*, January 28, 1982.

34. "U.S. Nuclear Extortion Threats Event List."

35. *Department of State (State), Department of Energy (DOE), and Department of Defense (DOD) Memorandum of Understanding (MOU) for Responding to Malevolent Nuclear Incidents Outside U.S. Territory and Possessions.*

36. "U.S. Nuclear Extortion Threats Event List."

37. Chambers, "Summary: A Brief History of NEST," p. 3.

38. Ibid.

39. John Noble Wilford, "Soviet Denies Peril from Satellite; U.S. Differs and Sets Up an Alert," *New York Times*, October 16, 2006, accessed from www.nytimes.com; John Noble Wilford, "Russian Satellite Falls Harmlessly over Indian Ocean," *New York Times*, January 24, 1983, accessed from www.nytimes.com.

40. Nicholas L. Johnson, *Soviet Military Strategy in Space* (London: Jane's, 1987), p. 97; Asif Siddiqi, "Staring at the Sea: The Soviet RORSAT and EORSAT Programmes," *Journal of the British Interplanetary Society*, 52 (1999), pp. 397–416.

41. Wilford, "Soviet Denies Peril from Satellite."

42. Ibid.; Wilford, "Russian Satellite Falls Harmlessly over Indian Ocean."

43. Wilford, "Soviet Denies Peril from Satellite."

44. Ibid.

45. Ibid.; "NEST Team Alert for Cosmos 1402 Descent to Earth," *Weekly Bulletin*, January 12, 1983, p. 2.

46. Timothy Aeppel, "Special Team's Challenge: Cleaning Up Nuclear Incidents," *Christian Science Monitor*, January 25, 1983, accessed from www.csmonitor.com.

47. Serge Schmemann, "Soviet Says Satellite Core Will Fall Next Month, but Doubts Danger," *New York Times*, January 16, 1983, accessed from www.nytimes.com; Genady Cherepanov, "An Introduction to Two-Dimensional Separated Flows," in S. M. Belotserkovsky (ed.), *Two-Dimensional Separated Flows* (Virginia Beach, Va.: Chapman & Hall/CRC Press, 1992), p. 4.

48. Schmemann, "Soviet Says Satellite Core"; "State Department's View," *New York Times*, January 16, 1983, accessed from www.nytimes.com.

49. Wilford, "Russian Satellite Falls Harmlessly over Indian Ocean."

50. Ibid.

51. William J. Broad, "Satellite's Fuel Core Falls 'Harmlessly,'" *New York Times*, February 4, 1983, accessed from www.nytimes.com.

52. "U.S. Nuclear Extortion Threats Event List"; Christopher Whitcomb, *Cold Zero: Inside the FBI Hostage Rescue Team* (New York: Warner Books, 2002), p. 198; "Exercise Equus Red," www.specialoperations.com/Domestic/FBI/Ops.htm, accessed February 10, 2005.

53. "Exercise Equus Red."

54. Ibid.

55. Chambers, "Summary: A Brief History of NEST," p. 3.

56. "U.S. Nuclear Events Threat List."

57. Ibid.; Ronald Reagan, National Security Decision Directive 135, "Counterintelligence and Security Precautions for the Summer Olympic Games," March 30, 1984.

58. Interview with William Chambers, Los Alamos, N. M., July 10, 2007.

59. "U.S. Nuclear Events Threat List"; "Bernhard Goetz," http://en.wikipedia.org/wiki/Bernhard_Goetz, accessed June 19, 2007.

60. "Bernhard Goetz"; "Bernard Goetz," www.heroism.org/class/1980/goetz.htm, accessed April 4, 2007.

61. "Bernhard Goetz."

62. "U.S. Nuclear Extortion Threats Event List"; Nonproliferation, Homeland and International Security, "Radiological and Nuclear Countermeasures," www.llnl.gov, accessed June 19, 2007.

63. Nonproliferation, Homeland and International Security, "Radiological and Nuclear Countermeasures"; U.S. Congress, Senate Committee on Armed Services, *Intelligence Briefing on Smuggling of Nuclear Material and the Role of International Criminal Organizations, and on the Proliferation of Cruise and Ballistic Missiles* (Washington, D.C.: U.S. Government Printing Office, 1996), p. 26.

64. Nonproliferation, Homeland and International Security, "Radiological and Nuclear Countermeasures"; see U.S. Congress, Senate Committee on Armed Services, *Intelligence Briefing on Smuggling of Nuclear Material and the Role of International Criminal Organizations, and on the Proliferation of Cruise and Ballistic Missiles*, pp. 26–27. In 1995 congressional hearings, the head of the CIA's Nonproliferation Center, Gordon Oehler, referred to an "early 1980s" threat to contaminate the New York City water supply by "a disgruntled citizen who tried to extort money." No threat against New York appears on the threats events list, so Oehler may have received a garbled version of the Goetz incident. See U.S. Congress, Senate Committee on Armed Services, *Intelligence Briefing on Smuggling of Nuclear Material and the Role of International Criminal Organizations, and on the Proliferation of Cruise and Ballistic Missiles*, p. 33.

65. "U.S. Nuclear Extortion Threats Event List."

66. Chambers, "Summary: A Brief History of NEST," p. 4.

67. Ibid.; Letter, Darwin J. Morgan to Jeffrey T. Richelson, Re: Freedom of Information Act (FOIA) Request NV2001-1231-02, March 1, 2002; Chambers interview.

68. "Camp Atterbury/Atterbury Range," http://www.globalsecurity.org, accessed May 2, 2007; "Camp Atterbury," http://en.wikipedia.org/wiki/Camp_Atterbury; Letter, Darwin J. Morgan to Jeffrey T. Richelson; Nelson interview.

69. Nelson interview.

70. Mode interview; Chambers, "Summary: A History of NEST," p. 4.

71. Chambers, "Summary: A History of NEST," p. 4; Nelson interview.

72. Nelson interview; Mode interview.

73. Dan Stober, "Missing Nuclear Data Is Vital to Bomb Sleuths," *San Jose Mercury News*, June 15, 2000, p. 1A.

74. "U.S. Nuclear Extortion Threats Events List."

CHAPTER FIVE: TARNISHED GOLD

1. "U.S. Nuclear Extortion Threats Event List," n.d. The list was provided to the author by a former member of NEST.

2. Ibid.

3. Sheila Grissett, "Enjoying Life in the Fest Lane," *New Orleans Times-Picayune*, October 16, 1994, pp. B1, B2; "Lafreniere Park," http//enwikipedia.org, accessed November 26, 2007; "History of Lafreniere Park," www.jeffparish.net, accessed November 26, 2007.

4. Federal Emergency Management Agency, *Exercise Mirage Gold After-Action Report*, March 1995, p. 7.

5. Danny O. Coulson and Elaine Shannon, *No Heroes: Inside the FBI's Secret Counter-Terror Force* (New York: Pocket Books, 2001), pp. 195, 204–205, 246.

6. Ibid., pp. 195–196, 204.

7. Ibid., pp. 208–209, 313.

8. Douglas Waller, "Nuclear Ninjas," *Time*, January 8, 1996, pp. 38–40; Andrew Cockburn and Leslie Cockburn, *One Point Safe: A True Story* (New York: Anchor Books, 1997), p. 86.

9. [Deleted], Re: Department of Energy (DOE) Nuclear Emergency Search Team (NEST) Full Field Exercise 1994 Codenamed "Mile Shakedown," August 3, 1992; Director FBI to SAC, New Orleans, [Subjects:] Mile Shakedown, Nuclear Terrorism Matter, Exercise Series, October 6, 1992, w/enclosure: Airtel to SAC, New Orleans Re: Mile Shakedown, Nuclear Terrorism Matter, Exercises Series, n.d.; [Deleted] to [Deleted], Re: "Mica Dig" TableTop Exercise, "Mile Shake-down" Exercise Series Counterterrorism Matter, November 25, 1992; [Deleted] to [Deleted], Re: "Mild Cover" Communications Exercise, "Mile Shakedown" Exercise Series Counterterrorism Matter, November 25, 1992; [Deleted] to [Deleted], Re: "Mile Shakedown", "Mica Dig," Nuclear Tabletop Exercise, December 16, 1993; Department of Energy, Nevada Operations Office, James K. Magruder, Assistant Manager for Operations, Subject: Mile Shakedown After-Action Report, September 1994, w/enclosure: Mile Shakedown After Action Report; From [Deleted], To: Mr. Bayse, Subject: "Mile Shakedown" Exercise Series; Communications Exercise "Mild Cover" Counterterrorism Matter, FBI Academy, Quantico, Virginia 11/17/92, December 24, 1992; Cockburn and Cockburn, *One Point Safe*, p. 86.

10. Cockburn and Cockburn, *One Point Safe*, p. 86; "Belle Chasse, Louisiana," http://en.wikipedia.org, accessed July 16, 2007.

11. COMJSOC [Commander, JSOC] to RUCJAA/USCINCSOC, Subject: Errant Knight Concept Modification, October 5, 1994.

12. Director FBI to SAC, New Orleans, [Subjects:] Mile Shakedown, Nuclear Terrorism Matter, Exercise Series, October 6, 1992 w/enclosure: Airtel to SAC, New Orleans Re: Mile Shakedown, Nuclear Terrorism Matter, Exercises Series, n.d.; W. Douglas Gow to [Deleted], October 9, 1992.

13. Department of Energy, Nevada Operations Office, *The Mile Shakedown Series of Exercises: A Compilation of Comments and Critiques*, February 18, 1995, p. 25; Federal Bureau of Investigation, *"Mirage Gold" Full Field Exercise, New Orleans, Louisiana, 10/16–21/94 FBI After-Action Report*, in U.S. Congress, Senate Committee on Governmental Affairs, *Global Proliferation of Weapons of Mass Destruction, Part III* (Washington, D.C.: U.S. Government Printing Office, 1996), pp. 184–209 at p. 186; Cockburn and Cockburn, *One Point Safe*, p. 87; From: SAC, CIRG, To: Director, FBI, Subject: "Mile Shakedown" Crisis Management Matter; Nuclear Exercise Series, July 27, 1994.

14. Department of Energy, Nevada Operations Office, *Mile Shakedown Series of Exercises*, p. 25; Federal Bureau of Investigation, *"Mirage Gold" Full Field Exercise*, in U.S. Congress, Senate Committee on Governmental Affairs, *Global Proliferation of Weapons of Mass Destruction, Part III*, p. 187; Cockburn and Cockburn, *One Point Safe*, pp. 86–87.

15. Department of Energy, Nevada Operations Office, *Mile Shakedown Series of Exercises*, p. 25; Federal Bureau of Investigation, *"Mirage Gold" Full Field Exercise*, in U.S. Congress, Senate Committee on Governmental Affairs, *Global Proliferation of Weapons of Mass Destruction, Part III*, p. 187; Cockburn and Cockburn, *One Point Safe*, p. 87; Fm: FBI Director To: FBI Anchorage . . . , Subject: "Mirage Gold" Nuclear Exercise 10/16–21/94, New Orleans, Louisiana, October 4, 1994; "KBR (company)," http://en.wikipedia.org, accessed November 12, 2007.

16. James K. Magruder, Assistant Manager for Operations, Nevada Operations Office, "Mile Shakedown After-Action Report," July 5, 1995, w/enclosure: Mile Shakedown After-Action Report; Waller, "Nuclear Ninjas."

17. Department of Energy, Nevada Operations Office, *Mile Shakedown Series of Exercises*, p. 25; Federal Bureau of Investigation, *"Mirage Gold" Full Field Exercise*, in U.S. Congress, Senate Committee on Governmental Affairs, *Global Proliferation of Weapons of Mass Destruction, Part III*, p. 187; Maj. Gen. Joseph W. Kineer, Deputy Commanding General, Fifth U.S. Army, Memorandum for: Commanding General, FORSCOM, Subject: Exercise Mirage Gold After Action Report, November 15, 1994, in U.S. Congress, Senate Committee on Governmental Affairs, *Global Proliferation of Weapons of Mass Destruction, Part III*, pp. 386–429.

18. Department of Energy, Nevada Operations Office, *Mile Shakedown Series of Exercises*, p. 26; Cockburn and Cockburn, *One Point Safe*, p. 88. The Department of Energy report gives the location of the airstrip as being off Magazine Road, but there is only a Magazine Drive.

19. Department of Energy, Nevada Operations Office, *Mile Shakedown Series of Exercises*, p. 26.

20. Ibid.

21. Telephone interview with Peter Zimmerman, November 20, 2007.

22. Cockburn and Cockburn, *One Point Safe*, p. 89; Department of Energy, Nevada Operations Office, *Mile Shakedown Series of Exercises*, p. 146; Telephone interview with Robert Kelley, November 20, 2007.

23. Department of Energy, Nevada Operations Office, *Mile Shakedown Series of Exercises*, p. 26; Federal Bureau of Investigation, *"Mirage Gold" Full Field Exercise*, in U.S. Congress, Senate Committee on Governmental Affairs, *Global Proliferation of Weapons of Mass Destruction, Part III*, p. 188; Federal Emergency Management Agency, *Exercise Mirage Gold After-Action Report*, p. 11.

24. Cockburn and Cockburn, *One Point Safe*, p. 90.

25. Federal Bureau of Investigation, *"Mirage Gold" Full Field Exercise*, in U.S. Congress, Senate Committee on Governmental Affairs, *Global Proliferation of Weapons of Mass Destruction, Part III*, pp. 184–210.

26. Federal Emergency Management Agency, *Exercise Mirage Gold After-Action Report*, pp. 13–14.

27. Interview with William Chambers, Los Alamos, N.M., July 10, 2007.

28. Department of Energy, Nevada Operations Office, *Mile Shakedown Series of Exercises*, pp. 37–38, 40.

29. Ibid., p. 41.

30. Ibid., pp. 44–45.

31. Ibid., pp. 53–54; Kineer, Deputy Commanding General, Fifth U.S. Army, Memorandum for: Commanding General, FORSCOM, Subject: Exercise Mirage Gold After Action Report.

32. Department of Energy, Nevada Operations Office, *Mile Shakedown Series of Exercises*, p. 54.

33. Ibid., p. 58.

34. Ibid., p. 96; U.S. Congress, Senate Committee on Governmental Affairs, *Global Proliferation of Weapons of Mass Destruction, Part III*, p. 9.

35. Department of Energy, Nevada Operations Office, *Mile Shakedown Series of Exercises*, pp. 59–60.

36. Ibid., p. 73.

37. "USS Minneapolis-Saint Paul, SSN 708," www.uss-saint-paul-ca.73.com/SSN708/ssn708.htm, accessed August 5, 2007; John T. Conway, Chairman, Defense Nuclear Facilities Safety Board, to Rear Adm. Charles J. Beers, August 23, 1995; Telephone interview with Adm. Charles J. Beers Jr., December 4, 2007.

38. Beers interview.

39. Rear Admiral Charles J. Beers, Deputy Assistant Secretary for Military Application and Stockpile Support, Defense Programs, Department of Energy, to Manager, Nevada Operations Office, Subject: Nuclear Emergency Search Team, January 25, 1995.

40. Ibid.

41. Ibid.

42. Interview with Alan V. Mode, Pleasanton, Calif., April 9, 2007.

43. Chambers interview; Interview with William Nelson, Alamo, Calif., June 9, 2007.

44. Beers interview.

45. Rear Admiral Charles J. Beers, Deputy Assistant Secretary for Military Application and Stockpile Support, Defense Programs, Department of Energy, to Manager, Nevada Operations Office, Subject: Nuclear Emergency Search Team.

46. U.S. Congress, Senate Select Committee on Governmental Affairs, *Global Proliferation of Weapons of Mass Destruction, Part III*, p. 70.

47. Nuclear Emergency Search Team Assessment Team, *Nuclear Emergency Search Team Assessment Team Report*, July 12, 1995, p. 1.

48. Ibid. The specific components of the Department of Energy headquarters, Nevada Operations Office, the FBI, and the Department of Defense from which representatives were interviewed were Office of the Deputy Assistant Secretary of Military Application and Stockpile Support, Office of Emergency Response, Emergency Management Operations, and Intelligence and Threat Assessment from the Department of Energy headquarters; the Office of the Manager, the Office of the Assistant Manager for Operations, Emergency Management and Nonproliferation Division, and Safeguards and Security Division of the Nevada Operations Office; the Counterterrorism Section, Domestic Counterintelligence Unit, and Critical Incident Response Group of the FBI; the Defense Nuclear Agency, Office of the Assistant Secretary for Special Operations, the Joint Chiefs of Staff Special Operations Division, U.S. Navy Special Operations, the Naval Explosive Ordnance Disposal Technology Division, and U.S. Army Forces Command 52 Ordnance Group of the Department of Defense.

49. Nuclear Emergency Search Team Assessment Team, *Nuclear Emergency Search Team Assessment Team Report*, p. iv; Mode interview.

50. Nuclear Emergency Search Team Assessment Team, *Nuclear Emergency Search Team Assessment Team Report*, p. 9.

51. Ibid., p. 11.

52. Ibid., p. 3; U.S. Congress, Senate Committee on Governmental Affairs, *Global Proliferation of Weapons of Mass Destruction, Part III*, p. 31.

53. Nuclear Emergency Search Team Assessment Team, *Nuclear Emergency Search Team Assessment Team Report*, p. 14.

54. Ibid., p. 17.

55. Ibid., p. 20.

56. Ibid., p. 25.

57. Ibid., p. 26.

58. Ibid., p. 27.

59. Ibid., p. 39.

60. Ibid.

61. Ibid., p. 43.

62. Ibid.

63. Ibid.

64. Ibid., p. 45.
65. Ibid.
66. Ibid, pp. 43–45, 59; U.S. Congress, Senate Committee on Governmental Affairs, *Global Proliferation of Weapons of Mass Destruction, Part III*, p. 346.
67. Ibid, p. 7; U.S. Congress, Senate Committee on Governmental Affairs, *Global Proliferation of Weapons of Mass Destruction, Part III*, p. 347.
68. Nuclear Emergency Search Team Assessment Team, *Nuclear Emergency Search Team Assessment Team Report*, p. 6.
69. Beers interview.
70. U.S. Congress, Senate Committee on Governmental Affairs, *Global Proliferation of Weapons of Mass Destruction, Part III*, p. 31; Beers interview.
71. "Statement of Victor H. Reis," in U.S. Congress, Senate Committee on Governmental Affairs, *Global Proliferation of Weapons of Mass Destruction, Part III*, p. 109.
72. Ibid.
73. Ibid., pp. 109–110.
74. Ibid., p. 110.
75. Lawrence R. Ackerly, Regional Manager, Western Regional Audit Office, Office of Inspector General, To: Manager, DOE Nevada Operations Office, Subject: Audit of Management of Department of Energy Nevada Operations Office Nuclear Emergency Preparedness Response Teams, January 5, 1996, p. 2.

CHAPTER SIX: PEOPLE, PAPER, AND MACHINES

1. Interview with William Chambers, Los Alamos, N.M., July 10, 1997.
2. "Lisa E. Gordon-Hagerty," www.sourcewatch.com, accessed August 5, 2007; Janet Pavasko, "An American Guardian Angel," http://www.kappakappagamma.org, accessed August 5, 2007.
3. "An American Guardian Angel"; Robert Windrem, e-mail, December 18, 2007.
4. Windrem e-mail.
5. Robert Windrem, *NBC Nightly News*, interview with Lisa Gordon-Hagerty, August 3, 1993.
6. Ibid.
7. Anthony L. Kinery, "Your Life May Depend on the Woman from NEST," *Insight on the News*, October 23, 1995.
8. The White House, "Fact Sheet: Combating Terrorism: Presidential Decision Directive 62," May 22, 1998; "The Role of Nuclear Power Speaker Biographys [*sic*]," http://npw.wlu.edu/bios.htm, accessed November 19, 2007.
9. Interview with William Nelson, Alamo, Calif., June 9, 2007; Chambers interview.
10. Telephone interview with Robert Kelley, November 20, 2007.
11. Telephone interview with Adm. Charles J. Beers, December 4, 2007.

12. Stephen Ronshaugen, "Standard NEST Briefing," n.d. (but circa 1995), p. 3; Ronald Reagan, Executive Order 12656, "Assignment of Emergency Preparedness Responsibilities," November 18, 1988, Part 7.

13. Ronshaugen, "Standard NEST Briefing," p. 3; Ronald Reagan, National Security Decision Directive 207, "National Program for Combatting Terrorism," January 20, 1986.

14. Ronald Reagan, National Security Decision Directive 207, "National Program for Combatting Terrorism"; William J. Clinton, Presidential Decision Directive 39, "U.S. Policy on Counterterrorism," June 21, 1995.

15. Department of Energy, DOE Order 5530.2, Subject: Nuclear Emergency Search Team, September 20, 1991, p. 3.

16. Ibid., p. 6.

17. Department of Defense Directive 3150.5, "DOD Response to Improvised Nuclear Device (IND) Incidents," March 24, 1987.

18. Ronshaugen, "Standard NEST Briefing"; Nuclear Emergency Search Team, *NEST Energy Senior Official's Reference Manual*, October 31, 1993.

19. Nuclear Emergency Search Team Assessment Team, *Nuclear Emergency Search Team Assessment Team Report*, July 12, 1995, p. 3.

20. Ibid.

21. Kelley interview; Department of Energy/Nevada, "Remote Sensing Laboratory," July 2006; "Nellis Air Force Base," http://en.wikipedia.org, accessed November 28, 2007.

22. Ronshaugen, "Standard NEST Briefing," p. 2, 5.

23. Ibid.; Raytheon, "Biography: Arthur W. Spooner," March 2007; "Company News; E&G Contract," *New York Times*, September 2, 1987, accessed from www.nytimes.com.

24. Nevada Operations Office, *Nuclear Emergency Search Team: Response to Nuclear Terrorism*, n.d., n.p.

25. Ronshaugen, "Standard NEST Briefing," p. 6.

26. Ibid., p. 8.

27. Ibid.; Nevada Operations Office, *Nuclear Emergency Search Team*.

28. U.S. Air Force Fact Sheet, "C-5 GALAXY," August 2007, www.af.mil/factsheets; "C-141B," www.fas.org, accessed November 28, 2007.

29. "C-141B."

30. Ronshaugen, "Standard NEST Briefing," p. 11.

31. E.J. Dowdy, C. N. Henry, R. D. Hastings, and S. W. France, Los Alamos Scientific Laboratory, LA-7108, *Neutron Detector Suitcase for Nuclear Emergency Search Team*, February 1978, p. 1.

32. Ronshaugen, "Standard NEST Briefing," pp.3–5.

33. Ibid., p. 11.

34. "PAH-1 BO 105," http://www.fas.org, accessed October 30, 2006.

35. "Ardmore Helicopters—Hughes H500 ZK-HUM," www.chopper.co.nz/H500.html, accessed November 28, 2007; E. L. Feimster, *Aerial Radiological Survey of Areas*

18 and 20 Nevada Test Site. Date of Survey: October–November 1980 (Las Vegas: EG&G Inc., November 1985).

36. "Beechcraft KingAir B200," www.hawkesbeechcraft.com.

37. "Cessna Citation II (CE-550)," www.aoc.noaa.gov/aircraft_cessna.htm, accessed January 2, 2006.

38. "Convair 580 Specifications," www.skzdalimit.com/rtw2004/fleet.html, accessed June 15, 2007; C. D. Hardwick, "NAE Convair 580 Aeromagnetics Program," *Quarterly Bulletin of the Division of Mechanical Engineering*, 4 (1979), pp. 1–16; "Convair NC-131H 'Samaritan,'" http//aeroweb.brooklyn.cuny.edu/specs/convair/nc-131h.htm, accessed June 16, 2007; "GPS Dropsonde," www.eol.ucar.edu/rtf/facilities/dropsonde/gpsDropsonde.html, accessed June 16, 2007.

39. Telephone interview with William Chambers, December 12, 2007.

40. Eileen Patterson, "Render Safe: Defusing a Nuclear Emergency," *Los Alamos Research Quarterly*, Fall 2002, pp. 22–23.

41. "When Terrorists Go Nuclear," *Popular Mechanics*, March 2002, accessed from www.popularmechanics.com.

42. Chambers interview, December 12, 2007.

43. Sandia National Laboratories, "Labs Accomplishments 2007: Nuclear Weapons," *Sandia Lab News*, February 2007, pp. 3–5; Under Secretary of Defense for Acquisition, Technology, and Logistics, DoD 3150.8-M, *Nuclear Weapon Accident Response Procedures (NARP)*, December 1999, p. 22; "Environmental Restoration, Protection, and Waste Management," *Newsline*, July 14, 2006, pp. 34–39.

44. "Liquid nitrogen," http://en.wikipedia.org, accessed November 29, 2007.

45. "30 mm caliber," http://en.wikipedia.org, accessed November 29, 2007.

46. ".50 Caliber Terror," www.50caliberterror.com/?page_id=2, accessed December 14, 2007; Violence Policy Center, *Sitting Ducks: The Threat to the Chemical and Refinery Industry from 50 Caliber Sniper Rifles*, 2002, Section 1, p. 1, available at www.vpc.org/studies/duckone.htm.

47. James H. Aubert, Andrew M. Kraynik, and Peter B. Rand, "Aqueous Foams," *Scientific American*, May 1986, pp. 74–82.

48. Sandia National Laboratories, Fact Sheet, "Aqueous Foam Containment," n.d.

49. Ibid.

50. National Aeronautics and Space Administration, "NASA's Mars Global Surveyor May Be at Mission's End," November 21, 2006, http://marsprogram.jpl.nasa.gov; John Noble Wilford, "Craft Is Launched to Explore Mars," *New York Times*, November 8, 1996, accessed from www.nytimes.com.

51. "Mars Pathfinder," http://en.wikipedia.org, accessed November 21, 2007; National Aeronautics and Space Administration, "Mars Pathfinder," www.nasa.gov, accessed November 29, 2007.

52. "Mars-96, Robotic Spacecraft Mission to Mars: Brief Descritpion," www.iki.rssiru/mars96/05_mars_e.htm, accessed November 21, 2007; "Russia's Mission to Mars Fails Hours after Liftoff," *New York Times*, November 17, 1996, accessed from www.nytimes.com.

53. James Oberg, "The Probe That Fell to Earth," *New Scientist*, March 6, 1999, p. 38.
54. "Russia's Mission to Mars Fails Hours after Liftoff"; "Mars Probe Expected to Fall within Hours," November 17, 1996, www.cnn.com/TECH/9611/16/russia.mars.update; Todd S. Pudrum, "Russia's Mars Craft Fails and Crashes in Southern Pacific," *New York Times*, November 18, 1996, accessed from www.nytimes.com; Oberg, "Probe That Fell to Earth."
55. "Mars Probe Expected to Fall within Hours."
56. Ibid.
57. Pudrum, "Russia's Mars Craft Fails and Crashes in Southern Pacific"; Telephone interview with Robert Kelley, November 20, 2007.
58. Kelley interview; Jeffrey T. Richelson, *The U.S. Intelligence Community*, 5th ed. (Boulder, Colo.: Westview, 2007), pp. 342–345.
59. Kelley interview.
60. Kelley interview; Pudrum, "Russia's Mars Craft Fails and Crashes in Southern Pacific."
61. Oberg, "Probe That Fell to Earth."

CHAPTER SEVEN: NEW ENEMIES

1. William J. Broad, "Seismic Mystery in Australia: Quake, Meteor, or Nuclear Blast?" *New York Times*, January 21, 1997, pp. C1, C8; Christel B. Hennet, Gregory E. van der Vink, and Danny Harvey, "IRIS Assists Senate in Investigation of International Terrorist Group," *IRIS Newsletter*, Fall 1996, www.iris.edu/news/IRISnewsletter/fallnews/senate.html.
2. Hennet, van der Vink, and Harvey, "IRIS Assists Senate in Investigation of International Terrorist Group"; "Sarin," http://en.wikipedia.org/wiki/Sarin, accessed August 29, 2007; U.S. Department of State, *Patterns of Global Terrorism 2000*, April 2001, p. 57; Office of the Under Secretary of Defense for Acquisition and Technology, *The Defense Science Board 1997 Summer Study Task Force on DoD Responses to Transnational Threats, Volume I, Final Report*, October 1997, p. 18.
3. Office of the Under Secretary of Defense for Acquisition and Technology, *Defense Science Board 1997 Summer Study Task Force on DoD Responses to Transnational Threats, Volume I, Final Report*, p. 18.
4. U.S. Department of State, *Patterns of Global Terrorism 2000*, pp. 57–58; "Shoko Asahara," http//en.wikipedia.org/wiki/Shoko_Asahara, accessed August 29, 2007; David E. Kaplan and Andrew Marshall, *The Cult at the End of the World: The Terrifying Story of the Aum Doomsday Cult, from the Subways of Tokyo to the Nuclear Arsenals of Russia* (New York: Crown, 1996), p. 190; U.S. Congress, Senate Committee on Governmental Affairs, *Global Proliferation of Weapons of Mass Destruction, Part I* (Washington, D.C.: U.S. Government Printing Office, 1996), p. 17; Sara Daly, John Parachini, and William Rosenau, *Aum Shinrikyo, Al Qaeda, and the Kinshasa Reactor: Implications of Three Case Studies for Combating Nuclear*

Terrorism (Santa Monica, Calif.: RAND, 2005), p. 10; Gavin Cameron, "Multi-track Microproliferation: Lessons from Aum Shinrikyo and Al Qaida," *Studies in Conflict and Terrorism*, 22, 4 (1999), pp. 277–309.

5. U.S. Congress, Senate Committee on Governmental Affairs, *Global Proliferation of Weapons of Mass Destruction, Part I*, pp. 16–18; Daly, Parachini, and Rosenau, *Aum Shinrikyo, Al Qaeda, and the Kinshasa Reactor*, p. 6.

6. Broad, "Seismic Mystery in Australia"; Daly, Parachini, and Rosenau, *Aum Shinrikyo, Al Qaeda, and the Kinshasa Reactor*, p. 18; Cameron, "Multi-track Microproliferation," p. 285.

7. Jeffrey T. Richelson, *The U.S. Intelligence Community*, 4th ed. (Boulder, Colo.: Westview, 1999), pp. 228–229.

8. Broad, "Seismic Mystery in Australia."

9. Ibid.; Hennet, van der Vink, and Harvey, "IRIS Assists Senate in Investigation of International Terrorist Group."

10. Cameron, "Multi-track Microproliferation," p. 286.

11. Kaplan and Marshall, *Cult at the End of the World*, p. 108; U.S. Congress, Senate Committee on Governmental Affairs, *Global Proliferation of Weapons of Mass Destruction, Part I*, p. 54; "AK-74," http://en.wikipedia.org/wiki/AK-74, accessed September 3, 2007; Daly, Parachini, and Rosenau, *Aum Shinrikyo, Al Qaeda, and the Kinshasa Reactor*, p. 14.

12. Kaplan and Marshall, *Cult at the End of the World*, p. 112.

13. Ibid., p. 192; Daly, Parachini, and Rosenau, *Aum Shinrikyo, Al Qaeda, and the Kinshasa Reactor*, p. 16.

14. Kaplan and Marshall, *Cult at the End of the World*, p. 192; Vasily Golovnin, Itra-Tass News Agency, "Aum Cult Implicated in Nuclear Information Stealing," March 29, 2000, and Anna Bazhova, Itar-Tass News Agency, "Russian Ministry Denies Aum Shinrikyo Had Access to Data," March 29, 2000, both at www.fas.org/sgp/news/2000/03/aum.

15. Daniel Benjamin and Steven Simon, *The Age of Sacred Terror* (New York: Random House, 2002), p. 229.

16. Bruce Hoffman, RAND Corporation, "Holy Terror—The Implications of Terrorism Motivated by Religious Imperative," May 1995, p. 1. Hoffman made a similar point in "Terrorist Targeting: Tactics, Trends, and Potentialities," *Terrorism and Political Violence*, 5, 2 (Summer 1993), pp. 12–29.

17. Hoffman, "Holy Terror," p. 2.

18. Ibid., with Hoffman relying on Amir Taheri, *Holy Terror: The Inside Story of Islamic Terrorism* (London: Sphere, 1987).

19. Kenneth Katzman, Congressional Research Service, *Terrorism: Near Eastern Groups and State Sponsors, 2002*, February 13, 2002, pp. 7–8; Gary Ackerman and Laura Snyder, "Would They If They Could?" *Bulletin of the Atomic Scientists*, May/June 2002, pp. 41–47.

20. Katzman, *Terrorism*, pp. 4–6; Ackerman and Snyder, "Would They If They Could?"

21. National Commission on Terrorist Attacks Upon the United States, *The 9/11 Com-*

mission Report: Final Report of the National Commission on Terrorist Attacks Upon the United States (New York: W.W. Norton, 2004), p. 55; Kenneth Katzman, Congressional Research Service, *Al-Qaeda: Profile and Threat Assessment*, August 17, 2005, p. 1.

22. National Commission on Terrorist Attacks Upon the United States, *9/11 Commission Report*, p. 55; Katzman, *Al-Qaeda*, p. 2.

23. National Commission on Terrorist Attacks Upon the United States, *9/11 Commission Report*, pp. 55–56.

24. Ibid., p. 56.

25. Ibid., p. 57.

26. Ibid., p. 58.

27. Ibid., p. 59.

28. CIA, "Usama Bin Ladin: Islamic Extremist Financier," 1996.

29. National Commission on Terrorist Attacks Upon the United States, *9/11 Commission Report*, p. 60.

30. Ibid., p. 70; Benjamin Orbach, "Usama Bin Ladin and Al-Qa'ida: Origins and Doctrines," *Middle East Review of International Affairs*, 5, 4 (December 2001), pp. 54–68 at p. 54; Simon Reeve, *The New Jackals: Ramsi Youzef, Osama Bin Laden, and the Future of Terrorism* (Boston: Northeastern University Press, 1999), p. 200.

31. National Commission on Terrorist Attacks Upon the United States, *9/11 Commission Report*, p. 70.

32. Ibid., p. 190; Reeve, *New Jackals*, p. 1.

33. Bob Port and Greg B. Smith, "'Suitcase Bomb' Allegedly Sought," *Seattle Times*, October 3, 2001, accessed from http://seattletimes.nwsource.com; Jonathan Spyer, "The Al-Qa'ida Network and Weapons of Mass Destruction," *Middle East Review of International Affairs*, 8, 3 (September 2004), pp. 29–45 at p. 38.

34. Mike Boettcher and Ingrid Arnesen, "Al Qaeda Documents Outline Serious Weapons Program," www.cnn.com, January 25, 2002.

35. Ibid.

36. "'Why We Fight America': Al-Qa'ida Spokesman Explains September 11 and Declares Intentions to Kill 4 Million Americans with Weapons of Mass Destruction," *MEMRI Special Dispatch Series*, 388 (June 12, 2002).

37. Nasir Bin Hamd al-Fahd, "A Treatise on the Legal Status of Using Weapons of Mass Destruction against Infidels," May 2003, pp. 2,4, http://clarityandresolve.com/wmd_fatwa.php.

38. Ibid., p. 5.

39. Ibid., pp. 9–11.

40. Ibid., pp. 13, 18.

41. "New York Subway Plot and al-Qaeda's WMD Strategy," http://jamestown.org/news_details.php?news_id=185, accessed September 11, 2007.

42. Cameron, "Multi-track Microproliferation," p. 288; John J. Goldman and Ronald J. Ostrow, "U.S. Indicts Terror Suspect Bin Laden," *Los Angeles Times*, November 5, 1998, p. A1.

43. Christopher Brown, "WMD Mystery," www.nationalreview.com, May 10, 2005.

44. Dan Darling, "Al Qaeda's Mad Scientist: The Significance of Abu Khabab's Death," *Weekly Standard*, www.weeklystandard.com, January 19, 2006; "Midhat Mursi," http://en.wikipedia.org/wiki/Midhat_Mursi, accessed September 12, 2007; Josh Meyer, "Al Qaeda Is Said to Focus Again on WMD," *Los Angeles Times*, February 3, 2003, pp. A1, A12; Alan Cullison, "Al Qaeda Posting Confirms Death of Weapons Expert," *Wall Street Journal*, August 4, 2008, p. A7.

45. Darling, "Al Qaeda's Mad Scientist."

46. Douglas Franz with David Rohde, "2 Pakistanis Linked to Papers on Anthrax Weapons," *New York Times*, November 28, 2001, pp. B1, B5; David Albright and Holly Higgins, "A Bomb for the Ummah," *Bulletin of the Atomic Scientists*, March/April 2003, pp. 49–55.

47. Albright and Higgins, "Bomb for the Ummah."

48. Ibid.

49. Ibid.

50. Ibid.

51. Ibid.

52. Kamran Khan and Molly Moore, "2 Nuclear Experts Briefed Bin Laden, Pakistanis Say," *Washington Post*, December 12, 2001, pp. A1, A23.

53. David Rohde, "Germ Weapon Plans Found at a Scientist's House in Kabul," *New York Times*, December 1, 2001, p. B4; Frantz with Rohde, "2 Pakistanis Linked to Papers on Anthrax Weapons"; Albright and Higgins, "Bomb for the Ummah"; "Bin Laden Got Nuclear Data," www.msnbc.com, December 20, 2001.

54. Albright and Higgins, "Bomb for the Ummah"; Arnaud de Borchgrave, "Al Qaeda's Nuclear Agenda Verified," *Washington Times*, December 10, 2001, p. A14; David Sanger, "Nuclear Experts in Pakistan May Have Links to Al Qaeda," *New York Times*, December 9, 2001, pp. A1, B5.

55. Reeve, *New Jackals*, p. 214.

56. Bill Gertz, "Terrorists Seek the Big Bang," *Air Force Magazine*, April 2002, pp. 58–61; Daly, Parachini, and Rosenau, *Aum Shinrikyo, Al Qaeda, and the Kinshasa Reactor*, p. 32.

57. Reeve, *New Jackals*, pp. 214–215.

58. Ibid., p. 215.

59. Daly, Parachini, and Rosenau, *Aum Shinrikyo, Al Qaeda, and the Kinshasa Reactor*, pp. 31, 33.

60. Adam Nathan and David Lappard, "Bin Laden's Nuclear Plot: Al-Qaeda's Men Held Secret Meeting to Build 'Dirty Bomb,'" *London Sunday Times*, October 14, 2001, accessed from www.freerepublic.com; Jeffrey Kluger, "Osama's Nuclear Quest," *Time*, November 12, 2001, accessed from www.time.com.

61. Ibid.

62. Bob Woodward, Robert Kaiser, and David B. Ottaway, "U.S. Fears Bin Laden Made Nuclear Strides," *Washington Post*, December 4, 2001, pp. A1, A18; Pavel Felgenhauer, "Do the Terrorists Have Nukes?" www.opinionjournal.com, November 11,

2001; Defense Intelligence Agency, Military Leadership Profile: General Colonel Igor Nikolayevich VALYNKIN, April 2002.

63. Bill Gertz, "Al Qaeda Pursued a 'Dirty Bomb'," Washington Times, October 17, 2003, pp. A1, A16; "Wanted the FBI Miami," www.fbi.gov/wanted/fo/mmwanted .htm, accessed September 15, 2007; Jerry Seper, "Al Qaeda Leader Identified in 'Dirty Bomb' Plot," Washington Times, October 5, 2004, p. A3.

64. Vice Admiral Lowell E. Jacoby, Director, Defense Intelligence Agency, Statement for the Record, Senate Select Committee on Intelligence, February 11, 2003, p. 3; George J. Tenet, Director of Central Intelligence, The Worldwide Threat in 2003: Evolving Dangers in a Complex World, February 11, 2003, p. 5.

65. Lieutenant General Michael D. Maples, Director, Defense Intelligence Agency, Statement for the Record, Senate Armed Services Committee, Current and Projected National Security Threats to the United States, February 27, 2007, p. 8; Edward Gistaro, National Intelligence Officer/Transnational Threats, and Michael Leiter, Principal Deputy Director, National Counterterrorism Center, Statement for the Record, U.S. Congress, House Permanent Select Committee on Intelligence and House Armed Services Committee, Implications of the NIE "The Terrorism Threat to the US Homeland," July 25, 2007, p. 2.

66. Hamid Mir, "Osama Claims He Has Nuke: If US Uses N-arms It Will Get Same Response," Dawn the Internet Edition, November 10, 2001, www.dawn .com/2001/11/10/top1.htm.

67. Walter Pincus, "Al Qaeda Aide: Radiation Bomb in the Works," Washington Post, April 23, 2002, p. A4; Philip Shenon, "Qaeda Leader Said to Report A-Bomb Plans," New York Times, April 23, 2004, p. A9; Sammy Salama and Lydia Hansell, "Does Intent Equal Capability: Al-Qaeda and Weapons of Mass Destruction," Nonproliferation Review 12, 3 (November 2005), pp. 615–653 at p. 620.

68. Steven Gutkin, "Terrorists Pursuing WMDs Capability," Washington Times, February 9, 2004, p. A14; Bill Gertz, "Reports Reveal Zarqawi Nuclear Threat," Washington Times, April 20, 2005, p. A3.

69. "Al Qaida Nukes Already in U.S.," www.worldnetdaily.com, July 11, 2005; Port and Smith, "'Suitcase Bomb' Allegedly Sought"; "Tancredo to Request al-Qaida Nuke Briefing," http://worldnetdaily.com, July 13, 2005; Jeffrey Kluger, "Osama's Nuclear Quest." The World Net Daily claims were based, at least in part, on Joseph Farah's G2 Bulletin and (at the time) a forthcoming book by Paul L. Williams, The Al Qaeda Connection: International Terrorism, Organized Crime, and the Coming Apocalypse.

70. David Smigielski, "A Review of the Suitcase Nuclear Bomb Controversy," RANSAC Policy Update, September 2003, p. 3.

71. Smigielski, "Review of the Suitcase Nuclear Bomb Controversy," p. 6; Bill Gertz, "Lebed Says Russia May Have Lost 100 Suitcase-sized Atomic Bombs," Washington Times, September 6, 1997, p. A21; R. Jeffrey Smith and David Hoffman, "No Support Found for Report of Lost Russian Suitcase-Sized Nuclear Weapons," Washington Post, September 5, 1997, p. A19; Kluger, "Osama's Nuclear Quest";

Felgenhauer, "Do the Terrorists Have Nukes?"; "Tancredo to Request al-Qaida Nuke Briefing." The last article cites Williams's *Al Qaeda Connection* as giving the weight of the suitcase nukes as between 110 and 176 pounds and capable of producing a two-kiloton blast.

72. Gertz, "Lebed Says Russia May Have Lost 100 Suitcase-sized Atomic Bombs"; Smith and Hoffman, "No Support Found for Report of Lost Russian Suitcase-Sized Nuclear Weapons"; Defense Intelligence Agency, "Biographic Sketch: General-Lieutenant Aleksandr Ivanovich Lebed," August 1994.

73. Smigielski, "Review of the Suitcase Nuclear Bomb Controversy," p. 6; Robert Windrem, e-mail, January 8, 2002.

74. Smigielski, "Review of the Suitcase Nuclear Bomb Controversy," p. 6; Anna Badkhen, "Al Qaeda Bluffing about Having Suitcase Nukes, Experts Say Russian Claim Terrorists Couldn't Have Bought Them," *San Francisco Chronicle*, March 23, 2004, accessed from www.sfgate.com.

75. Smigielski, "Review of the Suitcase Nuclear Bomb Controversy," p. 2; Windrem e-mail; Nikolai Sokov, James Martin Center for Nonproliferation Studies, "'Suitcase Nukes': Permanently Lost Luggage," February 13, 2004, http://cns.miis.edu/pubs/week/040213.htm.

76. Christina Chuen, "Don't Sweat the Suitcase," *Bulletin of the Atomic Scientists*, January/February 2005, pp. 69–70; Morten Bremer Maerli, Annette Schaper, and Frank Barnaby, "The Characteristics of Nuclear Terrorist Weapons," *American Behavioral Scientist*, 46, 6 (February 2003), pp. 727–744 at pp. 730–731. Also see Joseph C. Anselmo, "Defector Details Plan to Plant Nukes in U.S.," *Aviation Week & Space Technology*, August 17, 1998, p. 52.

77. Sokov, "'Suitcase Nukes'"; Chuen, "Don't Sweat the Suitcase."

78. Bill Gertz, "Terrorists Seek the Big Bang," *Air Force Magazine*, April 2002, pp. 58–61; Thom Shanker, "U.S. Analysts Find No Sign Bin Laden Had Nuclear Arms," *New York Times*, February 26, 2002, pp. A1, A10.

79. Jack Boureston, "Assessing Al Qaeda's WMD Capabilities," *Strategic Insight*, September 2, 2002; Julian Borger and Ewen MacAskill, "Bin Laden Is Looking for a Nuclear Weapon. How Close Has He Come?" *Guardian*, November 7, 2001, accessed from www.guardian.co.uk.

CHAPTER EIGHT: DANGER AND RESPONSE

1. Interview with Alan V. Mode, Pleasanton, Calif., April 9, 2007; Telephone interview with Robert Kelley, November 20, 2007; Graham Allison, *Nuclear Terrorism: The Ultimate Preventable Catastrophe* (New York: Times Books, 2004), pp. 14–15.

2. Government Accountability Office, GAO-07-404, *Nuclear Nonproliferation: Progress Made in Improving Security at Russian Nuclear Sites, but the Long-Term Sustainability of U.S.-Funded Security Upgrades Is Uncertain*, February 2007, p. 1. Lower estimates for an efficient implosion weapon are ten pounds of plutonium

or thirty pounds of HEU. See Matthew Bunn, Anthony Weir, and John P. Holdren, *Controlling Nuclear Warheads and Materials: A Report Card and Action Plan* (Cambridge, Mass.: Belfer Center for Science and International Affairs, 2003), p. 13. For a table specifying different fissile material requirements for both HEU and plutonium for different yields and different levels of technical capability, see Thomas B. Cochran and Christopher E. Paine, Natural Resources Defense Council, "The Amount of Plutonium and Highly-Enriched Uranium Needed for Pure Fission Nuclear Weapons," April 13, 1995.

3. J. Carson Mark, Theodore Taylor, Eugene Eyster, William Maraman, and Jacob Wechsler, Nuclear Control Institute, "Can Terrorists Build Nuclear Weapons?" n.d., www.nci.org/k-m/makeab.htm, accessed February 26, 2005. Also see Friedrich Steinhausler, "What It Takes to Become a Nuclear Terrorist," *American Behavioral Scientist*, 46, 6 (February 2003), pp. 782–795.

4. William Langewiesche, *The Atomic Bazaar: The Rise of the Nuclear Poor* (New York: Farrar, Straus & Giroux, 2007), pp. 65–66.

5. Peter D. Zimmerman and Jeffrey G. Lewis, "The Bomb in the Backyard," *Foreign Policy*, November/December 2006, pp. 32–39.

6. Charles D. Ferguson and William C. Potter, *The Four Faces of Nuclear Terrorism* (Monterey, Calif.: Center for Nonproliferation Studies, 2004), p. 141; U.S. Congress, Senate Armed Services Committee, *Intelligence Briefing on Smuggling of Nuclear Material and the Role of International Crime Organizations, and on the Proliferation of Cruise and Ballistic Missiles* (Washington, D.C.: U.S. Government Printing Office, 1996), p. 16. For a discussion of the alternative views of how easy or difficult it would be for a terrorist group to build its own nuclear weapon, see Robin M. Frost, Adelphi Paper 378, *Nuclear Terrorism after 9/11* (London: International Institute of Strategic Studies, 2005), pp. 25–40. Also see Steinhausler, "What It Takes to Become a Nuclear Terrorist."

7. John Deutch, Director of Central Intelligence, Statement for the Permanent Subcommittee on Investigation, Senate Committee on Governmental Affairs, *The Threat of Nuclear Diversion*, March 20, 1996, p. 6.

8. Marvin J. Cetron and Peter S. Probst, *Terror 2000: The Future Face of Terrorism* (Washington, D.C.: Department of Defense, 1994), pp. 1–8.

9. David Albright, "Securing Pakistan's Nuclear Weapons Complex," paper commissioned and sponsored by the Stanley Foundation for the 42nd Strategy for Peace Conference, Strategies for Regional Security (South Asia Working Group), Warrenton, Va., October 25–27, 2001.

10. Ibid.

11. Ibid.

12. Ibid.; Ferguson and Potter, *Four Faces of Nuclear Terrorism*, p. 78; David Wood, "Can Pakistan Keep Lid on Nukes?" *Seattle Times*, April 8, 2006, accessed from http://seattletimes.nwsource.com/html/nationworld/2002918442_paknukes08.html.

13. Wood, "Can Pakistan Keep Lid on Nukes?"; Seymour Hersh, "Watching the Warheads," *New Yorker*, November 5, 2001, accessed from www.newyorker.com.

14. Wood, "Can Pakistan Keep Lid on Nukes?"

15. Albright, "Securing Pakistan's Nuclear Weapons Complex."

16. Ibid.

17. Frost, *Nuclear Terrorism after 9/11*, pp. 63–68; Daniel Byman, "Iran, Terrorism, and Weapons of Mass Destruction," *Studies in Conflict & Terrorism*, 31, 3 (2008), pp. 169–181 at p. 178; Kenneth M. Pollack, *The Persian Puzzle: The Conflict between Iran and America* (New York: Random House, 2004), p. 419.

18. Graham Allison, "Worse Than You Think," *Los Angeles Times*, July 9, 2006, p. M5; Richard Clarke et al., *Defeating the Jihadists: A Blueprint for Action* (New York: Century Foundation Press, 2004), p. 137, cited in Michael Levi, *On Nuclear Terrorism* (Cambridge, Mass.: Harvard University Press, 2007), p. 23; Office of the Director of National Intelligence, "Acquisition of Technology Relating to Weapons of Mass Destruction and Advanced Conventional Munitions, 1 January to 31 December 2005," n.d., p. 6.

19. Judith Miller, "U.S. Experts Find Radioactive Material in Iraq," *New York Times*, May 4, 2003, p. 14; Government Accountability Office, GAO-05-672, *Radiological Sources: DOD Should Evaluate Its Source Recovery Effort and Apply Lessons Learned to Future Recovery Missions*, September 2005, p. 3.

20. Department of Defense, "Background Briefing on IAEA Nuclear Safeguards and the Tuwaitha Facility," June 5, 2003, pp. 3–4, www.defenselink.mil/transcripts/2003/tr20030605-0250.html.

21. Department of Defense, "Background Briefing on IAEA Nuclear Safeguards and the Tuwaitha Facility," p. 4; Barton Gellman, "Iraqi Nuclear Site Is Found Looted," *Washington Post*, May 4, 2003, pp. A1, A30; Barton Gellman, "Seven Nuclear Sites Looted," *Washington Post*, May 10, 2003, pp. A1, A19.

22. Gellman, "Iraqi Nuclear Site Is Found Looted."

23. Gellman, "Seven Nuclear Sites Looted."

24. Ibid.

25. Ibid.

26. James Glanz and William J. Broad, "Looting at Weapons Plants Was Systematic, Iraqi Says," *New York Times*, March 13, 2005, pp. 1, 12.

27. Geoff Brumfiel, "Iraqi Looters Spark Alert over Radiation Risks," *Nature*, May 22, 2003, p. 370.

28. Deutch, *Threat of Nuclear Diversion*, p. 2.

29. Graham T. Allison, Owen R. Coté Jr., Richard A. Falkenrath, and Steven E. Miller, *Avoiding Nuclear Anarchy: Containing the Threat of Loose Russian Nuclear Weapons and Fissile Material* (Cambridge, Mass.: MIT Press, 1999), p. 21; Ferguson and Potter, *Four Faces of Nuclear Terrorism*, p. 157; DCI Nonproliferation Center, *Kazakstan: A Proliferation Assessment*, January 27, 1997, p. 7.

30. Amy F. Woolf, Congressional Research Service, *Nuclear Weapons in Russia: Safety, Security, and Control Issues*, January 21, 2004, pp. 1–2.

31. U.S. Congress, Senate Committee on Governmental Affairs, Permanent Subcommittee on Investigations, *Staff Statement, U.S. Permanent Subcommittee on Inves-*

tigations (Minority Staff), Hearings on Global Proliferation of Weapons of Mass Destruction: Illicit Trafficking in Nuclear Materials, March 22, 1996, p. 12; Eugene E. Habiger, "Security of the Russian Nukes," *Air Force*, February 1998, pp. 74–76.

32. David Filipov, "Russia's Scattered Tactical Arms a Temptation for Terrorists," *Boston Globe*, June 18, 2002, accessed from www.bostonglobe.com. Woolf, *Nuclear Weapons in Russia*, p. 4.

33. Allison, Coté, Falkenrath, and Miller, *Avoiding Nuclear Anarchy*, p. 39.

34. Deutch, *Threat of Nuclear Diversion*, p. 9; Rensselaer W. Lee III, *Smuggling Armageddon: The Nuclear Black Market in the Former Soviet Union and Europe* (New York: St. Martin's, 1999), p. 124.

35. National Intelligence Council, *Annual Report to Congress on the Safety and Security of Russian Nuclear Facilities and Military Forces*, April 2006, n.p.; Allison, Coté, Falkenrath, and Miller, *Avoiding Nuclear Anarchy*, pp. 25, 36–39; Lee, *Smuggling Armageddon*, p. 42; "Leonid Smirnov, A Nuclear Thief," www.pbs.org/avoiding armageddon, accessed April 4, 2008.

36. Allison, Coté, Falkenrath, and Miller, *Avoiding Nuclear Anarchy*, pp. 25–27; Senate Armed Services Committee, *Intelligence Briefing on Smuggling of Nuclear Material and the Role of International Crime Organizations, and on the Proliferation of Cruise and Ballistic Missiles*, pp. 23–24; Lee, *Smuggling Armageddon*, p. 43.

37. Langewiesche, *Atomic Bazaar*, p. 25; National Intelligence Council, *Annual Report to Congress on the Safety and Security of Russian Nuclear Facilities and Military Forces*, n.p.; Government Accountability Office, GAO-07-404, *Nuclear Nonproliferation*, p. 2; Anna Badkhen and James Strengold, "Nuclear Theft Raises Fears about Russia," www.sfgate.com, November 23, 2003; Lawrence Scott Sheets and William J. Broad, "Georgia Says It Blocked Smuggling of Arms-Grade Uranium," *New York Times*, January 25, 2007, p. A13; David Felipov, "Conviction Underscores Threat of Nuclear Theft: Russian Fleet Official Stored, Tried to Sell Radioactive Material," *Boston Globe*, November 26, 2003, accessed from www.ransac.org.

38. National Intelligence Council, *Annual Report to Congress on the Safety and Security of Russian Nuclear Facilities and Military Forces*, n.p.

39. Joby Warrick, "Dirty Bomb Warheads Disappear," *Washington Post*, December 7, 2003, pp. A1, A28.

40. Joby Warrick, "Makings of a 'Dirty Bomb': Radioactive Devices Left by Soviets Could Attract Terrorists," *Washington Post*, March 18, 2002, pp. A1, A12; Malgorzata K. Sneve, "Remote Control," *IAEA Bulletin*, 48, 1 (September 2006), pp. 42–47.

41. Allison, *Nuclear Terrorism*, p. 83.

42. Danielle Brian, Lynn Eisenmann, and Peter D. H. Stockton, "The Weapons Complex: Who's Guarding the Store?" *Bulletin of the Atomic Scientists*, January–February 2002, pp. 49–55 at pp. 50–51; Nick Schwellenbach and Peter D. H. Stockton, "Nuclear Lockdown," *Bulletin of the Atomic Scientists*, November–December 2006, pp. 44–50 at p. 46.

43. Adam Zagorin, "Security Flaws Exposed at Nuke Lab," www.time.com, May 12,

2008; National Nuclear Security Administration, "Security Inspection of Livermore Lab Completed," May 9, 2008.

44. Schwellenbach and Stockton, "Nuclear Lockdown," p. 46.

45. Ibid.

46. Joby Warrick, "Smugglers Enticed by Dirty Bomb Components," *Washington Post*, November 30, 2003, pp. A1, A28; Stephanie Stoughton, Associated Press, "Nuclear Device Found in Virginia Beach," www.wtop.com, October 30, 2004; Bunn, Weir, and Holdren, *Controlling Nuclear Warheads and Materials*, p. 13; Joseph B. Verrengia, "'Dirty Bomb' Scenario Revives Nuclear Worries," December 18, 2001, www.msnbc.com/news/674098.asp; Joby Warrick, "NRC Warns of Missing Radioactive Materials," *Washington Post*, May 4, 2002, p. A13.

47. Lee, *Smuggling Armageddon*, pp. 6, 94–95; "Russia Says It Foiled Illegal Sale of Weapons-Grade Uranium," *New York Times*, December 7, 2001, p. A8; Karel Janicek, "Radioactive Material Seized in Czech Sting Operation," *Washington Post*, November 16, 2003, p. A28.

48. Government Accountability Office, GAO-03-483, *Nuclear Nonproliferation: DOE Action Needed to Ensure Continued Recovery of Unwanted Sealed Radioactive Sources*, April 2003, pp. 1–2. The NRC classifies low-level radioactive waste (waste not specifically classified as high-level waste, such as used fuel rods from nuclear power plants) as A, B, or C for purposes of disposal. Waste that exceeds NRC criteria for class C, known as "Greater than Class C" waste, generally cannot be disposed of at existing facilities. Class designations are based on the radionuclide (e.g., americium-241) and the concentration of radioactivity (often measured in curies per gram).

49. Ibid., pp. 3, 6.

50. Ibid., p. 15.

51. John A. Tirpak, "Operation Sapphire," *Air Force Magazine*, August 1995, pp. 50–53; Andrew Cockburn and Leslie Cockburn, *One Point Safe: A True Story* (New York: Anchor Books, 1997), pp. 143–144.

52. Tirpak, "Operation Sapphire."

53. Ibid.

54. Ibid.

55. Ibid.

56. Ibid.

57. Ibid.

58. Ibid.

59. Ibid.

60. Ibid.; Cockburn and Cockburn, *One Point Safe*, pp. 140–160.

61. Tirpak, "Operation Sapphire"; Cockburn and Cockburn, *One Point Safe*, p. 151.

62. Tirpak, "Operation Sapphire"; Cockburn and Cockburn, *One Point Safe*, p. 146.

63. Tirpak, "Operation Sapphire."

64. Tirpak, "Operation Sapphire"; Cockburn and Cockburn, *One Point Safe*, p. 160.

65. Walter Pincus, "U.S. Removed Radioactive Materials from Iraq Facility," *Wash-

ington Post, July 7, 2004, p. A16; Matthew L. Wald, "Radioactive Material Seized from a Nuclear Plant in Iraq," *New York Times*, July 7, 2004, p. A11; Government Accountability Office, *Radiological Sources in Iraq: DOD Should Evaluate Its Source Recovery Effort and Apply Lessons Learned to Future Recovery Missions*, September 2005, p. 4.

66. William J. Broad, "In Georgian Region, Race to Recover Nuclear Fuel," *New York Times*, February 1, 2002, p. A6.

67. Ibid.

68. Sneve, "Remote Control."

69. Joby Warrick, "Hunting a Deadly Soviet Legacy," *Washington Post*, November 11, 2002, pp. A1, A20.

70. Ibid.

71. George H. Friedman, Inspector General, Department of Energy, "Recovery of Highly Enriched Uranium Provided to Foreign Countries," February 9, 2004; Department of Energy, Office of the Inspector General, DOE/IG-O638, *Recovery of Highly Enriched Uranium Provided to Foreign Countries*, February 2004, p. 1.

72. George E. Friedman, Inspector General, Memorandum for the Secretary, Subject: Information: Audit Report on "Recovery of Highly Enriched Uranium Provided to Foreign Countries," February 9, 2004; Office of the Inspector General, DOE/IG-O638, *Recovery of Highly Enriched Uranium Provided to Foreign Countries*, p. 2. The twelve countries were Austria, Belgium, France, Iran, Israel, Jamaica, Japan, Mexico, Netherlands, Pakistan, South Africa, and the United Kingdom.

73. Thomas W. Lippman, "Uranium 'Take-Back' Operations a Success," *Washington Post*, September 24, 1996, p. A4.

74. Ibid.

75. Ibid.

76. Joby Warrick, "Risky Stash of Uranium Secured," *Washington Post*, August 23, 2002, pp. A1, A24.

77. Bill Gertz, "Yugoslavia Could Use Nuke-Laced Arms," *Washington Times*, April 16, 1999, pp. A1, A11; Warrick, "Risky Stash of Uranium Secured."

78. Warrick, "Risky Stash of Uranium Secured."

79. Ibid.

80. Susan B. Glasser, "Russia Takes Back Uranium from Romania," *Washington Post*, September 22, 2003, p. A16.

81. Peter Baker, "U.S.-Russia Team Seizes Uranium at Bulgaria Plant," *Washington Post*, December 24, 2003, p. A10.

82. C. J. Chivers, "Prague Ships Its Nuclear-Bomb Fuel to Russian Storage," *New York Times*, September 28, 2005, p. A3.

83. C. J. Chivers, "Uzbeks Ship Bomb-Grade Waste to Russia," *New York Times*, April 20, 2006, p. A8; John J. Fialka, "U.S. Shifts Uranium from Poland to a Secure Facility in Russia," *Wall Street Journal*, August 10, 2006, p. A4.

84. Ralph Vartabedian, "A Race with the Terrorists," *Los Angeles Times*, September 27, 2007, pp. A1, A10; Ralph Vartabedian, "High Enriched Uranium Removed from

Reactor in Deal with Vietnam," *Los Angeles Times*, September 16, 2007, p. A7; "Nuke Patrol," *Aviation Week & Space Technology*, September 24, 2007, p. 31.

85. Vartabedian, "Race with the Terrorists"; Vartabedian, "High Enriched Uranium Removed from Reactor in Deal with Vietnam."

86. Government Accountability Office, GAO-07-404, *Nuclear Nonproliferation*, pp. 2–4.

87. Ibid., pp. 6, 14; C. J. Chivers, "Securing Russia Nuclear Missiles? U.S. Is Set to Say Done," *New York Times*, October 31, 2007, p. A12.

88. Government Accountability Office, GAO-07-404, *Nuclear Nonproliferation*, p. 7.

89. Lee, *Smuggling Armageddon*, p. 11.

CHAPTER NINE: A NEW URGENCY

1. George Tenet with Bill Harlow, *At the Center of the Storm: My Years at the CIA* (New York: HarperCollins, 2007), pp. 118–119.

2. "Presidential Decision Directive-62," www.fas.org/irp/offdocs/pdd-62.htm, accessed October 15, 2007.

3. Shawn Reese, Congressional Research Service, "National Special Security Events," November 6, 2007, p. 2.

4. Ibid., pp. 4–5; The White House, Fact Sheet, "Combating Terrorism: Presidential Decision Directive 62," May 22, 1998; General Accounting Office, GAO-01-822, *Combating Terrorism: Selected Challenges and Related Recommendations*, September 2001, p. 65; Office of the Inspector General, Department of Justice, *A Review of the FBI's Investigative Activities concerning Potential Protesters at the 2004 Democratic and Republican National Political Conventions*, April 27, 2006, pp. 5, 6n16; The White House, HSPD 7, Subject: Critical Infrastructure Identification, Prioritization, and Protection, December 17, 2003; William Mullen, "NGA Expands Customer Base for Special-Security Events," *Pathfinder*, July/August 2006, pp. 18–19; Jamie Blietz, AABB *Interorganizational Task Force on Domestic Disasters and Acts of Terrorism—Task Force Update for the Advisory Committee on Blood Safety and Availability*, August 26, 2004, n.p.; Allen R. Myerson, "As Energy Council Gathers, Oil Industry Seeks Answers," *New York Times*, September 16, 1998, p. C23.

5. Catharina Wrede Braden, Center for Policing Terrorism, *Lessons Learned: An Analysis of WMD-Scenario Training Exercises*, April 30, 2004, p. 10; Jim McDonnell, *Exercise JAGGED WIND After Action Report*, n.d., n.p.; Lisa Cutler to Fred Kaplan, Subj: NEST info you requested, e-mail, June 8, 2002.

6. Oak Ridge Institute for Science and Education, *Exercise Package Satyr After-Action Report*, November 9, 1998, pp. 1, 3; Department of Energy, *Package SATYR*, August 4–7, 1998, n.p.

7. Oak Ridge Institute for Science and Education, *Exercise Errant Foe Ellipse Bravo 98 After-Action Report*, November 25, 1998, pp. 1, 3, 5.

8. Bill Belanger, Tom Hughes, and Steve Centore, *Vigilant Lion Exercise (VL-99)*

After Action Report (Washington, D.C., and Harrisburg, Pa.: Environmental Protection Agency and Pennsylvania Emergency Management Agency, May 2000), p. 4.

9. Ibid., p. 12.

10. Ibid., pp. 6, 18–19.

11. Ibid., pp. 19–20.

12. Cutler to Kaplan, Subj: NEST info you requested; General Accounting Office, GAO-01-822, *Combating Terrorism*, p. 74.

13. "Department of Energy (DOE) Nuclear Incident Response," *Beacon*, 1, 6 (May 16, 1999), pp. 1–3; "Statement of John A. Gordon, Under Secretary of Energy and Administrator for Nuclear Security National Nuclear Security Administration, U.S. Department of Energy, before the Committee on Appropriations, United States Senate," May 8, 2001, p. 3; General Accounting Office, GAO-01-822, *Combating Terrorism*, p. 146.

14. "Department of Energy (DOE) Nuclear Incident Response"; "Statement of John A. Gordon," p. 3; U.S. Department of Energy, National Nuclear Security Administration, "Nuclear Emergency Support Team (NEST)," 2002.

15. "Department of Energy (DOE) Nuclear Incident Response"; "Statement of John A. Gordon," p. 3.

16. "Department of Energy (DOE) Nuclear Incident Response"; "Statement of John A. Gordon," p. 3; Eileen Patterson, "Render Safe: Defusing a Nuclear Emergency," *Los Alamos Research Quarterly*, Fall 2002, pp. 22–23.

17. George H. Friedman, Inspector General, Memorandum for the Secretary, Subject: *Information*: Inspection Report on "National Nuclear Security Administration's Ability to Meet the Aircraft Requirements of the Joint Technical Operations Team," June 5, 2003.

18. Patterson, "Render Safe."

19. "Department of Energy (DOE) Nuclear Incident Response"; General Accounting Office, GAO-01-822, *Combating Terrorism*, p. 146.

20. Michael R. Anastasio, Director, Lawrence Livermore National Laboratory, *Establishment of the Department of Homeland Security, Hearing of the U.S. Senate Energy and Natural Resources Committee*, July 10, 2002, p. 5.

21. Department of Energy, *Package SATYR*, n.p.; Oak Ridge Institute for Science and Education, *Exercise Package Satyr After-Action Report*, p. 4; Belanger, Hughes, and Centore, *Vigilant Lion Exercise (VL-99) After Action Report*, p. 19; Oak Ridge Institute for Science and Education, *Exercise Errant Foe Ellipse Bravo 98 After-Action Report*, p. 3.

22. Peter Grier, "Got a Nuclear Crisis? Better Call NEST," *Christian Science Monitor*, June 22, 2000.

23. "Parks Official Retiring after Los Alamos Blaze," *New York Times*, June 11, 2000, accessed from www.nytimes.com.

24. Ibid.

25. Dan Stober and Ian Hoffman, *A Convenient Spy: Wen Ho Lee and the Politics of*

Nuclear Espionage (New York: Simon & Schuster, 2002), p. 308; Gary Milhollin, "The Real Nuclear Gap," *New York Times*, June 16, 2000, p. A33; James Risen, "Staff at Los Alamos Waited for 3 Weeks to Tell of Data Loss," *New York Times*, June 14, 2000, accessed from www.nytimes.com; James Risen, "Nuclear Secrets Reported Missing from Los Alamos," *New York Times*, June 13, 2000, accessed from www.nytimes.com.

26. Stober and Hoffman, *Convenient Spy*, p. 308; Risen, "Staff at Los Alamos Waited for 3 Weeks to Tell of Data Loss."

27. Risen, "Staff at Los Alamos Waited for 3 Weeks to Tell of Data Loss"; Brian Reynolds, "Breach at Los Alamos: Who'll Take the Blame," *New York Times*, June 16, 2000, accessed from www.nytimes.com.

28. Stober and Hoffman, *Convenient Spy*, p. 308; Milhollin, "Real Nuclear Gap"; "FBI Concludes Investigation of Hard Drive Incident at Los Alamos," January 18, 2001, www.energy.gov.

29. "FBI Concludes Investigation of Hard Drive Incident at Los Alamos"; Grier, "Got a Nuclear Crisis?"

30. "FBI Concludes Investigation of Hard Drive Incident at Los Alamos."

31. William M. Arkin, *CODE NAMES: Deciphering US Military Plans, Programs, and Operations in the 9/11 World* (Hanover, N.H.: Steerforth Press, 2005), p. 404, "RAF Fairford," http://en.wikipedia.org/wiki/RAF_Fairford, accessed November 16, 2007; "Base Overview," www.fairfordbase.org.uk, accessed November 16, 2007.

32. Oak Ridge Institute for Science and Education, *DOE Exercise 03-01 Jackal Cave After-Action Report*, n.d., pp. A-1, A-2.

33. Ibid., pp. 8–9.

34. National Commission on Terrorist Attacks Upon the United States, *The 9/11 Commission Report: Final Report of the National Commission on Terrorist Attacks Upon the United States* (New York: W.W. Norton, 2004), p. 32.

35. Ibid., p. 33.

36. George J. Tenet, Director of Central Intelligence, "We Are at War," September 16, 2001.

37. Keay Davidson, "Nuclear Terror Team on Standby," *San Francisco Chronicle*, September 16, 2001, accessed from www.sfgate.com/chronicle; ABC News, Transcript, "Loose Nukes on Main Street," October 11, 2005.

38. ABC News, Transcript, "Loose Nukes on Main Street."

39. Bob Woodward, *Bush at War* (New York: Simon & Schuster, 2002), p. 197; Robert D. McFadden, "A Nation Challenged: Threat; Tip on Nuclear Attack Risk Was Kept from New Yorkers," *New York Times*, March 4, 2002, accessed from www.nytimes.com; Massimo Calabresi and Romesh Ratnesar, "Can We Stop the Next Attack?" *Time*, March 11, 2002, accessed from www.time.com; "Blast Map—10110 Zip Code," www.nuclearterror.org, accessed December 19, 2007.

40. Woodward, *Bush at War*, p. 197; McFadden, "Nation Challenge"; Calabresi and Ratnesar, "Can We Stop the Next Attack?"

41. Robert D. McFadden, "Nation Challenged"; Michael Cooper, "A Nation Challenged: Threat: Officials Say U.S. Should Have Shared Tip," *New York Times*, March 2, 2002, accessed from www.nytimes.com.
42. Fred Kaplan, "Mobile Teams on Hunt for Atomic Threats," *Boston Globe*, June 9, 2002, accessed from www.bostonglobe.com; Douglas Waller, "The Secret Bomb Squad," *Time*, March 9, 2002, accessed from www.time.com.
43. Kaplan, "Mobile Teams on Hunt for Atomic Threats."
44. Waller, "Secret Bomb Squad"; Kaplan, "Mobile Teams on Hunt for Atomic Threats."
45. David Ruppe, "U.S. Response: Accelerate Nuclear Terrorism Response, Official Says," *Global Security Newswire*, July 3, 2002, accessed from www.nti.org; ABC News, Transcript, "Loose Nukes on Main Street."
46. Barton Gellman, "In U.S. Terrorism's Peril Undiminished," *Washington Post*, December 24, 2002, pp. A1, A6.
47. Ibid.; Barton Gellman, "Fears Prompt U.S. to Beef Up Nuclear Terror Detection," *Washington Post*, March 2, 2002, pp. A1, A18.
48. Gellman, "Fears Prompt U.S. to Beef Up Nuclear Terror Detection"; Douglas Waller, "Searching for the Dirty Bomb," www.time.com, March 12, 2002.

CHAPTER TEN: NEST AFTER 9/11

1. U.S. Department of Energy, National Nuclear Security Administration, "Nuclear Emergency Support Team (NEST)," 2002; Siobhan Gorman and Sydney J. Freedberg Jr., "Early Warning," *National Journal*, June 11, 2005, pp. 1744–1752.
2. Eric Lichtblau, Bob Drogin, and Josh Meyer, "U.S. Citizen Accused of Planning an Attack Using a 'Dirty Bomb'," *Los Angeles Times*, June 11, 2002, pp. A1, A14; Erich Lichtblau, "In Legal Shift, U.S. Charges Detainee in Terrorism Case," *New York Times*, November 23, 2005, pp. A1, A18.
3. Department of Justice, "Summary of Jose Padilla's Activities with Al-Qaeda," 2002, pp. 1–2.
4. Ibid., p. 2.
5. Ibid., pp. 2–3.
6. Ibid., p. 3.
7. Ibid., pp. 1, 3; Office of the Director of National Intelligence, "Summary of the High Value Terrorist Detainee Program," n.d., p. 1; "Abu Zubaydah," http//en.wikipedia.org, accessed October 26, 2007.
8. Office of the Director of National Intelligence, "Summary of the High Value Terrorist Detainee Program," p. 1; Office of the Director of National Intelligence, "Biographies of High-Value Detainees," n.d.; Private information; George Tenet with Bill Harlow, *At the Center of the Storm: My Years at the CIA* (New York: HarperCollins, 2007), p. 242.
9. Department of Justice, "Summary of Jose Padilla's Activities with Al-Qaeda," pp.

3–4; Bob Drogin, Eric Lichtblau, and Josh Meyer, "'Dirty Bomb' Probe Widens," *Los Angeles Times*, June 12, 2002, pp. A1, A24.

10. Department of Justice, "Summary of Jose Padilla's Activities with Al-Qaeda," p. 4.

11. Ibid., p. 4–6.

12. Lichtblau, Drogin, and Meyer, "U.S. Citizen Accused of Planning an Attack Using a 'Dirty Bomb'."

13. Ibid.

14. Department of Justice, "Summary of Jose Padilla's Activities with Al-Qaeda," p. 1.

15. President George W. Bush, *The Department of Homeland Security*, June 2002.

16. Ibid., p. 2; "Tom Ridge, Homeland Security Secretary 2003–2005," September 1, 2006, www.dhs.gov/xabout/history/editorial_0586.html.

17. "History: Who Became Part of the Department?" June 19, 2007, www.dhs.gov/xabout/history/editorial_0133.shtm.

18. Keith Bea, William Krouse, Daniel Morgan, Wayne Morrisey, and C. Stephen Redhead, Congressional Research Service, *Emergency Preparedness and Response Directorate of the Department of Homeland Security*, June 25, 2003, p. 5; National Nuclear Security Administration, Department of Energy, "Radiological Assistance Program," n.d.

19. Bea, Krouse, Morgan, Morrisey, and Redhead, Congressional Research Service, *Emergency Preparedness and Response Directorate of the Department of Homeland Security*, p. 5.

20. William K. Rashbaum, "In Sign of the Times, New York Begins Deploying Radiation Detectors," *New York Times*, June 29, 2002, p. A14.

21. Rashbaum, "In Sign of the Times, New York Begins Deploying Radiation Detectors"; Spencer S. Hsu, "Sensors May Track Terror's Fallout," *Washington Post*, June 2, 2003, pp. A1, A8.

22. Hsu, "Sensors May Track Terror's Fallout."

23. Ronald Smothers, "Navy Seals Join Federal Search of Cargo Ship," *New York Times*, September 13, 2002, p. A13.

24. Department of Homeland Security, *The Budget for Fiscal Year 2004* (Washington, D.C.: Department of Homeland Security, 2003), p. 142; Ronald Smothers, "Ship's Radiation Is Traced to Harmless Tiles," *New York Times*, September 14, 2002, accessed from www.nytimes.com; Smothers, "Navy Seals Join Federal Search of Cargo Ship."

25. Smothers, "Ship's Radiation Is Traced to Harmless Tiles"; Smothers, "Navy Seals Join Federal Search of Cargo Ship"; David McGlinchey, "Radiological Weapons: NEST Responds to Radiological Scare," *Global Security Newswire*, September 23, 2002, accessed from www.nti.org; Office of the Inspector General, Department of Justice, Audit Report 06-26, *The Federal Bureau of Investigation's Efforts to Protect the Nation's Seaports*, March 2006, p. 35.

26. Smothers, "Ship's Radiation Is Traced to Harmless Tiles"; Office of the Inspector General, Department of Justice, Audit Report 06-26, *The Federal Bureau of Investigation's Efforts to Protect the Nation's Seaports*, p. 35.

27. Office of the Inspector General, Department of Justice, Audit Report 06-26, *The Federal Bureau of Investigation's Efforts to Protect the Nation's Seaports*, pp. 35–36.

28. Edward Walsh and John Mintz, "Huge Homeland Security Drill Planned," *Washington Post*, May 5, 2003, p. A9; Sarah Kershaw, "Terror Scenes Follow Script of No More 9/11's," *New York Times*, May 13, 2003, p. A19.

29. Walsh and Mintz, "Huge Homeland Security Drill Planned"; Kershaw, "Terror Scenes Follow Script of No More 9/11's."

30. David E. Kaplan, "Nuclear Monitoring of Muslims Done without Search Warrants," www.usnews.com, December 22, 2005; Matthew L. Wald, "Widespread Radioactivity Monitoring Is Confirmed," *New York Times*, December 24, 2005, p. A11.

31. Kaplan, "Nuclear Monitoring of Muslims Done without Search Warrants."

32. "Mosques and Islamic Centers in the Greater Washington Area," www.aaagw.org, accessed December 15, 2007; "Chicago," www.internetmuslim.com/Community_Center/chicago_info.htm; "Los Angeles Area," www.internetmuslim.com/Community_Center/laarea_info.htm.

33. Kaplan, "Nuclear Monitoring of Muslims Done without Search Warrants."

34. Ibid.

35. Larry Margasak, Associated Press, "FBI Official Defends Radiation Monitoring," December 23, 2005, http://apnews.my.com; Kaplan, "Nuclear Monitoring of Muslims Done without Search Warrants."

36. Kaplan, "Nuclear Monitoring of Muslims Done without Search Warrants"; Richard A. Serrano, "FBI Monitor for Radiation at Some Mosques," *Los Angeles Times*, December 24, 2005, p. A16.

37. Supreme Court of the United States, No. 99-8508, 533 U.S. 27 (2001), *Opinion of the Court: Danny Lee Kyllo, Petitioner v. United States, On Writ of Certiorari to the United States Court of Appeals for the Ninth Circuit*, June 11, 2001, p. 1.

38. Ibid.

39. Ibid., p. 2.

40. Ibid., pp. 4–5.

41. Ibid., pp. 6, 10.

42. Kaplan, "Nuclear Monitoring of Muslims Done without Search Warrants"; Wald, "Widespread Radioactivity Monitoring Is Confirmed."

43. Supreme Court of the United States, No. 03-923, 543 U.S. 40 (2005), *Opinion of the Court: Illinois, Petitioner v. Roy I. Caballes, On Writ of Certiorari to the Supreme Court of Illinois*, January 24, 2005, pp. 1, 4.

44. Barton Gellman, "U.S. Reaps New Data on Weapons," *Washington Post*, March 20, 2003, pp. A1, A19.

45. Telephone interview with Robert Kelley, November 20, 2007.

46. Interview with William Nelson, Alamo, Calif., June 9, 2007.

47. John Mintz and Susan Schmidt, "'Dirty Bomb' Was Major New Year's Worry," *Washington Post*, January 7, 2004, pp. A1, A6; Greg Krikorian, "L.A. Checked as Possible 'Dirty Bomb' Attack Target," *Los Angeles Times*, January 7, 2004, p. A12.

48. Mintz and Schmidt, "'Dirty Bomb' Was Major New Year's Worry."

49. Ibid.; Christopher Lee, "DOE Bomb Squads' Exacting Mission," *Washington Post*, March 9, 2004, p. A21.

50. Mintz and Schmidt, "'Dirty Bomb' Was Major New Year's Worry"; "Baltimore Inner Harbor," www.baltimore.org/baltimore_inner_harbor.htm, accessed October 30, 2007.

51. Mintz and Schmidt, "'Dirty Bomb' Was Major New Year's Worry."

52. Ibid.

53. Ibid.

54. Jonathan Finer, "Reports of 'Dirty Bomb' Threat Mean High Anxiety in Boston," *Washington Post*, January 21, 2005, p. A8; Jerry Seper, "Terror Tip Sparks FBI Search," *Washington Times*, January 21, 2005, p. A3.

55. Finer, "Reports of 'Dirty Bomb' Threat Mean High Anxiety in Boston"; Seper, "Terror Tip Sparks FBI Search."

56. Finer, "Reports of 'Dirty Bomb' Threat Mean High Anxiety in Boston"; Seper, "Terror Tip Sparks FBI Search."

57. Seper, "Terror Tip Sparks FBI Search"; "F.B.I. Calls Boston Terror Plot Tip a False Alarm," *New York Times*, January 26, 2005, p. A9.

58. Nicholas Riccardi, "Colorado Springs Has Eye Out for Dirty Bomb," *Los Angeles Times*, December 25, 2005, p. A22.

59. Ibid.

60. Ibid.

CHAPTER ELEVEN: FOREIGN TRAVEL

1. Rensselaer W. Lee III, *Smuggling Armageddon: The Nuclear Black Market in the Former Soviet Union and Europe* (New York: St. Martin's, 1998), p. 88.

2. Ibid.

3. U.S. Congress, Senate Committee on Governmental Affairs, Senate Permanent Subcommittee on Investigations, Minority Staff Statement, *Hearings on Global Proliferation of Weapons of Mass Destruction: Illicit Trafficking in Nuclear Materials*, March 22, 1996, Appendix B, p. 3.

4. Lee, *Smuggling Armageddon*, p. 17; Michael Specter, "Russians Assert Radioactive Box Found in Park Posed No Danger," *New York Times*, November 25, 1995, accessed from www.nytimes.com; "Basayev, Shamil," *MIPT Terrorist Knowledge Base*, www.tkb.org, accessed November 11, 2007; "Basayev: Russia's Most Wanted Man," September 8, 2004, www.cnn.com; "Shamil Basayev," http://en.wikipedia.org, accessed November 11, 2007.

5. Specter, "Russians Assert Radioactive Box Found in Park Posed No Danger"; "Izmailovsky Park," www.moscow.info, accessed November 11, 2007.

6. Sarah Lyall, "Briton Tried to Buy A-Bomb, Prosecution in Trial Contends," *New York Times*, March 23, 2006, p. A14.

7. Melanie Phillips, *Londonistan* (San Francisco: Encounter, 2007), pp. 198, 213.

8. Steve Coll, "The Unthinkable," *New Yorker*, March 12, 2007, pp. 48–57.
9. Government Accountability Office, GAO-O5-547, *Olympic Security: U.S. Support to Athens Games Provides Lessons for Future Olympics*, May 2005, p. 10.
10. "2004 Summer Olympics," http://en.wikipedia.org, accessed November 12, 2007; "Athens 2004: Games of the XXVIII Olympiad," www.olympic.org, accessed November 12, 2007.
11. Department of State, *Strategic Plan for Interagency Coordination of U.S. Government Nuclear Detection Assistant Overseas*, August 5, 2004.
12. Ibid., p. 1.
13. Ibid., pp. 2–3.
14. Ibid., p. 4.
15. Nevada Operations Office, *NEST Energy Senior Official's Reference Manual*, October 31, 1993, pp. 4-1, 10-11–10-12.
16. Vassiliki Kamenopoulou, Panayiotis Dimitriou, Constantine J. Hourdakis, Antonios Maltezos, Theodore Matikas, Constantinos Potriadis, and Leonidas Camarinopoulos, "Nuclear Security and Radiological Preparedness for the Olympic Games, Athens 2004: Lessons Learned for Organizing Major Public Events," *Health Physics*, 91, 4 (October 2006), pp. 318–330.
17. Ibid.
18. Ibid.; Government Accountability Office, *Olympic Security*, pp. 3, 12.
19. Global Security Newswire, "China Purchases Radiation Sensors for Olympics," July 17, 2008, www.nti.org; Bill Gertz, "U.S. Nuke Spotters Sent to China," www.washingtontimes.com, June 20, 2008.
20. National Nuclear Security Administration, "U.S. and Russia Jointly Conduct Field Training for Radiological Emergency Response," November 5, 2007.
21. Ibid.
22. Ibid.
23. Coll, "Unthinkable."
24. Ibid.
25. Ibid.
26. Ibid.
27. Ibid.
28. Shaun Gregory, Pakistan Security Research Unit, Brief Number 22, *The Security of Nuclear Weapons in Pakistan*, November 18, 2007, p. 10; Private information.
29. Chairman of the Joint Chiefs of Staff, *National Military Strategy to Combat Weapons of Mass Destruction*, February 13, 2006, p. 7; Defense Science Board, *DSB Summer Study on Special Operations and Joint Forces in Support of Countering Terrorism, Final Outbrief*, August 16, 2002 p. 44.
30. Coll, "Unthinkable."
31. Office of the Assistant Secretary of Defense (Special Operations and Low-Intensity Conflict), *Nuclear Terrorism Intelligence: A Special Operations Perspective*, n.d., pp. 12–13.

32. Bruce G. Blair, "The Ultimate Hatred Is Nuclear," *New York Times*, October 22, 2001, p. A21; Peter R. Lavoy, Naval Postgraduate School, *Pakistan's Nuclear Posture: Security and Survivability*, n.d., p. 7.

33. "Nuclear Jihad: Can Terrorists Get the Bomb?" *Discovery Channel*, April 17, 2006; Ron Moreau and Michael Hirsh, "Where the Jihad Lives Now," *Newsweek*, October 29, 2007, pp. 27–34.

34. Bill Roggio, "The Second Coup," www.weeklystandard.com, November 4, 2007.

35. K. Alan Kronstadt, Congressional Research Service, *Pakistan's Political Crises*, January 3, 2008, pp. 10–11; "Prime Minister of the Republic of Pakistan," www.infopak.gov.pk/primeminister.aspx, accessed May 3, 2008.

36. Joby Warrick, "Pakistan Nuclear Security Questioned," www.washingtonpost.com, November 11, 2007; Greg Miller, "Pakistan's Nuclear Arsenal a U.S. Worry," *Los Angeles Times*, November 8, 2007, p. A10; David E. Sanger and William J. Broad, "U.S. Secretly Aids Pakistan in Guarding Nuclear Arms," *New York Times*, November 18, 2007, pp. 1, 12.

37. Warrick, "Pakistan Nuclear Security Questioned"; Sanger and Broad, "U.S. Secretly Aids Pakistan in Guarding Nuclear Arms"; Thomas F. Ricks, "Calculating the Risks in Pakistan," *Washington Post*, December 2, 2007, p. A20; Peter Wonacott, "Inside Pakistan's Drive to Guard Its A-Bombs," *Wall Street Journal*, November 29, 2007, pp. A1, A17.

38. Naeem Salik, Strategic Plans Division, Pakistan, *Nuclear Security Efforts in Pakistan and Handling Perceptions*, June 20, 2007.

39. "Nuclear Jihad: Can Terrorists Get the Bomb?"; David E. Sanger, "So, What about Those Nukes?" *New York Times*, November 11, 2007, Week in Review, p. 8; Miller, "Pakistan's Nuclear Arsenal a U.S. Worry."

40. John M. Glionna, "Pakistan Says Its Nuclear Arsenal Is Secure," *Los Angeles Times*, January 27, 2008, p. A9; "Pakistan to Keep Nuclear Control Structure," *Global Security Newswire*, April 9, 2008, accessed from www.nti.org.

41. Miller, "Pakistan's Nuclear Arsenal a U.S. Worry"; "Gen. Khalid Kidwai Retires," *Post*, October 7, 2007, accessed from www.thepost.com.pk; Scott Canon, "Nuclear Weapon Raises Stakes for the West; Unrest Could Help Terrorists Acquire The Bomb," *Kansas City Star*, September 20, 2001, www.nci.org/01/09/21-2.htm; Peter Wonacott, "Inside Pakistan's Drive to Guard Its A-Bombs," *Wall Street Journal*, November 29, 2007, pp. A1, A17.

42. David E. Sanger and Thom Shanker, "A Nuclear Headache: What If the Radicals Oust Musharraf?" *New York Times*, December 30, 2003, p. A3; Warrick, "Pakistan Nuclear Security Questioned."

43. "Pakistan Defends Its Nuclear Security," *Global Security Newswire*, November 9, 2007, accessed from www.nti.org; Sanger, "So, What about Those Nukes?"; Warrick, "Pakistan Nuclear Security Questioned"; Sanger and Shanker, "Nuclear Headache"; "Pakistani Military Likely to Secure Nuclear Arsenal if Musharraf Government Collapses, Analysts Say," *Global Security Newswire*, November 14, 2007, accessed from www.nti.org.

44. John Fox, "Bush Official Says Pakistan's Nuclear Weapons Safe," *Global Security Newswire*, January 23, 2008, accessed from www.nti.org.
45. Miller, "Pakistan's Nuclear Arsenal a U.S. Worry."
46. Warrick, "Pakistan Nuclear Security Questioned."
47. "Nuclear Jihad: Can Terrorists Get the Bomb?"
48. Ibid.
49. Danny Kemp, Agence France-Presse, "Pakistan Warns of Strong Response to Nukes Grab," December 11, 2007, http://yahoo.com.
50. "Pakistani Military Likely to Secure Nuclear Arsenal If Musharraf Government Collapses, Analysis Say"; Ricks, "Calculating the Risks in Pakistan."
51. Frederick W. Kagan and Michael O'Hanlon, "Pakistan's Collapse, Our Problem," *New York Times*, Week in Review, November 18, 2007, p. 16; Michael O'Hanlon, "What If a Nuclear-Armed State Collapses?" *Current History*, November 2006, pp. 379–384.
52. Robert Windrem, "Pakistan's Nuclear History Worries Insiders," www.msnbc.com, November 6, 2007; Sanger and Shanker, "Nuclear Headache."
53. Bruce G. Blair, "The Ultimate Hatred Is Nuclear," *New York Times*, October 22, 2001, accessed from www.nytimes.com.

CHAPTER TWELVE: CHALLENGES AHEAD

1. Lara Jakes Jordan, Associated Press, "Government Doubts Threat on NFL Stadiums," October 18, 2006, www.comcast.net; Emily Fredrix, Associated Press, "Stadium Hoax Was Prank by Grocery Clerk," October 21, 2006, www.comcast.net.
2. Jordan, "Government Doubts Threat on NFL Stadiums"; Emily Fredrix, Associated Press, "Football Stadium Threat a Hoax, FBI Says," October 19, 2006, www.comcast.net.
3. Fredrix, "Stadium Hoax Was Prank by Grocery Clerk"; Associated Press, "Man Pleads Guilty in Hoax to Attack NFL Stadium," February 28, 2008, www.usatoday.com.; Associated Press, "Local Clerk Sentenced in NFL Threat Case," June 5, 2008, accessed from www.jsonline.com.
4. John Mueller, "Radioactive Hype," *National Interest*, September/October 2007, pp. 59–65; William M. Arkin, "The Continuing Misuses of Fear," *Bulletin of the Atomic Scientists*, September/October 2006, pp. 42–45; John Mueller, "The Atomic Terrorist: Assessing the Likelihood," January 1, 2008, Paper prepared for presentation at the Program on International Security Policy, University of Chicago, January 15, 2008, p. 1.
5. Christopher Bodeen, "U.S. Terror Expert Says Nuclear Risk Low," June 1, 2007, http://sfgate.com; Robin M. Frost, Adelphi Paper 378, *Nuclear Terrorism after 9/11* (London: International Institute for Strategic Studies, 2005), pp. 7–10. For a critique of several of Frost's assertions, see Anna M. Pluta and Peter D. Zimmerman,

"Nuclear Terrorism: A Disheartening Dissent," *Survival*, 48, 2 (Summer 2006), pp. 55–70.

6. Graham Allison, "The Ongoing Failure of Imagination," *Bulletin of the Atomic Scientists*, September/October 2006, pp. 36–41; Bill Keller, "Nuclear Nightmares," *New York Times Magazine*, May 26, 2002, pp. 22ff; John Parachini, "Putting WMD Terrorism into Perspective," *Washington Quarterly*, 26, 4 (Autumn 2003), pp. 37–50; Glenn M. Cannon, Statement for the Record before the United States Senate Committee on Homeland Security and Governmental Affairs, "Not a Matter of 'If', But of 'When': The Status of U.S. Response Following an RDD Attack," November 15, 2007; Matthew Bunn, "The Risk of Nuclear Terrorism—And Next Steps to Reduce the Danger," Testimony for the Committee on Homeland Security and Governmental Affairs, April 2, 2008, p. 1; Kim Murphy, "El Baradei Warns about Extremist Nuclear Threat," *Los Angeles Times*, February 10, 2008, p. A4.

7. Charles Meade and Roger C. Molander, *Considering the Effects of a Catastrophic Terrorist Attack* (Santa Monica, Calif.: RAND 2006), pp. xv, 7.

8. Jasen J. Castillo, "Nuclear Terrorism: Why Deterrence Still Matters," *Current History*, December 2003, pp. 426–431.

9. Telephone interview with Robert Kelley, November 20, 2007.

10. Lieutenant General Michael D. Maples, Director, Defense Intelligence Agency, Statement for the Record, Senate Armed Services Committee, *Current and Projected National Security Threats to the United States*, February 27, 2007, p. 8; National Intelligence Council, *The Terrorist Threat to the US Homeland*, July 2007, Key Judgments; Mark Hosenball and Michael Isikoff, "A Sense of Unease," *Newsweek*, July 23, 2007, p. 36; Ronald Kessler, "FBI's Mueller: Bin Laden Wants to Strike U.S. Cities with Nuclear Weapons," www.newsmax.com, May 15, 2007; David Ignatius, "Portents of a Nuclear Al-Qaeda," www.washingtonpost.com, October 18, 2007; Rolf Mowatt-Larsen, "Statement before the Homeland Security and Government Affairs Committee," April 2, 2008, p. 2.

11. "Russian Warns of Dirty Bomb Attack," www.newsmax.com, October 5, 2007.

12. David Rising, Associated Press, "Iraq Terrorist Calls Scientists to Jihad," September 28, 2006, www.comcast.net.

13. "Men Tried for Seeking 'Dirty Bomb' Material," *Global Security Newswire*, November 8, 2007, accessed from www.nti.org.

14. Office of Public Affairs, "U.S. and Russia Sign Plan for Russian Plutonium Disposition," November 19, 2007.

15. Department of Energy, Office of Intelligence and Counterintelligence, *Human Capital Strategy and Workforce Plan Office of Intelligence and Counterintelligence*, September 8, 2006, p. 1, http://humancapital.doe.gov/pol/hcmp/pdf/cnhcmp.pdf.

16. National Nuclear Security Administration, "NNSA's Second Line of Defense Program," November 2007; National Nuclear Security Administration, "U.S. and Israel to Cooperate on Detecting Illicit Shipments of Nuclear Material," December 7, 2005; National Nuclear Security Administration, "NNSA Works with Cyprus

to Thwart Nuclear Smuggling," December 12, 2007; National Nuclear Security Administration, "Israel Begins Radiation Detection Efforts at Haifa Port," January 23, 2008; National Nuclear Security Administration, "U.S. and Malaysia Agree to Secure Seaport Cargo," February 27, 2008.

17. Government Accountability Office, GAO-05-840T, Statement of Gene Aloise, *Combating Nuclear Smuggling: Efforts to Deploy Radiation Detection Equipment in the United States and in Other Countries,* June 21, 2005, p. 5; Government Accountability Office, GAO-06-389, *Combating Nuclear Smuggling: DHS Has Made Progress Deploying Radiation Detection Equipment at U.S. Ports-of-Entry, but Concerns Remain,* March 2006, pp. 12–14; Department of Homeland Security, "Fact Sheet: Select Department of Homeland Security 2007 Achievements," December 12, 2007.

18. Eric Lipton, "New Detectors Aim to Prevent Nuclear Terror," *New York Times,* February 9, 2007, pp. A1, A18.

19. John Fox, "Radiation Detection Project under Way in Chicago," *Global Security Newswire,* November 16, 2007, accessed from www.nti.org; National Nuclear Security Administration, "NNSA Provides Aerial Detection Training to Chicago PD," January 29, 2008.

20. Government Accountability Office, GAO-06-1015, *Combating Nuclear Terrorism: Federal Efforts to Respond to Nuclear and Radiological Threats and to Protect Emergency Response Capabilities Could Be Strengthened,* September 2006, pp. 24–25; Mimi Hall, "Authorities Want to Survey City Radiation." *USA Today,* December 11, 2007.

21. National Academy of Sciences, "Speakers, Post-Cold War U.S. Nuclear Strategy: A Search for Technical and Policy Common Ground," August 11, 2004; Ralph Vartabedian, "U.S. Seeks to Make Stolen Nukes Useless," *Los Angeles Times,* December 5, 2006, pp. A1, A15.

22. "Director of the Domestic Nuclear Detection Office: Vayl Oxford," www.dhs.gov, accessed November 20, 2006; George W. Bush, National Security Presidential Directive 43 /Homeland Security Presidential Directive 14, Subject: Domestic Nuclear Detection, April 15, 2005, available at www.fas.org; Ralph Vartabedian, "Detecting Radiation an Arduous Job at Ports," *Los Angeles Times,* November 25, 2007, pp. A1, A20.

23. Bush, National Security Presidential Directive 43 /Homeland Security Presidential Directive 14, Subject: Domestic Nuclear Detection.

24. Vayl Oxford, Statement before House Homeland Security Committee Subcommittee, *Detecting Nuclear Weapons and Radiological Materials: How Effective Is Available Technology?* June 21, 2005, pp. 4, 7; Vayl S. Oxford, *Domestic Nuclear Detection Office (DNDO),* EFCOG 2007 Executive Council Meeting, February 21–22, 2007, pp. 11, 15–17.

25. Anthony Wier and Matthew Bunn, "Bombs That Won't Go Off," *Washington Post,* November 19, 2006, p. B7.

26. Government Accountability Office, GAO-07-404, *Nuclear Nonproliferation:*

Progress Made in Improving Security at Russian Nuclear Sites, but the Long-Term Sustainability of U.S.-Funded Security Upgrades Is Uncertain, February 2007; Government Accountability Office, GAO-07-282, *Nuclear Nonproliferation: DOE's International Radiological Threat Reduction Program Needs to Focus Future Efforts on Securing the Highest Priority Radiological Sources*, January 2007, pp. 5–8.

27. Gene Aloise, Director, Natural Resources and Environment, Government Accountability Office, Memo to Congressional Requesters, Subject: Combating Nuclear Smuggling: DNDO Has Not Yet Collected Most of the National Laboratories' Test Results on Radiation Portal Monitors in Support of DNDO's Testing and Development Program, March 9, 2007, p. 3; Government Accounting Office, GAO-07-581T, *Combating Nuclear Smuggling: DHS's Decision to Procure and Deploy the Next Generation of Radiation Detection Equipment Is Not Supported by Its Cost-Benefit Analysis*, March 14, 2007; Vartabedian, "Detecting Radiation an Arduous Job at Ports"; Robert O'Harrow Jr., "DHS 'Dry Run' Support Cited," *Washington Post*, September 18, 2007, p. A4; Government Accountability Office, GAO-07-1247T, *Combating Nuclear Smuggling: Additional Actions Needed to Ensure Adequate Testing of Next Generation Radiation Detection Equipment*, September 18, 2007, n.p.

28. Government Accountability Office, GAO-08-99T, Statement of David C. Maurer, *Nuclear Detection: Preliminary Observations on the Domestic Nuclear Detection Office's Efforts to Develop a Global Detection Architecture*, July 16, 2008, p. 2; Dana A. Shea, Congressional Research Service, *The Global Nuclear Detection Architecture*, July 16, 2008, p. 19.

29. Vartabedian, "Detecting Radiation an Arduous Job at Ports."

30. Ibid.

31. Ted Bridis, "Security Lapses Found at U.S. Ports," www.washingtontimes.com, March 12, 2006.

32. Liz Sidoti, Associated Press, " 'Dirty Bombs' Crossed U.S. in Borders Test," March 27, 2006, www.comcast.net; Gregory D. Kutz, Keith A. Rhodes, and Gene Aloise to Norm Coleman, Government Accountability Office, Subject: Border Security: Investigators Successfully Transported Radioactive Sources across Our Nation's Borders at Selected Locations, March 28, 2006, p. 5.

33. Mark Hosenball and Christopher Dickey, "A Shadowy Nuclear Saga," *Newsweek*, October 30, 2006, p. 48.

34. Matthew M. Aid, "All Glory Is Fleeting: Sigint and the Fight Against International Terrorism," *Intelligence and National Security*, 18, 4 (Winter 2003), pp. 72–120 at pp. 88, 92.

35. Ibid., p. 105.

36. Telephone interview with Peter Zimmerman, November 20, 2007.

37. George W. Bush, *National Strategy to Combat Weapons of Mass Destruction*, December 2002, p. 3; "Domestic Nuclear Detection Office Organization," www.dhs.gov, accessed December 8, 2007; Statement of John A. Gordon, Under Secretary of Energy and Administrator for Nuclear Security, NNSA, Department of

Energy, Before House Armed Services Committee, June 26, 2002, p. 6; "DOD Seeks Rapid Attribution of Domestic Nuclear Attack," *Secrecy News*, January 2, 2005.

38. See Jeffrey T. Richelson, *Spying on the Bomb: American Nuclear Intelligence from Nazi Germany to Iran and North Korea* (New York: W.W. Norton, 2006).

39. Caitlin Talmadge, "Deterring a Nuclear 9/11," *Washington Quarterly*, Spring 2007, pp. 21–34.

40. Ibid., p. 26.

41. Ibid.

42. Matthew Phillips, "Uncertain Justice for Nuclear Terror: Deterrence of Anonymous Attacks through Attribution," *Orbis*, Summer 2007, pp. 429–446. Also see Joint Working Group of the American Physical Society and the American Association for the Advancement of Science, *Nuclear Forensics: Role, State of the Art, Program Needs* (Washington, D.C.: American Association for the Advancement of Science, 2008).

43. Department of Homeland Security, "TOPOFF 4 Frequently Asked Questions," www.dhs.gov, accessed October 22, 2007; Northern Command, "Fact Sheet— Exercise VIGILANT SHIELD, 2008," 2008.

44. Interview with Alan Mode, Pleasanton, Calif., April 12, 2007; Interview with William Nelson, Alamo, Calif., June 9, 2007; Office of Inspector General, Department of Energy, DOE/IG-0605, *National Nuclear Security Administration's Ability to Meet the Aircraft Requirements of the Joint Technical Operations Team*, June 2003, pp. 3–7; Walter Pincus, "Nuclear Warhead Cut from Spending Bill," *Washington Post*, December 18, 2007, p. A2.

45. Steve Wampler, Lawrence Livermore National Laboratory, e-mail, December 3, 2007.

46. Office of Inspector General, Department of Energy, DOE/IG-0605, *National Nuclear Security Administration's Ability to Meet the Aircraft Requirements of the Joint Technical Operations Team*, pp. 3–7.

47. "When Terrorists Go Nuclear," *Popular Mechanics*, March 2002, accessed from www.popularmechanics.com.

48. Argonne National Laboratory, "Tiny Device Can Detect Hidden Nuclear Weapons, Materials," June 21, 2002, available at http://www.anl.gov.

49. Richard Stenger, "Cryo3 Could Spot 'Dirty Bombs'," www.cnn.com, June 10, 2002.

50. "Radiation Detection on the Front Lines," *Science & Technology Review*, September 2004, pp. 4–11.

51. Mark Wolverton, "Muons for Peace," *Scientific American*, September 2007, pp. 26–28.

52. "Mobile Mapping for Radioactive Materials," *Science & Technology Review*, October 2007, pp. 8–9.

53. John Fox, "FBI to Get Nuclear Weapon Neutralizer," *Global Security Newswire*, February 15, 2008, accessed from www.nti.org.

54. Telephone interview with Steven Fetter, November 29, 2007.

55. Ibid.; James Glanz, "Despite New Tools, Detecting Nuclear Material Is Doubtful," *New York Times*, March 18, 2002, p. A13; Department of Energy, Nevada Operations Office, *The Mile Shakedown Series of Exercices: A Compilation of Comments and Critiques*, February 18, 1995, p. 146.

INDEX

Page numbers in *italics* refer to maps.

Marine barracks bombing, 128
Maritime Security Act (2002), 189–90
Mark, J. Carson, 144–45
Markey, Daniel, 213
Mars Global Surveyor, 120
Mars 96 probe, 120–22
Mars Pathfinder, 120
Maslin, Evgeny, 153
Masri, Abu Ayyub al-, 219–20
Masri, Abu Khabab al-, 134
Materials Protection, Control, and
    Accounting (MPC&A) program,
    168, 220
Meir, Golda, 15
Menino, Thomas M., 197
Merritt, John C., 198
Messinger, Larry G., 8
Mexico, 13–14, 22–23, 140, 197, 221
Mica Dig exercise, 91–92, 98
Mighty Derringer exercise, 86, 91
Mikhailov, Viktor, 126
Mild Cover exercise, 91–92, 93, 98
Mile Shakedown exercises, 91, 99
Military Airlift Command, U.S., 56
Miller, John, 191
MINATOM (Atomic Energy Ministry),
    Russian, 141, 152, 165
Minneapolis–Saint Paul, USS, 99
Mir, Hamid, 139
Mirage Gold exercise, 91–106
    after-action reports on, 95–97, 235–36
    Beers's critique of, 99–101, 106
    classification problems in, 98
    component exercises of, 91–92
    deployment problems in, 96–97
    FBI in, 91–98
    FEMA in, 91, 93, 96, 99
    NEST equipment in, 93–95, 96, 98
    New Orleans scenario in, 92–93
    participating organizations in, 92
    Senate hearings on, 106–7
    small-scale exercises in, 98
    technical problems in, 97
Miron, Murray, 36, 39–40, 41, 76
Mirrored Image exercise, 171
Mobile and Human Portable Detection
    Systems, 223–24
Mobley, Mike, 65–66, 67
Mode, Alan V., xivn, 36, 74, 88, 100, 101,
    144, 233
Mohammad, Khalid Sheikh, 131, 185–86,
    187, 228
Moldova, 163
Mondale, Walter, 84

Monterey Institute of International Stud-
    ies, 142, 212
Mordhorst, John, 65–66, 67
Morgan, Darwin, 175
Morning Light Operation, 47–69, 120–21,
    206
    debris location and recovery in, 64–67
    destabilization and crash of Cosmos 954
        in, 50–58
    NEST in, 53, 56–61, 63–68
    reimbursement for, 69
    search missions in, 55–56, 58, 61–65,
        62, 68
    Soviet's US satellite program and, 47–48
    U.S. assistance in, 54–55
Morocco, 129
Morrison, Ira, 53, 81, 82
Morya-1, *see* US (Controlled Satellite) sat-
    ellite program
Moscow Institute of Physics and Technol-
    ogy, 81
Mossad, 14–15
Mowatt-Larssen, Rolf, 219
MS-13 (street gang), 140
Mueller, John, 217
Mueller, Robert, 219
Muhajir, Abu Hamza al-, 219–20
Mujahir, Abdullah al, *see* Padilla, Jose
Mukhtar, Mohammed Ali, 136
Mullen, Mike, 209
Mundaring Seismic Observatory, 123
Munroe effect, 75
muon radiography, 234
Murai, Hideo, 125
Musharrah, Pervez, 148, 208–9, 211, 212
Muslim Brotherhood, 128
Myre, Bill, 22

Nader, Ralph, 38, 40
narcotics, 226
National Aeronautics and Space Adminis-
    tration (NASA), 51, 120, 178, 206
National Command Authority, Pakistan,
    211
National Commission on Terrorism, 25
National Commission on Terrorist Attacks
    Upon the United States, 130
National Counterterrorism Center, 139,
    212, 227
National Disaster Medical System, 188
National Environmental Research Park, 44
National Football League (NFL), 216
National Guard, Indiana, 86
National Intelligence Council, 153, 155